Katharine J. Dell
The Book of Job as Sceptical Literature

Beihefte zur Zeitschrift für die
alttestamentliche Wissenschaft

Herausgegeben von
Otto Kaiser

Band 197

Walter de Gruyter · Berlin · New York
1991

Katharine J. Dell

# The Book of Job
# as Sceptical Literature

Walter de Gruyter · Berlin · New York
1991

*Printed on acid-free paper which falls
within the guidelines of the ANSI to ensure
permanence and durability.*

*Library of Congress Cataloging-in-Publication Data*

Dell, Katharine J. (Katharine Julia). 1961—
  The book of Job as sceptical literature / Katharine J. Dell.
    p.  cm. — (Beihefte zur Zeitschrift für die alttestamentliche Wissenschaft, ISSN 0934-2575 ; Bd. 197)
  Revision of the author's thesis (doctoral)—Oxford University, 1988.
  Includes bibliographical references and indexes.
  ISBN 3-11-012554-4 (alk. paper). — ISBN 0-89925-705-4 (U.S. : alk. paper)
  1. Bible. O. T. Job—Criticism, interpretation, etc.  I. Title.
II. Series: Beihefte zur Zeitschrift für die alttestamentliche Wissenschaft ; 197.
BS1415.2.D45    1991
221.6 s—dc20
[223'.1066]
                                                        91-14132
                                                           CIP

*Deutsche Bibliothek Cataloging in Publication Data*

**Dell, Katharine J.:**
The Book of Job as sceptical literature / Katharine J. Dell. — Berlin ; New York : de Gruyter, 1991
  (Beihefte zur Zeitschrift für die alttestamentliche Wissenschaft ; Bd. 197)
  Zugl.: Oxford, Oriel College, Diss., 1988
  ISBN 3-11-012554-4
NE: Zeitschrift für die alttestamentliche Wissenschaft / Beihefte

ISSN: 0934-2575

© Copyright 1991 by Walter de Gruyter & Co., D-1000 Berlin 30.

All rights reserved, including those of translation into foreign languages. No part of this book may be reproduced or transmitted in any form or by any means, electronic or mechanical, including photocopy, recording, or any information storage and retrieval system, without permission in writing from the publisher.
Printed in Germany
Printing: Werner Hildebrand, Berlin 65
Binding: Lüderitz und Bauer, Berlin 61

To my family

# Preface

My interest in Job began with a weekly essay, grew when I researched into the book further for an essay prize at St Hugh's College, Oxford and became the subject for my doctoral thesis at Oxford University. This monograph is a revised version of my thesis which was examined in 1988.

To Dr John Barton I owe a great debt of gratitude for providing so much encouragement, enthusiasm and intellectual stimulation throughout my Old Testament Studies. His assistance in the evolution of the ideas and structure of this work has been invaluable, as has his patience in reading though many versions. I have also been encouraged in my work by Professor Ernest Nicholson and Dr Rex Mason and by other members of the Theology Faculty.

I would like to thank Professor Otto Kaiser for agreeing to publish my work as a Beiheft for the Zeitschrift für die alttestamentliche Wissenschaft. I wish also to thank friends and associates from St Cross, Oriel and Ripon College, Cuddesdon for their interest and useful comments, particularly Dr Douglas Hamilton for his assistance with the production of this final copy. Finally I would like to thank my family for their encouragement - my parents, Robert and Molly, and my brother, Christopher and it is to them that I dedicate this book.

Oxford, December 1990                                   Katharine J. Dell

## Table of Contents

INTRODUCTION: 'Scepticism' as a description of *Job*     1

CHAPTER 1: Traditional and critical interpretations of the message of *Job*: Job the patient or Job the rebel?     5

Introduction     5
- a) Traditional interpretations of *Job*     6
  - i) Jewish interpretations     7
  - ii) The Job tradition in the earliest biblical tradition and ancient versions     12
  - iii) The apocryphal and pseudepigraphical Job tradition     17
  - iv) The ecclesiastical Job tradition     23
- b) Critical interpretations of *Job*     29
  - i) The innocent sufferer     29
  - ii) The doctrine of retribution     35
  - iii) The nature of God and man's relationship with Him     39
  - iv) Job as a protest     44

CHAPTER 2: The quest for an overall classification for *Job*: Wisdom and genre     57

- a) *Job* as 'wisdom' or 'wisdom literature'     58
- b) *Job* as 'wisdom literature'     63
  - i) Form     64
  - ii) Content     73
  - iii) Context     83
- c) The quest for an overall genre for *Job*     88
  - i) Genre levels     88
  - ii) The first pitfall - the assumption that the overall genre of *Job* is the most predominant 'smaller' genre     89
  - iii) The second pitfall - deciding the overall genre before studying the smaller genres which make up the whole     93
    - (1) Formal considerations foremost     93
    - (2) Considerations of content and meaning foremost     95
  - iv) Assessment of these findings     100
  - v) Small genres or forms in *Job*     103

## CHAPTER 3: A form-critical approach to *Job*: 'Parody' as an overall genre for *Job*    109

    a) The deliberate misuse of forms in *Job*    109
        i) The suggestions of scholars concerning the use of forms in *Job*    109
        ii) Passages in *Job* showing the deliberate misuse of forms    125
        iii) A pattern in the misuse of forms    136
        iv) The reuse and misuse of forms in Ecclesiastes    138
    b) A new overall genre for *Job*, the parody    147
        i) Definitions of 'parody'    148
        ii) Parody in *Jonah*    153

## CHAPTER 4: The 'sceptical' setting, content and structure of *Job*: The scepticism of Job and the author of the book    159

    a) The quest for a context for *Job*    159
        i) A wider intellectual setting for *Job*    160
        ii) *Job* - the product of a philosophical group    166
    b) The scepticism of Job as shown in the content of the book.    168
        i) Scepticism and the Greek sceptics    168
        ii) The dialogue section of *Job*    172
            (1) The first cycle of speeches    172
            (2) The second cycle of speeches    177
            (3) The third cycle of speeches    181
    c) The scepticism of the author of *Job* as shown in the overall structure of the book    184
        i) The interrelationship of structure and content    184
        ii) Secondary material    195
        iii) The prologue, epilogue and dialogue    199
            (1) The prologue and epilogue: Literary-critical questions    199
            (2) The interplay of structure and themes between the prose tale and poetic dialogue    203
        iv) The speeches of Yahweh and Job's replies    205
            (1) Literary-critical concerns    205
            (2) The juxtaposition of the dialogue, speeches of Yahweh and Job's reply    207
            (3) The epilogue    208

## CONCLUSION    213

Abbreviations    218

## BIBLIOGRAPHY    220

Indices    247

Introduction

## 'SCEPTICISM' AS A DESCRIPTION OF *JOB*

"[D]ieses Buch ist das Hohelied der Skepsis."[1]

This description by H Heine of the book of *Job*[2] did not have the profound effect upon interpretation of the book that it might have had because it was wrongly thought by scholars to refer to Ecclesiastes. It had important repercussions for the theological interpretation of Ecclesiastes which was, consequently, quickly perceived as 'sceptical' but not for that of *Job*, which was clearly not thought to fit such a description. Later scholars have gradually taken up the idea that *Job* is 'sceptical' literature, but not from Heine. M Jastrow, for example, wrote almost a century later:

"We must at the outset recognize that the Book of *Job* in its original form was a skeptical composition - skeptical in the sense of putting a question mark after the fundamental axiom in the teachings of the Hebrew prophets of the ninth and succeeding centuries, that the government of the universe rests on justice...its spirit is skeptical. The Book of *Job* arose out of a circle which was not content with the conventional answer to the question why the innocent suffer in this strange world."[3]

Heine had pointed to a fundamental understanding of *Job* ignored by his contemporaries and only acknowledged in recent times in a very general way;[4] Jastrow's contemporaries also glossed over such findings, and it is not until recent times that there is now a consensus amongst modern scholars that the

---

1  "This book is the Song of Songs of scepticism". H Heine in 'Spätere Note. Im Marz 1854', a note to his 'Ludwig Marcus. Denkworte. Geschrieben zu Paris, den 22. April 1844' - see F Ellermeier, 1965. I am indebted to Dr John Day for drawing my attention to this article.
2  In this monograph I shall use italics to indicate the book of *Job* and Roman script when I am referring to Job the character.
3  M Jastrow, 1920 (pp 28-29).
4  See the final section of chapter 1 (pp 44-52) on *Job* as 'protest literature' and chapter 4 (pp 210-212) on scepticism as a late stage in Hebrew thought.

'message' or content of *Job* is 'sceptical' in some sense, although this sense has not as yet been closely defined.⁵ A study of the dialogue sections of the book - notably of Job's speeches - confirms the impression that the book might be characterized as 'sceptical'. 'Sceptical' is one term amongst others (such as 'unorthodox', 'questioning' and 'protesting') that has been used by scholars to describe the untraditional stance that *Job* takes regarding the doctrine of retribution and the nature of man's relationship with God. However the book has not always been interpreted in this way, and both traditional and some modern readings of *Job* have either ignored this scepticism altogether or, after acknowledging some kind of sceptical element, have then drawn back from the *full* implications of seeing *Job* as sceptical literature. Furthermore, the classification of *Job* as sceptical in content has had little effect on scholarly judgements about literary aspects of the book (form, genre, structure), nor has it led to any fresh theories about the circles responsible for it. *Job* is merely regarded as having arisen out of an unconventional protest - either against conventional answers to innocent suffering, or against the doctrine of retribution, or against man's conception of the nature of God.

It has been widely assumed that *Job* is simply an example of 'wisdom literature': that is, that it belongs to one of the genres found also in proverbial and instruction literature in Israel and in other ancient Near Eastern cultures. Much of the language of *Job*, many of the forms and the prominent discussion of whether the righteous and wicked get their just deserts support this assumption. It has accordingly also been assumed that the author of *Job* belonged to 'the wise', understood as a social group in Israel concerned primarily with education. The fact that the contents of the book challenge many of the assumptions common in such circles leads scholars to see it (like Ecclesiastes) either as a development within mainline wisdom which

---

5  See G von Rad, 1965, Volume 1, pp 453-9: "...the point where contact with the action of Jahweh in history tended to be lost was always the point when faith was brought into the gravest danger. Accordingly a form of scepticism arose which was specific to Israel, not doubt about the existence of Jahweh - neither Job's despair nor that of the psalms of lamentation led to any dubiety about Jahweh's existence and power - but doubt about his readiness to interfere drastically in history or in the life of the individual." (p 453) However von Rad sees Ecclesiastes as being at the apex of sceptical literature and *Job* is only mentioned briefly, an emphasis I consider misplaced.

nevertheless challenged many of the presuppositions of wisdom,[6] or as a sideline of the main wisdom tradition which represents something of an anomaly or dead-end in the development of wisdom.[7] The realization that *Job* challenges traditional 'wisdom' beliefs has not however resulted in any more far-reaching assessment of its genre or authorship.[8]

In this study I shall argue that *Job* is sceptical in a more profound way than has previously been recognized and that this has implications for all areas of study connected with the biblical book. Simply because terms such as 'sceptical' are generally used to characterize the content or 'message' of *Job*, the meaning conveyed by formal, literary and contextual aspects of the book has been neglected. I shall suggest however that the form of *Job* expresses the author's scepticism just as much as its overt content and that the relation of form to content and context is a crucial key for understanding the book. These suggestions raise questions about classification, genre and context. If the forms used are discovered to be as atypical of 'wisdom' as the content clearly is, then this may call into question the traditional classification of *Job* as 'wisdom' and inspire a quest for more satisfactory terminology to characterize the book. The 'wisdom' setting of *Job*, in the sense of its origins within circles of 'the wise' as commonly defined, will then also come under discussion. Instead, the production of literature by a group of 'sceptics' or within a 'sceptical' tradition in Israel might be posited, particularly if other Old Testament literature not generally aligned with *Job* were found to contain similar strains of protest and forms which convey this protest on the level of authorship. Furthermore, the sceptical nature of *Job* is not confined merely to

---

[6] See R N Whybray, 1980, p 4. This development is then given a context in Israel's history so that, for example, H H Schmid, 1966, pp 173-195 (Israel), pp 74-78 (Egypt), and pp 131-143 (Mesopotamia), can talk of a 'crisis' in wisdom at a certain point in Israel's development parallelled by similar crises in the ancient Near East (for which there is also evidence of material of a questioning kind - see R N Whybray, 1980, p 4, and texts in J B Pritchard (ed), 1950, pp 405-410, 434-440). J F Priest 1968, p 319, writes "There was an informal kind of scepticism at all stages of Israel's history but...the formal, intellectual articulation does indeed come after the Exile."

[7] See G von Rad, 1972, pp 237-9.

[8] A recent trend has been to compare *Job* with Greek tragedy to underline the radically questioning nature of the book and to emphasize how different *Job* is from other Old Testament books. A recent contribution to this debate has been made by H Fisch, 1988. 'Tragedy' has also been suggested as a possible 'genre' for *Job* (see chapter 2, pp 98-100). However, as I shall show, such comparisons are of limited use when trying to characterize *Job*.

the unorthodox utterances of Job in the dialogue section; it is all-pervasive, accounting for the arrangement of the material in the whole book. Scepticism is expressed through the very structure of the book, and in the juxtaposition of its various parts. To take only one example of the many to be discussed: the careful mention of a patient Job in the traditional prose tale introduction is immediately and deliberately mocked in the opening line of Job's lament in chapter 3, "After this Job opened his mouth and cursed the day of his birth." (3:1)[9] This raises the question of the intention of the author(s) and/or editors of the book.

The arrangement of this monograph follows the pattern of the argument above. Chapter 1 contains a survey of traditional and critical interpretations of *Job* in order to discover how far scholarship has taken us in understanding the book as a whole and the major themes contained within it. I end the chapter with a reassessment of Job's rebellious sentiments. In chapter 2 I offer my own interpretation of *Job* emphasizing the problems raised by the quest for an overall classification for the book, both in relation to the traditional assignment to 'wisdom' and in relation to the quest for an overall genre. In chapter 3, I place an emphasis on a fresh, form-critical approach to *Job* which considers the use of forms made by the author. In the final chapter I demonstrate that the word 'sceptical' is more appropriate for characterizing *Job* than others, such as 'unorthodox' or 'protesting', not only on the level of content or 'message' but on the level of the author's use of genre, form and structure and in terms of a 'sceptical' tradition which provides a context for the book. A realization of the important interrelationship of context, content and structure assists an appreciation of the profound scepticism of the book. I shall therefore discuss in this study, the full implications of reading *Job* as sceptical literature.

---

9   In this monograph biblical quotations in English will be from the Revised Standard Version except where the Authorized Version is indicated.

## Chapter 1

## TRADITIONAL AND CRITICAL INTERPRETATIONS OF THE MESSAGE OF *JOB*

Job the patient or Job the rebel?

### INTRODUCTION

The book of *Job* contains a complicated interweaving of themes and many difficult contradictions. During the history of interpretation of *Job*, five major themes have in turn been seen as the key to an understanding of the book. As I will show below, traditional and early critical interpreters tried to find a unifying theme in the book and tended to gloss over contradictions, the former scarcely realizing they were there, and the latter anxious to stress the harmony of the book's various parts. Bolder literary critics emphasized the contradictions in *Job* but then explained them away (for example, as later additions or editorial interpolations) in order to retain the unity of the book's message. In more recent years, unity of message has not been a vital concern and the disjointedness of the book has been readily admitted. More recently still a unity of structure of the book has been sought which does not try to harmonize the various aspects of the message but seeks to find a unity in contradiction.

The major suggestions for a 'key' to the meaning of *Job* in terms of its message or content will be seen to correspond to changes in the concerns of scholars since the turn of the century. Furthermore, the interpretation of the message of *Job* is inextricably bound up with literary-critical conclusions regarding which parts of the book are primary and which secondary.[1] In this chapter therefore, I shall take the five main themes in chronological order, indicating briefly at each stage what the literary-critical concerns of scholars were and how they affected interpretation of the message of the book. This survey will conclude with my own assessment of the rebellious nature of Job's sentiments.

### a) TRADITIONAL INTERPRETATIONS OF *JOB*: Job, the pious and patient sufferer

"In the biblical tradition Job is sometimes impatient and rebellious. In the apocryphal tradition Job is always pious and patient as he is in the ecclesiastical tradition. And in the ecclesiastical tradition certain nearly blasphemous verses from the Book of Job are turned to devotional use, while the entire book of Job becomes the basis for exegetical reflections on Christian doctrine."[2]

For centuries Job was regarded as the model of steadfastness in the face of unexplained suffering - thus already in James 5:11 where the author refers to τὴν ὑπομονὴν Ἰώβ, the "patience of Job" (AV). This traditional, orthodox interpretation was based on a reading of the prose section which paid very little attention to the dialogue. The heavenly prologue - a conflict between God and Satan on the theme of disinterested righteousness - both sets the scene for and provides the reason for Job's afflictions. Job in turn demonstrates the proper manner of responding to undeserved suffering. He is the model of patience. Once Job has passed the various tests, his earlier state of blessing can be restored and doubled (42:10). The narrative in the prologue and epilogue of

---

1 Scholars often fall into a circular argument which leads to confusion. They argue that their interpretation of the message of *Job* is affected by their literary-critical conclusions, but they highlight themes in certain sections and omit others (in the absence of decisive literary-critical proof) according to individual interpretations of the message. Alternatively scholars argue that their literary-critical analysis is affected by their evaluation of the message, but they highlight particular parts to the neglect of others (in the absence of certainty as to the message) according to the literary-critical conclusions reached. Both starting-points lead to fragmentation of the text and of the message and to neglect of the important interrelationship between literary-critical concerns and the message of the book.

2 L L Besserman, 1979 (p 3).

*Job* therefore forms a unit which poses and answers the question whether there is such a thing as selfless piety.[3]

In the first half of this chapter I will discuss traditional interpretations of Job as a model of piety and patience in the first few centuries after the production of the book.

i) Jewish interpretations

"Jewish interpreters in the premodern period Judaized Job and Christian expositors Christianized him. Both sides...with exceptions, avoided a direct confrontation with the text of the book, in order not to be exposed (or not to expose the pious reader) to the bluntness of the hero's speeches and the shattering self-revelation of God in his answer to Job."[4]

In early rabbinic circles, the dialogue section of *Job* was largely ignored, being regarded as little more than a few musings on the nature of the punishment of sin and on the relation of the individual to the all-high God and being thought to have no fundamental effect on the book's overall message. The practical conclusion generally drawn was that it is not for man to question the ways of God or think that he himself always has the answer (as Job's three friends and the young Elihu suppose). Man can do only as Job finally does and repent in dust and ashes (42:1-2,6).

An extensive literature grew up which elaborated aspects of the biblical text which the rabbis considered important and toned down other parts. These elaborations in turn became so much a part of interpretation of *Job* that many features of the original text - particularly the less palatable ones - were forgotten. There was also a great deal of comparison of Job with other biblical figures - a debate associated with the desire to assert that Job was a historical

---

3 This story would probably have circulated independently in an oral tradition and been widely known in Israelite circles. Its existence would explain the reference in Ezekiel 14:12-14,19-20 to Job as a righteous man alongside Noah and Daniel. These allusions, if they come from Ezekiel himself, would precede the production, in perhaps the fourth century BC, of the present book of *Job* in its original form (without orthodox additions). Both because of their previous knowledge of a Job legend which did not contain unorthodox 'impatient' elements and because of a desire by orthodox editors of a later period to gloss over such sentiments, by the time *Job* as it is today was admitted into the canon people were reading the book in a way which ensured that it accorded with an orthodox view of divine justice.

4 N N Glatzer (ed), 1969 (p 11).

figure amongst the patriarchs[5] - which led to a distortion of the attributes of Job himself. Thus, interest in the *pious* Job of the traditional tale is reflected in rabbinic literature.[6] This literature treats Job as the most pious Gentile that ever lived[7] (although some exegetes considered him to have been a Jew) and as one of the seven prophets who prophesied to the nations of the world.[8]

The reasons for Job's ordeal, his reaction, and the extent of both his trials and his restoration were amplified by the rabbis by the addition of circumstantial and statistical details. For example, in haggadic legend, Satan, on seeing Job's prosperity, was filled with envy and so began to disparage Job's piety in the councils of heaven.[9] When a messenger told Job that the Sabaeans had seized his oxen, he armed his men and prepared to make war upon them. But when a second messenger came, telling him that a fire from heaven had destroyed his sheep, he said: "Now I can do nothing."[10] The wind that blew down his house was one of the three great winds whose power was sufficient to destroy the world.[11] Job was stricken by Satan with fifty different plagues.[12] These plagues forced Job to leave the city and sit down outside it upon an ash-heap.[13] His flesh was covered with vermin but if one

---

5   Job was associated with Abraham because of the patriarchal setting of the prologue, for example in Midrash Aggadath Bereshith 57.4. Others such as Abha b. Kahana saw him as a contemporary of Jacob or of Jacob's sons. One legend said that he was a grandson of Jacob's brother Esau and that after his trial he married Dinah, Jacob's only daughter, who became his second wife (Baba Bathra 15b; Jerusalem Targum on Job 2:9). Rabbi Levi said that Job lived in the time of Jacob's sons and lived 210 years, being born when Jacob and his children entered Egypt and dying when the Israelites left.
6   Unlike the Torah or the Five Scrolls *Job* (in the Writings) was not read officially at synagogue services so that few midrashim or homiletic commentaries on *Job* were written. But homiletic and ethical comments on the book appear in the Babylonian and Palestinian Talmuds and within various midrashic collections. A hypothetical Midrash Iyyobh, to which references are extant in mediaeval works, was reconstructed from references to Job in other midrash by S Wertheimer in his *Leket Midrashim*, 1904. For details of all these legends see L Ginzberg, 1913-38, volume II, pp 225-242 (notes in volume V, pp 381-390). See also I Wiernikowski, 1902.
7   Deuteronomy Rabbah II.4. Job is also described as one of "the saints among the Gentiles" (Baba Bathra 15b; Seder Olam 21).
8   Baba Bathra 15b.
9   Compare some talmudists who gave Satan's actions sacred intentions - Satan thought that God, in favouring Job, had forgotten the love of Abraham. When Satan heard this interpretation it is recorded that he came and kissed the interpreter's feet (Tanhuma Vayera 5; Baba Bathra 15b, 16a).
10  Leviticus Rabbah 4.
11  Genesis Rabbah 24.4.
12  Exodus Rabbah 23.10.
13  Testament of Job 4 (see below on the Testament of Job, pp 20-22).

of them tried to crawl away from him he forced it back, telling it to stay where it was until God found another place for it.[14] Job's sufferings lasted twelve months,[15] then God, yielding to the prayer of the angels, healed him and restored to him twofold what he had before. A small elaboration mentioned in Sotah 35a is that the whole world mourned Job's death. These legendary accounts extend also to Job's three friends who entered his house simultaneously, though they lived three hundred miles apart, and who each had a crown or, according to another statement, a tree on which their images were carved so that when a misfortune befell any one of them his image was altered.

Rabbinic treatment of Job contained an inherent tension within it. On one hand the rabbis wished to justify the biblical description of Job as pious and God-fearing and so elaborated upon many details of his scrupulous piety and numerous acts of charity.[16] On the other hand, there was a fear that his righteousness might place Abraham and other Jewish figures in the shade and so limits were put on Job's virtue.[17]

---

14  Testament of Job 5 (see below, pp 20-22); Abot de Rabbi Nathan, 164.
15  M. 'Eduyoth 2.10.
16  For example, Job is represented as a most generous man. Like Abraham, he built an inn at the cross-roads with four doors opening respectively to the four cardinal points, in order that wayfarers might have no trouble in finding an entrance, and his name was praised by all who knew him. His time was entirely occupied with works of charity, such as visiting the sick and, according to Raba, Job would take by force a field which belonged to orphans, make it ready for sowing and then return it to the owners. Job was represented as a man of exemplary piety. Like Abraham, he recognized God by intuition (Numbers Rabbah 14.7). Nothing in his possession had been acquired by rapacity, and therefore his prayer was pure (Exodus Rabbah 12.4). He, Melchizedek and Enoch were as spotless as Abraham (Midrash Tehillim to Psalm 37) and Job took great care to stay aloof from every unseemly deed. Samuel b. Isaac said: "He who received a 'perutah' from Job prospered in his affairs." Jose b. Hanina inferred from Job 1:10 that Job's goats could kill wolves; and Rabbi Johanan inferred from Job 1:14 that God gave Job a foretaste of the bliss of paradise (Baba Bathra 15a). According to Targum Sheni to Esther 1, Job's name was one of the seven engraved on the seven branches of the golden candlestick (See L Ginzberg, 1913-38, IV, p 158).
17  Whilst talmudists compared Job to Abraham in order better to understand Job's piety, others thought more highly of Abraham and asserted that whilst Job served God only from 'fear' (Job 1:1) (eg Johanan b. Zakkai - fear of punishment, Sotah 27a, J Sotah V 5), Abraham loved God. Some concluded that in both Abraham and Job 'fear' and 'love' were interrelated, whilst others believed Job's deeds to be motivated by pure love (eg Joshua b. Hyrcanus, Sotah 5:5: "That same day R Joshua b. Hyrcanus expounded: 'Job served the Holy One, blessed is he, only from love.'"). In the later midrashic work Abot de Rabbi Nathan Recension A, Job's generosity is stressed and yet it is said that God replied to Job's complaint that he was inadequately rewarded by saying to him, "Thy generosity has not yet attained to the half of that of Abraham" (Chapter 7).

A rare acknowledgement of Job's rebellious nature is found in Baba Bathra 16a where there is disagreement over whether Job's complaints were directed against God and constituted blasphemy or were directed against Satan and therefore justified.[18] It is recognised by Raba that under the impact of his tribulations Job became a rebel against God.[19] Raba states, for example, that Job blasphemed against God by using the word 'tempest' when he said, 'For he breaketh me with a tempest' (Job 9:17, AV). He notes that in the same verse Job accused God of confusing איוב (Job) with אויב (enemy) and thus multiplying his wounds 'without cause'. A more orthodox answer to this problem given by the rabbis was to assert that this 'tempest' mentioned by Job actually caused the confusion between איוב and אויב in Job's own mind - the blame was not on God's side. Raba says on the other hand that God answered Job out of the tempest in order specifically to refute Job's charge. In his answer to Job God gave examples of his fatherly providence, as shown in nature; how then could he mistake Job for an enemy?[20] The substance of Job's complaints is usually passed over by these interpreters. Job is seen as a rebel who spoke "as if there were an equality with heaven on the part of man." He, the servant, dared "to argue against his master."[21] God rebuked Job for his lack of patience when suffering was inflicted upon him, reminding him of the response to suffering of his biblical predecessors - notably Adam, whose sentence was death, Abraham, who was told his seed would be slaves in Egypt, Moses, who was prevented from entering the promised land, and

---

[18] Rabbi Eliezer said that Job blasphemed against God whilst Rabbi Joshua considered that Job spoke harsh words against Satan only. Abaye and Raba took up the discussion, the former following Joshua, the latter following Eliezer, inferring from the passage "and yet Job sinned not with his lips" (Job 2:10, AV) that Job nevertheless sinned in his heart.

[19] Raba remarks (Baba Bathra 16a), "Job's mouth ought to have been filled with dust on account of the offensive words he uttered against God." See also Midrash Tehillim to Psalm 26 - Job is described as having 'rebelled' - and Pesikta Rabbati Ahare Mot.

[20] Baba Bathra 16a. Raba saw Job's chief complaint as being the punishment of man even though he is driven to sin by the seducer, whom God Himself has created (cf Job 10:7). Eliphaz's answer is: "Thou castest off fear" (15:4, AV), meaning that God created not only the seducer but also the Torah by which a man can subdue the seducer. Yohanan of Tiberias, a third-century talmudist, actually learnt from Job that all are doomed to die, but "blessed is he who has grown in the Torah and who is giving pleasure to his Maker: he goes through life with a good name and with a good name departs from this world." (Berakhot 17a)

[21] Quotations from Baba Bathra 16a. In Baba Bathra 16b however, Job's outbursts are excused because "man is not held responsible for things done under duress."

Aaron whose two sons died.[22] God accused Job on New Year's Day, the day when God judges the good and evil deeds of man.[23] Whilst there was hostility between Job and his friends, God's stern rebuke was maintained. Once they had made peace with each other and Job interceded for his friends this situation changed.[24] However, had Job stood firm under trial, his name would have been included in prayer, and men would have called upon the "God of Job" as upon the "God of Abraham, Isaac and Jacob."[25]

Rabbinic circles thus more often portrayed Job, the character and the book, in a positive light than in a negative one. There was little concern with precise analysis of the text and there was much legendary embellishment of the tale. In general the sentiments expressed by Job were given less importance than his character and actions as they could be gleaned from the prose sections of the book. Of great significance was his personage in relation to other historical figures. He was viewed primarily as a saintly person who demonstrated great piety, and this image of him becomes developed in the legends about him.[26] There is however the realization at times that his piety was not perfect[27] and that even he required correction.[28]

---

22 Pesikta Rabbati 190a.
23 Targum on Job 1:6.
24 Pesikta Rabbati 190a.
25 Pesikta Rabbati 190a (commentary on Job 42:10).
26 For example, in later centuries, this tradition of Job as a man of perfect, unquestioning faith appears in an addendum to the midrashic work Abot de-Rabbi Nathan, a work compiled between the seventh and the ninth centuries AD. This addendum tells of a Job who throughout his troubles "acknowledged and praised the Lord for all His attributes" until "all the world believed that there was none like him in all the land." Satan does not succeed in destroying Job's trust in God and so is finally condemned and cast down from heaven. Job's trial lasts one full year (symbolic of a perfect unit of time) after which he is returned to his former estate (Addendum II to Version I of the work, pp 150-166 (especially p 164)).
27 In Semahot 8, for example, emphasis is laid on Job's lack of patience and on his audacity to argue with God.
28 Solomon ben Isaac ('Rashi' (1040-1105)) provides an example of a mediaeval Jewish commentator on the Hebrew Bible and Babylonian Talmud who overcame problems raised by the text by asserting that Job required correction. On Job 9:16 Rashi provided a reason for Job's unbelief, "because of my fear of Him, and how could I not fear him?" To 9:20 Rashi added to Job's statement that his mouth would condemn him, "fear [of Him] would silence my voice" and on 13:15 Rashi noted, "I shall not separate myself from Him and shall always trust in Him; therefore there is no rebellion and transgression in my words." On 13:16 Rashi commented, "As I am wholly with Him, so is He salvation to me." Rashi had Elihu pointing to man's insignificance in the cosmos (33:12) in order to correct some of Job's less easily muted utterances (eg 9:22

## ii) The Job tradition in the earliest biblical tradition and ancient versions

"The overriding interest of the age of faith in the Job of the prose tale is clearly reflected in the Ancient versions...The Ancient versions all testify to the enduring and widespread interest in Job the man, rather than in the book."[29]

A similar approach to *Job* can be found in early Christian circles. There was a one-sided reading of the book which placed emphasis on the prose story and character of Job rather than on the content of the book as a whole. This however is not the only reason why the figure of Job acquired his proverbial reputation for *patience* as well as piety. In Christian thought, the book of *Job* needs to be distinguished from the 'Job tradition' which grew up as a result of the book and which, although diverse, had a far-reaching influence exceeding that of the book itself. This Job tradition springs out of the biblical allusions to Job outside the book, in Ezekiel 14:12-14,19-20 and the Epistle of James 5:11, and out of the changes to the text made in the Septuagint version, allusions which supported the pious interpretations of orthodox Christians.[30] The sixth-century prophet Ezekiel, in one of his calls to repentance, warns his generation that its iniquity is so great that even if the three righteous men, Noah, Daniel and Job, were living in the land, their signal righteousness would avail to save them personally from catastrophe, but not their children, let alone the land as a whole. From this Ezekiel passage it is perhaps possible to reconstruct the oldest form of the Job narrative - a prose story about a man of exemplary righteousness. The author of the Epistle of James may have known only the popular legend concerning Job reflected in the Ezekiel passage - the folktale version of Job - since, like Ezekiel, he adduces the example of Job in terms which accord with the prose parts of the book. It is possible

---

and 13:21). He also had God pointing to Abraham, whose faith, in contrast to Job's, was perfect because it was unquestioning (comment on 38:2).

29 R Gordis, 1965 (pp 222 and 224).

30 I would argue that already in the later stages of editing of the book, there is evidence of orthodox tendencies - for example, a secondary stage in the development of the prose tale is marked by the introduction of Satan into the narrative (see chapter 4, pp 200-203); the Elihu speeches are clearly a later 'orthodox' addition (see chapter 4, pp 195-198); and some scholars even believe that the prologue and epilogue in their present form could have been added by the representatives of later orthodoxy. This view was defended by R Simon in 1685 (see K Kautzsch, 1900, for a history of the various theories). See also R H Pfeiffer, 1948; B D Eerdmans, 1939 and W B Stevenson, 1947.

however that he may have known the canonical book of *Job* and read it in the orthodox rabbinical way described above (though if this was the case one would perhaps expect the emphasis to fall on the piety rather than the patience of Job).[31] James exhorts his audience to "be patient" μακροθυμήσατε (5:7,8), for ἰδοὺ μακαρίζομεν τοὺς ὑπομείναντας τὴν ὑπομονὴν Ἰὼβ ἠκούσατε καὶ τὸ τέλος Κυρίου εἴδετε, ὅτι πολύσπλαγχνός ἐστιν ὁ Κύριος καὶ οἰκτίρμων.(5:11)[32] Both these biblical allusions to Job stressed aspects of his character that were palatable to later orthodoxy - Job's righteousness and his patience - and so they were taken up in the Job tradition.

The LXX translation of the Hebrew Bible initiated a new tradition which was to become more far-reaching than the one reflected in the passages described above. Changes were made by the translators of the Septuagint, but with what motives is an issue that is hotly debated. R Gordis[33] argues that the Greek translator omitted many stichs "because of the difficulty of the Hebrew which he often did not understand." He might also have abbreviated the Hebrew with the Greek reader in mind who was "unaccustomed to Semitic parallelism and would therefore find the Hebrew redundant." G Gerleman[34] argues, in a slightly different vein, that the translator's motives were to obtain a correct interpretation in difficult texts (not always achieved because of the

---

31 This idea is plausible in the light of arguments which place the author of James in a Jewish tradition. The epistle is generally classified as *paraenesis* which M Dibelius, 1976, describes as "a text which strings together general ethical admonitions." Dibelius argues that Christian churches used Jewish paraenesis when the need for ethical directives was felt with the delay of the parousia. Hence the need to consider the wider context of Jewish and Greek paraenetical traditions when assessing James. The authorship of James is often thought to have links with Jewish circles. F Spitta, 1896, pp 1-239, and L Massebieau, 1895, pp 249-283, stated that the epistle is a Jewish document which has undergone a quite superficial Christianization by some later hand through the addition of two references to Christ in 1:1 and 2:1. Kinship with Jewish concepts does not, of course, prove the Jewish provenance of the writing; it could suggest a Jewish-Christian milieu, one in which the break with Judaism was not so sharp. Alternatively, these chapters may have grown out of Diaspora Judaism, which would explain why Jewish material is passed on in only superficially Christianized form. The language of the book suggests that Greek was spoken in the milieu in which James was written so one might suggest that if the author of James knew the canonical book of *Job* - a real possibility if he read it without attention to the more rebellious speeches - he might have known it in the Septuagint version.
32 "Behold, we call those happy who were steadfast. You have heard of the steadfastness of Job, and you have seen the purpose of the Lord, how the Lord is compassionate and merciful."
33 R Gordis, 1965 (first quotation, p 222; second, p 223).
34 G Gerleman, 1946.

difficulties of the Hebrew), but he notes that the translator displays great stylistic freedom from the original, paraphrasing expressions foreign to Greek usage, stylistically polishing texts which present few difficulties and abbreviating long passages which were regarded as digressions from the main theme of the problem of suffering (for example Job 28 which is shortened and becomes a song of praise of God's power, illustrating religious and ethical truths). Gerleman also argues that the translator's Greek milieu affected his simplification or generalization of passages which was done in order to deprive them of their Hebrew colouring.

On a theological level Gerleman stresses that the translator reproduces satisfactorily the ideas of the Hebrew poet, with the exception of the portrayal of Job's friends and their points of view. The Hebrew poet represents them as preachers of the doctrine of retribution. In the LXX, whilst Job's friends maintain that punishment and reward correspond, respectively, to sin and righteousness, this correspondence is not represented as an inflexible law as in the Hebrew text, but rather as an ideal state to hope for. For example, in the LXX in Eliphaz's first speech (5:4), punishment of sinners is something hoped for by Eliphaz and all righteous people. Gerleman notes that this modification may reflect a different religious outlook on the part of the translator, although he is cautious in saying this, preferring to see the translator as in many places unable to grasp the problem and hence as providing simpler versions.

However D H Gard[35] does not share Gerleman's hesitation and takes up the idea of deliberate theological changes by the Greek translator. He argues that the translator who rendered the book of *Job* into Greek had a good knowledge of Hebrew and toned down offensive theological ideas. For example the arrogance of man before God is avoided (eg in Job 10:2, where in the Hebrew Job asks for an explanation of his misfortune, in the LXX he simply asks a question); the name of God is removed when its retention would detract from the perfect character of God (eg in 12:4 God is kept out of Job's statement thereby avoiding any idea of injustice regarding the dealings of God with man); prepositions are used to tone down offensive ideas (eg in 16:21a the

---

35   D H Gard, 1952 (pp 91-92).

translator objects to the idea of conflict with God, inferred from the use of עם, 'with' in the sense of 'against', so he replaces it with ἔναντι, 'before', 'in the presence of'), anthropomorphisms in reference to God are avoided (eg in 24:23 'his eyes' is omitted and the sense of the verse changed to convey the idea that there is retribution for the wicked - a far cry from Job's complaint that God does not take note of the wicked); references to God as conforming to human behaviour are also avoided (eg in 1:6 the idea of God's children is removed) as are references in general to his moral character (eg in 10:17 the translator eliminates concepts of God which portray him as acting like a human king with an army); and in fact anything that detracts from God's perfect character is changed - for example in 16:13-14 Job describes God's violent treatment of him:

36
יסבו עלי רביו
יפלח כליותי ולא יחמול
ישפך לארץ מררתי
יפרצני פרץ על־פני־פרץ
ירץ עלי כגבור

The translator removes God from the passage altogether. He changes the verbs from singular to plural so that whilst, in the Hebrew, God slays Job, in the Greek, indefinite enemies or troubles kill him:

"ἐκύκλωσάν με λόγχαις βάλλοντες εἰς νεφρούς μου οὐ φειδόμενοι, ἐξέχεαν εἰς τὴν γῆν τὴν χολήν μου· κατέβαλόν με πτῶμα ἐπὶ πτώματι ἔδραμον πρός με δυνάμενοι."[37]

Gard[38] argues that the translator follows an 'exegetical' method of approach to the Hebrew text: "He interprets passages or expressions according to a pattern which has a theological foundation." The word 'pattern' means in this context "an ideal concerning God and man's relationship to him which colours the exegesis of the translator." The question remains how far the differences

---

36 "His archers compass me round about; He cleaveth through my veins and doth not spare; He poureth out my gall upon the ground; He breaketh me with breach upon breach; He runneth upon me like a warrior." (English translation from Gard).
37 "They surrounded me with lances; Having thrown into my kidneys (and) not sparing, They poured out my gall upon the ground; They cast me down, misfortune upon misfortune; They ran into me, being powerful." (English translation from Gard).
38 D H Gard, 1952 (Both quotations from p 92).

are translational necessities and how far they represent a deliberate change. The truth may be a combination of both.

There is strong evidence therefore that changes were made to the plot and theology of *Job* in the Septuagint version which toned down and sometimes eliminated Job's most impatient, presumptuous and impious remarks and exerted a great influence on later traditions of Job. These changes are more than literary; they are theological in motivation. Gordis[39] suggests as a reason for this the desire of the writers of the Septuagint to appeal to the uneducated masses and thereby to transmit acceptable religious ideas to its readers and exclude heretical notions. Amongst the important additions is a genealogy for Job, the assurance to the reader that Job will be resurrected with other righteous men and the expansion of the character of Job's wife. An example of the greater role of Job's wife, is to be found in 2:7-9,11:[40]

"Ἐξῆλθεν δὲ ὁ διάβολος ἀπὸ τοῦ κυρίου καὶ ἔπαισεν τὸν Ἰωβ ἕλκει πονηρῷ ἀπὸ ποδῶν ἕως κεφαλῆς. καὶ ἔλαβεν ὄστρακον, ἵνα τὸν ἰχῶρα ξύῃ, καὶ ἐκάθητο ἐπὶ τῆς κοπρίας ἔξω τῆς πόλεως. Χρόνου δὲ πολλοῦ προβεβηκότος εἶπεν αὐτῷ ἡ γυνὴ αὐτοῦ Μέχρι τίνος καρτερήσεις λέγων Ἰδοὺ ἀναμένω χρόνον ἔτι μικρὸν προσδεχόμενος τὴν ἐλπίδα τῆς σωτηρίας μου; ἰδοὺ γὰρ ἠφάνισταί σου τὸ μνημόσυνον ἀπό τῆς γῆς, υἱοὶ καὶ θυγατέρες, ἐμῆς κοιλίας ὠδῖνες καὶ πόνοι, οὕς εἰς τὸ κενὸν ἐκοπίασα μετὰ μόχθων. σύ τε αὐτὸς ἐν σαπρίᾳ σκωλήκων κάθησαι διανυκτερεύων αἴθριος. κἀγὼ πλανῆτις καὶ λάτρις τόπον ἐκ τόπου περιερχομένη καὶ οἰκίαν ἐξ οἰκίας προσδεχομένη τὸν ἥλιον πότε δύσεται, ἵνα ἀναπαύσωμαι τῶν μόχθων καὶ τῶν ὀδυνῶν, ἅι με νῦν συνέχουσιν. ἀλλὰ εἰπόν τι ῥῆμα εἰς κύριον καὶ τελεύτα... Ἀκούσαντες δὲ οἱ τρεῖς φίλοι αὐτοῦ τὰ κακὰ πάντα τὰ ἐπελθόντα αὐτῷ παρεγένοντο ἕκαστος ἐκ τῆς ἰδίας χώρας πρὸς αὐτόν, Ἐλιφας ὁ θαιμανων βασιλεύς, Βαλδαδ ὁ Σαυχαίων τύραννος, Σωφαρ ὁ Μιναίων βασιλεύς..."

---

39 R Gordis, 1965, p 223.
40 "Thereupon Satan withdrew from the presence of the Lord, and smote Job with foul ulcers from head to foot, so that he took a shell to scrape away the ichor, and sat down on a dunghill without the city. And much time having elapsed, his wife said to him, How long wilt thou persist saying, Behold I will wait yet a little longer, in hope and expectation of my deliverance? For behold the memorial of thee - those sons and daughters, whom I brought forth with pangs and sorrow, and for whom I toiled in vain, are vanished from the earth; and thou thyself sittest among the putrifaction of worms, all night long in the open air, while I am wandering about, or working for wages, from place to place and from house to house, wishing for the setting of the sun, that I may rest from the labours and sorrows I endure. Do but say something for the Lord and die. Now when his three friends heard of all the calamities which were come upon him, they

This passage introduces small details that are not specified in the Hebrew text but which feature in the later Job tradition Notable features are Job's seat on a dunghill outside the city (in the Hebrew text Job sits in ashes, whether inside or outside the city is not specified), his affliction with worms and the idea that his comforters are kings. These motifs and others from the Septuagint can be found in numerous Western literary and artistic renderings of Job.

### iii) The apocryphal and pseudepigraphical Job tradition

"In the apocryphal tradition Job is always pious and patient." [41]

The existence of a parallel tradition which begins with the Septuagint is of importance in seeing how the biblical book of *Job* was read from earliest times. Many early Christian churches would possess only the Septuagint version of *Job*, whilst many people would have access to the story only through their own churchgoing or through their knowledge of popular legend; they would therefore not know of the truly unorthodox nature of the book. References to Job in the apocrypha and pseudepigrapha and in church liturgy confirmed this traditional misunderstanding of Job as the patient sufferer.

One work from the Apocrypha which contains overt references and extended analogies to Job is the Vulgate version of the Book of Tobit,[42] a work popular in the Middle Ages. Tobit, a virtuous Hebrew exiled by the Assyrians, living in Nineveh and having the outstanding virtue of attending to the burial of the dead, is tried for his patience in 2:10-23:

" [10]contigit autem ut quadam die fatigatus a sepultura veniens domum iactasset se iuxta parietem et obdormisset [11]ex nido hirundinum dormienti illi calida stercora insiderent super oculos eius fieretque caecus [12]hanc autem temptationem ideo permisit Dominus evenire illi ut posteris daretur exemplum patientiae eius sicut et sancti Iob [13]nam cum ab infantia sua semper Deum timuerit et mandata eius custodierit non est contristatus contra Deum quod plaga caecitatis evenerit ei [14]sed immobilis in Dei timore permansit agens gratias Deo omnibus diebus vitae suae [15]nam sicut beato Iob insultabant reges ita isti parentes et cognati eius et inridebant vitam eius dicentes [16]ubi est spes tua pro qua elemosynas et sepulturas faciebas [17]Tobias vero increpabat eos dicens nolite ita loqui [18]quoniam filii sanctorum

---

came to him each from his own country, namely, Eliphaz the king of the Thaimanites, Bildad the sovereign of the Saucheans and Sophar the king of the Minaians."
41 L L Besserman, 1979 (p 3, cited above).
42 Not to be confused with the LXX version of Tobit. The basic story of Tobit is itself from a combination of two Jewish folk tales, supplemented by tales from biblical material. See sections on Tobit in J C Dancy, 1972 and R H Charles, 1913.

sumus et vitam illam expectamus quam Deus daturus est his qui fidem suam numquam mutant ab eo [19]Anna vero uxor eius ibat ad textrinum opus cotidie et de labore manuum suarum victum quem consequi poterat deferebat [20]unde factum est ut hedum caprarum accipiens detulisset domi [21]cuius cum vocem balantis vir eius audisset dixit videte ne forte furtivus sit reddite eum dominis suis quia non licet nobis ex furto aliquid aut edere aut contingere [22]ad haec uxor eius irata respondit manifeste vana facta est spes tua et elemosynae tuae modo paruerunt [23]atque his et aliis huiusmodi verbis exprobrabat ei."[43]

Features which appear in this story recall strongly the prose tale of *Job*. Tobit is cast in the character of Job. Resemblances are found in the resigned and pious speeches of Tobit while he is suffering, the role of his wife, and the blasphemous questions of his would-be comforters. Thus the sufferings of Tobit make him suspicious and, like those of Job (2:9), set up friction between him and his wife. This passage is followed by Tobit's prayer (3:1-6), which recalls Job 7:15 in which he asks to be put out of his personal misery by death. However there are clear variations, for example the expansion of the role of his wife and the reference to the comforters as 'kings'. These additional elements in the story point to the existence of a tradition parallel to but different from the biblical narrative. Elements of the story are reminiscent of the Septuagint version of *Job* - notably the expansion of the role of Job's wife - which suggests that the Septuagint stands at the beginning of this tradition.

L L Besserman[44] maintains that the 'Job tradition', which I have argued was initiated by the Septuagint, originated before the Septuagint and was

---

43 "Now it happened one day, that being wearied with burying, he came to his house, and cast himself down by the wall and slept. And as he was sleeping, hot dung out of a swallow's nest fell upon his eyes, and he was made blind. Now this trial the Lord therefore permitted to happen to him, that an example might be given to posterity of his patience, as also of holy Job. For whereas he had always feared God from his infancy, and kept his commandments, he repined not against God because the evil of blindness had befallen him. But he continued immoveable in the fear of God, giving thanks to God all the days of his life. For as the kings insulted over holy Job: so his relations and kinsmen mocked at his life, saying: Where is thy hope, for which thou gavest alms, and buriedest the dead? But Tobias rebuked them, saying: speak not so: For we are the children of saints and look for that life which God will give to those that never change their faith from him. Now Anna his wife went daily to weaving work, and she brought home what she could get for their living by the labour of her hands. Whereby it came to pass that she received a young kid, and brought it home: And when her husband heard it bleating, he said: Take heed, lest perhaps it be stolen, restore ye it to its owners, for it is not lawful for us either to eat or to touch anything that cometh by theft. At these words his wife being angry answered: It is evident thy hope is come to nothing, and thy alms now appear. And with these and other such like words she upbraided him."

44 L L Besserman, 1979 (pp 39-40).

available to its translator in oral or written form as well as to the author(s) of Tobit. He argues that this oral tradition was early enough to have influenced the Epistle of James and possibly even Ezekiel. Presumably this original oral or written Job tradition which Besserman isolates is separate from the oral tradition which was appropriated by the author of the dialogue of Job when he put together the book in virtually the form we have it. Besserman cites in support of his argument Theodore of Mopsuestia (died 428), disciple of Diodorus of Tarsus and the most influential teacher of the theological school of Antioch,[45] who wrote "de beato Iob historiam maximam et claram, quae in ore omnium similiter ferebatur, non solum Israelitici generis sed et aliorum."[46] This "true history" Theodore contrasted with the Hebrew book of *Job*, which he considered a fiction composed by an author who wanted to gain repute. Job's speeches in the biblical story, said Theodore, are unworthy of a man "qui cum tanta sapientia et virtute et reverentia suam vitam gubernasset"[47] and an author has clearly fabricated the contest between Satan and God. In my opinion, however, these words of Theodore could be taken to refer to the original folk story of *Job* (which did not necessarily include references to Satan - see chapter 4, pp 200-203) which circulated independently and, even after being incorporated in the biblical book of *Job*, may have continued to circulate in groups familiar with popular legends. In such a form, allowing for a few alterations and elaborations, this tradition may have been familiar to the translator of the Septuagint. I see the motive for the changes made by the Septuagint writer as predominantly theological, and so do not need to posit a separate oral tradition to account for the differences between the Septuagint and the Hebrew text. Besserman therefore adds another oral tradition, which unnecessarily complicates our understanding of the pattern of literary dependence here. He writes:[48]

---

45 J D Mansi (ed.), *Sacrorum conciliorum nova et amplissima collectio* IX, 1759-98, cc 223-225. Quotation c 225.
46 This denotes "an outstanding and much esteemed history of the saintly Job, which circulated everywhere orally, in substantially the same form not only amongst people of Jewish race but also amongst other peoples."
47 J D Mansi (ed.), *Sacrorum conciliorum nova et amplissima collectio* IX, cc 223-225. "who governed his life with such great wisdom and virtue and piety."
48 L L Besserman, 1979 (pp 39-40).

"Although Theodore's views were not accepted by the Church, his testimony is further proof of the existence of a history of Job quite different from the one preserved in the Hebrew Bible...The Septuagint in several respects reflects this other tradition of Job: there is a raising of Job's hope for and belief in an afterlife and a proportionate lowering and mitigation of his righteous rebelliousness...the Septuagint's theological hallmark."

Rather than the Septuagint reflecting this other tradition of Job, I would argue that it is its beginning.

Better evidence of the influence of the Septuagint on later works based on the Job story is provided by the pseudepigraphical *Testament of Job* [49], an anonymous, apocryphal work which survives in four Greek manuscripts, in an Old Church Slavonic version and in an incomplete Coptic version, and which was written between the first century BC and the first century AD. It presents the story of Job in the form of a last will and testament. The original language of the *Testament* is most likely to be Greek although Hebrew has been suggested.[50] Job relates his trials to his ten children who were born to him after his restoration to his former estate. Like the Septuagint, the Testament of Job embellishes some features of its Hebrew original and simplifies others. As in the addition to the Septuagint, Job is called Jobab here and his wife is given the name Sitis.[51]

Many details of Job's charity, paralleled in rabbinic sources, can be found in the *Testament*, as well as an expansion of the relationship between Job and his wife. When destitution overtakes Job, his wife sells her hair in order to secure three loaves of bread for her ill and starving husband. Later on, she pleads with the friends to help her bury her children, who lie crushed under the ruins of their home. In the *Testament*, Job understands the reason for his trials from the beginning and he learns from an angel of his guaranteed reward at the end of his suffering. There is no wager between God and Satan; rather Job is

---

[49] The Greek Text was first published by Cardinal Mai in Volume VII of his *Scriptorum Veterum Nova Collectio*, Rome, 1825-38, edited from a single manuscript. M R James, *Apocrypha Anecdota* (ii), 1877, published a slightly different text from an eleventh century Paris manuscript which is thought to be older. Both texts are needed for an accurate picture of the work to be obtained.

[50] For a detailed discussion of the original language in which the *Testament of Job* was written and for the text of the *Testament*, see J H Charlesworth, Volume 1, 1983.

[51] C C Torrey, 1945, p 145 makes the suggestion that her name is originally *Ausitis*, 'the woman from Ausitis or Uz', Job's native land.

said to have brought the suffering upon himself by antagonizing Satan but with the knowledge that only the body can suffer, while the soul will be safe. Awkward themes found in the Hebrew are dropped in the *Testament* - for example Job's rebelliousness in the face of suffering - in favour of a constant stress on Job's perfect patience and endurance. As Besserman writes[52]:

"Here Job becomes as the imagery of the Testament would have it, an athlete or wrestler *for* God; he is no longer the righteous rebel *against* God whom we meet in the Bible."

In the *Testament* the roles of Job and the friends are reversed - Job upholds the notion of divine justice, even echoing the divine speeches from the Hebrew book of *Job* at times (38:1-8), whilst it is his friends who are besieged by doubts. There is a strikingly negative attitude in the *Testament* towards Elihu, also paralleled in rabbinic sources.[53] Basing itself on the text of the epilogue, which declares that Job won forgiveness for Eliphaz and his two companions (42:7-9), but which makes no mention of Elihu, the *Testament of Job* explicitly states that Elihu was not pardoned. Indeed, he is described as "the evil one...the son of darkness, the lover of the Serpent, the Northern one, the hater of the saints who is cast down to Sheol."[54]

A few colourful details are added in the *Testament:* for example, Job plays instruments and sings to cheer up his servants and educate those benefiting from his charity in the love of God (14:1-5) and later he gives two of his daughters musical instruments as gifts (52:2). These elaborations are the origin of the mediaeval tradition that made Job the patron saint of music - a far cry from the original story![55]

In the *Testament of Job* women are generally portrayed in a negative light,[56] Job's maidservants and doormaid, and his wife who begs for bread on her husband's behalf but at the same time berates him. Only Job's daughters are regarded in a completely positive way. The *Testament* contradicts the Hebrew

---

52  L L Besserman, 1979, p 49.
53  Thus R. Akiba identifies Elihu with the heathen prophet Balaam, who is the enemy of Israel (J Sotah V, 30d).
54  K Kohler, 1897, equates this epithet with the Hebrew צפוני, from צפון 'north'. R Gordis, 1965, suggests that it is an erroneous retroversion in the Greek of the Hebrew צפעוני 'asp, serpent'; cf Isa 11:8; 59:5; Jer 8:17; Prov 23:32.
55  See D J A Clines, 1983 and the books listed in his commentary, 1989, p cvi.
56  See P W van der Horst, 1986 and the list in D J A Clines, 1989, pp cv-cvi.

Bible's equal division of Job's possessions amongst his sons and daughters, probably because this was not the custom in the writer's day. Instead the sons receive the property and each of the daughters receives a magical band which the Lord gave to Job from the whirlwind when he was healed. Besserman suggests that the reason for this embellishment was probably the failure of the biblical account to mention how Job was healed. The author may also have wanted to portray Job as able to initiate others in secrets concerning God.[57]

In later ages Job is represented as a wise man, prophet or philosopher and, although there is sufficient basis in the Hebrew for this portrayal of Job in the biblical and ecclesiastical traditions - for example in the wisdom poem in chapter 28 - it is possible that the Testament contributed to this emphasis in its mention of the magical bands.

Thus the later Job tradition sustained misconceptions about the character of Job as a patient sufferer and about the true nature of his trials. Furthermore the original folk tale (still preserved in outline in the prologue and epilogue of the biblical book) inspired not only Jews (see above) and Christians (see below) but also Moslems and it was elaborated on and expanded to form independent literary creations of a legendary nature. The Islamic sources and later traditions extol Job as the pious and righteous servant of Allah and the recipient of revelation, as were Abraham, Ishmael and Isaac and Jacob, Jesus and Jonah, Aaron, David and Solomon (Qur'an 4:161).[58]

At the base of traditions of Job as a patient saint in Judaism, Christianity and Islam lies the simple prose tale that forms the prologue and epilogue to the drama in the biblical book of *Job*. Fascination with the figure of the submissive, trusting, pious sufferer led to the expansion of this tradition along legendary lines whilst the awkwardnesses of the biblical book led writers and interpreters to prefer this single aspect of the biblical Job. The theme of the just sufferer can be traced through many centuries of the book's interpretation.[59] This image of Job thus infiltrated the interpretation of the

---

57 For good discussions of issues relating to the *Testament of Job* see C C Torrey, 1945, pp 140-145, R H Pfeiffer, 1949, pp 70-72 and M A Knibb and P W van der Horst, 1989.
58 For literature on Islamic versions of the Job story, see list in D J A Clines, 1989, p civ.
59 See discussion in N N Glatzer (ed), 1969.

main part of the book and modified the rebellious character of Job depicted there. This interpretation was supported by the Christian tradition which was largely ecclesiastical and which marked the beginning of exegetical study of the biblical text of *Job*.

iv) The ecclesiastical Job tradition

"It can be maintained that, generally speaking, Christianity was in a more advantageous position than Judaism in approaching the book of *Job*. It saw in Job a type, symbol, prefiguration of Jesus and could concentrate on and elaborate this understanding of the book. Judaism, on the other hand, had no corresponding focus of interpretation. This made for a greater variety of outlook and greater freedom of exposition, but militated against a singleness of purpose such as is evident in the Christian reading of *Job*."[60]

The early Christian church maintained the ideal of a saintly Job. This interpretation was based on the prose tale, possibly on Jewish readings of the book and certainly on the New Testament allusion to the patience of Job in the Epistle of James 5:11. The First Epistle of Clement to the Corinthians (AD 100) refers to Job as the "righteous and blameless, true worshipper of God." He is accompanied by Abraham and Moses, Elijah and Elisha, Ezekiel and the other prophets, who were "heralding the coming of Christ" and whose piety and humility are to be imitated by the faithful.[61] The Apocalypse of Paul (end of the fourth century) [62] has Job afflicted by a terrible plague for thirty years - "and in the beginning the blains that came forth from my body were as grains of wheat; but on the third day they became like an ass's foot, and the worms that fell from them were four fingers long:" The devil appears to Job three times and says, "Speak a word against the Lord and die." But Job says, "If thus be the will of God that I continue in the plague all the time of my life until

---

60 N N Glatzer (ed), 1969 (p 24).
61 1 Clement 17; *The Apostolic Fathers*, (Loeb Classical Library), translated by K Lake, London, 1930.
62 Greek original in *Apocalypses Apocryphae Mosis Esdrae, Pauli, Johannis*, ed C Tischendorf, 1866, pp 34-69. English translation from M R James, 1924, pp 525-555. James remarks in a footnote that "it seems as if the author had read the Testament of Job...in which are very similar details." See also E Hennecke and W Schneemelcher (eds), Volume II, 1963, pp 533-536, and their section on textual history. The Syriac version of the Apocalypsis Pauli contains a few extra details, for example it has the evil one prompting Job's sons to make their father blaspheme against the living God.

I die, I will not rest from blessing the Lord God, and I shall receive the greater reward. For I know that the sufferings of this world are nought compared with the refreshment that is thereafter." When Paul sees Job he appears to him "very beautiful in the face, and smiling and his angels singing hymns."[63]

The ecclesiastical tradition is to be found in patristic and later exegetical writings. A sixth century work which had a great influence on Christian interpretation of *Job* in the Middle Ages and after was Gregory the Great's *Moralia in Iob*.[64] Gregory's work is a commentary on every verse in *Job*, stressing either its literal and historical level, or its allegorical level, or its moral level - or all three, depending on the verse. For example he interpreted on an allegorical level any verse in *Job* which he considered 'typical', ie which he took to refer to Christ or to the church. An example of this allegorical interpretation is provided by Moralia I, Book 1 ix, 15 on Job 1:

"*Vir erat in terra Hus, nomine Job:* Haec per historiam facta credimus sed per allegoriam jam qualiter sint impleta, videamus. Job namque, ut diximus, interpretatur dolens. Hus vero consiliator. Quem ergo alium beatus Job suo nomine exprimit, nisi eum, di quo Propheta loquitur, dicens *Dolores nostros ipse portavit?* [Isaiah 53:4] Qui Hus terram inhabitat, quia in corda populi consiliatoris regnat. Paulus quippe ait: *Christum Dei virtutem, et Dei sapientiam* [I Cor 1:24]. Atque haec ipsa Sapientia per Salomonem dicit: *Ego sapientia habito in consilio, et eruditis intersum cogitationibus* [Prov 8:12]. Hus ergo terram inhabitat Job: quia Sapientia, quae pro nobis passionis dolorem sustinuit, corda vitae consiliis dedita sibimet habitationem fecit.*" [65]

---

63 All quotations taken from paragraph 49 of the Apocalypse of St Paul (M R James, 1924, p 552). The pseudo-Clementine "Apostolic Constitutions" contains a "Form of Prayer for the Ordination of a Bishop." which dates from around the same time as the Apocalypse. "[Thou] who hast fore-ordained priests from the beginning for the government of Thy people - Abel in the first place, Seth and Enos, and Enoch and Noah, and Melchisedeck and Job." (Quoted in ANCL XVII, pp 214-215). A Syrian version also exists - Constitutiones Apostolorum, Syria, ca AD 380.

64 Gregory the Great, *Moralia in Iob* (text in *Morales sur Job*, Paris, 1950). For detail on Gregory's method see N N Glatzer, 1969, pp 27-32.

65 "*There was a man in the land of Uz whose name was Job:* We do not doubt the historical value of this narrative, but let us see how, by allegorical interpretation, it was fulfilled. Job, as we have said, signifies 'the sufferer' and Uz 'the counsellor'. Therefore the blessed Job expresses by his name the one of whom the prophet said: *Surely he has borne our griefs?* He lives in the land of Uz because he rules the hearts of the people of the counsellor. Saint Paul said: *Christ is the power of God and the wisdom of God* and from the mouth of Solomon Wisdom herself said: *I, wisdom, dwell in council and am found in judicious thoughts.* Thus Job lives in the country of Uz because wisdom, which has for us suffered a painful passion, has chosen to live in hearts which surrender to the councils of life."

As Besserman writes:[66]

"Gregory's exegetical method enabled him to by-pass contradictory or otherwise vexing verses in the Book of Job and to reconstitute the story of Job into a comprehensive statement on Christian dogma and morality."

Gregory had more concern for expounding Christian doctrine than for representing contradictions which he regarded as superficial, and he takes little note of the theme of Job's righteous rebelliousness. He is at pains to explain away Job's blasphemous remarks, focusing on the patient Job of the prologue. Thus the Job of the Moralia is, on the historical and moral levels, a patient Christian saint and on the allegorical level he is a type or prefiguration of Christ.

These two themes of Job's patience and his prefiguration of Christ dominate the entire exegetical Job tradition. Some recognize Job's problematic vehemence in protesting his fate. For example Ambrose in *De interpellatione Job et David* wrote:

"David ac Jobum pro nostris infirmitatibus interpellasse, unde hujus operis argumentum." (625, Introduction)

and:

"Quod idem ante ipsum fecerat sanctus Job: sed iste moralius, ille vehementius." (626.3).[67]

However most stress Job's perfect patience - for example Tertullian in *De Patientia:*

"O felicissimum illum quoque, qui omnem patientiae speciem adversus omnem diaboli vim expunxit, quum non abacti greges, non illae in pecore divitiae, non filii uno ruinae impetu adempti, non ipsius denique corporis in ulcere (14) cruciatus a patientia et fide Domino debita (15) exclusit, quem diabolus totis viribus frustra caecidit (Job 1). Neque enim a respectu Dei tot doloribus avocatus ille est; sed constitit nobis in exemplum et testimonium, tam spiritu quam carne, tam animo quam corpore patientiae perpetrandae (16); ut neque damnis saecularum, nec amissionibus carissimorum, nec corporis quidem conflictationibus succidamus (i)."[68]

---

66 L L Besserman, 1979 (p 55).
67 Ambrose, *De interpellatione Job et David*, PL 14 (cc 797-811).
68 Tertullian, *De patientia*, PL 1, cc 1249-1274; piece on Job cc 1270-1271 (chapter XIV). Footnote (i) reads "*Quasi in illo viro feretrum Deus diabolo exstruxit.* Sic veteres libri. Est autem feretrum, νεκροφορειον quo mortuus effertur. Itaque dicitur Jobus feretrum fuisse Diabolo, quia in Jobi patientissimi corpus omnes Satanae impetus sic usque

Thus the complex character of Job in the biblical narrative is lost.

The role of Job in the liturgy of the Catholic Church, notably in the Office of the Dead,[69] shaped people's view of him and made him popular. Readings from *Job* were spread through the three nocturns of Matins (the Dirige proper): the first nocturn included Job 7:16-21; 10:1-7 and 10:8-12, the second nocturn Job 13:23-8; 14:1-6 and 14:13-16 and the third, Job 17:1-3,11-15; 19:20-27 and 10:18-22[70].

In the later Middle Ages in France and England these verses came to be read together as a 'Le petit Job': 'Pety Job' or 'Little Job', a shorter version of the book of *Job*. This 'Little Job' can be found in the English primer, the layman's prayer book, as well as in Latin service books. This indicates how widely available this version of the Job story was compared to the version in the Vulgate. The last lesson from *Job* in the 'Little Job' is out of biblical order (Job 10:18-22 following Job 19:20-27) and we do not know why this is so nor why it was chosen (nor, indeed, do we know why the others were chosen). All nine passages are spoken by Job and are not linked in any

---

contusi sunt et commortui." Cyprian and Augustine also stress Job's patience: Cyprian, *De bono patientia*, PL 4, cc 645-662, esp c 658, Chapter XVIII (634); Augustine, *De Patientia*, PL 40, cc 611-626, comment on Job cc 615-616, Chapter XI.

69  The Office of the Dead was a major liturgical observance in mediaeval times. From the eighth century onwards the office was recited in monasteries, then in cathedrals, then among the secular clergy and by the devout everywhere. Clergy could supplement their income by reciting this office, a particularly fruitful activity during the plague of 1349. G. Chaucer in *The General Prologue* (lines 477-528), when describing the parson, refers to the recitation of memorial services for pay as a common practice - an abuse of which his parson is not guilty. Lines 507-11 read "He sette nat his benefice to hyre I And leet his sheep encombred in the myre I And ran to Londoun unto seinte Poules I To seken him chaunterie for soules I Or with a bretherhed to been withholde" (cited in F N Robinson (ed), 1974).

70  According to L L Besserman (pp 57-58) the forerunner of the Office of the Dead in the liturgy was the Commendatio Animae in which mention of Job was simply in connection with a plea for deliverance - "Deliver us as you have delivered Job". Besserman cites in his footnote (30) "A Muratori (ed), *Liturgia romana vetus*, Venice, 1748, 1, 750. Text from Sarum use." I have been unable to find this reference. In the Commendatio Animarum which is found in the Sarum Breviary (Manuale ad usum percelebris ecclesiae sarisburiensis from edition printed Rouen 1543, compared with those of 1506 (London), 1516 (Rouen), 1526 (Paris), Chichester, 1958 (Henry Bradshaw Society Volume XCI)) there is no mention of Job and the Commendatio is not presented as a forerunner of the Office of the Dead - they are often used together. If this reference to *Job* in the Commendatio Animae does exist it may provide the reason why further passages from *Job* were included in the Office of the Dead. On the spread of the Office of the Dead and related growth of the liturgy see Edmund Bishop in *The Prymer or Lay Folks' Prayer Book*, (ed. H Littlehales, 1891).

obvious progression, and none is marked by any narrative detail. Besserman[71] reproduces a text from an early fifteenth-century English primer following the Sarum Use and it is from this that I quote the first set of lessons in the 'Little Job':

"Leccio .1ᵃ: Parce michi domine!

Lord, spare þou me, for my daies ben not! / what is man, for þou magnifiest him? eþer what settest þou þin herte towardis him? / þou visitist him eerli; and sodeynli þou preuest him. / hou longe sparest þou not me, neþer suffrest þat y swolewe my spotele? / y haue synned, o þou keper of men, what shal y do to þee? whi hast þou set me contrarie to þee? & y am maad greuouse to my silf? /whi doist þou not awey my synne? & whi takest þou not a-wey my wickidnesse? lo, now, y slepe in poudur; and if þou sekest me eerli, y schal not abide. (Job 7:16-21)

leccio iiᵃ: Tedet animam.

It anoieþ my soule of my lyif; y schal lette my speche azenes me, y schal spekein e bitternesse of my soule. / y schal seie to god, 'nyle þou condempne me; schewe þou to me whi þou demest me so. / whe þer it semeþ good to þee, if þou falseli chalengist & oppressist me, þe werk of þin hondis, & if þou helpe þe counseil of wickid men. / wheþer fleischli izen ben to ee? eþer as a man seeþ, also þou schalt se? / wheþer þi daies ben as þe daies of man; & þi zeeris ben as mannes tymes, / þat þou enquere my wickidnesse, & ensserche my synne, / & wite þat y haue do no wickid þing, siþen no man is þat mai delyuere fro þyn hond?' (Job 10:1-7)

leccio iijᵃ: Manus tue.

Thyne hondis maden me, & han formed me al in cumpas; & þou castist me doun so sodeynli! / y biseche þee haue þou mynde þat þou madist me of cley, & shalt brynge me azen in-to poudur. / wheþer ou hast not softid me as mylk; and hast cruddid me to-gideres as chese? / þou hast clopid me wiþ skyn and flesch; & þou hast ioyned me to-gideres wiþ bones and synewes. / þou hast zoue liyf and merci to me; & þi visitacioun haþ kept my spirit. (Job 10:8-12)"

In the first set of lessons Job confesses he has sinned and prays for the remission of his sins and wickedness. Sometimes the English follows the Latin so closely it ends up being obscure (eg 10:1). Elsewhere the English departs from the Vulgate wording or word order. These problems however do not affect our overall understanding of the passage. This passage resembles closely those psalms which precede the texts from *Job* in the Office of the Dead, especially Psalm 6, one of the penitential psalms. In the second set of lessons there is a reversal. Job complains that he is not guilty of sin and that

---

[71] See L L Besserman, 1979, pp 59-62. His text is reproduced from H Littlehales (ed), *The Prymer or Lay Folks' Prayer Book*, 1891, pp 56-70. Chapter and verse are according to the Vulgate.

God has been unfair. The English follows the Latin original fairly closely but there is a tendency to tone down a few of Job's most rebellious remarks - for example in 17:15 the Vulgate reads, "Ubi est ergo nunc praestolatio mea? Et patientiam meam quis considerat?" Job's rhetorical questions are turned into hopeful declarations of faith when the Office adds in at the end "my lord god þou it ert!" [72] In the third set of lessons there is a movement back to repentance from protest. Grief leads to resignation which then leads to hope - this was clearly the message which the writers of the office wished to convey. Not all the original *Job* is lost, for example, in the seventh lesson, Job 17:2, "y haue not synned", despite the confession in other passages that he had sinned. But the psalms placed between the nine lessons from *Job* all stress penance and trust in God's justice and so colour the way the verses from *Job* are read. *Job* also featured in other parts of the liturgy although only in small measure - for example, selected verses from chapters 1 to 7 were read in the office in the first two weeks of September.

The combined effects of both the apocryphal and ecclesiastical traditions about Job can be seen in the popular veneration of Job in the Middle Ages as the patron saint of sufferers from melancholy, worms, venereal disease, leprosy and other skin diseases and as the patron saint of musicians. These developments clearly spring from the Job tradition which began with the Septuagint as outlined above, for they are certainly not implied in the biblical narrative. They were no doubt sustained by the important place that Job had in the ecclesiastical tradition and by the significant role given to him by exegetical writers of the time as the model of patience and as a type of Christ himself. The later Christian interpreter read *Job* as an allegory, as a text that calls for symbolic analysis.[73] For this interpreter, *Job* was but a testimony to the central event in Christianity and to some of the theological and moral teachings of the Church. Only a rare mediaeval philosopher like Maimonides or Gersonides would turn to *Job* for ideas bearing on God and the problem of evil. Not until modern times does Job the rebel, the hero of the dialogue, become the prime focus of attention.

---

[72]  See L L Besserman, 1979, p 61.
[73]  See discussions of Chrysostom and Jerome in N Glatzer (ed), 1969.

In the second section of this chapter I shall turn to modern critical evaluations of the message of Job. From ecclesiastical traditions in the Middle Ages to modern critical scholarship is a considerable leap and it is not meant to suggest that there was nothing of note written on *Job* in the intervening period.[74] However the picture of Job which had come about by the end of the Middle Ages, and indeed long before - that of Job as the pious and patient sufferer - persisted throughout the centuries until the modern period.

## b) CRITICAL INTERPRETATIONS OF *JOB*

### i) The Innocent Sufferer

"The primary theme is the suffering of the innocent. For the overwhelming majority of readers and commentators this is, and always has been, the problem of the book." [75]

At the beginning of the book, Job, a righteous, prosperous and innocent man (as God himself testifies) suffers as a result of a heavenly conflict on the theme of disinterested righteousness about which he knows nothing. God says to Satan: "Have you considered my servant Job, that there is none like

---

[74] For example, among the reformers, Luther, 1524 (see *The Works of Martin Luther*, 1932, pp 383f), wrote a preface to *Job* when he translated it into German and argued that the theme of the book was "whether misfortune can come to the righteous from God." For him the chief message is "that God alone is righteous and yet one man is more righteous than another even before God". The book was written "for our comfort, in order that we may know that God allows even His saints to stumble." Luther's Job is thus a man tempted by God. The elements of rebellion in the book are reduced in scope and the speeches of God are not seen as the answer to Job. Calvin, 1569, wrote a sermon on virtually every chapter, eg in Sermon 147 on God's answer to Job from the whirlwind (chapter 36) Calvin argues that it is because of our rebellion that God must show himself in a terrrible manner. God speaks to us out of a whirlwind because when he spoke to us graciously we did not hear him. When God perceives man's hardness of heart, he must cast us down from the start. Calvin's argument is that if a saint like Job, who humbled himself in the face of God's majesty, needed to be rebuked, how much more do we need to be made obedient to him? Man needs to be made to recognize his inferiority so that he is ready to accept God's goodness. Job speaks "without knowledge" - in the same way, man is full of meaningless talk and should not presume to answer God, rather man should listen in fear to God's word. Calvin is clearly using the book as a foil for his own views about pride rather than analysing it objectively, which was neither his aim nor his method. See discussion in N N Glatzer, 1969 (cf N Glatzer 1966).

[75] M Tsevat, 1966 (p 364).

him on the earth, a blameless and upright man, who fears God and turns away from evil?" (1:8). But Satan denies the possibility of genuine religious devotion when he remarks, cynically, "Does Job fear God for naught?" (1:9) implying that Job's piety depends solely on favourable external circumstances. God on the other hand insists that Job's fear of God rises above selfish interests. The suffering which befalls Job thus provides the means for adjudicating between these two opposing convictions.

After the first set of trials "Job did not sin or charge God with wrong" (1:22) and even after the second set, when his wife encourages him to "curse God and die" (2:9), Job's reply is, "Shall we receive good at the hand of God and shall we not receive evil?" (2:10). Despite disaster Job does not give up his trust in God. The result is a foregone conclusion. G von Rad[76] calls this outcome:

"the...simple, self-illuminating logic of a faith in which he [Job] is unassailably secure... Without knowing it [the heavenly prologue to his suffering] Job, with his two confessions of faith, justified the 'word of honour' with which God had answered for him in advance. Thus the narrative portrays Job as a fitting witness to God."

Whilst innocent suffering functioned as a secondary theme to that of the pious and patient sufferer in traditional thought about *Job*, it came to prominence in the early critical period, hand in hand with the themes of disinterested righteousness and the doctrine of retribution. It is still advocated as the central theme of the book by some modern scholars,[77] although, today, whilst most scholars would acknowledge that *Job* airs the problem of innocent suffering in some form, few would see this as providing the key to the

---

76  G von Rad, 1972 (pp 207-208).
77  eg M Tsevat, 1966, reproduces the older view. More recent scholars shift the emphasis of this central theme, eg G Fohrer, 1962, argues that the problem of *Job* is not why the righteous man suffers but what the proper conduct of man in suffering is - not theodicy, but man's own behaviour, cf S Terrien, 'Job', 1962, pp 897 and 902, and 1963, pp 35f and 45-49. D J A Clines, 1979, asserts that, since the reason for suffering is not satisfactorily answered in *Job*, it is not the primary question being addressed. The problem answered is whether there is such a thing as innocent suffering or whether it is always a matter of desert. However, Clines' own position is that the essential problem in *Job* is 'How can I suffer?' and the answer is twofold - either calm acceptance (prologue/epilogue) or bitterness and anger towards God (dialogue).

interpretation of the book.[78] The problem with early scholarship was that there was a tendency to read the whole book in the light of the prologue and epilogue.[79] There was an overemphasis on this section, notably on the heavenly wager between God and Satan concerning Job's motives for worshipping God. Job was pictured as the righteous man to whom undeserved suffering came as a result of this wager. The prologue answers the question of whether there is such a thing as unselfish virtue and shows, by the example of Job's response, how man should respond to suffering. The epilogue rewards Job's patience and vindicates his suffering. Whilst it was occasionally noted that the prologue/epilogue and dialogue sections were different in style and content, scholars were keen to retain the unity of the book and find an overall message for it. Thus the dialogue was seen as airing the problems of the relationship of suffering to the individual and to the world order.[80]

Certain questions concerning suffering were especially considered by scholars: for example that of God's ability to bring suffering upon a good man, not necessarily because he has sinned;[81] that of innocent suffering in relation to the goodness and omnipotence of God;[82] how man should respond while suffering to such apparently arbitrary treatment by God;[83] and the

---

[78] eg J L Crenshaw, 1982, who sees the theme of innocent suffering as confined to the narrative parts of *Job*. In the prologue he sees it as secondary to the theme of disinterested righteousness, cf G Fohrer 1963.

[79] These were usually read together as a unit but E König, 1929, rejected the originality of the prologue. K Fullerton, 1924 and L Finkelstein, 1938, doubted the early date of the epilogue. M Buttenweiser, 1922 and A Alt, 1937, argued that the epilogue is added by a later hand. E König, 1893; M Jastrow, 1920; L Finkelstein, 1938; J Lindblom, 1945 and R H Pfeiffer, 1948, question the originality of the scenes in heaven.

[80] On the relationship of the prose story to the dialogue see K Kautzsch, 1900. K Fullerton, 1924, regards the dialogue as containing a discussion of 1) the relationship of suffering to the individual and 2) the relationship of suffering to the world order (the problem of theodicy).

[81] S R Driver, 1906, wrote, "The problem is this: *Why do the righteous suffer?* and the principal aim of the book is to controvert the theory, dominant at the time when it was written, *that suffering or misfortune is a sign of the Divine displeasure and presupposes sin on the part of the sufferer*" (p vii).

[82] eg W O E Oesterley and T H Robinson, 1937, who conclude: "The suffering of the righteous may raise the question of the justice of God's government of the world, but the contemplation of the divine creative work brings man to a deeper apprehension of God and he comes to see that God is concerned with something more than the mere punishing and rewarding of men; and thus there is generated a clearer sense of the proportion of things" (p 316).

[83] A S Peake, 1904, finds this issue at the centre of interest in *Job*.

possibility of a deeper understanding of God through the experience of suffering.[84] Job is often seen as the model of the innocent sufferer, a type either of the class of suffering, righteous men or of the suffering remnant during the Exile.[85] The author is regarded as having experienced innocent suffering himself and is put into a situation in Israel's history when this might have occurred.[86] The book is often compared to conceptions of suffering in other Old Testament books[87] and regarded as "the most thorough, frank, and honest discussion which the subject [the problem of suffering] has ever received."[88] In general *Job* is seen as a tract on the problem of the innocent suffering of the righteous to which it attempts to provide an answer. Some scholars find the answer in a particular section of the book which they highlight,[89] others find various answers but often conflict over what precisely these are,[90] and others find no answer at all.[91]

Any discussion of the message of *Job* is inextricably related to literary-critical factors and the literary-critical standpoint taken affects the interpretation of the message of the book. The reading of *Job* which focuses on the issue of

---

[84] eg S R Driver and G B Gray, 1921, argue that Job shows how man can serve God not for outward things and, in asserting that man is not always punished because he has sinned, Job places the findings of personal experience foremost. The theme of the triumph of experience over theory is then expanded in the dialogue section.

[85] eg A Davidson, 1884; and E Kellett, 1939-40 who argues that Job stands for Israel in a similar manner to the suffering servant of Isaiah.

[86] eg A Davidson, 1884. See discussion of authorship in chapter 4, pp 160-161.

[87] eg the 'confessions' of Jeremiah. It is often supposed that the author of *Job* is the first to perceive that all suffering is not self-entailed - but in fact Jeremiah 12:1 gives expression to this sentiment too.

[88] eg W O E Oesterley and T H Robinson, 1937 (2nd edition, p 347).

[89] eg in Chapter 19 - G Fohrer, 1963, p 318f (in 19:25-27) and K Fullerton, 1924, pp 116 and 136; in Chapter 28 - discussed by C Kuhl, 1953, H H Rowley, 1958-9, pp 167-207 and N H Tur-Sinai, 1957 (a number of scholars who accept this place Chapter 28 at the end of the Yahweh speeches); in the Elihu speeches - K Budde, 1896; and in 38:1-42:6 - M Tsevat, 1966, who argues that the speeches are a replacement of the original answer of the poem, cf G Fohrer, 1963, pp 37 and 538.

[90] eg R B Y Scott, 1972 finds three answers to the problem of the suffering of the innocent on three different levels - in the prologue/epilogue, in the dialogue and in a more general religious solution. W O E Oesterley and T H Robinson, 1934, find three solutions to the problem of "the inequality of suffering and its apparent injustice" in *Job* (p 175).

[91] E Montet, 1947, writes, "After having examined studiously and profoundly without result, he [the author] subjects himself to the mysterious and enigmatic will of God. Resignation and submission to the divine arbitrator, that is the last word of the poem; it does not bring any solution whatever to the sorrowful question posed." (p 7) Sometimes the finding of no answer leads scholars to assert that this is not therefore the central theme of the book, eg O Procksch, 1949.

innocent suffering thus affects the literary-critical standpoint of its advocate. Whilst some early scholars recognised the disjointedness of the book and based their assessment of the message on prior conclusions regarding literary-critical issues[92], most focused on the prologue and epilogue as a result of their assessment of innocent suffering as the primary theme of the book.[93]

The most significant contribution in this period was that of K Budde who managed to combine both approaches.[94] He emphasized the importance of the prologue/epilogue and his assessment of its relationship to the dialogue dictated his view of the book's message. However he did not find the message of the dialogue to be in contradiction to that of the prose narrative and so was able to assert the unity of the book. The weakness in his attempt to harmonize the message of the book was the necessity to remove verses and correct the text to fit his conception of the author's overall message or purpose. He thus decided literary-critical issues before attending to the message and then adapted the finer literary-critical details of the text to the demands of a unified message. Thus Budde posited the original circulation of the prose story in written form in popular tradition, known by and referred to in Ezekiel (14:14-20), which depicted Job as a model of righteousness. The author of the present book adopted the prose story and inserted his own additions to present a very different, impatient Job, guilty of spiritual pride in believing himself guiltless. Budde defined the aim of the original folk story as being to exhibit the suffering Job's unswerving constancy and thus to point to the impending

---

[92] The Elihu speeches provide a good illustration of this. They were often regarded as secondary on literary-critical grounds for there is no mention of Elihu in the prologue/epilogue but rather a long justification of his appearance in 32:6-22 and his speeches and contribution are ignored both in the Yahweh speeches and in the epilogue. See brief discussion of the authenticity of the Yahweh speeches below (pp 40,43) and in chapter 4 (pp 205-207).

[93] eg E F Sellin, 1923, finds three solutions (or four with chapter 28) to the problem of suffering in *Job* and concludes from this that the book is not a unity. He goes on to argue that the prologue and epilogue are not by the same hand as the dialogue and that the author of *Job* has, with poetic freedom, taken over an earlier popular book and made it the setting of his poem. He finds, however, no tension between the prologue/epilogue and dialogue.

[94] K Budde, 1876, p 39, and 1896, pp viii ff. The idea of the author adapting a popular story for his own didactic purposes is also to be attributed to J Wellhausen, 1871, p 555; B Duhm, 1897, p vii; and T K Cheyne, 1887, p 66. cf M Vernes, 1880; G Bickell, 1894; J C B Mohr, 1897; L Laue, 1896; D B MacDonald, 1895; L Gautier, 1914; P Volz, 1921; A Lods, 1934; J Lindblom, 1945; W O E Oesterley and T H Robinson, 1934.

defeat of Satan who had sought to overthrow Job's integrity. The purpose of the dialogue, Budde argued, is to show that Job's piety was not without a flaw; this is demonstrated by his violent language, although God testifies that he is innocent. On this reading, Budde was able to support the view of the friends and maintain the unity of the book. The secret fault which lurked in Job's heart, unsuspected by himself, is brought to light and he is led to penitent humiliation on account of it and so to a strengthening of his piety. Budde differed from other scholars in both recognizing the composite nature of the book, and trying to maintain the unity of its message. Other scholars were wary of admitting this compositeness because it seemed to pose a threat to the book's unity.[95] Scholars advocating the unity of the message had opposed the idea that the prose story was to be attributed to a different hand and once circulated independently.[96] Budde continued to stress the importance of the author, arguing that he had formed an *imposed* unity from previously disparate parts.[97] A new emphasis on the author's role in including the dialogue in the prose story emerged, an emphasis which has been taken up again in the modern period.[98] Budde's ideas on author's intention were forward-looking for his day.

To conclude, early scholarship tended to focus on innocent suffering as the primary theme of Job. This caused the prologue/epilogue to be at the forefront of interest. Both the assessment of the message of *Job* and literary-critical conclusions can be seen to have influenced scholars' evaluation of *Job* at this time.

---

[95] eg S Davidson, 1862 and A Davidson, 1884, rejected only the Elihu speeches on the ground of disunity of theme with the rest of the book.

[96] eg W H Green, 1897, who wrote: "It is quite insupportable that this introduction and conclusion which are so precisely adjusted to the rest of the book could have been written by a different hand with a totally different design." He is wary of Budde's approach and even more so of scholars such as G Studer, 1881, who found seven different writers in *Job*. It is clear that the carving up of the text was taken too far by Studer.

[97] In a similar vein, H W Robinson, 1937, made a bid for the unity of the book and a reconciliation of differences between the prose sections and the dialogue by appealing to the design of the author. He held that since the author wrote, adopted or adapted the prologue and made it a significant part of the book, he must have regarded it as "the sufficient explanation of the debate" (p 153).

[98] See discussion in chapter 4, pp 184-194.

## ii) The doctrine of retribution

"The book of Job is a discussion of the problem of retribution - the apparent contradiction between the doctrine of the justice of God and the facts of human experience. If God is just, why is it that the innocent sometimes suffer, and the wicked prosper?"[99]

The attention of scholars shifted slowly in the direction of a fuller appreciation of the dialogue section of *Job* so that by the 1940s this was commonly emphasized as the key section of the book. Many found the central message of *Job* in the discussion between Job and the friends on the nature of retributive suffering.[100] This raised the deeper question of theodicy - how can the suffering of a good man be reconciled with the moral government of God?[101] *Job* was seen as a discussion of the apparent contradiction between the doctrine of the justice of God, which led to a hardened doctrine as represented by the friends, and the facts of human experience, as represented by Job's suffering. The question is raised: If God is just, why is it that the innocent suffer and the wicked prosper? This was seen as a 'wisdom' question[102] since the old dogma, characteristic of early wisdom and found in Proverbs[103] and some wisdom psalms,[104] was that the good prosper and the wicked are punished. This old wisdom doctrine had however become

---

99 E J Kissane, 1939 (p xv).
100 In 1906 S R Driver argued that the principal aim of *Job* was to controvert the theory that suffering was a sign of the divine displeasure, cf S R Driver and G B Gray, 1921. A large number of scholars from the late 1930s-1960s have followed this view, eg H W Robinson, 1937, who writes, "The subject of the book is the suffering of the innocent and the prosperity of the wicked - ie the justice of God as based on the principle of exact moral retribution within this world" (p 154). See also E Jones, 1966; O S Rankin, 1936; F Delitzsch, 1866; R Gordis, 1971 and S H Blank, 1962, who writes of *Job*, "Its author does not deny providence - that would be leaving the orbit of religion. What he denies is the simple arithmetic of divine justice; so doing, he attacks the arrogance of the fortunate and reassures all persons (like Job) who are perplexed by adversity." (p 858)
101 G F Moore, 1913, writes, "The author means to controvert the dogma that all suffering is retributive and to show in the instance of Job how this doctrine may drive a godly man to the denial of God's justice altogether." (1948, p 212)
102 By, for example, P Volz, 1911; J Fichtner, 1933; B Gemser, 1937; H Gese, 1958 and R B Y Scott, 1972, pp 136-140.
103 eg Proverbs 11, 25-29 - see discussion in K Koch, 1955.
104 eg Psalms 1, 32, 37 and 128 in which, according to J K Kuntz, 1977, "rewards and punishments for specific human conduct issue according to an underlying principle of justice unfailing in its concrete application" (p 228). Kuntz does not however find this rigid system at work in all psalms featuring this theme.

individualized.[105] The friends cherish the view that suffering is a sign of divine displeasure and thus conclude that since Job suffers he must be a sinner - any other interpretation impugns the justice of God - but Job asserts that whereas striving for good ought to be rewarded in fact it is not: for example, in 9:22 he asserts, "It is all one; therefore I say, he destroys both the blameless and the wicked." His experience thus leads him to question God's justice and hence to question the doctrine of retribution. He maintains the right of the sufferer to complain; asserts that the friends' doctrine is heartless in the way it reproves rather than comforts the sufferer; and argues that, although one cannot rebel against a supreme God, his omnipotence does not prove his justice. He refuses to admit guilt when he is innocent and maintains his right to appeal to God as the only arbiter. However the key element in this reading of *Job* is that he is in fact praised by God who says to the friends, "you have not spoken of me what is right, as my servant Job has." (42:7) and the conclusion generally drawn was that this demonstrates the necessity of breaking out of old dogmatic ways of thinking. It also emphasizes that personal experience is more relevant than dogma.

Realization of the increased importance of the dialogue when assessing the message of *Job* was accompanied by a fuller awareness of the tensions between the prologue/epilogue and the dialogue which led to their being seen as two unconnected compositions.[106] In the characterization of Job, the prologue and epilogue show Job obediently submissive to God's will even if it

---

[105] It is often asserted that the view of the friends was the orthodox view in Israel as a whole, not just in the wisdom literature, until the author of *Job* challenged it (eg J Meinhold, 1919; L W Batten, 1933; I G Matthews, 1947). The doctrine of retribution is therefore often given a historical context. The Deuteronomistic theory of history is that the nation always got what it deserved - in Judges religious defection is regularly given as the cause of foreign oppression (eg Judges 2:2-3,11-15,20-23). In the time of the author of *Job*, it was said (eg by E J Kissane, 1939), this doctrine was individualized, a process which created many new problems for theology. It led to the hard doctrine of the friends against which Job protests. K Koch, 1955, sees *Job* and Ecclesiastes as decisive in changing the doctrine of retribution. He writes, "It was when skepticism gained the upper hand that there was a *radical reassessment of the concept that there was a powerful sphere of influence in which the built-in consequences of an action took effect*" (1973, p 79).

[106] eg W B Stevenson, 1947, points out the differences in Job's character in the two parts and shows how the dialogue, notably the words of Job, has been misunderstood when read in the light of the prose tale. He blames 42:7 for causing much prejudice and prefers to read the poem without it.

means unexplained sufferings: "In all this Job did not sin with his lips" (2:10). The dialogue, on the other hand, portrays a much less submissive and accepting Job who is self-reliant and defiant. In 19:6-7 Job says to his friends "know then that God has put me in the wrong and closed his net about me. Behold, I cry out, 'Violence', but I am not answered, I call aloud, but there is no justice." Some scholars have seen this as evidence of two different Jobs.[107]

Furthermore the prose narrative gives no satisfactory conclusion to the issues raised in the dialogue. It is not (to us at least) satisfactory for a man suffering great agonies and bereft of everything, whilst assured of his innocence, to be given no explanation and merely have his possessions doubled as a reward for his steadfastness. The speeches of God which should constitute the theological climax make no attempt to answer the questions originally discussed such as whether and why the innocent suffer or whether God has a purpose in tormenting man. They merely state his power: "Where were you when I laid the foundation of the earth?" (38:4); "Shall a faultfinder contend with the Almighty? He who argues with God let him answer it" (40:2). The orthodox answer appears to be that if one understands the greatness of the Creator one will not ask these questions - God's justice is better than ours (the line taken by the friends). But more probably these speeches simply stress that God is unknowable, whether good or bad (thus supporting the line taken by Job himself).

---

[107] H L Ginsberg, 1969, isolates two Jobs whom he calls 'Job the patient [JP] and Job the impatient [JIP]'. He reconstructs two separate sources found throughout the present book of *Job*. The flaw in his work is that he presupposes the division JP/JIP without providing any detailed reasons for doing so and then juggles with verses to fit the awkward ones into either one part or another, positing missing sections where there are omissions. His merit is that he does see that the two portrayals are inconsistent. P Volz, 1911, noted the contrast between the patient and impatient Jobs - "der Hiob der leidenschaftlichen 'Klage' (K. 3f) und der geduldige Hiob der 'Erzählung' (K. 1f, 42:10-17)" (p 1) - and wrote "Es ist unmöglich, daß der eine Hiob sich in den anderen gewandelt hätte." ("The one Job could not possibly have changed into the other.") (p 1). B S Childs, 1979, has recently pursued arguments similar to Ginsberg's for two continuous narratives running through *Job*: he argues that *Job* has two functions and poses two sets of questions for two different readers. The first set is for the reader who looks at the dialogue from the perspective of the framework, and the second is for the reader who decides to share Job's ignorance of the divine will to pursue his questions. He sees a theory of unintentional corruption as inadequate to describe the present literary shape of the book and finds the reason for its present shape as seeking to instruct the reader in the true purpose of wisdom.

Thus the dialogue section of *Job* was given a fresh appraisal and assigned a new importance during this period of scholarship, and the prose tale and dialogue were often seen as separate compositions.[108] The concern to emphasize the dialogue sometimes led to neglect of the prose parts[109], although some scholars continued to argue for the importance of the prose sections in providing a framework for the book.[110]

The usual classification of *Job* as 'wisdom' is linked with this emphasis on the importance of the doctrine of retribution in *Job* since retribution is held to be a characteristic 'wisdom' doctrine and *Job* is seen predominantly to contain a dialogue which airs this theme. This link gave momentum to studies of wisdom literature in this period which was accompanied by a mounting interest in the 'wisdom' movement, notably in the social setting of wisdom, largely fostered by discoveries of parallel ancient Near Eastern material.[111]

---

108 R Marcus, 1949-50, regards the prose and dialogue as separate compositions (the former used by the author of the latter) and argues that the author of the latter tried to answer the problem raised in the prologue of why the righteous suffer. Two different answers are given, the more profound one being given by God in the dialogue - that he is so involved in trying to control the universe that he has no time to notice, let alone persecute, Job.

109 O J Baab, 1951, writes, "He [the writer of the article] cannot accept as genuine any part of the book which flatly contradicts the basic thesis with which the Dialogue so radically deals...Thus the Epilogue...is utterly contradictory to the author's purpose as seen in the Dialogue as is the ascription to Satan of Job's troubles." (p 334)

110 eg O Eissfeldt, 1934; and E Jones, 1966, who finds the prologue as of the greatest significance since in it the author gives the key to a fuller solution of the dilemma created by the suffering of a good man, ie disinterested piety. H A Fine, 1955, tries to show that Chapters 27 and 28 of *Job* are consistent with the portrayal of Job in the prose parts of the book.

111 A study of ancient Near Eastern parallels to *Job* shows that there was traditionally a certain current of literature from the edges of 'wisdom' of a persistent and questioning kind which dwelt upon suffering and injustice and voiced questions from personal experience about the order of the world. This opinion is supported by H Gese, 1958; H H Schmid, 1966; and J L Crenshaw, 1981. Attempts have been made to prove dependence of *Job* on Egyptian literature (P Humbert, 1929); on Ugaritic and Phoenician sources (M Noth and D W Thomas, 1960) and on Babylonian parallels (W Baumgartner, 1933 and 1951, cf discussions in H Duesberg and I Fransen, 1966 and J Gray, 1970). The Babylonian Theodicy, for example, is a friendly dialogue about the validity of the act-consequence relationship which takes place between a sufferer and his companion who is a representative of traditional wisdom. The sufferer denies that this system works whilst his comforter argues that it does and urges patience. The remoteness of the gods and the inscrutability of their ways is emphasized and the sufferer complains that the gods made humans prone to injustice. The Babylonian Job (J B Pritchard, 1950, pp 434-437) offers a parallel to *Job* since the sufferer is a pious king who is stricken by disease, mocked by his friends and eventually restored. However whilst this sufferer cries to God for relief from suffering, the cause of which he does not understand, he is prepared to accept that in some way he has offended God.

Considerations of form and social setting also led to *Job* being classified as 'wisdom' since it contains forms which are paralleled in other 'wisdom' books in Israel and the ancient Near East; and it contains ideas thought to be characteristic of wise men, who may have existed in Israel as well as in other ancient Near Eastern countries. *Job* is seen as part of the wisdom literature of the Old Testament, along with Proverbs, Ecclesiastes, Sirach and the Wisdom of Solomon, and is regarded, with Ecclesiastes, as a radical strain within wisdom thought.[112] In the next chapter I shall examine the evidence for wisdom forms, ideas and social setting in *Job*.

In conclusion, the doctrine of retribution was highlighted in this period as a result of a greater emphasis on the dialogue section and a fuller awareness of the tensions between the prologue/epilogue and the dialogue. This emphasis coincided with a new interest in the wisdom movement. Before turning to a consideration of the classification of *Job* as 'wisdom literature', I shall examine two further stages of critical assessment of the message of *Job*.

iii) The nature of God and man's relationship with him

"Because, in spite of everything, he [Job] cannot give up his faith in divine justice, it is not easy for him to accept the knowledge that divine arbitrariness breaks the law. On the other hand, he has to admit that no one except Yahweh himself is doing him injustice and violence. He cannot deny that he is up against a God who does not care a button for any moral opinion and does not recognize any form of ethics as binding. This is perhaps the greatest thing about Job, that, faced with this difficulty, he does not doubt the unity of God."[113]

---

In *Job*, Job's protestation of innocence is a central theme. Hence, H Gese, 1958, argues that in such ancient Near Eastern works there is no question of accusing God, rather restoration to health follows submission to the divine will. All ancient Near Eastern 'Job' texts answer the question of what to do when unmerited suffering comes. Their answer is to advise turning to guardian gods who will certainly help. No question of divine 'righteousness' arises. There is no one striking parallel to *Job* and connections and similarities which have been detected do not solve questions about *Job* because we do not know how far the author was aware of them and, if he was, how far he has used their ideas or even adapted their forms in order to express something different.

112 G von Rad, 1972 and R B Y Scott, 1972, who classifies both *Job* and Ecclesiastes (and the Sayings of Agur, Proverbs 30:1-4) as 'wisdom in revolt', although he acknowledges that the two revolts of *Job* and Ecclesiastes move in opposite directions. On the Sayings of Agur, see O Plöger, 1984.

113 C Jung, 1952 (1954, p 10). See discussion of Jung's approach to *Job* in chapter 4, pp 189-190.

In recent times there has been an emphasis on the content of the speeches of Yahweh and the issues raised by the portrayal of an omnipotent and largely indifferent Creator. *Job* raises the issue of the character or nature of God and how man can respond to him.[114] There is a conflict in the dialogue between traditional doctrines of God and Job's experience of him. This is exacerbated further in the Yahweh speeches where God appears to rely on the fact that he is the stronger - how then can a man argue with God on rational terms?[115]

Evaluations of the importance of the Yahweh speeches have varied enormously. It has been argued in justification of the speeches that they are the climax of the meaning of *Job* and raise the problem of Job's suffering onto a higher level by calling on him to rise above the vantage point of man.[116] Many scholars, however, regard God's reply to Job as inadequate since the speeches make no reference to the theme of man's suffering. This has led some to assume that the work was left unended and that some other writer added these chapters which are therefore irrelevant.[117]

Others argue that the book of *Job* was originally confined to a discussion of Job's misfortunes and grew to its present size via successive editions.[118] However, those scholars who place an emphasis on the themes raised by the speeches generally have a high opinion of their place in the book as a whole.

---

114 This includes the issue of theodicy in *Job* - the vindication of the divine providence in view of the existence of evil. See A P Hastoupis, 1951 and R H Pfeiffer, 1948.

115 K H Miskotte, 1967, finds a dualism between power and justice in *Job*. In the dialogue the friends think they interpret God's judgement and Job cannot contradict them since he has evidence of his suffering at God's hand. He slowly realizes that he is being confronted with God's power rather than his justice.

116 R Gordis, 1964, writes of the speeches of Yahweh, "Their purpose is not the glorification of nature, but the vindication of nature's God" (p 117). He appeals to the literary greatness of the chapters, and to the fact that throughout the dialogue Job has demanded an answer from God so that it would not have made sense for there not to have been an answer in the original book; cf R H Pfeiffer, 1948.

117 eg M Jastrow, 1920, sees the speeches of Yahweh as a series of four independent compositions which are not a part of the original composition but which have been added to counterbalance the sceptical trend of the original book. A slight variation on this is proposed by D B MacDonald, 1895 and 1933. In 1895 he argued that the speeches may have been written by the same poet at an earlier point in his development before the problem had assumed for him the complexity it did later. In 1933 he held that "the whole philosophical attitude to the world and to man of the Speech of the Lord is different from that of the Colloquies" (p 31).

118 See footnote 127, pp 42-43.

Job's case gives rise to philosophical questions concerning the character of the deity.[119] Karl Barth[120] discusses the problem that Job faces when he finds that the character of God is not as he and the friends had supposed. He writes:

"The clearly declared meaning of the Book of Job is that he [Job] put himself both in the right and also in the wrong in so doing [ie, in making his complaint against God]. On the one side Job respects the freedom of God both to give and to take. On the other, he does so with a resignation which defiantly insists that God ought really to have exercised his freedom very differently...The theme of Job's complaint is the change in the divine form which found concrete manifestation and expression in the blows of fate which he had suffered. God had obviously adopted this new form in exposing him to these blows. His wrath and curse had replaced his blessing. Job does not doubt that he still has to do with the same God...Yet he cannot see to what degree he has to do so. His complaint thus rises against God in this hiddenness like the unceasing surge of the ocean against the sea-coast. Questioning, petition, protest, and finally the cry of bitter resignation succeed one another."[121]

Finally through the Yahweh speeches and Job's response:

"God spoke to Job and Job heard him...Thus the circle closes as it opened, namely, with man's liberation by and for the free God: by the free God since it is He who is the Witness speaking against Job yet also for him and for the free God, since Job, set in the wrong by Him yet also in the right, proves to be the faithful witness of this God."[122]

It is clearly important that God answers Job, but so is the way Job reacts to God. God is vindicated to a certain extent, despite what he says, by the fact that he appears. Thus the meaning of the book has been found in encounter with God rather than in theology.[123] The conduct of man in the face of suffering is the other aspect of the book's message that is often

---

119 R H Pfeiffer, 1948.
120 K Barth, *Church Dogmatics*, Vol. IV 3 1st half, 1961, pp 406, 407 and 422.
121 K Barth, 1961 (p 434).
122 K Barth, 1961 (p 434).
123 For example H H Rowley, 1970, finds the meaning of the book in religion (encounter with God) rather than in theology and writes, "A false theology sapped the springs of religion when religion was most needed" (p 19). God does not reveal to Job why he is suffering because he does not want to enter into theological debate. Rather he reminds Job of the mysteries of nature and leaves him to realize that innocent suffering is one of these. To Job the important factor is that God came to him in his suffering which showed him that when he most needs God, he is with him. Job's words of repentance are the climax to the book. In them he repents of the foolish things he had said in the dialogue. It is of the essence of the message of *Job* that Job found God *in* his suffering. His suffering was therefore enriched by the presence of God.

emphasized.[124] Others see the transformation of Job himself as the key issue of the book.[125]

A fuller appraisal of the place of the Yahweh speeches in the book of *Job* led to a subordination of other parts of the book to the one theme of the appearance of God. It was argued, for example by R Laurin,[126] that an ancient tale was retold in order to raise the problem of the view of God as an absolute sovereign who can do what he wants with the lives of men but to whom men can only show unquestioning obedience, and to raise the difficulties for faith which this view brings. The author wanted to ask whether or not one could find a meaningful faith in God in the light of this kind of theological perspective. The author's theological climax is in chapters 38-42. He wants to show that faith finds its basic ground only in a personal encounter with God. Only after encounter with God was Job reconciled to his own suffering and the suffering of others.

The issue of primary and secondary material in *Job* and of stages in the composition of the book was raised again in conjunction with this reappraisal of the message of *Job*. Each separate section was studied both in isolation and in relation to other parts of *Job*, and this led to the idea of various stages of composition or of editing by a number of authors.[127] The suggestion that

---

[124] G Fohrer, 1963, argues that the problem of *Job* is not 'Why does the righteous man suffer?' but 'What is the proper conduct of man in suffering?' The emphasis should be put on the character of Job and his relation with God. J B Curtis, 1983, talks in terms of two types of God one of which Job accepts, another which Job repudiates. Job rejects the "transcendent god" but affirms personal religion in terms of his "personal god" (cf S Mowinckel, 1925; G H Box, 1932; E G Kraeling, 1938; S Terrien, 1957; W A Irwin, 'Job's redeemer', 1962; M H Pope, 1965). S Terrien, IB, 1962, argues that man's knowledge of God (ie What is the meaning of faith?) is the central issue and Job's merit is that he "looked beyond the wisdom of men and sought the wisdom of God" (p 897).

[125] R A F MacKenzie, 1979, sees Job's transformation as taking place in three stages, the final and decisive stage being God's appearance which establishes a new relationship between them.

[126] R Laurin, 1972.

[127] Such reconstructions are a good idea in theory but have led to little agreement. N Snaith, 1968, argues for one author, but three distinct stages in the development of the author's thought and in the book's themes. The first intention was to tell a story in Hebrew comparable with the story of the Babylonian Job. The author rewrote the 'ancient folk tale' of the righteous Job in a traditional form inserting a long poetic piece into a prose tale, a normal practice of wisdom writers. Snaith's first edition - a 'prose tale' - consisted of a prologue and epilogue and a long poetic soliloquy by Job followed by a speech of God (chapters 1-3, 29-31, 38-42). Snaith then detects a second stage prompted by the author's having further thoughts about his orthodox first edition. He

cycles of sources were involved seemed in many ways more plausible than the idea that one author compiled the whole in view of the disjointed structure and contradictions contained within the book. However, scholars have differed greatly on the relative dates of the various strata in the book and how such strata evolved. Attempts to solve these problems have tended to result in an overvaluation of the original form of the book and in a devaluation of later additions. There is no manuscript evidence for an earlier version, so that reconstructions have rested entirely on the individual scholar's opinion of how different parts fit together or how one element makes sense in relation to another.[128]

In conclusion, this section has shown how there was an emphasis in a third stage of scholarship on the themes of the nature of God and man's relationship with him as the central message of *Job* which led to a corresponding reappraisal of the Yahweh speeches and Job's reply. Questions regarding the character of the Deity and the possibility of a response by man to an indifferent Creator were at the forefront of interest and other themes in the book were

---

added the dialogues of the three friends in which a new attitude appears which asks 'Why has Job suffered so much?' - to which these 'aged wise men' reply in the orthodox tradition (chapters 4-28). Finally, a third edition (chapters 32-37) emerged, again a result of dissatisfaction with his solution, and this represents a last attempt to solve the problem of a gap between the High God and mortal man. This was achieved by introducing the character of Elihu; but the problem was in fact left unsolved. Snaith's reconstruction rests on tenuous foundations in its claim to be able to reconstruct stages of thought in an author's mind; for one could easily argue for a different chronological order of thought-development, and then his structure would collapse. V Maag, 1982, finds two sources, the first an independent novel about an Aramean Job (1:1-2:10 and 42:11-17) and the second an account of an Edomite Job that framed the main poetic section (2:11-13 and 42:7-9). When a later compiler joined these two works much material from both stories was lost. Thus Maag detects two original strata each of which gave an orderly and satisfying account of Job the redeemed sufferer. He attributes the complications in the text and message of the book to the interference of a spurious orthodoxy.

[128] The Yahweh speeches, for example, are evaluated highly by scholars who regard them as the climax to the book, eg K Budde, 1896; C Cornill, 1907 and G Wildeboer, 1895 who defended the immediate and original unity of these speeches with the rest of the work on the ground that without them the book offers no solution whatever of the problems raised by Job in the dialogue section. The authenticity of the speeches is also defended by S R Driver and G B Gray, 1921 (only the first speech); E J Kissane, 1939 and H H Rowley, 1970. Others regard God's reply as inadequate and underplay the significance of the speeches - R A F MacKenzie, 1959, calls them "a huge irrelevance" (p 27); others reject them on literary-critical grounds, eg W E Staples, 1925; O S Rankin, 1936. Each of the speeches tends to be evaluated separately by scholars, the authenticity of Yahweh's second speech being the most frequently questioned (eg S R Driver and G B Gray, 1921). See discussion in chapter 4, pp 205-207.

44   Traditional and critical interpretations of the message of *Job*

subordinated to these concerns. The issues of man's encounter with God and conduct in the face of suffering are also raised.

iv) *Job* as a protest

"The failure in actual experience of the orthodox teaching that God would reward the righteous and punish the wicked gave rise in later times to a whole literature of dissent ranging from the disturbed and melancholy psalms, the ambiguous attitude toward the Deity in stories like Jonah, to the complaints of Ecclesiastes and the full-scale protests of Job."[129]

In 1854 H Heine[130] noted the radical and questioning nature of *Job*. Radical statements are made about God and man's relationship to him that go beyond what has previously been said or experienced. This realization sprang from an appreciation of Job's own sentiments in the dialogue section of the book. Heine attributed the inclusion of *Job* in the canon of scripture to the foresight of those who saw the necessity of including doubt and despair in the Bible. Heine wrote:

"Wie kommt es, daß bei der Rückkehr aus Babylon die fromme Tempelarchivkommission, deren Präsident Esra war, jenes Buch in den Kanon der heiligen Schriften aufgenommen? Ich habe mir oft diese Frage gestellt. Nach meinem Vermuten taten solches jene gotterleuchteten Männer nicht aus Unverstand, sondern weil sie in ihrer hohen Weisheit wohl wußten, daß der Zweifel in der menschlichen Natur tief begründet und berechtigt ist und daß man ihn also nicht täppisch ganz unterdrücken, sondern nur heilen muß. Sie verfuhren bei dieser Kur ganz homöopathisch, durch das Gleiche auf das Gleiche wirkend, aber sie gaben keine homöopathisch kleine Dosis, sie steigerten vielmehr dieselbe aufs ungeheuerste, und eine solche überstarke Dosis von Zweifel ist das Buch Hiob; dieses Gift durfte nicht / fehlen in der Bibel, in der großen Hausapotheke der Menschheit. Ja, wie der Mensch, wenn er leidet, sich ausweinen, wenn er sich grausam gekränkt fühlt in seinen Ansprüchen auf Lebensglück; und wie durch das heftigste Weinen, so entsteht auch durch den höchsten Grad des Zweifels, den die Deutschen so richtig die Verzweiflung nennen, die Krisis der moralischen Heilung. - Aber wohl demjenigen, der gesund ist und keiner Medizin bedarf!"[131]

---

129 R B Sewall, 1959 (pp 22-23). Sewall refers to *Job* as protest literature but makes this assessment on the basis of comparisons with Greek tragedy.
130 H Heine in 'Spätere Note. Im März 1854', a note to his 'Ludwig Marcus. Denkworte. Geschrieben zu Paris, den 22 April 1844' Quoted in full by F Ellermeier, 1965 (p 93), cf Introduction, p 1.
131 "How did the pious Commission on Temple Archives, presided over by Ezra, come to include this book in the canon of the Holy Scriptures after the return from Babylon? I have often wondered. My conjecture is that these divinely illuminated men did not act

Heine thought that the author of *Job* made his book sceptical and also that the canonizers acted wisely in including it in the Bible. The modern approach is to state the intention of the author only and to attribute the inclusion of doubt in *Job* to the author who is seen to have reasons for presenting certain ideas in this way (see discussion in chapter 4, pp 184-194). Thus the book is seen as a structural unity, each part contributing to a co-ordinated whole[132]. There is an accompanying awareness of the importance of inconsistencies in the overall form of the book. Thus, for example, rather than the author's being accused of providing a variety of unsatisfactory conclusions to the problem of suffering in both the prologue/epilogue and dialogue sections, he is seen as deliberately employing irony in using the folk tale as the context for his own theological discussion in the dialogue.[133] The less palatable parts of the book are thus

---

in ignorance, but because (in their sublime wisdom) they knew very well that doubt has a profound basis and justification in human nature, and that it should not be ponderously repressed, but needs to be healed. The cure they used was thus a homeopathic one, working by healing like with like; but the dose was not a homeopathic one - rather, they piled it on as much as they could; and the book of Job is just such an exaggerated overdose. In the great domestic medicine-chest of the Bible, this poison needed to have its place. Just as a man must weep his fill when he suffers, so he must also doubt his fill when he feels desperately cheated in his claims to life's happiness. The crisis of moral healing comes about precisely through the highest degree of doubt and despair, just as it does through profound weeping. Still, happy is the man who is healthy and needs no medicine!"

132 N C Habel, 1985, for example, looks for a unity of theme in the book which transcends inconsistencies of message and literary-critical questions. He argues for a "forceful underlying plot". He sees the narrative as having been constructed in three movements (1:1-2:10; 2:11-31:40; 32:1-42:17) indicated by "prose markers" in the text. He concludes that the prologue is "not an independent story (even if some such story once circulated orally), and not a simplistic pretext for the dialogue which follows, but the first movement of a complex plot which foreshadows and requires the subsequent movements for its appropriate development and resolution." (p 29) He sees the appearance of Elihu, for example, as logical in the development of the narrative plot - he is the arbiter whom Job summoned. The Elihu speeches say that God no longer intervenes directly in human lives as he did in patriarchal times, and yet directly after these speeches God does appear to Job. Thus there is a deliberate anticlimax in the presence of the Elihu speeches which heightens the surprise element of God's eventual appearance. It leads the audience to expect a plot development which is the opposite of what actually happens. See further discussion of Habel and other like-minded scholars such as R M Polzin, 1974, in chapter 4, pp 191-194.

133 R D Moore, 1983, on the basis of a detailed analysis of Chapter 3, which he regards as a key chapter in which the poet joins his materials, argues that: "The poet, in presenting Job, has not sought thematic continuity with the narrative but rather thematic disjunction...The poet has denied integrity to his character and we should deny thematic integrity to the book." (pp 30-31) Moore also finds a unity in the book which transcends literary-critical questions, which takes account of inconsistencies in the

seen as an integral part of the book's structure. The idea of deliberate irony on the part of the author of *Job* as a clue to the resolution of difficulties in the literary-critical interpretation of the book will be discussed more fully in chapter 4. This possibility reinforces the idea that *Job* is to be characterized as protest or dissent literature since the author can be seen as deliberately stepping outside literary conventions to make a protest.

In modern times there has also been a reappraisal of the message of *Job* as protesting and unorthodox.[134] *Job* has been compared with material of a protesting kind in the Old Testament (material outside the bounds of the wisdom literature). Two modern scholars lead the field in regarding *Job* as a protest - J L Crenshaw[135] and R Davidson[136] - and each places a different emphasis on what precisely that protest is.

Crenshaw emphasizes the tension that he finds in *Job* which he calls "Job's dilemma".[137] He argues that Job's realization that there is no reward for virtue and his consequent probing into "the mystery of God's demeanour" takes two forms. In one sense Job thinks that God has withdrawn from him (eg 23:3,8-9); yet in another sense he thinks of God as oppressively near, for example in chapter 7 where there is a parody of Psalm 8's glorification of God's watchful eye.[138] In 10:20 also Job begs to be left alone rather than being the object of God's solicitude. It is this view of God as an *oppressive presence* that is the unifying factor in all of the passages Crenshaw appeals to. He writes:

"Job imagines that God has become his enemy...a cherished relationship has gone sour, and Job knows he is not to blame for the change. He can only think the deity has betrayed a trust, even though the very idea of God proving untrue was more than the mind could bear."[139]

This is the nature of Job's protest.

---

character of Job and in the message of the book in its canonical context. He also affirms the integrity of Job on a theological level.
[134] R B Sewall, 1959, (pp 23-24) refers to *Job* as 'protest' literature on the basis of comparisons with Greek tragedy (see chapter 4, footnote 21, pp 163-164).
[135] J L Crenshaw, 1984.
[136] R Davidson, 1983 (cf R Davidson, 1968-9).
[137] J L Crenshaw, 1984 (p 60).
[138] cf M H Pope, 1965, who writes on Job 7:17-18: "What in happier circumstances would be regarded as providential care is here ironically presented as overbearing inquisitiveness and unrelenting surveillance" (2nd edn. p 61).
[139] J L Crenshaw, 1984 (p 61).

Crenshaw sees Job's agonies in the context of the framework of the story - the reader knows that Job is undergoing a test of his integrity but Job does not. He points out the ways in which Job reacts under the test, such as his obsession with finding God and proving his innocence in a face-to-face confrontation:

"The pathos of Job's trust arises from the fact that such assurance [ie that he can endure the nearness of God] can exist only if God rewards good deeds and punishes sinful conduct...As a matter of fact, Job has no case at all against God apart from an operative principle of reward and retribution, for in a world devoid of such a principle good people have no basis for complaining that the creator has abandoned the helm and thus allows the ship to wander aimlessly amid submerged rocks."[140]

As Job's language becomes more heated and outspoken he is perhaps beginning to realize that his claims concerning a moral deity are losing credibility. God becomes a hostile deity and appears to have launched a personal attack on Job[141] and yet Job retains his integrity and learns from bitter experience that God does not reward virtue or punish vice according to a fixed idea of retribution.[142] Crenshaw's study emphasizes the radical nature of the content of *Job* - notably Job's own protests - and shows how diverse it is. The view of God as an oppressive presence shows that questioning taken to its limit becomes virtually blasphemy.

Davidson's study is much wider in scope. He deals with a general theme rather than a specific radical element. Davidson uses *Job* as an example of what he calls "rethink". He writes:

"Where doctrine and history, either communal or personal, clash, an attempt may be made to resolve the tension in one of two ways: either by rewriting the history in such a way that it conforms more closely to what doctrine demands or by taking a long, hard look at doctrine, being prepared to rethink it in the light of experience...In its starkest form this issue is faced in the book of Job."[143]

Davidson studies at some length the conflict between Job and his three friends in the dialogue and comes to two main conclusions. The first is Job's

---

[140] J L Crenshaw, 1984 (p 62).
[141] Job perceives God as a personal enemy in 6:4; 7:12-14,17-21; 9:17-24; 10:8,16-17; 13:24-28; 16:9-14; 19:5-12,22; 23:16-17; 27:2; 30:19-23, cf G von Rad, 1972 (pp 216-217).
[142] cf M Tsevat, 1980 (pp 1-37).
[143] R Davidson, 1983, (p 174).

increasing awareness from his own experience that "life does not always fit the religious script from which the friends are working".[144] He appeals to human experience in general to verify that there is much evidence pointing in the opposite direction from the pious assertions of the friends. Job declares his innocence (27:2-6) and if that is not to be sacrificed, then the theology of the friends stands in need of radical revision or 'rethink'. Davidson's second conclusion concerns the doctrine of God which has to be revised in the light of Job's experience. He asks:

"What kind of God is it possible to believe in, in a world where the traditional religious script no longer makes sense, and where there seems no explanation of the harshness of life's experience?"[145]

Job has no answers, but despite his tempestuous relationship with God he never doubts God's omnipotence and he feels sure that his plea for an arbitrator will be heard and that he will be vindicated (19:25-6). He reaches out to an elusive God,[146] wondering whether he is merely a plaything in the hands of a capricious God whose ways he can neither understand nor justify. Thus Davidson concludes from *Job* that the reassessment of traditional doctrines and dogmas in the light of experience, experience which refuses to be placated by remonstrations of the pious, is of chief importance. Davidson regards such rethinking as the way to a deeper faith - but is Job ever given the chance to understand what has happened to him and what the answers to his questions are? This depends on how one interprets God's reply and Job's response.[147] True, Job's desire to be answered is fulfilled by the appearance of God. His encounter with God is the most meaningful part of the experience since God's reply really confirms all that he had suspected, that he can never

---

144 R Davidson, 1983, (p 179).
145 R Davidson, 1983, (p 180), discussion pp 180-182.
146 S Terrien, *The Elusive Presence*, 1978. Terrien argues that "It is the theology of presence, not the problem of suffering which lies at the core of the poem" (p 362). The argument moves on three levels. Presence is first beyond grasp, then beyond time and then beyond honour when it unexpectedly rushes in as "the voice from the whirlwind" (38:1ff); its obtrusiveness shatters man's imagination of God" (p 362). He concludes, "The *Masque of Job* began in revolt, but it ended in faith, without the old illusion about the self and with a new lucidity about God." (p 373).
147 Is Job crushed by God's power (R P Carroll, 1975-6) and faced with a God beyond morality (M Tsevat, 1980) or is Job spoken to in his suffering and restored from his alienation (H H Rowley, 1970, M H Pope, 1965)?

understand God's ways. The main lesson he learns is that it is better to question than to rest on tradition - God himself says that Job is in the right (42:7). As Davidson writes:

"He struggled to grasp the God who was beyond the God of current theology. In the outcome his protests, his bitter wrestling with God, were justified. There was more faith in such deeply questioning protests and scepticism than in the pious affirmation of untroubled, but blind, certainty."[148]

Davidson's approach to *Job* clearly outlines the radical content of the book. The author of *Job* is challenging both traditional doctrines of just retribution and the traditional doctrine of God, and at the end of it all he shows that the only real solution to the problem of Job's situation is to continue questioning and accept God's unfathomableness. Both studies affirm that the content of *Job* can be well characterized as 'protest' literature in the sense that everything that tradition had passed down is questioned, criticized and doubted. Both Crenshaw and Davidson however see *Job* as only part of a whole tradition of questioning within the Old Testament. Interestingly, these authors ignore traditional groupings of Old Testament material into 'prophecy', 'wisdom', etc and realign passages and books according to different criteria.

The criteria for J L Crenshaw's selection of texts are those which trace "a growing animosity on God's part...and an accompanying change in human response."[149] The believer is convinced that God has become a personal enemy who frustrates the cause of truth, who has trifled with man's affections and who has become indifferent for no apparent reason whilst the believer has remained constant. The texts he assembles all convey this sense of 'God-forsakenness' although the kind of deity portrayed varies. He includes both texts which involve humans putting God to the test and texts which introduce the notion of divine testing (eg Psalm 26:2; Judges 2:20-23; Judges 3:1,4; Deut 13:1-3; II Chron 32:31; Deut 33:8; Deut 8:2,16; Exod 20:18-20; and

---

148 R Davidson, 1983 (p 183).
149 J L Crenshaw, 1984 (p ix). In an article on dissent literature Crenshaw, 1976, asserts that "Dissent characterizes the Hebrew Scriptures from first to last." (p 235) He finds different levels of dissent - *Job* and Ecclesiastes are at the apex, but certain Psalmists, Jeremiah, Habakkuk, Jonah, Abraham and Moses all display comparable tendencies. In an earlier article, Crenshaw, 1970, used a different criterion for aligning material - the questioning of the justice of God. This included *Job* and Ecclesiastes and a number of ancient Near Eastern parallels.

Gen 22:1,12).[150] At the apex of divine testing, for example, is the story of Abraham and Isaac in Genesis 22 which portrays "a deity who trifles with what humans consider most precious".[151] Crenshaw finds as the most astonishing thing about this story Abraham's ready acceptance of the divine word which contains no objection. Nor is there any irony in the way God is presented. Crenshaw describes it as a "monstrous test".[152]

R Davidson[153] uses the terminology of 'doubt' and his study covers a wide range of texts from the Psalms, the prophets, patriarchal narratives, Mosaic traditions, *Job* and Ecclesiastes. We can detect two types of passage amongst Davidson's selection - those which display brief moments of doubt and in which healthy questioning leads to a deepening of faith (for example, Davidson places the patriarchal narratives alongside the psalms of lament and the wisdom psalms as reflecting a religious tradition in which the experience of God was often ambiguous and where trust in God often demanded that questions be faced and doubts expressed)[154] and those of extended doubting in which radical things are said about God and the human condition which do not automatically lead to a deepening of faith (for example the confessions of Jeremiah[155] and Ecclesiastes[156]). When characterizing protest literature one

---

150 See J Licht, 1973 on the concept of divine testing. A detailed examination of the traditions of divine testing during the wilderness experience is undertaken by G W Coats, 1968. He argues that the wilderness traditions are dominated by a negative presentation of a people who 'murmured' about their circumstances. At times God saw to their needs and ignored the murmurings, but at other times he punished them.
151 J L Crenshaw, 1984 (p ix). Against this view see K R R Gros Louis, 1982, who emphasizes the long history of a relationship between Yahweh and Abraham which prepared Abraham to trust God in this experience.
152 J L Crenshaw, 1984 (p 9).
153 R. Davidson, 1983.
154 An example from Davidson's selection is the strange story of Jacob's struggle with God at the ford of Jabbok (Genesis 32) which results in Jacob's being blessed with the name 'Israel' (v 28). Davidson sees this outcome as evidence that questioning and struggling has a significant place in Israel's faith. See Davidson, pp 55-56.
155 Davidson notes a recurring sense of failure and loneliness in Jeremiah's confessions which testify to personal pressures which, added to his role in the community as a prophet of doom, led the prophet "to the very brink of cognitive and spiritual collapse" (p 127). This took several forms - deep personal despondency, most dramatic in 20:14-18, and defiance which made him speak out vehemently against God. On another level of his experience Jeremiah is "consciously and self-reflectively raising questions about the meaning of his relationship with God, opening the door to doubts which the bitter ambiguity of his ministry forced him to face" (p 129). Thus, for example, 12:1-6 airs the problem of the prosperity of the wicked for which Jeremiah holds God directly responsible. Jeremiah discusses this question in personal terms - those who ignore the

needs to be aware of these two levels. The raising of doubts and recognition of human life as a struggle leads to an increased awareness and understanding in which religion flourishes. It is clear that the questioning and doubting of God and man's relationship to him was deeply embedded in Israel's religion from an early time.

Along similar lines another scholar, S H Blank,[157] makes a selection of protest literature based on a slightly different criterion - he draws together figures who demonstrate 'Promethean' elements in their prayers.[158] This element is found amongst those who stand up to an apparently arbitrary or tyrannical God in prayer and demand their own due and that of others. Blank considers two biblical passages - Jeremiah 15 and Ezekiel 14:14,20 both of which contain lists of Israelite figures who have particular influence with God, notably Moses,[159] Samuel, Noah, Daniel and Job. He writes:

---

Lord and his word prosper whilst the prophet, the mouthpiece of God's word, makes no impact at all - what then is the meaning of the prophet's ministry? Jeremiah feels betrayed by God. A recent discussion of the authenticity of the confessions of Jeremiah within the book can be found in K-F Pohlmann, 1989.

156 Davidson draws an interesting contrast between the authors of *Job* and Ecclesiastes. He writes, "Whereas the author of Job insists on struggling to save faith in a just world order, Qoheleth gives up the struggle. It doesn't make sense, cries Job, but it *must* make sense. It doesn't make sense, says Qoheleth, accept that it doesn't make sense...Job still believes that a living personal relationship between God and man is possible, even if God at times seems elusive. It is for him a stormy relationship ...Qoheleth can no longer believe that God is interested enough to fire arrows...For Qoheleth the experiential side of religion has dried up; he believes still in religious etiquette, but no longer in personal faith." (pp 201-202) See discussion of Ecclesiastes as part of the development of wisdom in chapter 2 and discussion of forms in Ecclesiastes in chapter 3, pp 138-147. For a recent assessment of Ecclesiastes as a sceptical work see D Michel, 1989.

157 S H Blank, 1953.

158 The parallel of Job with Prometheus is drawn in connection with a comparison of the radical sentiments of *Job* with Greek tragedy, notably with Aeschylus, *Prometheus Bound*. See chapter 2, pp 98-100, especially footnote 139.

159 Blank argues that the name of Moses leads all the rest - "for he more often than others and more successfully takes issue with God." He sees Exodus 32:12 as suggesting that God is capable of evil. In Exodus 32:12 Moses says to God "Turn from thy fierce wrath and repent of this evil against thy people" at the point when God is about to destroy Israel for making a golden calf - a bold plea which is answered in these words: "and the Lord repented of the evil which he thought to do to his people". Blank asks whether God acceded to Moses' request because of the cogency of his argument or because it was Moses who presented it.

"It is not, indeed, among the rebels that we find them [ie Promethean figures] but among the faithful. They hold fast to God even while they question his decrees. Though they defy, they do not deny him."[160]

Before concluding this chapter, I will indicate the nature of Job's rebellious remarks from a reading of the text. It is this kind of assessment of the dialogue section of *Job* that has led scholars to classify *Job* as 'protest literature'.

Elihu summarizes Job's position in 34:5-6: "Job has said, I am innocent, and God has taken away my right; in spite of my right I am counted a liar; my wound is incurable, though I am without transgression." Elihu refuses to accept Job's view and accuses Job of saying "it profits a man nothing that he should take delight in God" (34:9). This is not doing full justice to what Job has said. Certainly he consistently affirms his innocence. He describes himself as 'blameless' (9:21), in word (6:10; 6:30) and deed (10:6-7) but his conclusion is "It is all one; therefore I say he (God) destroys both the blameless and the wicked." Job argues therefore that it makes no difference whether a man is wicked or righteous for he is punished in both cases if God so decides (10:15). This is a surprising statement for Job to make since the traditional line was that the righteous and wicked get their just deserts. Job also states quite categorically in chapter 21 that, contrary to pious belief, the wicked are not punished in this life by God. Many of them reach old age, their children are established, their houses are safe, and finally they die honourably and have a splendid burial, praised by all (21:7-9,13-15). "How often is it" asks Job, "that the lamp of the wicked is put out?" (21:17) He implies that the wicked are not often punished by God. Later in the dialogue - 27:13-23 - he changes his position and begins to say that God does punish the wicked - apparently a strange contradiction. But this appears to be the result of dislocation in the third cycle of speeches.[161] In general he persists in

---

[160] S H Blank, 1953, (p 2).
[161] The speeches between Job and his three comforters follow a formal pattern for two rounds but when the third begins the speeches are of disproportionate lengths and people seem to be contradicting themselves. Rounds 1 and 2 follow the same pattern: Job speaks and the first comforter, Eliphaz, replies; Job answers and the second comforter, Bildad, replies; Job speaks again and the third comforter, Zophar, replies. All the speeches in these rounds are between roughly 20 and 50 verses in length. Eventually in chapter 21 a third round starts and again Eliphaz answers, but to the second comforter

maintaining that the wicked are not punished but go to their graves in honour. This position is in opposition to the orthodox line as represented by the three friends. Job also challenges traditional ideas about the justice of God which the friends presuppose - he thinks God should be bound by some conception of justice but his experience teaches him otherwise. In fact, God shows in the Yahweh speeches that he is not bound by such considerations.

Nowhere does Job deny God's power to punish or reward as he wishes. Indeed this is a point on which all the speakers in the dialogue agree, with many vivid illustrations of how God exercises his power through nature. None of the speakers says anything on this subject which is not fully in accord with God's reply to Job in chapters 38-41. But Job's dilemma is that whilst he acknowledges fully both God's power to punish and his right to do so he

---

the text ascribes only a short speech of six verses followed by an extremely long one of 161 verses by Job in which he contradicts what he has previously said. It seems likely therefore that part of what is ascribed to Job should belong to the third-round speeches of Bildad and Zophar and that some material has been lost. There are a large number of suggested reconstructions which differ in their details. An example is R Gordis, 1978, who reconstructs the third cycle of speeches as follows: Job's reply - 24:1-3,9,21,4-8,10-14b,15,14c,16,17; Bildad - 25:1-6; 26:5-14; Job - 27:1; 26:1-4; 27:2-7; Zophar - 27:8-23; 24:18-20,22-25. Gordis considers the second group of Job's speeches to be the only parts of an original longer speech which have survived. Similarly with the last speech of Zophar, the pieces are thought to be fragments. Other rearrangements are listed by G A Barton, 1911; S R Driver and G B Gray, 1921; A Regnier, 1924; R H Pfeiffer, 1948; M P Reddy, 1978. Many older scholars excised verses, but it is interesting to note that K Budde, 1896, who often followed this approach, accepted the given text, with no substantial changes, as genuine. Thus, it is generally agreed by scholars that there was possibly a complete third cycle but that part has been lost and what has survived is out of order. An alternative suggestion put forward by N Snaith, 1968, is that a complete third cycle of speeches was never written by the author. He argues that the author began fitting fragments together, as evidenced in the opening speech of Job in chapter 23, but he did not complete the process either because he died or because he found them too difficult to fit into the scheme and gave up the attempt. Another suggestion is that by reducing the contributions of the friends in the third cycle, the author wanted to convey the impression that the friends had run out of arguments (H Möller, 1955; K Fullerton, 1924). A further possibility is that this dislocated third cycle of speeches is not to be attributed to an author, rather a later editor may have tried to tone down Job's heretical statements by attributing to him sections lifted out of the third speeches of Bildad and Zophar and by censoring Job's reply to Zophar, see S Terrien, 1962; cf M Jastrow, 1920 and K Fullerton, 1924, who writes, "it is difficult to escape the conclusion that the speeches have been reshuffled in order to give a more orthodox tone to Job's closing words" (p 122). Whilst this solution is attractive, a final alternative is also possible - that there may have been scribal error involved in transmission or disarrangement of pages of the manuscript. Although this kind of solution is often seen as a last resort by literary-critics, it may provide the answer in this case. For a recent discussion of the problem of the third cycle of speeches see J-J Hermisson, 1989.

cannot admit to sin which he has not consciously committed. He recognizes that God can put him in the wrong despite his many good deeds in the past. In 29:15-16 Job recalls how he was "eyes to the blind, feet to the lame (and) a father to the poor". But now "God has cast me into the mire" (30:19), God has become cruel to Job: "when I looked for good, evil came, and when I waited for light, darkness came" (30:26). So he asks God to crush him (6:9) although "there is no violence in my hands and my prayer is pure" (16:17). God must either forgive his transgression (whatever it is) (7:21) or give an answer to Job's case. Job is bold enough to stand up to God and question his ways. He is not content to accept punishment without knowing the cause. His attitude is one of questioning and defiance. He recognizes that no man is fully just before God: "though I am innocent I cannot answer him, I must appeal for mercy to my accuser" (9:15) but he needs an answer: "Make me know my transgressions and my sin" (13:23). His conclusion is that "God has put me in the wrong and closed his net about me" (19:6) implying that God has behaved unjustly towards him: a dangerous accusation which shocks Job's orthodox comforters and which confirms his unorthodox attitude, which so contrasts with the accepting, unquestioning Job found in the prologue.

The three friends maintain their position throughout that Job must have sinned or God would not have punished him: "Who that was innocent ever perished? Or where were the upright cut off?" (4:7) Job should be grateful that God is reproving him for his own good: "Behold, happy is the man whom God reproves, therefore despise not the chastening of the Almighty. For he wounds, but he binds up, he smites, but his hands heal" (5:17-18). They see Job as obstinate in refusing to acknowledge that it is for his own sin that calamity has befallen him: "How long will you say these things? Does God pervert justice?" (8:2-3) and they deny that Job has any grounds for complaint: "God exacts of you less than your guilt deserves" (11:6). There are only hints of a deeper response by two of the comforters. Eliphaz in response to Job's protestations of innocence goes deeper than the orthodox view which they have all been upholding when he asks in 22:3: "Is it any pleasure to the Almighty if you are righteous or is it gain to him if your ways are blameless?" He is perhaps hinting that their idea of righteousness falls short of the reality of it in God's eyes and this is not far from Job's emerging position. Bildad takes this up in asking: "How then can a man be righteous before God?" (25:4)

Thus there is no doubt that what Job is saying is for the most part a radical departure from the position represented by the friends and found in wisdom literature. This realization demands an assessment of the nature of wisdom and the role *Job* plays within that classification which I shall attempt to do in the next chapter.

In conclusion, the quest to find a central, unifying message in *Job* in order to make sense of its various themes and different parts both in relation to each other and to the whole has proved largely fruitless. Perhaps the book is just an accidental jumble of literary forms and themes, of parts written at different times and of misinterpretation by subsequent editors. However this is clearly not an attractive conclusion. I will argue in the rest of this monograph that an approach to the material that breaks out of the confines of traditional modes of thought about the literary history and message of *Job*, whilst it will not claim to solve every problem ever raised in connection with the book, will prove more helpful in trying to understand it.

The starting point in the next chapter will be the suggestion that rather than seeking an overall unifying message for *Job*, we look at the possibility of an overall classification on a literary level. The usual classification of *Job* as 'wisdom' will be assessed along with other suggestions for an overall *genre* for the book. Such classifications will be seen to have limitations. *Job* is not such a normative 'wisdom' book as scholars have supposed and the quest for an overall genre for *Job*, whilst a useful exercise, is subject to methodological pitfalls.

In chapter 3 I shall suggest that a form-critical approach which works from the smallest genre level, that of individual forms, builds up a picture of how forms are being used in the book to convey a 'scepticism' which breaks out of traditional modes of thought. This method enables the author to work within the confines of an established tradition, and, at the same time, criticize that tradition. I shall suggest 'parody' as a possible genre classification for the book.

In chapter 4 I shall look for a context for the work of such an author in a 'sceptical' tradition which remained detached from the 'wisdom' tradition.

I shall look again at the message of *Job* to determine its 'sceptical' nature; at traditional literary-critical conclusions; and at the structure of the whole which conveys the 'scepticism' of the author in its juxtaposition of various parts. This approach attempts to provide a fresh unity to the book to be gleaned from its disparate themes and various literary units in terms of the intention of the author and the methods he employed in constructing a profoundly sceptical work.

The sense in which I am using the word 'sceptical' is clearly important here. In the last section of this chapter (iv)) 'sceptical' could easily have been used to replace a number of terms, such as 'unorthodox' and 'radical' used to describe the protesting content of the book of *Job*. I have avoided using the term to prevent confusion at this stage. In what follows I shall explore the possibility that 'sceptical' is in fact a more appropriate word than others to use in reference to *Job* (particularly in view of its early meaning in Greek culture) and I shall link ideas concerning the 'sceptical' nature of the content to the issues of genre, setting and overall structure of the book.

## Chapter 2

## THE QUEST FOR AN OVERALL CLASSIFICATION FOR *JOB*

## Wisdom and Genre

"The supreme masterpiece of Israel's wisdom tradition is, ironically, one in which none of the principal characters is an Israelite, in which the name of Israel's God is for the most part avoided, and which contains the most radical critique of the fundamental thesis of the Israelite wisdom schools, and indeed, of much else in the Old Testament as well."[1]

It is argued by J A Baker[2] that *Job*, by these very features, remains strictly faithful to the ideals of the wise: to their internationalism and their realism which led them to face facts and take the consequences. But this statement presupposes that *Job* is 'wisdom' and that wisdom can be characterized by internationalism and realism on the part of sages, who are presumed to be those engaged in 'wisdom'. It then sees the challenge that *Job* offers to traditional wisdom as 'ironical'. However, what if these presuppositions were themselves to be laid open to scrutiny? Could *Job* then be seen as 'the supreme masterpiece of Israel's wisdom tradition'? In the first part of this chapter I shall question the traditional classification of *Job* as 'wisdom' or 'wisdom literature', attempting, in the process, to define these terms. In the second part, I shall examine other genres to which scholars have tried to assign *Job*. A study of the question of *Job* as 'wisdom' raises the important issues of

---

1   J A Baker, 1978, (p 17).
2   J A Baker, 1978.

the definition of 'wisdom' and the classification of *Job* which provide a suitable starting-point for a fresh approach to the study of the book.

## a) *JOB* AS 'WISDOM' OR 'WISDOM LITERATURE'

Confusion in terminology and difficulty in characterizing 'wisdom' makes assessing whether *Job* is 'wisdom', and in what sense, a difficult task. When we talk of 'wisdom' in the Old Testament we immediately think of the group of books which make up the main body of wisdom *literature*: Proverbs, Ecclesiastes, *Job*, Sirach and the Wisdom of Solomon. If asked, "Why are these books called 'wisdom'?", we would reply that they contain certain marked similarities in form and content, and that they share the same background or social setting which corresponds to similar settings in Egypt and Mesopotamia where 'wisdom' had long been practised by circles of sages. However there is no one easy definition characterizing the wisdom in these books, not even in comparison with ancient Near Eastern works of a similar type, because later wisdom books differ markedly from earlier ones; for example the Wisdom of Solomon is very different from Proverbs.

If one confined oneself solely to Proverbs and ancient Near Eastern parallels such as the Egyptian 'Instructions' one might define 'wisdom' as, (1) in form, single or double line sentences; (2) in content, analogies between nature and human experience in an attempt to secure life and master it; whilst (3) in origin, 'wisdom' appears to be the distillation of long experience. However, there are problems with all these categories when we wish to include later wisdom books in the definition of 'wisdom'.

(1) By the time of Sirach and the Wisdom of Solomon rarely does a proverb appear in a simple form without an accompanying interpretation, and, instead of the proverb, the didactic essay and hymn and prayer forms are prominent. Forms characteristic of later wisdom are often thought to have developed from those in the earlier wisdom literature.[3] There is a danger here of defining the

---

3   W Baumgartner, 1933, argued for a development in wisdom into which, in the later stages, salvation-history elements in Israelite tradition were worked. He writes (1951) "According to the methodical type-analysis (Gattungsforschung) of Gunkel, the single

limits of 'wisdom' itself on the basis of new forms which appear which are thought to be a development from earlier forms but may, in fact, not be. Furthermore, such a wide range of forms become eligible for inclusion as 'wisdom' that we start to find 'wisdom forms' in parts of the Bible that are not generically 'wisdom' (eg Baruch 3:9-4:4[4]).

(2) As regards content: in these later works, 'wisdom' is hypostatized (the development of hints in Proverbs 8) and a link with Israel's sacred history has been formed. A specifically Israelite theological flavour appears which was lacking in Proverbs. This observation has led to the idea of a development in the concerns of wisdom from experiential to theological ones.[5] However, once this is posited, such a wide range of ideas have a claim to be included under the title of 'wisdom' that the boundaries of the literature can easily become confused. Again, we find 'wisdom ideas' in texts which are clearly not 'wisdom' in the same sense that Proverbs is 'wisdom' or the Wisdom of Solomon is 'wisdom'. Examples of this are found in I Esdras 3:1-5:3,[6] a late historiographical work, and in some Psalms.[7] Thus, the limits of the wisdom

---

māšāl developed into groups of aphorisms, extended maxims, and didactic poems of still greater length, ending up on the one hand with the collection of aphorisms and on the other with a considerable didactic poem such as Job" (p 210) (reference to H Gunkel, 1933). J Schmidt, 1936, argues for a development from sentence to instruction in Proverbs against which W McKane, 1970, argues strongly.

4   A hymn in praise of wisdom, Baruch 3:9-4:4 draws heavily upon canonical language, imagery and concepts from Proverbs, Sirach and Job 28 and so is often included in the category of wisdom literature. However only this section of the book of Baruch shows signs of 'wisdom'.

5   J L Crenshaw, 1981, finds evidence of secular and theological wisdom which can be clearly distinguished from each other, although he argues that a strict line of development from experiential concerns to theological ones cannot be proved. Rather the two existed together from an early period, as evidenced in Proverbs (cf R N Whybray, 1965).

6   There are echoes of Proverbs in the description of wine's power over its victims (I Esdras 3:18-24, cf Proverbs 20:1-2; 23:29-35) and in the speech in honour of wisdom (I Esdras 4:35-40, cf Proverbs 8:4-36). I Esdras 4:7-12 echoes the listing of polarities found in Sirach 43:1-5 and 17:31-2 and Ecclesiastes (eg 3:1-9). The final praise of truth in I Esdras 4:38-41 resembles the Egyptian Instruction of Ptahhotep. I Esdras 3:1-5:3 contains experiential and theological wisdom in a largely narrative form which contains no proverbial material. I Esdras 3:1-5:3 may be an old anecdote serving a new didactic purpose. A wise man with wider interests than just 'wisdom' may have added it, or a sage with a theological purpose in mind when he added the speech about truth. It is clearly not 'wisdom literature' in a narrow sense and yet it springs from the same wider quest as 'wisdom', especially in its content.

7   Considerable 'wisdom' influence can be found in some Psalms, eg 37, 49 and 73, but, unless a psalm shows it in great measure, it is confusing to classify all psalms containing 'wisdom' influence as 'wisdom psalms'. See discussion in J K Kuntz, 1974

literature become hard to define because of the breadth of texts that can be included under the criterion of content. J L Crenshaw,[8] for example, asserts that 'wisdom' as 'non-revelatory speech' would cover anything that is not to be categorized as divine speech. This would include all historiography since it seeks to understand the course of human events by the use of human reason.[9] Wisdom thinking is seen as anthropocentric in that it exposes man's deepest feelings and hopes. This definition allows further scope for including even more of the Old Testament within the category of wisdom - for example, the Primaeval History (Genesis 1-11), the Joseph narrative (Genesis 37-50), the Succession Narrative (2 Samuel 9-20, I Kings 1-2) and Esther.[10] In addition:

"once a didactic tendency is recognized as clear evidence that a sage has been at work, additional literature enters the discussion, especially Tobit, Judith, I Esdras 3-4, and Ahiqar."[11]

A humanitarian concern might also reveal a wisdom origin; thus Deuteronomy can be seen as "the legal expression of the sages".[12] Other texts such as Habakkuk 3, Amos, Deuteronomy 32 and Exodus 34 have also been seen as having been influenced by wisdom, as have specific texts in Isaiah, Jeremiah and Hosea. Comparisons have been made between wisdom thought and apocalyptic giving rise to the idea that Daniel is wisdom literature (especially since Daniel is called a 'wise man').[13] Finally the airing of problems of innocent suffering and divine justice have led some scholars to

---

    and R B Y Scott, 1965 and 1971. Kuntz tries to classify psalms as 'wisdom' by a study of typical forms, vocabulary, themes and Gattung or Sitz im Leben of wisdom. This approach is instructive when it comes to defining 'wisdom' in general as I shall show in this chapter.

8  J L Crenshaw, 'Wisdom', 1974; cf J L Crenshaw, 1969.
9  J L McKenzie, 1967, argues that the historical books were composed as guides to decision. He writes, "These books are not so much historical narrative as reflections on the human condition, the explanation...of an existing situation by its origins...From the events of the past and the wise sayings of the elders, the Israelite might learn how to meet the present reality, which was still the encounter of Yahweh with man" (p 8).
10  G von Rad, 1958 (1966); R N Whybray, 1968; S Talmon, 1963.
11  J L Crenshaw, 'Wisdom', 1974, p 226.
12  J L Crenshaw, 'Wisdom', 1974, p 227; cf M Weinfeld, 1961, who argues for wisdom influence on Deuteronomy rather than Deuteronomic influence on wisdom.
13  C Rowland, 1982, suggests a link between apocalyptic and mantic wisdom (notably with Daniel), p 203f; cf G von Rad, 1965, p 306f, and 1972, p 280f who links apocalyptic with wisdom; and J M Schmidt, 1969.

include certain psalms in the wisdom corpus, for example Psalms 37, 49, and 73.[14]

Thus one begins to wonder if any books in the Old Testament are free from wisdom influence.[15] The term 'wisdom' has now begun to be used in a very general sense to describe a certain set of ideas which characterize a wisdom movement rather than defining the scope of the wisdom literature itself. The criteria for distinguishing 'wisdom' texts have become so diverse that one wonders if one can really establish any criteria at all.

(3) Finally the limits of a wisdom setting are also hard to define. If a wisdom context merely means evidence of the interests and work of sages a great number of texts could be included.[16] On the other hand, if a wisdom context requires the text to show a particular purpose of instruction, a narrower definition might be possible. Some traditional wisdom books, such as *Job* and Ecclesiastes, might on this definition be excluded. Can these books really be said to have as their purpose *instruction*? It is arguable that *Job* is more predominantly narrative and dialogue than 'proverbial' and comes down against traditional wisdom teaching as exemplified in Proverbs, whilst Ecclesiastes is more of an individual observation on life than a piece of instruction. Furthermore, if wisdom forms and ideas can be seen to have developed, the historical context of 'wisdom' texts may well have changed too and their purpose may be hard to define. It is possible that each text has its own purpose and distinctive context, in which case this classification gets us no further.

These categories of form, content and context, taken individually, generally suffer from being too wide. However if we narrow the discussion to texts which show strong evidence of all three categories, we may be able to define the limits of the 'wisdom literature' and come closer to a definition of what the

---

[14] J L Crenshaw, 1981, calls these psalms, plus Psalm 39, 'discussion literature' since they question divine justice in view of the apparent prosperity of the wicked. They are more usually classified as 'wisdom' psalms, although, as with 'wisdom literature' the limits are hard to define, cf J K Kuntz, 1974.

[15] It has been argued that Israel's legal and wisdom traditions are related (E Gerstenberger, 1965, and W Richter, 1966) and that passages in prophecy are influenced by wisdom - see below, footnote 34.

[16] For example, the Joseph story and the Succession narrative, see E W Heaton, 1974; cf G von Rad, 1958 and R N Whybray, 1968.

essence of 'wisdom' is. R N Whybray[17] evaluates the three criteria for detecting 'wisdom influence' - subject matter, form and style, and vocabulary - which he finds in the work of other scholars. He finds subject matter too broad and subjective and sees form-criticism as an inadequate method unless a form is closely matched by characteristic 'wisdom' ideas. He finds vocabulary the most satisfactory criterion and pursues this line of research. His purpose in evaluating these criteria is to argue for a broad definition of 'wisdom' as an intellectual movement rather than for a narrower classification of texts. Wisdom as a 'style of intellectual and spiritual quest', as an overall category divorced from literary questions, may be a more satisfactory 'broad' definition.[18] Wisdom is seen on this level as 'eine bestimmte Geistesströmung'[19] or as an 'intellectual movement'[20] rather than as a literary corpus or as the product of a distinct class of sages.[21] J L McKenzie argues that wisdom is viewed too narrowly when it is viewed as wisdom *literature* and that wisdom was a 'living tradition'. He writes:

"Wisdom is much more than a literary form, much more than a way of life...It was also a way of thought and a way of speech, which was by no means limited to the schools and the writings of the sages."[22]

Thus in order to capture the 'essence' of 'wisdom' a broad definition is helpful. However in order to contain the sphere of reference of the discussion, we need to define the limits of 'wisdom literature'.[23] We need some precise

---

17  R N Whybray, 1974.
18  R N Whybray, 1974 argues that 'wisdom' denotes "superior intellectual ability whether innate or acquired, in God, men or animals" (p 11).
19  'A stream of ideas' - W Baumgartner, 1933, p 282.
20  H Gese, 1958, p 1.
21  E W Heaton, 1974. See discussion in R N Whybray, 1974, pp 15-54.
22  J L Mc Kenzie, 1967 (p 2).
23  J L Crenshaw, 'Wisdom', 1974, attempts a narrow definition of 'wisdom' based on the five traditional wisdom books. This begs the question of how the corpus is to be identified since he defines the scope of the wisdom literature on the basis of this definition of 'wisdom'. He is thus in danger of a circularity in his argument. H H Schmid, 1966, realizes this danger but sees it as inevitable. He argues that to recreate an exact picture of wisdom it is essential to limit oneself to wisdom literature proper whilst realising that this inevitably results in a circle. He writes, "Was zur Weisheitsliteratur gehört, welche literarischen Werke ihr zuzurechnen sind, wird sich seinerseits erst ergeben müssen." (p 7) - "what is to be reckoned as wisdom literature, which literary works belong to this category, will in turn be a result of the enquiry."

categories to cover parts of the bible which not only show the influence of such an intellectual and spiritual quest, but also employ some distinctive forms and are concerned with particular types of questions throughout the book. Such categories would exclude works which simply showed the influence of 'wisdom forms' or 'wisdom ideas' on small parts of the material. In the next section I shall consider the traditional classification of *Job* as 'wisdom'. Whilst *Job* can perhaps be classified as 'wisdom' in a broad sense, it can be seen as 'wisdom literature' only if it displays strong evidence of wisdom forms, content, and overall didactic purpose or context in wisdom circles.

## b) *JOB* AS 'WISDOM LITERATURE'

In order to provide points of comparison by which to assess *Job* it is essential to know what forms and content are typical of other books that are generally assumed to be 'wisdom literature'. It is beyond the scope of this monograph to assess whether each of the traditional 'wisdom' books (excluding *Job*) can be considered as 'wisdom literature' according to the criteria outlined above. This is an assumption that will have to be made and examples of traditional forms and ideas in the 'wisdom literature' will be used as points of reference by which to measure the 'wisdom' element of *Job*. I shall assess, on the basis of Proverbs, Ecclesiastes, Sirach, Wisdom of Solomon and some 'wisdom' Psalms,[24] what the major features of wisdom are and then assess whether *Job* displays strong evidence of such features. Ecclesiastes is a particularly interesting book for comparison because it stands closer to *Job* in its questioning of traditional modes of thought and yet, as I shall show in chapter 3 (pp 138-147), it stands closer to mainline wisdom than *Job* in its use of forms and its social setting.

---

24 See J K Kuntz, 1974, for a full discussion of which psalms to include as wisdom.

i) Form

Wisdom literature (excluding *Job*) is characterized by forms[25] common to all or some of the wisdom books and to ancient Near Eastern material.[26] First, there are onomastica or lists such as are found in Egyptian Instructions. This is one of the earliest forms of proverbial material which is still found relatively unchanged in the later works; for example, compare Ecclesiastes 3:2 with Psalm 104:12-21 or Sirach 43. A form of onomasticon is the numerical proverb[27] which is found in Proverbs (eg Proverbs 30:18, "Three things are too wonderful for me; four I do not understand.") and a few Psalms (eg Psalm 62:11, "Once God has spoken; twice have I heard this...") but not in the other three works, and which also appears in ancient Near Eastern material. By their universality[28] they have a claim to an early date. These are both part of the wider category of proverbial-type sentences and, whereas the onomasticon cannot really be said to have developed in form, the proverb has. In Proverbs there are simple proverbial sayings - the single-line, the thought-rhyme and the various parallelistic proverbs as well as numerical proverbs and onomastica. By the time of Ecclesiastes, proverbs of these types were being used but a new element has appeared - the citation of proverbs in order to refute them (eg Ecclesiastes 2:24 refutes 2:18-19).[29] Sirach too introduced an innovation, the interpretation accompanying the Proverb (eg 33:14-15; 39:33-34); but the persistence of the proverbial form throughout shows it to be basic to the forms of wisdom. Only in the Wisdom of Solomon is there little evidence of proverbial material (although there is a possible list in 7:17-20 where the author alludes to the entire curriculum of the wise man). In the wisdom

---

25  A genre differs from a form only in the fact that form and content are included, not form alone. On the level of small forms the terms are virtually interchangeable. See discussion of genre later, pp 88-89.
26  The simple proverb in Proverbs resembles closely the 'Instructions of Onchsheshonqy' (B Gemser, 1976 (60)). Literary dependence of Proverbs 22:17-23:11 on the Egyptian 'Instruction of Amenemope' (J B Pritchard, 1950, pp 421-5) seems likely - for a recent discussion of the relation of these, see D Römheld, 1989.
27  cf W M W Roth, 1965. See A H Gardiner, 1947, for a collection of ancient Egyptian onomastica.
28  See W M W Roth, 1965 for a list of books containing numerical sayings.
29  This citation of proverbs in order to refute them was first noticed by H-P Müller, 1978. See discussions in R N Whybray, 1981 and R Gordis, 1951. See discussion in chapter 3, p 141.

psalms proverbial sayings provide one of the main criteria for deciding which psalms to include as 'wisdom' (eg Psalm 37:16, cf Proverbs 15:16).[30]

In *Job*, a few isolated numerical sayings and proverbs can be found - the former in Job 5:19-21; 13:20-22 and 33:14-30[31] and the latter in Job 6:5-6; 8:11-12; 12:12-13 and 17:5. Proverbs often appear with an explanation, as in 8:11-13, or are apparently contradicted immediately after they have been quoted, for example 12:12-13: "Wisdom is with the aged, and understanding in length of days. With God are wisdom and might; he has counsel and understanding." The simple proverbial form is at the heart of all wisdom literature.[32] The simple form and its developments characterize the book of Proverbs. Ecclesiastes and Sirach feature more advanced stages of the proverb, often with an accompanying interpretation. This is clearly not the case in *Job* where examples of proverbs are few and can only be found on the smallest genre level.[33] Many other books in the Old Testament contain occasional proverbs, including some prophets, such as Amos and Isaiah.[34] This consideration leads us into a broad definition of 'wisdom' in which we could include all texts containing such hints. On a narrower definition of the genre it is clear that such small evidence of a traditional wisdom genre in a work does not make it 'wisdom'.

Another important form which can be found and seen to develop is the 'autobiographical narrative'. In Proverbs this appears in a rudimentary form as 'autobiographical stylization' and may be defined as an entirely personal discovery or experience on the part of the author, eg Proverbs 7:6-27; 24:30-34. In Ecclesiastes the form comes to full fruition in the autobiographical

---

30  E Gerstenberger, 1974, uses three criteria to decide which psalms to include as wisdom psalms - the criteria of form, didactic intention and content.

31  W M W Roth, 1965, finds a further example in 2:11a but I consider his inclusion of this passage forced.

32  G von Rad, 1965, Volume 1, p 418f writes, "what preponderates in Israel's [wisdom] is the maxim which states and affirms, that is, the genuine form of the proverb proper." (p 430)

33  R N Whybray, 1974, argues that the speeches of Job and his friends "abound" in poetical units which would fit well into Proverbs as individual sayings (and longer didactic poems). However, he gives only a few examples which largely correspond to the references I gave above in the section dealing with proverbs and numerical sayings.

34  On Amos and wisdom see J Fichtner, 1949; S Terrien, 'Amos and Wisdom', 1962; H W Wolff, 1964. On Isaiah and wisdom see E Gerstenberger, 1962; J W Whedbee, 1971. On the relationship between prophecy and wisdom in general see R E Clements, 1975; J A Emerton, 1979 and R N Whybray, 'Prophecy and Wisdom', 1982.

narrative or 'royal testament' (Ecclesiastes 3:10-15), again a legacy of personal experience from one generation to another, paralleled in ancient Egypt where Pharaohs or their viziers collected their insights as to the correct behaviour before gods and men of young, aspiring rulers. The refrains also emphasize the personal message of the author, thus giving a unity to diverse materials. In Sirach however this autobiographical style has disappeared; and yet even more than the others this book is a personal testimony, for Sirach constantly gives us his own interpretation with the proverbs he cites, and uses refrains for emphasis (2:5-6). The trend towards prophecy found in Sirach is also a personal element for, in the style of prophecy, the author personally exhorts the people, and warns and admonishes them to behave in the way he is advocating (2:7-18). These later trends can be witnessed in the Wisdom of Solomon where we have warnings and admonitions in a semi-prophetic style (eg 2:1-20 and 5:3-13) which are similar to the 'imagined speech' form found in Proverbs (eg 1:19; 1:22-23).[35] This demonstrates the move towards wider interests by the wise man. This includes an interest in the cult, as evidenced by the production of wisdom psalms. It also shows that wise men were by this time learned in 'scripture' in general, including the 'prophetic' books whose style they were by now versatile enough to imitate.

Although *Job*, in its depth of emotion in the dialogue section, has been regarded as a personal testimony by a suffering individual,[36] there is no real evidence of this in the forms found in the book. Von Rad[37] argues that in the summary sentences in Job 1:22 and 2:10b, the narrator addresses the reader from outside the narrative. I shall argue in chapter 3 that in *Job* there is evidence of an author at work, using forms in a distinctive way. However the author does not reveal himself, give any kind of personal testimony or directly involve himself in the action or characterization.

In all wisdom books there is a didactic element in the proverbial sayings; this also appears in the instruction forms in Proverbs and then in Sirach in the didactic essay and ancient debate forms (Sirach 15:11) and in the didactic

---

35 J L Crenshaw, 'Wisdom', 1974.
36 For example R Potter, 1969, argues, with many older scholars, that the book reflects the real experiences of the author.
37 G von Rad, 1972.

poetry in Proverbs, Ecclesiastes, Sirach and the Wisdom of Solomon. At times the poetry is lyrical rather than instructive, as in Ecclesiastes (eg 1:4-9; 3:2-8), but such lyricism could well have developed out of the more matter-of-fact types of poetry of the earlier period, eg Proverbs 1:10-19, the long didactic poem containing a warning against bad company, and Proverbs 2:1-22, a description of what wisdom has to offer.[38] Again the Wisdom of Solomon contains poetry of a more imaginative type whilst in Sirach didactic elements abound (eg Sirach 1:1-20 and 4:11-19, poems about wisdom, and 16:24-30 and 17:1-12, poems about the creation of man). Related to the poetic forms are prayers and psalms. The psalms themselves are a kind of prayer or hymn, even if they are sometimes non-cultic,[39] whilst prayers are found from Proverbs (30:7-9) to the Wisdom of Solomon (9:1-18). However the prayer features very little in these two books in comparison with Sirach where the form of the prayer is accorded much more importance, eg 23:1-6 (compare with the simple request in Proverbs 30:7-9 for a balance between poverty and wealth). This form can be seen to have developed from small beginnings; in fact it was probably taken over from some other area of religious life, for example the cult, in the expansion of the wise man's field of interest.

*Job* contains didactic elements, for example, interrogative questions such as Job 8:11, which could well have come from an educational context (cf Amos 3:3-8). G von Rad[40] argues that the form of 'long didactic poem' features four times in *Job* in the speeches of Job's three friends as well as in Proverbs 1:10-19 and 2:1-22. However even von Rad admits that the Proverbs passages are dissimilar to those in *Job*. It is arguable that the form is restricted to *Job*. The entire book of *Job* could be seen to serve as a didactic lesson to those who suffer, or to those who question God's justice - depending on how one interprets the message. Von Rad emphasizes the didactic aspect of *Job*; for example he labels the prose narrative in *Job* 'didactic narrative' because

---

38 G von Rad, 1972, compares these long didactic poems in Proverbs with the four didactic poems which he finds in *Job* in the speeches of Job's three friends. The Proverbs passages are however short and poor comparisons to these and one is led to question whether they can indeed be classified as long didactic poems.
39 S Mowinckel, 1962, (p 111f, 138f) calls wisdom psalms 'non-cultic' or 'didactic poetry'. He describes the prayers in Sirach as 'learned psalms'.
40 G von Rad, 1972, pp 38-40.

"it is the events, the spoken word, which instruct"[41] and he tries to relate to this a didactic emphasis which he finds in Proverbs 7:6f where an event is described which a wise man has observed in the street. The link between *Job* and Proverbs here seems tenuous, and furthermore, since these are the only examples von Rad can find of didactic prose narrative in Proverbs, it is clearly not a common enough feature of the book to be allotted much importance. There is a didactic 'hymn' to wisdom in Job 28 the claims to authenticity of which are questionable.[42] There are no prayer forms in *Job*, although the line between these and lament forms is thin and it could be argued that some of the laments in *Job* resemble prayers.

A final prominent form is the hymn to wisdom found in Proverbs (1:20-33 and 8), Sirach (24:1-22) and the Wisdom of Solomon (6:12-22; 7:22-8:21). This form remains constant throughout the literature although the content, the way Wisdom is perceived, develops. There is also the general hymn form found only in the later material - Sirach 42:15-43:33 and small hints in the wisdom psalms - which again could well be the product of borrowing from other sources (Sirach, for example, borrowing from the Psalms). The border between hymn forms and wisdom forms is thin and I shall show later (pp 71-72, 104-105) how hymnic forms feature to a considerable extent in *Job*. A straightforward didactic hymn is found in Chapter 28 which teaches where wisdom is to be found (or not found). The presence of this hymn in *Job* has enhanced the impression that *Job* is wisdom. There are some forms in the early material which do not reappear, for example the riddle (eg Proverbs 30:29-31) and the fable and allegory which, even in Proverbs (eg in Proverbs 5:15-23), are late developments[43] and then die out in wisdom literature. There is a hint of allegory in Ecclesiastes (12:1-8) but this seems to be an isolated example. Again there are a few forms which appear only in the later material, some under the influence of prophecy or of prophetic interests by wise men, eg Sirach 24:30-34[44] and others under Hellenistic influence: for example the

---

41  G von Rad, 1972 (p 46).
42  The authenticity of chapter 28 in Job is questioned on literary-critical grounds - see discussion in chapter 4, pp 195-198.
43  W McKane, 1970.
44  See W Baumgartner, 1914.

mention of authorship in Sirach 50:27;[45] the Summary Appraisal in Psalm 49 (see also Psalm 45:1); and the didactic exhortation in the Wisdom of Solomon.[46] Some forms have scarcely developed at all, whereas others have developed considerably. However, there is no one line of development but various parallel ones.

Thus it is clear that much of the material in other 'wisdom' books either varies considerably from what is to be found in *Job* or does not appear in *Job* at all: even the basic proverbial form at the heart of 'wisdom' is uncommon. The predominant forms of mainline wisdom, certainly in their earliest stage of development, are not found in *Job*. A possible reason is simply that *Job* is historically later than Proverbs and forms have developed. However, we have not found much evidence of highly developed wisdom forms in *Job* either. The author of *Job* was clearly familiar with the forms in which the teaching in Proverbs is expressed, but he did not choose to use these forms predominantly in his book. Conversely, there appear forms in *Job* which have been classified as 'wisdom' probably on that account, but which are absent from these mainline wisdom books.[47] For example, there is no hint in Proverbs of the dialogue form which makes up the largest part of *Job* (ie chapters 3-42:6), nor is there any substantial prose narrative.

The dialogue form is paralleled in ancient Near Eastern wisdom, notably, it is argued, with the Babylonian Theodicy although this comparison has led to no far-reaching conclusions.[48] One reason for this is the lack of order in

---

45 See M Hengel, 1973.
46 See J M Reese, 1970.
47 G von Rad, 1972, distinguishes between old wisdom, the product of a radically secular age, and later wisdom, which seldom uses the sentence form but uses the didactic poem, hymn, dispute and autobiographical narrative and deals with the individual.
48 The Babylonian Theodicy - text in W G Lambert, 1960, pp 63-91, and J B Pritchard, 1950, pp 438-40; cf B Landsberger, 1936. G B Gray, 1919-20, for example, finds a parallelism of form between *Job* and the Babylonian Theodicy. He writes of the latter, "In it we find dialogue used for the purpose of discussing aspects or problems of life. It has also another formal resemblance to Job, viz. its schematic character. But in both respects the differences are not less striking" (p 442). He then goes on to enumerate the differences which certainly seem to outweigh the similarities. Furthermore the similarities he does find are only of a very general nature. In his conclusion he acknowledges that there is still a great gap in form between *Job* and other wisdom works, including the Babylonian Theodicy. A Bentzen, 1948, notes the alignment of the content of *Job* with the Babylonian 'I will praise the lord of Wisdom' (J B Pritchard, 1950, p 434) and suggests that this work is a combined psalm of lamentation and of thanksgiving. He writes, "*the parallel poems in dialogue form are only a further*

subject matter in the dialogue and the constant interruption of dialogue with lament.[49] The dialogue form is not found elsewhere in the Old Testament[50] and, whilst it has been suggested that this form is derived from a practice of holding disputations in wisdom 'schools' by professional teachers,[51] there is no evidence for this in the Old Testament. Such suggestions generally rest on the assumption that ancient Near Eastern texts provide close parallels to *Job*. It has been argued that the riddling between Solomon and the Queen of Sheba in its disputation style is a parallel to the dialogue form in *Job*, but it is hardly comparable. The dialogue in *Job* is not strictly a disputation in that the speeches do not follow logically one from another.[52]

Further examples of forms common to *Job* but lacking in Proverbs are those of the debate[53] and lament;[54] nor does Proverbs contain any material directly addressed to God or directly spoken by God as *Job* does. Furthermore, there is nothing in Ecclesiastes which resembles the debate in dialogue form found in *Job*, nor is there prose narrative of any length in either Proverbs or Ecclesiastes, the latter containing only anecdotes from personal experience (eg 2:1-11) and a two verse story in 9:14-15 used to illustrate a point in 9:16, "But I say that wisdom is better than might, though the poor man's wisdom is

---

*development of the situation of the psalm of lamention and its forms...the dialogue is a "dramatization" of the psalms of lamentation*, more accurately of the "prayers of the accused" placed in the frame of a narrative" (p 182). He then draws a comparison with *Job* envisaging the author as having developed a conversational form which allowed him to bring psalms of lamentation into a dialogue framework alongside his introduction of the friends. An Egyptian work 'The Dialogue between the World-Weary and his Soul' (in H Gressmann, 1926, pp 25ff), a conversation between two vultures concerning retribution, could, from its title, be thought to be a dialogue along similar lines to *Job* (cf also the Babylonian dialogue of a nobleman and his slave (H Gressmann, 1926, pp 287f)) but, unless one includes all conversational forms in this category, there are no formal parallels.

49  See G von Rad, 1972, pp 40-41.
50  Thus A Bentzen, 1948, writes when comparing *Job* with psalm forms, "The forms of the psalms are of great importance for the understanding of the forms used in the speeches of the Book of Job...Its peculiar form, the *dialogue*, has no parallels in the OT, eg not in the discussion speeches of Malachi." (1952, volume 2, p 181)
51  H Gunkel, 1928, O Eissfeldt, 1934, and G Fohrer, 1963 and 1970.
52  G von Rad, 1972, points out that the dialogue of *Job* is presented not as a series of disputes (Streitgespräche) but as a series of conversations (Gespräche) between an afflicted man and his friends, in which he laments and they try to comfort him.
53  The Sayings of Agur in Proverbs 30:1-4 could be seen as an exception to this statement since it contains a short debate, though scarcely of the magnitude of the debate in *Job*.
54  C Westermann, 1956, (1981) has highlighted the importance of the lament in *Job* and in the whole Old Testament (C Westermann, 1974).

despised and his words are not heeded." *Job* also lacks certain features essential to Ecclesiastes, for example his use of proverbs the importance of which is suggested in Ecclesiastes 12:9-11 where the author's activity is described as "weighing and studying and arranging proverbs with great care." Furthermore the whole of Ecclesiastes is presented as an autobiographical testament, it bears a very personal stamp and the reader is often addressed from within the narrative. In *Job*, on the other hand, no outside comment appears - no doubt because of its narrative framework.

Small wisdom forms are dotted around *Job*.[55] These are not enough on their own to characterize the whole book as wisdom, especially when it is noted that forms from other areas of Israelite life also feature in the book. To take a random chapter as an example: Chapter 5 contains a number of small wisdom forms. It opens with a rhetorical question and continues with a wisdom saying in support of the question (possibly being a quotation of an existing saying). Then in 5:3 there is a typical wisdom-form - a first person account - as in Psalm 37:25 or Proverbs 24:30, but with an unusual ending resembling endings in Ecclesiastes (eg Ecclesiastes 1:14). In 5:3-5 there is an example story about the punishment of evildoing and in 5:6-7 wisdom sayings, if rather unorthodox ones, concerning man's trouble. But, in this chapter, and in others, we find that many of the forms are more typical of hymnic forms than wisdom, for example 5:8-13 is a hymnic description of God to whom *Job* should appeal, cf I Samuel 2:1-10. Verses 10-13 are a doxology typical of the psalms. In 5:17-21 there are further wisdom forms, in 5:17-18 a 'happy is the man' saying with a motive clause, and in 5:19-21 a graded numerical saying concerning divine deliverance. In the next chapter, as well as wisdom and hymnic forms, there are echoes of questions and claims

---

55 For example in the dialogue section *Job* contains short wisdom sayings, eg 4:10-11; 5:2,6-7; 12:11-12; 15:34-35; quasi-acrostic features, 4:2-6; 5:3-7; arguments characteristic of wisdom style, 4:3-6,7-9; example stories, 5:3-5; numerical sayings, 5:19-21; proverbs, 6:5-6; 12:12-13; ridicule of opponents, 15:2-3,7-11; 16:2-6; accusations, 15:12-16; appeals to ancient tradition, 8:8-13; 15:17-19; descriptions of the fate of the wicked, 18:5-21; 20:4-29; 21:7-33; 27:13-23; summary appraisal formulas, 18:21; 20:29; 27:13; and rhetorical questions, 20:4-5; 21:17-18. In the Yahweh speeches there are examples of nature wisdom, eg 38:4-39:30 (ironic questions about creation and its creatures) and 40:15-41:16 (a sarcastic challenge to Job concerning control of Behemoth and Leviathan).

that would characterize a legal hearing, (eg 6:21-30), and legal forms appear in chapter 8 (eg 8:2-4). G Fohrer[56] argues that the first strophe of verse 2 is totally determined by the elements drawn from parties in litigation. Ridicule is followed by a counterclaim. In verse 2 a rhetorical question ridicules the opponent and in verse 3 Bildad's thesis is presented in the form of a rhetorical question. In verse 4 proof of the thesis in the form of the treatment of Job's children is provided.

Thus wisdom, hymnic and legal forms appear to be accorded equal importance in the book. Narrative forms predominate in the prose sections. This observation will be discussed further at the end of this chapter (pp 103-107). In mainline wisdom books, on the other hand, there is no such mixture of forms. In Ecclesiastes wisdom forms predominate, even though they are used in an unorthodox way (see chapter 3, pp 144-147). This evidence supports the idea that *Job* cannot be viewed decisively as 'wisdom literature'; it could be the product of a mixture of traditions, since so many forms are represented from other areas of Israel's life.

In conclusion, either 'wisdom' thinking expresses itself in very diverse forms of literature[57] and *Job* should be seen as 'wisdom', even if it is not mainline wisdom; or we can attempt a narrower definition of 'wisdom literature', but exclude *Job* from it since the book does not contain a predominance of mainline wisdom forms. However we cannot come to any decisive conclusion regarding whether *Job* is 'wisdom' before examining wisdom ideas in *Job* and a possible wisdom setting. All that can be stated from the findings of this section on forms is that *Job* is not characteristically 'wisdom' in terms of major forms used in the book and that it contains many forms from other areas of Israelite life.

---

[56] G Fohrer, 1963.
[57] H H Schmid, 1966, stresses this diversity of forms in wisdom and opposes 'narrow' interpretations that exclude Job as 'wisdom' because a certain form (eg the didactic poem) does not feature or because it deals with an individual rather than a general problem.

## ii) Content

What applies to form applies also to content. A comparison needs to be made between the content of *Job* and that of earlier wisdom. Scholars have largely based their assessment of *Job* as wisdom literature on the fact that the book airs the doctrine of retribution, an early wisdom concern.[58] However, one immediately striking difference is that *Job* questions, in contrast to the serene authoritativeness of earlier wisdom. It is because *Job* calls into question many traditional wisdom stances[59] and raises doubts about the validity of the wisdom exercise that it is usually regarded, with Ecclesiastes, as a development within wisdom, on the edges of the wisdom tradition.[60] *Job* is described as 'wisdom in revolt'.[61] The traditional doctrine is seen to have hardened into a dogma of which Job underlines the limitations, providing a personal wisdom which does not accept things at face value. Thus H H Schmid[62] argues that *Job* represents a genuine wisdom solution to the problem

---

58 eg O S Rankin, 1936, sees the purpose of *Job* as being to lodge a protest against the current dogma of retribution, but *Job* does not question the general validity of the Deuteronomic theory which provides the background against which the author sought to present his picture.

59 B Duhm, 1897, p x and R B Y Scott, 1972, who asserts that Job abandons the theory of an exact retributive justice, if he ever held it at all.

60 D Bergant, 1982, sees the purpose of *Job* as being to show the limitations of the wisdom exercise - the attempt to find 'order' in daily life and its underlying principles and to master and understand that order. She writes, "Job is an example of a challenge thrown in the face of the claim of an ordered world." (p 20). R B Y Scott, 1972, argues that *Job* represents a wisdom debate - "a wisdom rooted in shattering personal experience revolts against scholastic dogma" (p 136).

61 R B Y Scott, 1972. See chapter 1 note 112.

62 H H Schmid, 1966 writes "Er verlangt, daß die Weisheit offen sei, auch neue, zum Problem werdende Gegebenheiten zu verarbeiten und mit den früheren Erkenntnissen in Verbindung zu setzen." This Schmid sees as the key to 'genuine' wisdom. But the friends have lost the ability to think in this way and have fallen into systematic dogmatic wisdom: "Ihre Weisheit ist abgerundet und abgeschlossen. Was einmal gültig war, muß für sie immer gültig sein...Auf der Basis dieser grundsätzlichen Differenz ist eine Verständigung nicht möglich." The first speech of Yahweh is a genuine wisdom response to the problem of the innocent sufferer - Job's suffering is not explained rationally, as the three friends and Elihu have tried to explain it, instead Job is instructed to see his own fate within the horizons of cosmic order and to accept it in that context, order being the presupposition of wisdom thinking. In real wisdom the quest for this order has constantly to be renewed as fresh experiences challenge what has hitherto been accepted. Dogmatic wisdom thinks it knows the answers already and cannot perceive any experience as new. In Chapters 40-41, Yahweh's second speech, God is not meant to be comprehensible and Job's powerlessness is stressed - the question of justice is not addressed and wisdom questioning is silenced. Schmid suggests that chapters 40-41 are redactional, added at the time when the synagogue was

of innocent suffering over against the dogmatic wisdom represented by the friends, which became the way in which wisdom developed. Sometimes this questioning is accommodated within the bounds of traditional wisdom and is not seen to change it much.[63] Others however see it as marking a profound change in the nature of wisdom.[64]

There is clearly an awareness of the wisdom tradition in *Job*, since the whole dialogue revolves around a discussion of the righteous and the wicked and their just deserts along traditional lines. However this teaching is not peculiar to Proverbs, *Job* and Ecclesiastes but is presupposed generally in the Old Testament. I shall argue below that an evaluation of *Job* as 'wisdom' contributes little to the full appreciation of *Job*'s more radical ideas, which break outside the bounds of traditional wisdom beliefs. First, however, it is necessary to look at the characteristic themes of 'wisdom' contained in traditional wisdom books and compare *Job* with them.

As with wisdom forms, wisdom ideas developed over a long period of time and various specific developments can be traced. However, in general terms, by the later period wisdom had been lifted off the plane of everyday human experiences of life on to a more theological plane and into closer association

---

    developing, to make *Job* eligible for canonicity. He finds this trend paralleled in the wisdom of other nations. "Wie in Ägypten und Babylon ist auch in Israel die ursprünglich durchaus zeit- und situationsbezogene Weisheit erstarrt und als überzeitliches, dogmatisch-axiomatisches Formelgut verwendet worden. Sowohl in Ägypten wie in Babylon sind die Versuche, wieder neu weisheitlich zu denken, von dieser Dogmatik überfahren worden...Die Hiobdichtung hat mit Kap. 38f. einen Weg aus der Krise anvisiert, aber ihre Stimme wird mit Gewalt [cc. 40-41] zum Schweigen gebracht." Thus Schmid describes the message of *Job* in terms of structurally distinct forms of wisdom in confrontation with each other: "Die Hiobdichtung ist eine eindrückliche Abweisung der dogmatischen Weisheitsform und ein Versuch, die Welt wieder neu genuin-weisheitlich zu verstehen." Generally it is argued that *Job* is meant to show that human wisdom cannot discover the justice of God, so that revelation is needed - the fact that God appears then matters more than what he says. Schmid argues that the revelation of a genuine wisdom solution by God is what matters.

63  G F Moore, 1913; R B Y Scott, 1972; S H Blank, 1962; W A Irwin, 1952.
64  J F Priest, 1963, argues that such questioning led, on the one hand, to "a loss of belief in the dependability of life and the consequent assertion that life was meaningless or... unknowable" (p 227). On the other hand, such questioning led to "a new orientation for life's meaning which transcended the moral, optimistic outlook of the sages without remaining in the abyss of the pessimist" (p 227). He finds a parallel development in Egypt and quotes T O Lambdin, 1961: "the confident affirmation in the worldly order of the Old Kingdom is replaced by a period of doubt and searching for a new way and finally by one in which trust in a resourceful and gracious divine power dominates" (p 292f).

with the need for faith in God. Schmid[65] argues against this kind of secular-to-theological development, maintaining that theological ideas can be found in the earlier material. However, even if this is the case, the theological ideas can still be seen as coming to a fuller development in the later material. In the secular world wisdom achieved greatness but, as Ecclesiastes found, such wisdom was not enough by itself to give meaning to life at a deeper level. A more profound theologization enabled wisdom to survive. At each stage, wisdom provides the necessary tools for man to be able to cope with life;[66] initially by means of intuition born of experience, but later by means of a deeper understanding of the ways of God. More specifically, I have identified six themes, each of which can be found in some or all of the wisdom books and which are closely interlinked. These themes develop but remain integral to a definition of the content of wisdom literature:-

1. The first theme is that of *order in the world* - whether it can or cannot be found and whether it is to be gained by human experience or from God. In Proverbs there is a positive assessment of an order apparent in the world through man's experience. Knowledge of this world order led to a search for analogies of an essentially practical nature.[67] Man could attempt to match this order with his own behaviour.[68] Ecclesiastes contradicts these positive assertions by claiming that a rational rule cannot be discovered in the universe[69] and man cannot secure his future existence since God's activity is unpredictable and unknowable (11:5). Although meaningful events occur, man has not the knowledge to match the deed with the occasion (7:23-29). He has no confidence in the knowledge gained from experience, for all knowledge

---

65 H H Schmid, 1966.
66 A Caquot, 1978, with reference to the Ugaritic texts from Ras Shamra, defines 'hokma' as 'ability to cope', the fountain of life, a human and divine capacity rather than a current of thought or a literary genre.
67 eg 'Like' proverbs such as Proverbs 25:23 which link very different phenomena: "The north wind brings forth rain; and a backbiting tongue, angry looks."
68 To assist this Proverbs contains experiences of types of behaviour that occur with such regularity that a rule may be recognized, eg Proverbs 14:20. Proverbs also concern man's inner life and its relation to his outer one; how he can either broadcast or conceal it, eg Proverbs 14:13. Many proverbs deal with cause and effect, eg Proverbs 16:18: "Pride goes before destruction, and a haughty spirit before a fall", although some pay attention to the fact that an action is only often appropriate in a certain situation, eg Proverbs 25:11: "A word fitly spoken is like apples of gold in a setting of silver."
69 As stated repeatedly in the refrain, "...all was vanity and a striving after wind and there was nothing to be gained under the sun" (2:11).

comes from God (2:26; 3:11). He shows that the answers given in Proverbs do not satisfy a deeper questioning.[70] Sirach however is more positive. He asserts that one can know the right behaviour at the right time, though it is God who allocates the time[71] and human experience is not enough on its own to find it out.[72] He asserts that there are no limits to man's possible knowledge as long as God is at the centre. The fear of God is the beginning of wisdom (eg 1:16; 1:27) and is also linked with the torah (eg 1:26; 6:37; 19:20; 21:11; 23:27).[73] In the Wisdom of Solomon this same emphasis on God is found in a discussion of the theological implications of man's relationship with God.[74] The distinctively 'wisdom' element is merged with historical concerns regarding Israelite history and the election of the chosen people and religious concerns such as the polemic against idols and theological concerns such as repentance. There is also in the Wisdom of Solomon a full development of the theological implications of wisdom in relation to God and man. In the wisdom psalms (which probably belong before the time of Sirach and represent an earlier stage in the development) God is in control even when calamity strikes (Psalm 37); he is the source of all knowledge and an indispensable guide to life. There is the idea of an order that can be known and an emphasis on experience. A development can therefore be traced in this material away from concern with an order that can be found through experience, into an emphasis that all knowledge comes from God and can be obtained only through communion with him. This development was prompted by the realization that the type of knowledge found in Proverbs was not at a deep enough level to satisfy fully the needs of those searching within it for life's meaning. On the

---

[70] He tests various answers to life's meaning and whilst he concedes that some have a fleeting significance (eg 2:24) he expresses a preference for death since that fate awaits both the wise man and the fool (2:14,18-21).

[71] The goodness of God's decrees is stressed, Sirach 33:13-15.

[72] In Sirach 21:6 trust in God is advocated.

[73] In his attempt to legitimate and interpret Torah from the realm of understanding characteristic of wisdom, Sirach starts to regard the functions of wisdom in a different way from his predecessors. See discussion of Sirach 24 in G von Rad, 1972, pp 147f, 170f.

[74] For example, the stress on God's mercy in 3:9 and on God's divine foreknowledge (7:7-8) and forebearance. Such concerns lead him to condemn human perversions, eg idol worship in 13:1-15:19.

other hand, Proverbs contains a simplicity and directness which is often lacking in the theologization of the later material.

In *Job* man's confidence that he can influence God's actions towards him is shattered. Man cannot predict what will happen (eg 9:11-12) - even if he behaves in the way that God has indicated that a righteous man should act, he is not saved from the arbitrary punishment of God, nor has he any right of appeal (eg 9:13-20). However, Job is not resigned, as Ecclesiastes is, to an unknowable order in the universe. He tries desperately to understand God's action (eg 6:24) and cling to his belief that it is not arbitrary, yet his experience tells him otherwise.[75] Thus *Job*, like Ecclesiastes, provides a critique of the traditional wisdom stance, but, unlike Ecclesiastes, Job holds on to his faith in God and tries to understand God's action within this framework.

2. The first theme is closely related to the second - *the ambiguity of events and of the meaning of life*. In Proverbs, although much can be known through experience (which tended to be the wise man's starting point (22:17-24:20)[76]), the ultimate meaning of events is unknowable apart from Yahweh, in whom man must trust[77]. There is thus a tension between fear of God and man's knowledge of God (Proverbs 2:1,5).[78] In Ecclesiastes this takes a more negative form - a deep understanding of the meaning of life is totally denied to man, for God's activity is unknowable (11:5). In Sirach however there is the same tension as in Proverbs between self-reliance and the fear of God.[79]

---

75 See discussion of Job's own position in relation to the orthodoxy of the friends in chapter 4, pp 172-183.
76 Compare 22:17-22 with the Instruction of Amenemope, chapter 1. "Give thy ears, hear what is said, Give thy heart to understand them. To put them in thy heart is worth while, [But] it is damaging to him who neglects them." (J B Pritchard, 1950, pp 418-419). In the Egyptian instruction there is not the emphasis on God found in Proverbs - "Incline your ear, and hear the words of the wise, and apply your mind to my knowledge; for it will be pleasant if you keep them within you, if all of them are ready on your lips. That your trust may be in the Lord, I have made them known to you today, even to you." (Prov. 22:17-17)
77 G von Rad, 1972, argues that Proverbs are "marked by the same tension between a radical secularization on the one hand and the knowledge of God's unlimited powers on the other. At one point, man's life was seen to be bound up in orders which themselves were not entirely free from a certain amount of control. Then again it was seen to be dependent on God's benevolence." (p 98)
78 See discussion in G von Rad, 1972, pp 53-73.
79 Sirach advocates self-trust but hastens to place it under a greater obligation, the necessity to pray for divine guidance (37:12-16). Thus, for example, Sirach both endorses traditions about wisdom being a cosmic entity and maintains that human effort

There is seen to be an order that is hidden and to some extent ambiguous.[80] It is the task of the wise man to find this order out so that it can be known at the right time and on the right occasion and so that appropriate action can be taken.[81] This is a positive assessment of the seeming ambiguity of events - such ambiguity does not prevent man from understanding and controlling his life as long as he is in close contact with God.[82]

Job strains to obtain a deeper understanding of life (eg 10:2-17) and yet his questions are not directly answered in the speeches of Yahweh. Even in his repentance, one wonders if he has obtained any deeper understanding - his response may rather be the result of personal communion with God. Whilst he is returned to prosperity at the end of the book, he is none the wiser as regards the reason for his suffering. Thus the outcome of the book is negative and challenges the positive attitude of traditional wisdom ideas.[83]

3. A third theme is that of *punishment and reward.* In Proverbs a just and individual accounting and balancing takes place, the wise and righteous man prospers and is rewarded by God whilst the foolish and wicked man is punished. Good and evil are seen as forces which are linked to behaviour.[84] In Ecclesiastes however there is no confidence in God's disposition to reward virtue or punish vice for there is a loss of trust in God's goodness. The author's experience is that the wicked prosper just as much as the good, if not

---

first grasped wisdom which, initially a yoke, becomes a beautiful bride (6:18-31). There is a debate over whether the fear of God is identified in Sirach with the Mosaic law (J L Crenshaw, 1982) or with Wisdom as both a primaeval order and a wisdom needed by man but which he cannot acquire without God's assistance (G von Rad, 1972) (Sirach 19:20).

80  In fact Sirach enjoys contrasting things to heighten their ambivalence, eg in 41:1-2 he shows how there are two sides to death, one bitter, the other sweet.
81  God allocates to man 'his time' (39:16-35) which man must discover to know, for example, when to speak and when be silent, eg verse 33: "The works of the Lord are all good and he will supply every need in its hour." There is an underlying order to life; everything comes in pairs, 33:7-15.
82  Unlike earlier wisdom, Sirach does not regard God as a limit imposed on human attempts to master life. Rather piety and a secure religious relationship with God are most important to Sirach.
83  See discussion in chapter 4, pp 172-183 and 203-209.
84  A strong contrast is drawn between the wise man and the fool, the latter being unable to adhere to the order taught by the wise. A further concern is with the effect of the act on its author, eg Proverbs 11:21 which contrasts the blessing of the righteous and the curse of the wicked (cf Proverbs 24:16), a theme aired in *Job*. See G von Rad, 1972, and K Koch, 1955, on the 'act-consequence' relationship and B Gemser, 1937 and P Volz, 1911, who prefer to speak of a doctrine of retribution.

more so. God is seen as indifferent to human conduct.[85] In Sirach there is an emphasis on a right religious relationship as the goal of his educational endeavours and he encourages pious behaviour (32:14-24). The idea of predestination also comes into play and sets up a conflict between predestination and man's control over his life by the choices he makes (eg 15:16). Yet in the midst of the ambiguities, the wise man must find the right way of looking at things and so will obtain the ability to do the right thing in God's sight.[86] In the Wisdom of Solomon there is a confidence in the beneficial effects of correct human behaviour which is expressed in the maxim that a person's being virtuous is always stronger than the power of vice.[87] Virtue includes full faith in God (1:2-5). In Proverbs merit was based on wise or foolish actions; here however, a more theological emphasis on repentance is introduced. The idea of God's compassion for the elect stands in tension with a desire to emphasize God's love for everyone so that all can repent - in 11:15-20 the same lenience is granted to the Egyptians. In the wisdom psalms there is an emphasis on retribution,[88] possibly even in the afterlife (Psalm 49:16-17)[89] - another theological development. On this view, inconsistencies in the principle that the good are rewarded and the wicked punished are countered by the admonition not to worry at these inconsistencies but to look to the 'end' when all will get their just deserts.

In *Job* it is the very fact that the rule of just deserts is broken that is the cause of the suffering and of the questioning. Job realizes that it is often the wicked that prosper whilst the innocent suffer - God's treatment of good and bad alike is arbitrary (eg 12:13-25). By questioning such maxims Job loses

---

[85] Different passages in Ecclesiastes seem to suggest an ambiguity in the author's attitude towards reward and retribution - 3:17 and 8:13 support the traditional understanding; 7:15 and 8:14 contradict it. He maintains that God is hidden and advises caution in dealing with God (5:1-6) yet he often makes assertions about God's will and activity, (eg 9:7).

[86] Sirach however expresses awe at man's ability to differentiate between good and evil (17:6f).

[87] An example is the way the Wisdom of Solomon extends the old maxim that progeny is an indication of God's favour to include barren women (3:13, 4:1) and eunuchs (3:14) as long as they are virtuous. Creation itself fights on behalf of the righteous (5:15-23; 16:17; 16:24).

[88] This emphasis especially regards the prosperity of the righteous and punishment of the wicked, eg Psalms 37; 49 and 73.

[89] G von Rad, 1972, regards Psalm 49:16-17 as "the expression of a hope for a life of communion with God that will outlast death." (p 204)

the 'wisdom' framework of his life and is forced to push the frontiers of his knowledge (or lack of it) further.[90]

4. Linked to this is the fourth theme - *life as the supreme good*. This idea is a presupposition in Proverbs, 'life' meaning a long existence characterized by good health, many friends, children, possessions and wisdom as the staff of that life (3:9-18). Men are instructed to gain or preserve life and that is the totality of all achievements. In Ecclesiastes, on the other hand, life is empty and at times the author would rather be dead than alive, or better still have never been born.[91] However, the author of Ecclesiastes appears to contradict himself, and there are times when he admits that life is still good and advocates enjoying it to the full (7:14). In Sirach the emphasis has shifted for the law is seen as the way to life. True wisdom is hidden in the Mosaic law and so sacred history is integrated into sapiential discourse (eg Sirach 44:1-50:21). Good actions are no longer enough, they have to be according to the law (28:1-7) and since the law is from God, man has to be in close communion with God to achieve his reward. Thus the emphasis is on an individual's relationship with God. There is no doubt that God is good (33:13-15) and there is a positive assessment of the possibility of such a relationship. As in Proverbs, so in the Wisdom of Solomon, good and evil are seen as very real forces linked theologically with the frail sphere of the flesh and the creative wisdom of the spirit. There is a detailed description of all the terrors and hallucinations which assailed the enemies of the people of God "shut up in a prison not made of iron" (17:16), a prison of their own anxieties (17:17-21).[92] The theological emphasis found in Sirach is apparent here too - there can be no reward without adherence to God and an attempt to forge a relationship with him - experiential wisdom is not enough to satisfy a deep religious need. An emphasis in the Wisdom of Solomon is on intellectual love - a relationship between man and wisdom as well as man and God. In the wisdom psalms the hope that life will be just is thrown into the future and the psalmists look to the

---

[90] See discussion in chapter 4, pp 172-183.
[91] In Ecclesiastes 7:1 the day of death is better than the day of birth.
[92] G von Rad, 1972, argues that in the Wisdom of Solomon the world is for the first time divided into a benevolent one ruled by God and a malevolent one ruled by evil.

end time, even if this only means the moment when injustices will end rather than an afterlife (eg Psalm 37:37; 73:23-26).

Job curses the day of his birth, he wishes he had never been born and he wishes he was dead (eg Job 3) - this is because his life has been made a mockery. His experience leads him to the realization that a life without order or meaning is worthless. First, the order given to his life by his past belief in the doctrine of retribution has been shattered. Secondly, his faith in God gave his life meaning and an inability to understand God's actions and the loss of communion with him has led to feelings of betrayal and anger. Yet he still clings to his old beliefs and the contradictions in his thought - a desire both to affirm and deny God - betray his confused state of mind. He is nevertheless led to question that life is the supreme good, one of the major presuppositions of the wisdom tradition.[93]

5. The fifth theme is *confidence in wisdom*. In Proverbs the search for knowledge is man's goal in life. Its acquisition is open to all and its application is universal. Any knowledge that cannot be acquired is part of a divine mystery controlled by God. God is seen as being in ultimate control and yet confidence in the knowledge that can be gained by human experience is high (Proverbs 22:17-24:22). Ecclesiastes, as usual, provides a complete contrast. For the author, the wisdom exercise is bankrupt (1:3,17,18; 7:23-9) for the knowledge wanted is inaccessible (3:11). The negative side of the issue is heightened here and yet the author of Ecclesiastes appears to contradict himself and sometimes sees wisdom as a prize to be gained (7:12,19) providing a positive appreciation of wisdom's worth. Sirach's positive confidence in wisdom resembles that found in Proverbs and yet in Sirach wisdom is closely linked to the law and to the fear of God which has developed away from its simple meaning in Proverbs to express the need for fulfilment of ancient covenantal obligations expressed in the Torah (eg 1:26; 6:37; 19:20; 21:11; 23:27). However, this appeal is universal whilst in the Wisdom of Solomon there is a new element in the emphasis on the elect (3:9; 15:1-2) - knowledge is available only to the chosen few, partly because its acquisition is now seen to be much more dependent on faith in the God of

---

[93] See discussion in chapter 4, pp 172-183 and 203-209.

Israel; a large secular, experiential knowledge is no longer valued so highly. Yet this author realizes that ideas of election cannot be fully defended since no one can call God to task for his conduct (12:12-18). Thus there is a tension apparent in his work.[94] Wisdom here is very central to life, not only to education and the pursuit of knowledge but to an understanding of history. Wisdom has a part in history guiding the chosen people,[95] and she becomes more and more glorified as she attains further attributes. This is connected with the hypostatization of wisdom in the Wisdom of Solomon (see theme 6 below). Finally in the wisdom psalms Yahweh is the source of all knowledge and the divine order he represents is the indispensable guide to life.[96] Wisdom is again closely related to the fear of Yahweh and to the praise of his name, eg Psalm 111:10, if this can be regarded as a wisdom psalm.[97]

*Job* marks the failure of wisdom - it defines the limits of the exercise when experience proves that life does not follow a strict pattern of justice. In his reliance on his own experience Job is obeying the rules of wisdom and yet his experience proves that an order cannot be known through man's experience, nor can God be known. Thus *Job* negates the quest for order, both in the human sphere and in the divine realm, a quest which is the keynote of the wisdom exercise.[98]

6. The last theme is that of the *personification* of wisdom which starts in a small way in Proverbs but which, by the Wisdom of Solomon, pervades all wisdom thinking and the entire assessment of the value of the wisdom exercise. This whole development, even in Proverbs, is a very theological one and becomes more so in the later works. In Proverbs wisdom is personified - in Chapter 8 wisdom is a woman standing at the gate crying out for men to hear her voice and reference is made to her having been "created at the beginning: before the beginning of the earth" (8:22-23). In Sirach, wisdom is linked with creation, notably the creation of the law which brought wisdom

---

94 eg 3:1 - all the souls of the righteous (not just the elect) rest in God's hand.
95 Chapters 10-19 are a midrashic exposition on the Exodus experience.
96 eg Psalm 119. On Psalm 119 as a wisdom psalm see discussion in J K Kuntz, 1974.
97 On Psalm 111 as a wisdom psalm, see J K Kuntz, 1974 (p 218).
98 See discussion in chapter 4, pp 172-183 and 203-209.

into being.⁹⁹ In the Wisdom of Solomon there is a very rich imagery of wisdom which has developed out of the view of it in the earlier books. Here however wisdom is hypostatized rather than merely personified and there is much emphasis on her relationship to God. She is the manifestation of God to humans, an emanation of divine attributes (7:22). She is the orderer and creator of all things (8:1,6) as well as the teacher of virtues such as self-control and justice (8:7) and the supplier of all instruction (7:17-22)¹⁰⁰. The personification of wisdom does not appear in the wisdom psalms, Ecclesiastes or *Job* (except in chapter 28). Developments inherent in the earlier material can be seen to have come to full expression in the later material and, at the same time, to have acquired new elements that make their continued existence possible. Such developments can usually be explained in the light of the weaknesses of earlier wisdom.

Thus on all these issues, *Job* clearly provides a critique of the wisdom exercise. In order to criticize any tradition, the protagonist needs to be aware of its conventions. However one is led to question whether the book can be seen as strictly 'wisdom' in its content, in the same sense as the other 'wisdom' books. *Job* questions the wisdom tradition to such an extent that it breaks outside its bounds.

iii) Context

The most common suggestion for a social context for the author of *Job* is a wisdom setting.¹⁰¹ Once it was discovered that schools of wisdom existed in

---

99  Sirach reinterprets the older tradition of wisdom, found in Proverbs, as the life-giving law providing food for the devout and evil for sinners. Instead of the law being inherent in creation, the creation of the law brings it into being (Sirach 24).
100 On the typology of Wisdom see B L Mack, 1973.
101 We cannot name the author and so have to rely on what we can deduce from the concerns and ideas expressed in the book. The author was clearly an educated person with knowledge of Israel's religious traditions but the international flavour of his work suggests that he saw his book as having a wider application than just an Israelite audience. The presence of unique words, considerable Aramaic and some Arabic in *Job* has led to suggestions that the book was originally written in Arabic (H Foster, 1982-83, E F F Bishop, 1973, and A Guillaume, 1963) or Edomite and translated into Hebrew. A R Ceresko, 1980, widens the philological scope of the vocabulary in *Job* to include Eblaite, Ugaritic and Phoenician. A study of the language used does not provide much support for these tenuous conclusions except to enhance the possibility of an extra-Israelite setting for production of *Job*. Against this J Barr, 1985, states that such

the ancient Near East,[102] *Job* was regarded by many scholars as a product of such schools.[103] A few scholars prefer to talk not of wisdom schools but of an intellectual or religious context for the book,[104] whilst others, such as R Gordis,[105] regard *Job* as from a group of dissidents on the fringe of the main wisdom tradition. He writes:

> "[They] had been trained to apply observation and reasoning to the practical problems of daily life. They would use the same instruments to solve the more fundamental issues that intrigued them, the purpose of life, man's destiny after death, the basis of morality, the problem of evil. When they weighed the religious and moral ideas of their time by these standards, they found some things they could accept, but much that they felt impelled to reject as either untrue or unproved."

Gordis sees the authors of *Job* and Ecclesiastes as trained in the 'wisdom academies' and utilizing the conventional religious vocabulary of the schools to express both ideas they agreed with and ideas they wanted to modify or oppose. Job is regarded as a product of circles of 'the wise' but there is hesitation in attributing the book to the orthodox mainstream of activity of such a group.

It was seen above that rather than teaching maxims in an authoritative manner, Job questions the teaching and does not replace it with any more positive answers. This does not imply a didactic context. It is true that, in a sense, in its movement away from tradition, it teaches the reader the limitations of the wisdom exercise when faced with man's experience and with an

---

defective spellings are balanced by a mass of contrary evidence within *Job*, the proportion of them differing only in tendency and degree from what is found in Jeremiah, Ezekiel, some Psalms and in Proverbs. An absolute date for the book cannot be found. Majority opinion prefers a post-exilic date, around the fourth century BC and I shall suggest in chapter 4 that *Job* can perhaps be assigned to the period immediately preceding the Hellenistic era (see discussion pp 160-168).

102  T N D Mettinger, 1971 and J P J Olivier, 1975.
103  D Cox, 1981, argues that "the dialogues in the book of *Job* are an often dramatic evocation of a classic wisdom position. They are not a personal statement but they represent the point of view of a school of thought." (p 55)
104  I G Matthews, 1947, talks in terms of the post-exilic religion of the intellectuals consisting of philosophic, legalistic or priestly and apocalyptic strains rather than of 'wisdom' and places *Job* in this context. J J M Roberts, 1977, argues for the influence of both cultic and wisdom traditions on *Job*.
105  R Gordis, 1944, (1971, p 161). Gordis argues that *Job* and Ecclesiastes modified the tradition by means of a 'use of quotations' technique. See R Gordis, 1949, (1971, pp 104-159) and discussion of this technique in chapter 3, pp 123-124.

arbitrary God. But this latter kind of teaching hardly resembles didactic or wisdom teaching, rather it undermines wisdom teaching.

*Job* is clearly not didactic in the same sense as Proverbs: R N Whybray[106] argues this case. After demonstrating the positive didactic attitude of Proverbs, he writes:

> "This positive and confident didactic tone, which is imitated, only to be attacked, in the speeches of Job's 'friends', is entirely different from that of the book of *Job* considered as a whole. It has often been remarked that the book offers no clear-cut solution to the problems which it raises. This is surely due not to the author's inability to make his conclusions clear to the reader, but to his basic intention, which was not didactic in any strict sense, but was to air and discuss certain problems to which he knew of no answers, in order to provoke reflection. This may have been the intention of some sayings in Proverbs; but in *Job*, considered as a single literary work, the method is quite different, and the scale of the enterprise quite beyond comparison with anything in Proverbs. Moreover the confident tone of Proverbs is entirely lacking in *Job* except where it is imitated for the purpose of showing its falsity."[107]

Therefore, if the book of *Job* could be shown to have sprung from 'wisdom circles' and to typify the activity of the 'wise man'[108] it could reasonably be

---

106 R N Whybray, 1974.
107 R N Whybray, 1974 (p 62). Such imitation for the purpose of showing the falsity of the confidence of Proverbs is found by Whybray in the speeches of Elihu (eg in 33:9-11; 34:5,9; 35:2f where Job's statements are cited to try to demonstrate their falsity). He considers these speeches secondary and cites scholars who have argued that this section shows signs of being the work of professional wise men (G Fohrer, 1970, says that Elihu "uses the rhetorical form of the lecture delivered by a wisdom instructor" (p 330) and A Weiser, 1951, sees him as a wisdom teacher using the form of *Streitgespräch*). He notes that, whilst Elihu's speeches have more the character of a disputation than other parts of *Job*, there is nothing to suggest that their author was a wise man. Furthermore Elihu's claim to special inspiration (32:8-9) and assertion that in general God speaks to man through direct revelation (33:14-18) shows that this author's thought is removed from 'wisdom', which is based on the principles of inherited professional lore and learned reflection upon it.
108 See E W Heaton, 1974, who posits 'schools' of wise men as in Egypt. These 'schools' trained the administrators of Solomon's government as well as producing literature - 'wisdom' was practical as well as academic. They emerged when Israel became a strong national state for which a highly articulate, professional and ambitious bureaucracy was needed. Egypt already had such a system which Israel was able to imitate. Heaton finds a reference to an Israelite school in Sirach 51:23 and evidence of borrowing from the Egyptian Instruction of Amenemope in Proverbs 22:17-23:14. He includes amongst the literature of the scribes, the Joseph narrative, the Succession narrative and the Yahwist's history. In Heaton's view, these are connected by the view taken of the relationship between human freedom and divine control, a characteristic of Egyptian wisdom, eg the Instruction of Merikare (J B Pritchard, 1950, pp 414-418) which displays a theology of the hidden God.

assumed to have a didactic purpose. But, if *Job* can be shown not to have been composed by sages, this may be used as evidence that the book lies outside the wisdom tradition, for, although the author clearly understands the presuppositions of the wisdom tradition (a necessity for providing a critique of it) this need not mean that he is a traditional wise man (the implications of this argument are pursued in the next chapter). The very fact of the author's critique suggests that he no longer stands within the tradition but has broken out of it.

Of course, the 'wise' need not only refer to a specific 'class' of educated people in Israel; it can also refer to people of skill or education who have in common a similar intellectual tradition.[109] 'Wisdom circles', even if they did exist in an earlier period, gradually became very loosely defined and turned into circles of general intellectual culture.[110] *Job* would certainly fit such a wider definition of 'wisdom circles' but not the narrower one which is usually implied when the work is called a 'wisdom' book.

It has been seen above that the more strictly 'wisdom' grouping does not do justice to the forms and themes found in the book. This is supported by the fact that *Job* does not contain any traditional attribution in terms of authorship to famous wisdom teachers whereas the other 'wisdom' books do. With regard to ostensible authorship, the attribution of wisdom books to well-known 'wise' men reinforces the idea that these books were composed in circles of 'the wise', even if the books cannot really be attributed to great figures such as Solomon. Three wisdom books are attributed to Solomon - Proverbs, Qoheleth and the Wisdom of Solomon - and all three attributions are thought, on the level of actual authorship, to be spurious. Proverbs, for example, does not contain the type of proverb that Solomon is supposed to have excelled in concerning phenomena of the plant and animal world (I Kings 4:32-34), whilst in Ecclesiastes the mention of Solomonic authorship does not persist throughout the work but disappears after the section on the royal experiment. The Wisdom of Solomon is from a period much later than the

---

[109] R N Whybray, 1974, argues that 'the wise' did not exist as a distinct professional class but that wisdom was an 'intellectual tradition'.
[110] An alternative to this kind of development is to envisage one in which the three classes of prophet, priest and wise man (Jeremiah 18:18) become more closely interlinked, the differences becoming almost insignificant.

time of Solomon and so, on grounds of chronology alone, could not have been written by him. The book was probably attributed to Solomon, as the symbol of the greatest wisdom thinker, to add more weight to the content of the book. In fact this may well be the case with all three attributions. In the same way, all the law is attributed to Moses and all the psalms to David, including those usually labelled wisdom psalms. Sirach too is attributed to an author - Jesus, the son of Sirach - in 50:27 "Instruction in understanding and knowledge I have written in this book, Jesus the son of Sirach, son of Eleazer of Jerusalem, who out of his heart poured forth wisdom." This is the only wisdom book which is not attributed to a great hero of Israel's past and hence a claim to actual authorship by this 'ostensible' author is strong. Thus each of these books is assigned to an author, whether it be a correct attribution or not; a feature which is missing from *Job*.

It is highly probable that the actual authors of all the books discussed here were from within the wisdom tradition.[111] Little attention needs to be paid to the claims to authorship in the texts themselves (with the exception of Ecclesiastes), except that such assignations affirm the tradition that such books are 'wisdom'. That such claims are not found in *Job* may be significant and may strengthen the argument that *Job* is very much on the edge of the wisdom context in the same way that the book does not display evidence of mainline forms and content of wisdom.

In conclusion to this section on the form, content and social context of wisdom and *Job*'s position in this tradition, it can be seen that on a narrow definition *Job* fails as a 'wisdom' text. It contains a radical questioning of the 'wisdom' tradition; it does not embody the literary categories of wisdom forms, ideas and setting to a sufficient extent to qualify it as belonging to 'wisdom literature'; nor does it fit into the mainline development within 'wisdom' which I have traced. However on a broader definition of 'wisdom' it is essential to include *Job*, because of the realization that it springs from the same intellectual and spiritual quest as other 'wisdom' books. Thus H H Schmid[112] lays emphasis on the fact that the book is 'marked' ('geprägt') by

---

[111] See the discussion of a possible context for the author of *Job* in chapter 4, pp 159-168.
[112] H H Schmid, 1966, p 185-186.

wisdom thinking, and this stress allows him to classify *Job* as 'wisdom'. The observations made here concerning the social setting or context of *Job* support the idea that the book is part of a wider intellectual quest and context, but not part of a narrow 'wisdom' circle such as might have been found at an earlier stage of the wisdom tradition. The book could represent part of a more general intellectual exercise. The need then would be to try to define which part of this wider intellectual milieu provides a context for *Job*. An alternative to trying to find a corner of a general intellectual tradition in which *Job* can be placed is to try to isolate a different mainline tradition from wisdom which was at work in Israel and may even represent a separate 'group' in existence at the time. If this is the case we will have to discuss what kind of author or group could have produced this literature, where and when. This question will be pursued in chapter 4. In the second part of this chapter however I continue the discussion of the quest for an overall classification for *Job* by considering the suggestions of scholars regarding an overall literary genre for the book. I examine the possibility of finding an overall genre, discuss the scope of the term and assess the different levels on which 'genre' operates.

### c) THE QUEST FOR AN OVERALL GENRE FOR *JOB*

i) Genre levels

The term 'genre' has a wide sphere of application and this often leads to confusion. It can be used to refer to the distinctive identity of both a whole work and a small section of the whole. Thus the very smallest 'genre' may be little more than a 'form' or turn of phrase or *Gattung*; complete chapters and entire speeches may be ascribed to particular genres; and, finally, an overall classification of a complete book may be called the book's genre. A genre differs from a form by the fact that form and content and context (*Sitz im Leben*) need to correspond. For example, to be classed as a 'lament' in genre or *Gattung* a psalm needs not only to be in the same form as other laments, but needs to contain also the content traditionally found to accompany such a form and to derive from a *Sitz im Leben* in which such a form would be relevant and comprehensible.[113] An awareness of the different levels on which the term 'genre' operates avoids much confusion. In my discussion of 'wisdom' above, I argued that the presence of forms of 'wisdom', without corresponding wisdom 'ideas' and a wisdom setting for the production of the book, are not enough to classify a whole text as 'wisdom literature'. Thus the presence of small 'wisdom' genres in the text is not sufficient to classify the whole as (generically) 'wisdom'. In the same way, deciding the overall genre of a book does not depend on finding a predominance of one type of 'smaller genre' and reading the whole in the light of this interpretation; for example, classifying a book as 'a lament' merely because lament forms predominate in it. It means gathering evidence of different smaller genres and then trying to assess the greater whole to which they contribute. Thus it is equally as fallacious to assume that a book is 'a lament' because it contains a lot of small lament genres as it is to classify all the smaller forms within it as lament genres because one has already decided that overall the book is generically 'a lament'. These are the two major pitfalls into which interpretations of the genre of *Job* have fallen.

ii) The first pitfall - the assumption that the overall genre of Job is the most predominant 'smaller' genre

An example of this is provided by C Westermann's interpretation of *Job*.[114] His suggestion for the overall genre of *Job* springs from a consideration of certain key words found within it. For Westermann the dominant form in *Job* is the lament. He starts from the observation that the dialogue or 'Streitgespräch' as he calls it, in chapters 4-27, is encased between the lament in chapters 3 and 29-31. He argues from this observation that the literary genre of *Job* is a "dramatization of a lament", for Job does indeed lament (unlike the three friends, who argue). Westermann writes:

"The dialogue is supposed to become a consoling conversation in which the speech of the one partner would have to be lament and that of the other consolation (for example 16:2;

---

113 For a discussion of why genres are important for exegesis see G W Coats, 1985.
114 C Westermann, 1956, (1981).

21:34). Controversy replaces the consolation offered by the friends and this leads to arguments."[115]

In Job's speeches the lament remains the dominant form but alongside this there is opposition to the friends which makes the whole (except the narrative sections and lament) a disputation. In the lament however God is addressed and the controversy moves to a higher court when God is summoned in 31:35-37 - he alone can resolve the controversy. In fact another dispute takes place in chapters 38-42, this time between God and Job. All this is placed in the framework of the prose narrative in chapters 1-2 and 42:7-12 which tells of a real event that befell a human being and so makes the dialogue more than just illustrative. The usual three figures in a complaint - self, God and enemies - which correspond to the three parts of the lament, are to be found here in the figures of Job, God and the three friends. Chapter 28 is a transitional passage from one act to another in the drama in the way that it interrupts the dialogue or disputation, reminding the friends that wisdom is not so easily attained as they claim.

Westermann is right to isolate the genre of 'lament' and the fact that it has a role to play in *Job*; but this term generally designates relatively small genre units in the book (usually only a chapter, eg 6:2-27, or occasionally two, eg 23:2-24:25). It is inadequate to provide a classification of the entire work, and so he suggests the category "dramatization of the lament" as a genre for the whole book. But this category suffers from the opposite drawback; it is too wide to be useful as a literary term. There is a similarity between laments such as are found in the psalms of lament and sections of *Job* (eg complaints or laments are contained in 3:11-16,17-26; 6:2-27; 9:25-35; 10:1-22; 13:17-27; 14:1-22; 16:7-17:16; 19:13-22; 19:23-27; 23:2-24:25; 30:1-31). However, in my opinion, this one category is inadequate as an assessment of the genre of the whole book, for its application to parts of *Job* clearly distorts their meaning: for example, although Westermann tries to argue that the dialogue or disputation sections have developed away from lament/consolation forms to something more argumentative, the genre of disputation is clearly separate from that of lament, and although this theory is plausible for the friends'

---

[115] C Westermann, 1956, 1981 (p 12).

dialogue passages, it is less easy to apply it to the dispute between Job and God - there is very little consolation in God's reply.

A second example of the method that decides the overall genre of the book of *Job* by finding a predominance of a small genre on grounds of form and arguing that it characterizes the whole is the work of H Richter.[116] He argues that the genre of the book is that of a judicial process:

"Der alles tragende Grund des Hiobdramas sind die Gattungen des Rechtlebens."[117]

The speeches of Job, for example, often make use of the language of litigation where Job accuses God of a breach of contract, eg. 9:13-24; 19:1-12. Legal terminology is present in the accusations, and in chapter 31 where there is an oath of innocence that has its closest parallels in the negative confession within Babylonian literature. Richter counts 444 verses as belonging to judicial genres as opposed to 346 which are wisdom genres and argues that it is the former that intrinsically characterize the book whilst the latter are largely used for ornamental purposes. In Richter's view, chapters 4-14 comprise a preliminary attempt at reconciliation; chapters 15-31 represent a formal legal effort at reconciling Job and his friends and Job's prayer for a divine answer is later provided in the secular lawsuit of the Yahweh speeches (38:1-42:6). Chapters 32-37 contain Elihu's 'appeal' of the case and chapters 38-41 a secular lawsuit between God and Job, God's judgement leading to Job's withdrawal of the accusation. For evidence of these various legal processes in Israel, Richter looks at small pieces of evidence elsewhere in the Bible. This evidence is rather too sparse to support his conclusions. Richter's interpretation clearly rests on finding a predominance of one small genre or form (in this case various judicial ones), and reading the whole in the light of this. The isolation of judicial genres in certain passages in *Job* clearly has a contribution to make when discussing the lower-level genres within the book. However, this is not a satisfactory method for interpreting the whole work. Just as the presence of many wisdom forms in a work does not make such a work 'wisdom' in genre, so the presence of judicial forms does not make a

---

116 H Richter, 1959.
117 H Richter, 1959 (p 131) - "The all-pervasive basis of the drama of Job are the genres taken from law."

work 'judicial' in genre. Such attempts to find an overall genre for *Job* which work from the enumeration of small genres may well shed light on the interpretation of certain passages in *Job*; but neither Richter's nor Westermann's attempt, in its onesidedness, provides a satisfactory answer to the question of the genre of the whole book, for in each theory there are certain passages or ideas which do not fit. We can see the value of their contribution in their detailed interpretation of passages without accepting their claim to have found that which characterizes the whole work.

A further pitfall related to these is the attempt to take one of the categories of 'smaller' genre and lay emphasis on its importance for the overall genre of the book on the grounds that *Job* is similar to the representative book of that smaller genre. Thus A Bentzen[118] and G I Davies[119] point out that *Job* is akin to the psalms. Bentzen sees the dialogue in *Job* as a "*dramatization of the psalms of lamentation*...of the 'prayers of the accused', placed in the frame of a narrative", whilst Davies, expressing the views of H-P Müller, writes:

"while 'wisdom' thinking and juridical forms of speech have certainly contributed to the poet's stock of ideas and expressions, it is the parallels with the psalm genres which take the reader closest to the point of departure and purpose of the dialogue between Job and his friends."

Other scholars such as J L Crenshaw[120] and E Kellett[121], on the other hand, stress the similarities between *Job* and Deutero-Isaiah. Crenshaw argues that *Job* is akin to Deutero-Isaiah:

"The prophetic *Streitgespräch* which differs as to intensity of argumentation and purpose, namely self-vindication of the prophet, has contributed to the genre as found in Job, and explains the kinship with II Isaiah."[122]

---

118 A Bentzen, 1948, p 182.
119 G I Davies, 1983 (p 367). H-P Müller, 1978, actually wrote: "In der künftigen Forschung wird es darauf ankommen, die weisheitlichen und juridischen Motive des Dialogs in die Grundstruktur einer eher psalmistischen Klage zu integrieren..." (p 100). His argument is that psalm genres deal better with the problems raised by a so-called dialogue (in which Job rarely addresses the others and argues with God) and by an unexpected climax consisting of an exchange of words between Job and God.
120 J L Crenshaw, 1970.
121 E Kellett, 1939-40, regards Job as a metaphor for Israel during the Exile and argues that the picture of Job's sufferings is dependent upon the particular psalms and prophets in which similar themes are aired. This viewpoint is based on considerations of message and contributes little to a form-critical investigation.
122 J L Crenshaw, 1970 (p 389).

Crenshaw does not however go as far as to say that this is an overall genre for *Job* for he argues that:

"In reality...Job is rooted in wisdom and prophetic theology both as to literary genre and final resolution of the problem by a theophany."[123]

*Job* has been regarded as an allegory on the basis of similarities with the innocent sufferings of Deutero-Isaiah.[124] This suggestion along with many others regarding overall genre is old-fashioned in its method and is not based on firm literary foundations.

iii) The second pitfall - deciding the overall genre before studying the smaller genres which make up the whole

The second approach to the question of genres in *Job*, which leads to an equal amount of distortion, is that which decides on an overall genre and then attempts to fit all smaller genres into this picture. Among these attempts to begin by identifying the overall genre of *Job,* some have their starting points in formal considerations, sometimes in conjunction with comparative studies, and others take as their starting point content and meaning with very little attention paid to form.

(1) Formal considerations foremost

An example of the first of these approaches is provided by the view that *Job* is a *Streitgespräch*, a view formulated from the observation of close similarities between *Job* and Babylonian disputation literature, notably with the Babylonian Theodicy.[125] A *Streitgespräch* is a controversy dialogue made up of a mythological introduction, a debate between two friends, and a divine resolution of the issue. Job is thought to have been influenced by the function of self-vindication which the *Streitgespräch* fulfils within prophetic literature, a function which leads him to use the *Streitgespräch* as a weapon for his own

---

123 J L Crenshaw, 1970 (p 389).
124 eg C F Aked, 1913. who saw *Job* as a dramatic poem but also as a work of imagination and J F Genung, 1891, who called *Job* an epic poem but provided little argumentation for it. W H Green, 1897, saw *Job* as a drama, the action taking place in the soul of Job.
125 See W Lambert, 1960, pp 63-91. See discussion above, pp 69-70.

vindication. Thus the key to *Job* is 13:16 - "This will be my salvation, that a godless man shall not come before him." The prologue and epilogue are regarded as the mythological introduction and legendary conclusion of popular origin antedating the dispute itself which utilizes three formal traditions (wisdom disputational material, legal terminology associated with the lawsuit, and cultic laments).

G Von Rad[126] has objected to viewing *Job* as a *Streitgespräch* on the grounds that the dialogue is between a sufferer and his 'friends', complaints being expected from one side and comfort from the other. Both sides become very heated, even openly quarrelsome, but this is not the main characteristic of these dialogues - in the lament psalms too, friends sometimes become enemies. He supports the close alignment of the dialogue with the psalms of lament and writes:

"It is particularly surprising to note how Job...even with regard to details, adopts the style and the subject-matter of the psalms of lament. There is very little in the speeches of Job which, from the point of view of form-history, is really new poetry without analogy, and yet from the whole something completely new and unique has emerged by means of a certain shift of emphasis or of a radicalization of traditional forms of speech, especially, however, by means of the skilful manner of composition."[127]

These formal units are simply placed side by side: the transition of thought is often sudden, Job is the only developed character and the argument is slow to progress - "The speeches are repetitive and, to a certain extent, move forward only in a circular fashion."[128] God is present from the beginning as the third party and his speech is well-prepared in advance. Von Rad emphasizes that the difference between Job and his friends is theological: the friends stress the order of the universe, whereas Job is concerned about the relationship between himself and God. Job's God has become his personal enemy; he who was God's glory and pride has become the object of his wrath. J L Crenshaw, however, argues against von Rad's interpretation. He writes:

"The single issue of Job, von Rad argues, is *Yahweh pro me*. Nevertheless, he is obliged to admit that the dissent between Job and his friends was greater at the end than in the

---

126  G von Rad, 1972.
127  G von Rad, 1972 (p 209).
128  G von Rad, 1972 (p 210).

beginning, so that his refusal to recognize the intensity of strife, the basis for rejecting the Streitgespräch as descriptive of the book, carries little weight."[129]

Another suggestion which is again based on formal and comparative concerns is that of H Gese[130] that Job is a "paradigm of the answered lament" (*Klageerhörungsparadigma*). He bases his understanding of this literary form upon the Babylonian, Ludlul bel nemeqi (I will praise the Lord of wisdom),[131] and the Sumerian, Man and his God. In all three texts the main figure is one who is suffering, apparently without cause. All relate a complaint by the sufferer, who is eventually restored by the divinity. This literary form is characterized by two features: a 'lament' and a trusting appeal to God from one in distress. The sequence is: distress, complaint, divine response, restoration. Gese claims that the author of *Job* took over this form but with the intention of changing it. The mechanical theory of retribution is replaced by a theology of God's transcendence. Gese does not class "paradigms of answered laments" as 'wisdom' but leaves the question of genre and classification open, saying that they could belong to wisdom literature. The weakness of this approach is that the relation of *Job* to the Mesopotamian models is not as close as Gese makes out. W G Lambert writes of the Ludlul bel Nemeqi:

"Quantitatively the greater part of the text is taken up with showing how Marduk restores his ruined servant, and only a small part with trying to probe the reason for the suffering of the righteous. In places the writer deliberately sheers away from plainly facing this problem because of its blasphemous implications." [132]

The restoration of Job takes place in the very short epilogue, and Gese places much emphasis on its role in the book and can be accused of overrating it in the understanding of the whole.

(2) Considerations of content and meaning foremost

The second approach to finding an overall genre for *Job* is that which has its starting point in questions of content and meaning, paying little attention to

---

129  J L Crenshaw, 'Wisdom', 1974 (p 255).
130  H Gese, 1958.
131  W G Lambert, 1960, pp 21-62. This is often called the 'Babylonian Job' since it airs the problem of the suffering of the righteous and the conflict of this with the idea of a just God.
132  W G Lambert, 1960 (p 27).

form. The analysis of *Job* by J W Whedbee[133] as belonging to the genre of comedy is an example of this viewpoint. Whedbee writes:

> "In my judgement, the category of comedy is sufficiently broad and comprehensive to embrace the wealth of disparate genres and traditions which have long been noted in the book of Job."

Comedy must contain two elements - a vision of incongruity that involves the ironic, the ludicrous and the ridiculous, and, most evident in *Job*, a basic story line in which ultimately the hero arrives at happiness and is restored to a harmonious society. Thus the prologue gives the story line in the way it describes Job's righteousness and in its explanation of the divine conflict which causes Job's distress and which is unknown to Job and the friends. The epilogue restores Job to more than his state in the prologue and provides a 'comic upturn'. Incongruity, manifested in irony and the ridiculous, appears throughout the work. It is first seen in the prologue when God admits to Satan, " you moved me against him to destroy him without cause"(2:3). This is a hint of the 'underside' of God that Job's speeches go on to develop (chapters 7, 9, 12). In chapter 3 the incongruity of the Job of the prologue and the Job of the dialogue is made apparent in Job's initial complaint. The friends provide the author with an opportunity for caricature. They begin with silence (2:13), to which Job later refers as their only wisdom (13:5). Eliphaz is a parody of the 'wise counsellor'. His description of Job's "ripe old age" (5:26) is an ironic anticipation of the epilogue. The friends advocate traditional wisdom teaching concerning the righteous and the wicked, but it turns to their own ridicule as Job rejects these platitudes and cuts down their moralizing with harsh words (12:2-3; 13:12; 16:2-5; 26:2-4). The friends thus represent not the 'wise man' but the 'alazon', the classical comic figure of the fool or imposter. Elihu, the interloper, is another 'alazon' whose prosy and turgid style suits his platitudes. However, Job's real enemy is not 'the friends' but God to whom Job addresses several attacks; for example, he parodies Psalm 8 in 7:17-18, and he turns the traditional song of praise to God as creator into a song to the God of terror and destruction (9:2-10). In the Yahweh speeches there is irony in the questions addressed to Job (38:2-5; 40:1-2,6-14; etc) but

---

133   J W Whedbee, 1977 (p 1).

there is double irony in Job's anticipation of how God would act in 9:3-4,11-12. The theophany provides Job with two visions: one of God and the other of the world from God's point of view (as von Rad[134] has pointed out, God lets nature speak for him in these speeches). Whedbee sees the two divine speeches and the two replies of Job (40:3-5 and 42:1-6) as a "two-stage movement" from silence to repentance; Job's reaction, whilst genuine, is paradoxical in that he has seen God but has not seen all nor understood what he has seen.

This attempt to fit *Job* into the genre of comedy clearly involves reinterpretation of many passages, and the danger of distortion of detail in the service of an overall interpretation can clearly be seen. It involves imposing an artificial overarching unity of genre on the diversity of smaller genres within the book, and thus represents the opposite danger to that seen in Richter's work. Further examples of this approach can be seen in the work of D B MacDonald[135] who classifies *Job* as a dramatic lyric, the purpose of which is "to fill all the functions filled in other literatures by the drama, the epic and the didactic poem."[136] He reaches this conclusion from a consideration of the dramatic content of *Job* rather than from any considerations related to form and, at the same time, creates his own very broad classification to include all other more specific classifications. Another example of an approach working from content alone is that of L Alonso Schökel[137] who talks of *Job* as 'dramatic'. He does seem, however, to realize the weakness of his own approach when it comes to genre classification. He sees *Job* as a drama - but not necessarily in the narrow sense of genre, "probably because our concept of the literary genre 'drama' is very precise and limited."[138] He sees it as 'dramatic' however in a more general sense and thinks that this interpretation, whilst not the only possible one, enhances the richness of the book and is therefore valuable. He does not claim the exclusive explanation of the book's overall genre, as most scholars do when on this quest. He is aware of the

---

134 G von Rad, 1972, p 225; cf K Barth, 1936-81, (1961, p 430).
135 D B MacDonald, 1933.
136 D B MacDonald, 1933 (p 14).
137 L Alonso Schökel, 1977; cf W J Urbrock, 1981.
138 L Alonso Schökel, 1977 (p 45).

inadequacies of such a view as his to one concerned with genre in the strictest sense of the word.

A more realistic approach is pursued by those who compare *Job* with Greek tragedy. It is widely recognized that *Job* is not a tragedy; yet a comparison between *Job* and works such as Aeschylus' *Prometheus Bound* is illuminating.[139] Thus J Barr[140] considers the general atmosphere of *Job* to be tragic, but notes the absence of action in *Job* and the small amount of characterization. For example, there is no individual characterization of the three friends - they all say much the same thing and uphold the same orthodox view. Both action and characterization are fundamental to the literary genre of tragedy. In his Hannah Arendt Memorial Lecture at the University of Southampton, George Steiner compared *Job* with Greek tragedy.[141] He outlined the story of the Antigone observing that "it is in the moment of remorse that Creon pulls down upon himself irremedial horror and catastrophe. Not so Job."[142] When he is faced with "the almost mocking, unanswerable speech of the Lord God out of the whirlwind of his ironic

---

139 For a comparison of Job and Prometheus, see J Lindblom, 1939 and G Murray, 1940 (Greek text in M Griffith (ed), Aeschylus: *Prometheus Bound*, Cambridge, 1983). Some argue for borrowing by the author of *Job* from Prometheus, eg J J Slotki, 1927-8 and W A Irwin, 1950, who suggests that "literary dependence, in one direction or the other, may not unreasonably be postulated" (p 92). H Kallen, 1918, argues that *Job* was written as an imitation or echo by a Hebrew genius of a Euripidean tragedy and that our present work is the result of editorial interpolation and disarrangement (see also J J Slotki, 1927-8; W A Irwin, 1950; H G May, 1952 and R B Sewall, 1959, pp 9-24). W A Irwin, 1950, argues that there are a number of radical statements in *Job* which go further than Prometheus and contradict both Hebrew tradition and Greek belief; for example, Job's bold outburst against God's arbitrary behaviour towards the just and innocent in the midst of his pain. Irwin maintains that Job is much bolder since Israel's God is higher than Zeus, who is an upstart who had wrested power from his father. He argues that the most profound difference is the note of triumph in *Job* concerning the nature of God and the realization that suffering contributes to man's purification. He writes: "With all its greatness Aeschylus' answer to man's most poignant question seems, by contrast, adolescent." (pp 101-2) In a similar vein J Barr, 1971-2, writes of Job: "Though he does not 'curse God' the preference for death is itself something verging on the blasphemous." (p 45) Others see the sentiments in *Job* as tame compared with some of the Greek questioning. Interesting comparisons have also been made between *Job* and Oedipus (eg M Fortes, 1983) and, on the subject of the use of irony, with the *Dialogues of Plato* (Text in English in B Jowett (tr), *The Dialogues of Plato*, Oxford, 1964 (4th edition). See K Fries, 1904; O Holzmann in B Stade, 1887; G B Gray, in S R Driver and G B Gray, 1921).
140 J Barr, 1971-2, pp 40-41. Barr argues that there is no literary dependence between the two, which is the assumption of the majority of scholars.
141 G Steiner, 1979.
142 G Steiner, 1979 (p 508).

omnipotence" he repents and humbles himself. Job recognizes his folly in questioning "the transcendental, the incomprehensible reasons for God's action"[143] and as a result his suffering is repaired by God. Steiner sees the 'happy ending', which scholars have regarded as an addition, as vital to the Jewish conception of God without which the book would not have been a Hebraic composition. He writes:

> "There are, in a number of Psalms, in Ecclesiastes and, above all, in the questions of Job to God, questions which have rung down the ages, absolute tragic values; there are insights into the self-destructive nullity of human life. But they are...not *official* insights and they are hedged about within the Bible by constant and eloquent elements of reassurance, of the unalterable belief that finally, even in its anguish, the universe makes sense and that the punishments which God visits upon us are justified or deserved. Above all, and contrary to the world of Creon, there is the assurance that if we repent there will be reparation."[144]

Thus the possibility of real tragedy is ruled out by the nature of Judaism. D D Raphael[145] argues that in the early biblical narratives there is abundant material for tragedy, yet these stories are not presented as tragedy but as moral lessons. In the psalms too there are protests, but it is never doubted that all will come right in the end - the main complaint is that God's fulfilment of justice seems overlong. There is no feeling of 'wasted goodness' which, as A C Bradley[146] argued, is essential to tragedy. *Job* comes closer to the spirit of the Greek tragedians by raising questioning doubts about suffering without accompanying answers, than, for example, Deutero-Isaiah who faces the same problem of unmerited suffering and provides answers without first raising questions and doubts. In *Job*, as nowhere else in the Bible, "the problem of evil raises doubts and no solution is provided."[147] This comes near to tragedy. Yet Raphael acknowledges that *Job* is not a tragedy because "the grandeur of the hero is deliberately shrunk to nothing before the sublimity of the power he has questioned."[148] Furthermore Raphael argues that when Job does contend with God he opposes only his *understanding* to God's justice. There is never any question of opposing his will, of refusing to accept the

---

143 G Steiner, 1979 (p 508).
144 G Steiner, 1979 (pp 508-510).
145 D D Raphael, 1960, (1968, pp 51-55).
146 A C Bradley, 1904.
147 D D Raphael, 1960, (1968, p 52).
148 D D Raphael, 1960, (1968, p 53).

order of the world. He questions its justice but he submits to it willingly."[149] As Raphael writes:

"Job joins the questioning intellect of a Greek with the submissive faith of a Hebrew."[150]

The fundamental difference between tragedy and religion is that tragedy glorifies human resistance to necessity, religion praises submission - "Prometheus defies Zeus: Job lays his hand upon his mouth".[151]

iv) Assessment of these findings

It seems that most of the suggestions of scholars concerning overall genre, whilst they are worth making in that they enhance our understanding of *Job*, do not provide the *key* to its genre. The major, more convincing suggestions have been discussed and whilst all can be shown to suffer from one of the pitfalls outlined above, no one proposal being conclusive, some provide better solutions to the problem of finding an overall genre than others. A view such as Westermann's,[152] for example, has been quoted and even presupposed by many students of *Job* and has received a large amount of support and acclaim. Nearly every modern commentary on *Job*[153] mentions at some length Westermann's analysis of the genre of *Job* as a "dramatization of a lament", although it is nowadays ranked *alongside* other suggestions for overall genre and shown, with them, to provide only part of the answer.[154] Westermann's book has greatly illuminated genre-based studies of *Job* but does not, in my opinion, provide the key to interpretation of the whole.

N C Habel mentions Westermann and the lament genre, but he then points out hymnic materials and other diverse genres within *Job* and shows how

---

149 D D Raphael, 1960, (1968, p 54).
150 D D Raphael, 1960, (1968, p 54).
151 D D Raphael, 1960, (1968, p 55).
152 C Westermann, 1956, (1981). His view is based on findings of other scholars - P Volz, 1911; A Weiser, 1951; J Fichtner, 1950; A Bentzen, 1948; F Baumgartner, 1933 and M Buttenwieser, 1922, who all see the lament as the chief component of *Job* and question its classification as 'wisdom literature' on the basis of that observation. This view received particular acclaim at a time when the true character of the lament in the Old Testament had not been sufficiently investigated.
153 eg N C Habel, 1985.
154 eg See the discussion in O Kaiser, 1969 (75) pp 391-394.

recognition of the diversity of genres within *Job* has led to more general suggestions as to overall genre, for example the idea of *Job* as a festal tragedy (Terrien[155]) and *Job* as a serious comedy (Whedbee[156]). He then looks at ancient Near Eastern prototypes which, he argues, "clarify the genre of *Job* as a whole" in that they have "the same skeletal plot structure."[157] But he sees the author of *Job* as working on a different plane from these ancient Near Eastern writers as he has "adapted and expanded each component of this plot to highlight the existential complexities and theological paradoxes involved in exploring this plot."[158] Such a conclusion shows a clear movement away from a straightforward search for one genre so Westermann's[159] suggestion for an overall genre for *Job* no longer holds the field as it once did and his method has been superseded. One should perhaps add that the very variety of views that this method of searching for a single overall genre has produced reduces the possibility of an answer being found by this approach. A kind of amalgamation of suggestions is now being propounded and it is generally concluded that, since no one suggestion provides an answer, the quest for an overall genre is in vain and should perhaps be dropped. Thus Habel writes:

"The creative literary work of Job, however, does not conform to any single traditional genre structure. Traditional forms are incorporated, adapted, and transcended through the integration of curses, disputation, lament, trial speeches, wisdom poems, and hymnic materials into an underlying narrative plot."[160]

Older scholars reached a remarkably similar conclusion when they saw *Job* as "*sui generis*" as regards overall genre. According to M. Pope,[161]

"there is no single classification appropriate to the literary form of the Book of Job. It shares something of the characteristics of all the literary forms that have been ascribed to it, but it is impossible to classify it exclusively as didactic, dramatic, epic or anything else. The book viewed as a unit is *sui generis* and no single term or combination of terms is adequate to describe it."

---

155 S Terrien, 1963.
156 J W Whedbee, 1977.
157 N C Habel, 1985 (p 45).
158 N C Habel, 1985 (p 45).
159 C Westermann, 1956, (1981) (p 45).
160 N C Habel, 1985.
161 M H Pope, 1965, (p xxx).

It is true that the very variety of suggestions for an overall genre for *Job* shows that the book does not neatly fit into any genre classification. The lack of success by scholars to capture an overall genre would appear to reinforce Pope's judgement.[162] Thus in order to avoid the pitfalls outlined above into which scholarly work on genres in *Job* has fallen a new methodology is required. Rather than seeking to find a genre for the whole book we need to break it into smaller genres and gradually build up a complete picture, but not by merely adding up the numbers of forms represented and deciding on that basis what the overall genre should be, as Richter[163] and Westermann[164] do. Rather the idea of finding an overall genre should be laid aside whilst the book is studied in small blocks at the various genre levels. This method would involve no twisting of the evidence at the lowest genre level in order to fit it to a wider interpretation. Each section could be taken as it stands.[165]

R. Murphy[166] argues that one should not carry out an exact and careful analysis of forms and motifs without a sense for the broad perspective for "Not many clear and simple genres retain their separate identity within a speech."[167] He sees it as "unhelpful" to separate them from their larger setting. However in my view this reaction is an attempt to gloss over difficulties posed by the variety of small genres in the book because an overall interpretation is being sought. We can extend the search for smaller genres by having no presuppositions about what the genre of the whole book is and by

---

162 A S Peake, 1905, argues that no literary label can be found for *Job*; "it is itself" (p 41). E Jones, 1966, finds elements of drama, epic poem and philosophical debate in *Job*, but none characterizes the whole. R H Pfeiffer, 1948, argues that *Job* is not exclusively lyric, didactic, reflective or dramatic unless cut down to fit a particular literary category. R Aharoni, 1979, asserts that, whilst *Job* contains elements characteristic of a number of literary genres, it cannot be classified according to normal literary standards. He writes, "In its structural patterns, artistry, aesthetic texture, subtleties, complexity and particularity of formulation, it emerges as a unique literary composition: Job" (p 13).

163 H Richter, 1959.

164 C Westermann, 1956, (1981).

165 The designation 'smaller genres' would include, for example, certain wisdom genres which no one would ever think of extending to the classification of the whole book; for instance, the 'appeal to ancient tradition' located by N C Habel, 1976. The basic structure of this 'smaller' genre is the appeal itself, the citation of the tradition, and its application; cf. 8:8-13; 12:7-12; 15:17-35; 20:4-29. Another candidate is the 'Summary Appraisal' pointed out by B S Childs, 1967 which takes the form: 'Such is...' (Job 8:13; 18:21; 20:29).

166 R E Murphy, 1981.

167 R E Murphy, 1981 (p 18).

deliberately concentrating on small passages isolated from their context, but with an eye to how they are being *used* in the wider context of the whole book. Then at the end we can decide whether there is such a variety of genres that any attempt to classify *Job* as a whole is inappropriate or whether there is some helpful categorization which will enhance our understanding of the book. One aim of this detailed study of smaller genres is to show that *Job* is not so typical a wisdom book as scholars have assumed - the presence of small wisdom genres in the book does not make the whole a piece of wisdom literature. But in the same way the presence of some of the other genres that scholars have suggested does not mean that the whole can be easily categorized according to these genres. The mere occurrence or even predominance of certain smaller genres is not enough to determine the literary genre of the whole work. As G Fohrer[168] writes:

"The contrast between form and function shows that the form used does not necessarily correspond to the content or provide any clue as to its nature. This must be remembered in a formal analysis of the book of Job as a whole."

v) Small genres or forms in *Job*

Deliberate concentration on small passages in *Job* taken in isolation from their context and concentration on finding small genres rather than an overall one for whole chapters, or for the whole book, reveals a striking variety of different genres in *Job*.[169] In many cases this cannot be distinguished from the diversity of forms found in the book and mentioned earlier in this chapter, although sometimes a 'smaller' genre might be larger than simply an individual form. This diversity can be illustrated by selecting a few random chapters from the dialogue section of *Job* in which it is chiefly found within relatively short passages - for example, chapter 11 which contains only twenty verses. Within the context of the dialogue section as a whole this speech of Zophar has the genre 'disputation speech'. But, if we divide the speech into more specific smaller genres, on the very smallest genre level of individual forms, there is evidence in chapter 11 of rhetorical questioning (v2) and quotation (v4). We

---

168 G Fohrer, 1968 (1970, p 333).
169 R E Murphy, 1981.

need to look at a small group of verses which forms a unified whole within the larger context and which has its own genre. Thus in verses 2-6 of this chapter we find judicial elements. Zophar opens his speech in the style typical of litigation (such as is also found in Job 8:2-4). Evidence for this is the rhetorical question in due process style in verses 2-3 and the quotation of the opponent's claim in verse 4. This small section can therefore be said to belong to a 'legal' genre. Yet in verses 7-12 the genre changes, for here we have a hymnic description of God's superiority. This is not a straightforward hymn in that it is shaped in a didactic way by the rhetorical questions that are designed to heap ridicule on Job and move him from his convictions (vv7-8). From 'hymn' we then pass to a 'wisdom' genre in verses 13-20. These verses contain conditional advice offered to Job with a description of the results of heeding the advice. This advice is couched along the lines of wisdom teaching and culminates in the contrast of the just (v14) with the wicked (v20).

The genres apparent in chapter 11 - 'legal', 'hymnic' and 'wisdom' - recur throughout the book of *Job*. Other smaller genres of this kind can also be found in *Job*, for example: 'narrative' in 1:1-2:12 and 42:7-16 - the prologue and epilogue sections; a 'curse' in 3:3-10; a 'summary appraisal' in 5:27; an 'appeal to ancient tradition' in 8:8-13; 'prophetic' elements in 22:6-14,23,28-30; 'liturgical' elements in 22:26-27; the 'discourse' form in 27:1 and other introductions to speeches; the 'purificatory oath' in 31:1-40; 'nature wisdom' in 38:4-39:30 and 40:15-41:26; and the 'confession' in 42:1-6. There may even be evidence of a 'vision' or 'apocalypse' in 4:12-21. These other genres, with the exception of that of 'narrative', occur infrequently, often only in the one place cited. The rest of the book is dominated by 'legal' genres, by 'hymnic' genres - perhaps better termed 'cultic' so as to include laments and complaints which generally have a hymnic form - and by 'wisdom' genres, none of which predominates to any significant extent.

In almost every chapter of the dialogue there is a good mixture of these genres, for example in chapters 12 and 13, part of a speech by Job, 12:2-6 uses various 'legal' genres (verse 2, ridicule of the opponent, verse 3 Job's claim to wisdom); 12:11-13 uses wisdom sayings and proverbs; 12:13-25 contains a hymnic description of God's wisdom and power and so combines 'cultic' or 'hymnic' genres and 'wisdom' genres; 13:1-5 contains 'legal' genres with elements of 'wisdom' genres; 13:6-16 contains 'legal' genres; 13:17-27 largely comprises a complaint which belongs to the group of 'cultic' genres but Job again draws on legal procedure - in verse 18 he makes the formal claim that he is in the right and in verse 23 he challenges God for a bill of particulars.

Another chapter which provides good examples of the variety of genres is chapter 34, Elihu's second speech: verses 2-9 contain 'legal' genres (Job summons 'the wise' to hear him, proclaims his innocence and is then ridiculed); verses 10-15 contain 'wisdom' genres (eg affirmation of divine justice) and verses 16-20 contain 'hymnic' genres; verses 21-33, 'wisdom' genres again; whilst 'legal' elements reappear in verses 23-27 and finally echoes of the 'cultic' complaint are found in verses 31-37. There is nothing new about these genre classifications but they have generally been noted in order to be fitted into a wider interpretation and have not previously been isolated from their context in this way. They all in principle demand different settings and do not fit together to provide any overall single genre for the book. Furthermore *Job* defies exclusive classificiation as only one of these things, since none is dominant.

The range of genres in the dialogue of *Job* was noted by G Fohrer who writes:

"Die Auseinandersetzung zwischen Hiob und seinen Freunden hat hinsichtlich ihrer Form drei Vorbilder und wählt ihre Formelemente im einzelnen aus drei Formbereichen. Einmal geht sie auf die 'Streitgespräche der Weisen' zurück und bedient sich häufig der Einzelformen der Weisheitslehre...Ferner setzt der Dialog die 'Parteireden vor der Rechtsgemeinde' voraus und verwendet häufig die Einzelformen des Rechtsverfahrens...Als dritte Gruppe von Formelementen treten die Rede- und Stilformen der Psalmen in Erscheinung, die in ziemlich großem Ausmaß zu erkennen sind."[170]

---

170 "The discussion between Job and his friends has three prototypes in respect of its form, and selects formal elements from three spheres. (i) First, it goes back to the 'debates of the wise' and uses many individual forms from wisdom teaching... (ii) Secondly, the dialogue presupposes the 'speeches of the parties in court', and uses many forms from legal proceedings... (iii) The third group of formal elements are the speech-forms and stylistic features of the Psalms, of which many examples can be found." G Fohrer, 1963 (p 50).

Fohrer asserts that the argument between Job and God in the dialogue section is composed in a different way from the arguments of Job with his friends. He writes:

"Die Herausforderungsreden Hiobs folgen dem Vorbild der Klagepsalmen, in denen der Beter die 'Erzählung' seiner Not und die eidliche Beteuerung seiner Unschuld vorbringt. Der 'Erzählung' liegt das Motiv des 'Einst und Jetzt' zugrunde, das aus dem Leichenlied stammt, in seinem ersten Teil (Kap. 29) aber mit Hilfe eines Weisheitsliedes ausgeführt wird. Der Erweis der Unschuld verbindet eine von der Weisheit aus dem apodiktischen Recht übernommene Reihe von Vergehen mit dem Eid vor der Rechtsgemeinde. Insgesamt zielen die Reden nicht auf ein der Klage folgendes kultisches Jahweorakel ab, sondern richten eine rechtliche Herausforderung an Gott. Diese aber bezweckt nicht ein Gottesurteil im Rechtsverfahren, sondern drückt den dringlichen Wunsch nach einer persönlichen Begegnung mit Gott aus."[171]

As well as small genres, the different sections of *Job* can be characterized on the level of genre, as is attempted by Fohrer who discusses the God-speeches and the final response of Job in terms of genre. He writes:

"Die Gottesrede entspricht formal dem Jahweorakel nach der Klage oder dem Gottesurteil im Rechtsverfahren, ist aber im Unterschied zu beiden nicht eindeutig positiv oder negativ gehalten. Tatsächlich ist sie, für sich genommen, der Form nach eine Streitrede, wie Einleitung und Schluß zeigen. Ihrer Aufgabe nach bildet sie eine große Frage an Hiob, die ihn vor letzte Entscheidungen stellt. Zur Ausführung dessen hat sich der Hiobdichter in Einleitung und Schluß der Rechtsformen, im Schluß ferner hymnischer Formen, im großen Mittelteil aber der Listenwissenschaft der Bildungsweisheit bedient."[172]

---

[171] "Job's challenges follow the model of the psalms of lament, in which the suppliant presents a 'narration' of his distress and a statement on oath of his own innocence. This 'narration' rests on the motif of 'then and now' which comes from the funeral lament but (in its first part in chapter 29) is executed with the help of a wisdom poem. The proof of innocence joins together a series of misdemeanours (taken over by wisdom from apodictic law) and an oath before the court. The speeches are not designed to elicit a cultic oracle from Yahweh as a response to the complaint, but constitute a legal demand to God. However, this is not a demand for a divine judgement in a legal action, but expresses the urgent wish for a personal encounter with God." G Fohrer, 1963 (p 51).

[172] "The speech of God corresponds formally to the oracle of Yahweh after a lament, or to the divine judgement in legal proceedings; but, in contrast with either of these, it is not unambiguously either positive or negative in tone. In itself it is formally a disputation speech as is shown by the introduction and conclusion. But its function is to form a great question to Job, and so to confront him with ultimate decisions. To achieve this the Job-poet used legal forms in the introduction and conclusion (and, in the conclusion, hymnic forms too), but in the large central section the learned lists that belong to educational wisdom." G Fohrer, 1963 (pp 51-52).

"Die Wende Hiobs entspricht formal dem ursprünglichen dritten Teil des Klagepsalms, in dem der Beter nach Klage und positivem Orakel seinen Dank oder die Gewißheit der Erhörung aussprach, oder der Aneignung des Urteils durch den Rechtsuchenden im Rechtsverfahren. Sachlich wird die radikale Umkehr Hiobs nach der an ihn gerichteten Entscheidungsfrage umschrieben, wobei sich im einzelnen Weisheits-, Rechts- und Psalmenformen feststellen lassen."[173]

Thus either *Job* as a whole has no genre and is an accidental jumble of small genres; or its various sections can be characterized in terms of genre, but the whole belongs to a genre that has not yet been isolated and identified. Or perhaps the whole is a hybrid which defies classification under any 'genre' in the strict sense. This may be a deliberate move on the part of the author of *Job*. Perhaps in order to demonstrate the fully radical nature of the book, it was made to defy traditional ideas in its content and to follow no one traditional genre in its form. However the author's technique is probably more subtle and far-reaching than this. To come to the conclusion that *Job* is a hybrid seems to me to be very close to saying, as Habel[174] does, that *Job* is an amalgamation of genres, or saying, as Pope[175] does, that it is "*sui generis*", and that conclusion seems to me to be unsatisfactory. In the next chapter therefore I shall investigate the possibility of finding a pattern on the form-critical level of individual forms or 'smaller' genres.

---

173 "From a formal point of view Job's conversion corresponds either to the original third part of a lament psalm, in which the suppliant, after his lament and the positive oracle that followed, expressed his thanks or the conviction that he was heard, or else to the acceptance of the verdict by one of the parties in a legal suit. But so far as content is concerned Job's radical repentance is described as following the questions that have been directed to him, questions demanding a response in the form of a decision, and a detailed study reveals forms from wisdom, legal, and psalm forms in this." G Fohrer, 1963 (p 52).
174 N C Habel, 1985.
175 M H Pope, 1965.

# Chapter 3

# A FORM-CRITICAL APPROACH TO *JOB*

## Parody as an overall genre

"Um seine Gedanken auszusprechen, standen dem Hiobdichter nur die begrenzten Stil- und Ausdrucksmöglichkeiten des Hebräischen zur Verfügung. Daß er dennoch ein Werk schaffen konnte, das zu den größten der Weltliteratur gehört, verdankt er der geschickten Anwendung verschiedener Methoden. Außer der Benutzung des altorientalischen Bildungsgutes und der reichen Bildsprache sind darunter die Grundsätze der formalen Komposition zu nennen. Die formgeschichtliche Untersuchung zeigt, daß a) die Reden nach dem Grundsatz der Gattungsmischung komponiert sind, b) der Hiobdichter den Anwendungsbereich der Gattungen vergrößert hat, indem er sie in einer anderen als ihrer eigentlichen Funktion verwendet."[1]

### a) THE DELIBERATE MISUSE OF FORMS IN JOB

i) The suggestions of scholars concerning the use of forms in *Job*

In this chapter I shall argue that *Job* belongs to a genre - 'parody' - that has not yet been isolated or identified, but one which is unlike standard literary genres in the way it uses other genres for its own purpose. This suggestion arises from the observation that a characteristic feature of *Job* is that it

---

[1] G Fohrer, 1963 (p 50) - "To express his thoughts the Job-poet had only the limited resources of style and expression of Hebrew available to him. He owes his success in nevertheless creating a work which belongs among the greatest in world literature to his skilful use of various methods. Alongside the use of ancient Near Eastern educational material, and the rich language of images, principles of formal composition must also be mentioned. A form-critical examination reveals that (a) the speeches are composed according to the principle of a mixture of *Gattungen*, and (b) the Job-poet has increased the range of use of the *Gattungen* by employing them in functions other than those proper to them."

constantly *misuses* the forms it contains. Traditional forms from legal, cultic and wisdom spheres are deliberately misused by the author to convey his scepticism. R E Murphy[2] makes an observation which, when taken out of context, clarifies this point. He writes:

"How are the genres used? Often there is a contrast between the use of a genre and its ordinary function and one has to stand away from the work in order to appreciate this."[3]

He makes this point in order to stress that one must look at the overall genre of a work rather than at smaller genres in isolation. For our purposes however the comment may suggest that how a genre is used by an author may be just as important as classifying the genre itself. As G W Coats[4] argues, there may be a conscious alteration of the characteristics of a genre, for example a changing of the setting in which the genre originally appeared, which reveals a unique intention by an author who can employ a genre in new and creative ways. Thus, although looking for an overall genre classification for Job has led us down a blind alley, a unifying feature can possibly be found in the way the author of *Job* uses - or rather deliberately misuses - disparate smaller genres.

I distinguish here between the 'misuse' of forms and the 'reuse' of forms, the former referring to a traditional form being used with a different content and context and thus having a different function; the latter retaining its form and content but being placed in a different context with a different function. Both these techniques of form occur in *Job* and should be distinguished from each other. Both involve a form being divorced from its usual content, the 'misuse' of a form involving a change of context which often brings about a change of meaning in the content and the 're-use' of a form involving a change of content alone. We need to distinguish therefore between a form, its content and its function in a certain context. In *Job*, the disparity between these is fundamental to the structure of the book and the intentions of its author. This has already been noted by scholars but perhaps without their fully realizing its significance. Some examples will make this clear.

---

2   R E Murphy, 1981.
3   R E Murphy, 1981 (p 17).
4   G W Coats, 1985.

(1) C Westermann[5] notes that the lament and consolation forms that are supposed to characterize the dialogue are spoiled in *Job* because in the place of the consolation expected from the friends, controversy arises which leads to arguments. The lament becomes a disputation and the original form is spoiled. Westermann finds disputation passages in the speeches of the friends - in 4:2-19; 5:1-27; 8:2-22; 11:2-20; 15:2-35; 18:2-21; 20:2-29; 22:2-30.[6] On Job's side the lament is dominant but opposition to the friends adds elements of disputation, notably in 13:4-13 and chapter 21. Westermann tries to stress the predominance of the lament form in spite of the disputation elements. He emphasizes that the disputation is found alongside laments in chapters 3 and 29-31 which name the third party, God, who is summoned in 31:35-37 and expected to solve the controversy. The lament is dramatized and then put into a narrative framework. However, in recognizing the misuse of a traditional form Westermann has stumbled across an important point for discovering the key to this author's thought, although he has simply used this insight to argue for his own overall genre classification for *Job* - the 'dramatization' of the lament. It is the quest for an overall genre for *Job* which has largely thrown up genre elements which do not quite fit into a traditional classification. But this has caused scholars merely to modify their genre classifications whereas, in fact, they should have been looking at the untraditional elements themselves for a clue as to the author's intention. The work of two scholars illustrates this:

(a) A Bentzen[7] classifies the dialogue of *Job* as a 'dramatization' of the psalm of lamentation. The dialogue form is seen to be merely "a further development of the situation of the psalm of lamentation and its forms so the dialogue in a natural way grows under the hand of the poet, and in this situation he is able to use the many forms, especially of psalms of lamentation, which he displays in his lyrics."[8] This discussion has as its aim an attempt to

---

5   C Westermann, 1956, (1981).
6   C Westermann, 1956, distinguishes between personal and substantive elements in the speeches of the friends and Job. He argues that over the course of the three sets of discourses, personal accusation becomes much more dominant. The personal address itself divides into two elements, the altercation and the admonition. He writes, "The disputational speech...is by no means *one* definite form of speech. On the contrary, it includes all the forms which one can use in opposition to another" (1981, p 20).
7   A Bentzen, 1948.
8   A Bentzen, 1948 (1952, p 182).

find an overall classification for *Job* and, in doing so, has to modify the original 'psalm of lamentation' genre to fit the dialogue of *Job*. In fact, what is of interest is that the author has used traditional genre elements in an untraditional way, thus defying classification in familiar terms.

(b) H Gese[9], in his attempt to find an overall genre for *Job* remarks on the use of the *Klageerhörungsparadigma,* "paradigm of the answered lament", in the book saying that the author of *Job* took over this form with the intention of changing it, notably by replacing a theory of retribution by a theology of God's transcendence. This raises the important issue of the author's intention in relation to the way forms are presented in *Job*.

(2) D Cox[10], concerned with the structure of chapters 29-31 of *Job*, notes that in a traditional lament genre, as found in these chapters, the lament is followed by a declaration of 'clearance'; whereas in Job 31:35-37 the author reverses the style, turning the expected prayer into an accusation. He writes:

"This modification highlights the author's particular purpose. He is using a familiar literary form to achieve an unusual end. The first part of the lament - remembrance of past happiness - describes the conventional notion of human values familiar to all wisdom literature. This convention is now contrasted with the reality of human life as experience finds it. This is a recapitulation of the thrust of the book - the crisis of faith."[11]

Cox thus notes, within a few chapters, a reversal of a traditional form by the author, an idea already taken much further by G Fohrer.

(3) G Fohrer[12] notes the skill of the author of *Job* and argues that he achieves his effects by the use of three methods. First, the author proves himself a learned man by his use of rich imagery - Fohrer envisages the author as having learned these from the techniques of the wisdom movement. Secondly, the author uses a mixture of genres - from the wisdom literature, from legal contexts and from the psalms, as argued above. Lastly, forms are used so that they go beyond their original functions. Fohrer argues that this is characteristic of much of the Old Testament. Fohrer distinguishes between the

---

9  H Gese, 1958.
10  D Cox, 1981.
11  See discussion of chapter 31 later in this chapter, pp 133-134.
12  G Fohrer, 1959.

*Sitz im Leben* of a form - its original use - and the *Sitz im Buch* - its immediate context.[13] *Job* is full, he argues, of examples of a new use for old forms.

Fohrer puts into groups the different ways in which traditional forms are used with a new purpose.

(a) His first classification is of forms which are inherently capable of use in different situations and functions: forms which are easily adaptable for use in different arguments. For example, traditional wisdom material about the fate of the righteous and the wicked is generally used in *Job* to teach about order in the world - see Job 15:17-35 which uses the form in a traditional way but identifies such teaching as based both on personal experience and on tradition. The same form is used in the psalms, but instead of balancing pairs comparing the lot of the good and bad, sayings on the fate of the wicked there find their way into the psalms of lament, whilst sayings on the prosperity of the righteous are found in psalms of beatitude, eg Psalms 1, 91 and 128. Fohrer argues that the author of *Job* uses both types of source for these sayings. He uses wisdom sayings in 4:7,8-11; 5:2-7,8f; 8:5-7,8f; 11:17-19,20; 18:5-21; 20:4-29; 21:7-13; 29:7-17,21-25 and psalm-sayings in 4:10-11 and 11:10. This category of Fohrer's is not a 'misuse' but a 'reuse' of forms - borrowing or imitation of forms from other areas of life.

(b) Fohrer's second category is of forms deliberately modified to make them usable in a new context. The form is changed slightly to convey a different meaning and the content remains virtually unchanged. However a new context conveys a different meaning. Sayings about the righteous and the wicked have been changed, so that, for example, in 21:17-18 commonplaces about the fate of the wicked are made into questions expecting the answer 'no' (whilst commonplaces are found in the mouths of the friends, cf 18:5-6,12).

---

13 In his 1963 commentary Fohrer distinguishes between the *Sitz im Leben* of a *Gattung* and its *Sitz in Rede und Buch*. The latter is important for establishing the function given to the forms in their respective contexts, which can be very different from their original meaning. He notes that sometimes the use of forms in a function different from one which corresponds to the *Sitz im Leben* is not a creation of the author of *Job*. Instead the forms have a diversity of function inherent in them, for example where the motif of the end of the wicked and the prosperity of the pious is used to provide warnings and advice, eg 4:7-11; 5:1-11; 8:5-7,11-22; 11:13-16. But sometimes it is the author who has made recognizable changes in the forms used and given them a different function, eg in speech-forms taken from wisdom teaching (cf 21:7-13,17-18; 22:15-16; 29:7f), laments (cf 10:18f) and hymns (cf 7:12; 11:7-9).

Job 29:7-17,21-25, is based on a traditional form concerned with the success of the pious and provides a parallel to the poem on the fate of the wicked in 18:5-21 and 20:4-29. It properly belongs to a wisdom context (compare 29:2 with Psalm 49:5 and 78:2) and would normally refer in the third person to the present or future prosperity of the righteous; but the poet has made it refer in the first person to the past prosperity of Job which no longer obtains, for example verses 21-22, "Men listened to me, and waited, and kept silence for my counsel. After I spoke they did not speak again, and my word dropped upon them." 21:7-13 presents the prosperity of the wicked in a parody of a wisdom poem which would normally have described the prosperity of the righteous, thus in verses 7-8, "Why do the wicked live, reach old age, and grow mighty in power? Their children are established in their presence, and their offspring before their eyes." Complaints about the good luck of the wicked in the lament-psalms provide evidence that this kind of parody was common with reference to the wicked, for example Psalm 10:5-6; 73:3-9. Job 10:18-19 picks up the lament of chapter 3 and turns it into a 'why' question, which amounts to a complaint against God; and in 11:7-19 hymnic forms are used but adapted so as to change them from a praise of God's incomprehensible majesty into an interrogation of Job, making him (or trying to make him) realize that he cannot understand God. In 7:12 Job uses similar forms to affirm his own dignity instead of their appearing in the mouth of God.

(c) The most important category (in my view) that Fohrer isolates is his third one of forms being *used* in a context different from their original *Sitz im Leben*. Under this category, Fohrer has five subgroups.

(i) The first is of forms that are transferred to a different area of life. For example, in 21:23-26 Job uses a wisdom saying about death (v 26) - that happy and unhappy alike are united in death - in order to show that the wicked escape punishment, since the righteous die just as they do. Hence in contradiction to what the friends claim, death is not a punishment which shows God's enmity to the wicked. Legal forms are used in the dialogue, in which no legal action is actually taking place. These forms then take on the function of a rejection of false rules for living, eg 6:22-23; 6:24; 6:26-29; 13:4-12; 19:2-4; 19:28-29, where speech-forms that originally belong to the accusation in court against an opponent on the grounds that he is a sinner, or forms that properly call upon the defendant to change his ways, are used in debate to urge the friends to give up their false beliefs about retribution and to stop 'persecuting the righteous' in the sense of challenging Job's innocence. The friends also use legal forms in this transferred sense, eg 8:2-4; 11:2-3; 18:2-4; and in his debate with God, Job uses such forms in three ways in speaking to God: i) to accuse God of behaving in a hostile way towards him (9:2f,14-16,19-21,24,28b; 10:4-7,14-15,17); ii) to defend his own conduct and position (13:3; 16:8; 27:3-4); and iii) to summon God to act in defence of his innocence (13:13-28; 16:19-22; 19:25; 16:18; 17:3). God is made to use legal forms to show Job the error of his ways (38:2-3; 40:2,8). In his 1963 commentary, Fohrer remarks on the reason for this transfer of the function of legal forms:

"In den Reden Hiobs dienen sie der Bestreitung von für falsch gehaltenen Lebensregeln und der Abwehr der Freunde, in den Freundesreden der Ablehnung des Verhaltens Hiobs und der nachdrücklichen Einführung der eigenen Lehre."[14]

Thus forms from the law court here appear in a debate which is really about life-questions rather than legal ones. In these examples the change of context alters the meaning of the saying to such an extent that the original form is barely recognisable.

(ii) Fohrer's second subgroup is of forms which are used in a context that gives them the opposite meaning from that which they would have had in the proper *Sitz im Leben*. This category comes closest to the misuse of forms technique I am trying to emphasize. For Fohrer this technique is one among many others. He does not highlight it nor does he work out any implications of his findings. In 21:32-33 "words about the peaceful and honourable end of the pious man come to be referred in a parodic way to the happy end of the sinner simply through the context in which they are placed".[15] This occurs particularly with lament forms. Thus in 3:11-13, 21f; 6:8-10 laments are not

---

14  G Fohrer, 1963 (p 52) "In Job's speeches these legal forms serve to challenge rules for living which are regarded as false, and thus to rebut the friends: in the friends' speeches they are used to decry Job's conduct and to introduce the friends' own teaching in an emphatic way."

15  G Fohrer, 1963 (p 69).

an attempt to improve the sufferer's situation, but are a complaint that he is still alive. In 7:15 the wish for healing becomes a wish for death (cf also 7:3; 6:11-13; 7:5-8; 9:25-26; 17:11-16). Lament is not linked with a confession of sin, but with a protestation of innocence (30:25-26). The lament is *about* God, rather than directed to God (3:20-23). 'Remember ' is not an appeal, but an accusation or reproach (7:7-8 - contrast Psalm 74:2; 89:50-51; 103:14).

In 3:3-10 the curse on the day of birth is in effect a self-curse. A curse on enemies becomes a curse on friends, who have proved faithless (6:15-21; 19:22) - cf Psalm 31:11-12; 38:11; 41:9; 55:13-15; 69:8-12; 88:8,18, where this has already happened - or on God (16:9a; 16:12-14). Job 30:12-14 is a curse against the demon of sickness, which amounts in context to a curse on God. Even hymn forms are parodied: 3:17-19; 7:17-18 (cf Psalm 8:5; 144:3) - פקד, which in Psalm 8:5 means 'visit in mercy' here means 'visit in anger', 'call to account.' In 9:12-13; 10:8-12,13-17; 23:13 hymnic sentences are used as laments or reproaches.

(iii) Fohrer's third sub-group is of forms which are diverted from their proper function into a paraenetic or didactic use. In my opinion, this should be called a reuse of forms rather than a misuse. Job 4:12-16 uses a form proper to prophecy, but in order to convey a 'wisdom' content (cf 4:17-21) rather than a real 'revelation'. Job 22:19-20 uses the psalm of thanksgiving form (cf Psalm 52:8-9; 58:11; 69:33; 107:42) to threaten the 'sinner' (Job) that the righteous will rejoice over him; then 22:27 is a promise, but it uses the forms proper to psalmic requests and thanksgivings: see also 5:9,11,12-16, where formulae of praise of God become warnings or advice. In 40:9-14 the author uses a hymn of praise as an ironic warning to man to know his proper place.

(iv) Fohrer's fourth sub-category is of wisdom forms which are given a direct reference to Job's situation - again a reapplication of old forms, not a misuse. Thus in 15:17-35 the portrayal of the life and fate of 'the wicked' by Eliphaz is meant as a direct description of Job rather than a general truth. Job 22:6-9 uses a similar generalized description to accuse Job of sins which (according to 4:3-4) he cannot have committed - the suggestion is an argument from first principles: since Job must be a sinner, he must have done these things. Prophetic forms, which were already being taken over into 'wisdom', are used to justify not coming judgement but suffering which has already occurred (22:13-14).

(v) Fohrer's final subgroup is of forms which are used as a justification for some point that lies outside them: for example the lament, which properly is an attempt to get God to save the sufferer, is used in 7:9-10 to justify the reproach addressed to God in 7:11. In 9:4 Job's fear that a legal contest with God cannot possibly succeed is grounded in a hymnic description of God. In 15:7-8 a mythical text about the first man is used to justify the condemnation of Job in 15:9-10. Thus Job tries to justify his actions before God and justify his own attitude to God by reference to God's actions. This again is not a 'misuse' of traditional forms but a clever aligning of forms in order to make a new point.

(4) Fohrer has a fourth category of the way old forms are used in a new way. This category does not refer to individual forms, but to whole sections of discourse which are given a fresh function. Examples are the wisdom poems in 15:17-35; 18:5-21; 20:4-29 and 29; the three sections preparing for the oath of innocence (21:6-34; 23:2-12; 27:2-6) and Job's lament in 14:1-22 which is used as part of a challenge to God to enter into a law-suit. The oath in 31:1-34,38-40 contains two formulaic elements. First, Job proves his innocence with twelve examples (constructed, according to Fohrer, out of an original list of ten - hence some dislocations in the text). This form belongs properly in wisdom or in apodictic law - for example in the Decalogue. Secondly, Job asserts his innocence through a negative confession, not in the form found in Egyptian funerary or cultic texts but more probably in a form used in Israelite law-courts, an oath of innocence taken by the accused (cf Exodus 22:7,9f). These two forms are joined together, the immediate intention being to justify Job's demand (which is met) to encounter God directly, and to fill out Job's assertion that once all was well with him (29:2). Job 31:35-37 has the same function. Thus the forms are used to call on God to give an oracle or favourable judgement - but even this is adapted, since what Job actually wants is a personal encounter. Yahweh's reply to Job ought to be either a divine oracle or a judgement on the case before the court; but in fact the first Yahweh speech is neither. It is neither positive nor negative and does not give judgement in favour of either party. Formally it is a disputation-speech

*(Streitrede)* as is shown by the introduction (38:2-3) and conclusion (40:2,6-14); yet its content is actually a question not an assertion. Within this overall question, the author uses other forms; for example list-type wisdom (onomastica) which properly belongs to the realm of control of the world through encyclopaedic knowledge, but here is used to convince Job of the limits of wisdom. Job's submission in 40:3-5; 42:1-6 is formally like the third section of a lament-psalm (where the psalmist gives thanks that his prayer has been heard) or the acceptance by the accused of his sentence (in a law-court), but its function here is actually to describe the means by which a person achieves fulfilment in life - the goal to which the whole book has been moving. So even in the last section the form is dislocated from the content. Thus Fohrer concludes:

"Die Annahme, daß die verwendete Form dem Inhalt entsprechen müsse oder auf ihn schließen lasse, erweist sich dem nach in dieser verallgemeinernden Art als irrtümlich. Gewiß trifft sie häufig zu. Aber die Form kann ebenso einem ganz anderen Inhalt dienen, als es ihrem Sitz im Leben entspricht, und also eine andere Funktion erhalten."[16]

Fohrer also applies this idea to the prophets with a certain amount of success. He argues that the prophets imitated many alien speech forms, using them for their own proclamation. A distinction must be made between the original meaning of a genre and its use in a certain context, ie between its form and its function in prophetic proclamation. He writes:

"The duality of form and function, or original 'Sitz im Leben' and modified 'use in discourse' is nowhere more evident as in the words of the prophets...To a surprisingly great extent the prophets borrowed rhetorical forms from other realms of life and used them in new functions."[17]

Fohrer talks of drinking songs and love songs imitated by the prophets - for example an antithesis to the Song of Solomon in Ezekiel 16:23f in which the

---

16   G Fohrer, 1959 (1963, pp 76-77), "The assumption that the form which is used must always either correspond to, or provide a clear indication of, the content can be seen, as a generalization, to be mistaken. Usually it is true enough, but it is also possible for a form to serve as a vehicle for a quite different content than is appropriate to its [normal] Sitz im Leben, and thus to acquire a quite different function." cf G Fohrer, 1961, "A distinction must...be made between the original meaning of a genre and the way in which it is utilized, that is, between the form and its function" (p 312).

17   G Fohrer, 1970 (pp 356-357), cf his article on modern interpretations of the prophets - G Fohrer, 1961.

form and content of the love song are used in a different context. He talks of hymnic style, hymns and wisdom forms borrowed by them, for example communal laments in Jeremiah 3:21-25; 14:7-9,19-22; Hosea 6:1-3; 14:2b-3 and rhetorical wisdom forms in Isaiah 28:23-29 and Amos 3:3-6.[18] Finally he talks of taunt songs and dirges which are given a new function by the future event depicted in them being referred to as having already taken place, for example, Isaiah 47; Amos 5:1-3. He writes, "In this way the prophet intensified his threat of disaster: it is so sure to take place that its results can already be mourned."[19] A clear distinction should be made, one that Fohrer himself does not emphasize, between places where the prophets are imitating or borrowing a form (giving it a new context) and those places where they are employing a form with not only a new function, but an opposite meaning as well (the content is changed to contradict the form's original use and to make a new point). In the latter, the newness of the prophets' message is emphasized but within the forms of tradition. This most closely resembles my own findings in *Job* as I shall go on to discuss.

In *Job*, conclusions about the 'original' *Sitz im Leben* must not be deduced from the identification of particular forms, taken out of context. Fohrer writes:

"Dem Verfasser war nicht an der Verwendung einer bestimmten Gattung, sondern an der Behandlung eines bestimmten Themas gelegen, in deren Rahmen die einzelnen Redeformen eine auf das Ganze bezügliche Funktion erhalten."[20]

This distinction between form and function, Fohrer argues, is crucial for the whole understanding of *Job*. He regards *Job* neither as a treatment of a legal theme (as Richter [21] maintains), nor as a dramatized lament (Westermann [22]), but as a work in which both legal and lament genres are used in the service of a discussion of the correct way for man to behave whilst suffering. He writes in his 1963 commentary:

---

18  Noted by J Lindblom, 1955.
19  G Fohrer, 1968 (1970, p 276).
20  G Fohrer, 1959 (p 77), "The author was not committed to the use of a particular genre *(Gattung)* but the treatment of a particular theme, within which individual speech-forms acquire a function in relation to the whole work."
21  H Richter, 1959.
22  C Westermann, 1956, (1981).

"Der Unterschied zwischen Form und Funktion zeigt, daß die verwendete Form nicht immer dem Inhalt entspricht oder auf ihn schließen läßt. Dies ist für das formale Gesamtverständnis des Buches Hiob zu bedenken. Gewiß stellt das Buch weder ein Epos noch ein Drama dar, ebensowenig ein reines Weisheitsbuch oder eine reine Lehrdichtung. Man kann es aber auch nicht als Verhandlung einer Rechtssache oder dramatisierte Klage bezeichnen, indem man einseitig einen einzigen Formbereich ohne Berücksichtigung der funktionellen Verwendung heranzieht.

Das Buch Hiob ist insofern ein Lebensbuch, als Hiob in seinen Reden ein bestimmtes Verhalten lebt, deswegen von den Freunden bekämpft und schließlich zu einem anderen Verhalten geführt wird. Es ist insofern eine Lehrdichtung, als die Freunde den Hiob über sein Verhalten belehren und das Ganze naturgemäß als beispielhaft für andere Menschen im Leide bestimmt ist. So läßt das Buch sich als ein Dichtwerk mit Rahmenerzählung bezeichnen, in dem sich in Leben und Lehre eine Auseinandersetzung über das rechte Verhalten des Menschen im Leide abspielt."[23]

The work of Fohrer is clearly crucial in any assessment of literary techniques in *Job*.[24] He does not however work out fully the wider implications of his isolation of the form/function technique,[25] nor does he cite many examples of traditional *Sitze im Leben* for the original forms, which are seen as being used in a new function, a method which would strengthen his

---

23 G Fohrer, 1963 (p 53), "Differences between form and function show that the form which is used does not always correspond to the intended content, or enable one to decide what this must be. This must be borne in mind in attempting to grasp the book of Job as a formal whole. It is certainly true that the book does not amount either to an epic or a drama, and equally it is not a pure wisdom book or didactic poem. But nor can it be classified as a trial or a dramatized lament, by one-sidely stressing a single formal sphere, and paying no attention to the way the forms are used." "The book of Job is a book of life, inasmuch as Job embraces certain styles of conduct in his speeches, and is consequently attacked by his friends and eventually led to a different kind of conduct. It is a didactic poem, inasmuch as the friends 'teach' Job about his way of living, and the whole book is intended as exemplary for other sufferers. Thus the book may be seen as a poetic work with a narrative framework, in which, through life and through teaching, a discussion takes place about the right way for man to live in times of suffering."
24 R N Whybray, 1974, mentions the work of G Fohrer when criticizing his over-reliance on form-criticism for trying to detect the influence of one tradition on another. Whybray writes of Fohrer that he "has pointed out that even when it can be shown that a speaker or writer has in fact made use of extraneous forms, this does not necessarily mean that his thought has been significantly influenced by them. His intention may merely have been to refer to a well known saying or mode of speech in order to communicate more effectively with his audience." (p 73)
25 Fohrer draws no conclusions from his findings in his 1959 work but goes a little further in his commentary in trying to link the findings of his form/function technique to his conception of the message of *Job* - see quotation above. However, these ideas are still not followed up in depth.

arguments. Neither does he distinguish between the reuse and misuse of forms - he tends to muddle his categories. He describes the use made of old forms by an author, using the expression 'form/function technique' in a wide sense. Only two of his classifications of forms correspond to the deliberate 'misuse of forms' technique which I have isolated. I hope to show that this technique is much more common in *Job* than Fohrer has discerned and that it is crucial to an understanding of the profound scepticism of the author. In what follows I shall show how in the dialogue section of *Job*, the misuse of forms technique is operating in a profound way and has implications both for the assessment of *Job* as sceptical literature and for an assessment of the overall genre of the book.

First, however, it is important to look briefly at how different literary techniques are employed by the author of *Job* in order to demonstrate the diversity of his literary skill and show that positing a 'misuse of forms' technique makes sense in relation to this author and in fact highlights the importance of the author in the production of the book. Specific literary techniques have been found in certain chapters or verses of *Job*, techniques designed to have a particular limited effect; others have a wider range of application.[26]

Effective use of 'double-entendre' by the author of Job at key points is found by K Fullerton, notably in 40:3-5,[27] in the prologue,[28] in chapters 9 and 10[29] and in Eliphaz's first speech (chs 4-5).[30] Fullerton argues that these passages were written in such a way that the orthodox reader would approve of them whilst the less traditional reader would find in them an indirect

---

[26] An example of the former is provided by the work of K Fullerton, 1924, 1930, 1938, discussed in the next section. An example of the latter is given by P W Skehan, 1961, who finds a prime literary technique by the author of *Job* in the strophic structure of the poems in the book. His analysis affects only Job 3:3; 24:11 and tentatively the third cycle of speeches in *Job*. He argues that the editor of Proverbs and Ben Sira wrote in similar patterns and that such a technique is a normative wisdom technique. With respect to Job, this analysis provides a measuring rod for the relative integrity of the text and the proportion of flaws in its transmission and an objective framework for the task of textual criticism.

[27] K Fullerton, 1924.
[28] K Fullerton, 1924.
[29] K Fullerton, 1938.
[30] K Fullerton, 1930.

criticism of the orthodox position.[31] Job 40:3-5 would be read by the orthodox as a confession of repentance (especially when aligned with 42:1-6); but the author in fact conveys his view that nothing further can be said on the subject. In 40:3-5 Job does not apologize or confess as in 42:6, he merely says that he is unable to argue with God and will debate no longer. Fullerton writes:

"This confession of Job at 40:3-5 *could* be very easily construed as *the cryptic conclusion of the author himself, his own confession* that the problem which he had raised is insoluble. Thus the Confession at 40:3-5, in its present position after the Speeches of Jahweh and in its present wording, is capable of a double sense, one pious, one sceptical. Is this double sense intentional?"[32]

The orthodox reader would find in the Yahweh speeches a well-deserved rebuke of Job's daring criticism of God, but the author also suggests that the problem of suffering is insoluble. The speeches have an ironical tone and whilst the irony of the speeches is ostensibly directed against Job, in fact it is really directed against the orthodox readers who think they have the answer to the problem of suffering.

In the prologue, Fullerton notes a mixture of irony and of piety. He argues that the prologue did take up a conventional tale, satisfactory to the orthodox. However the author reformulated it. Fullerton writes:

"The *pious reader* would see in the Prologue the suggestion that suffering came from God and would be content with that ...the *thinker* would see that this is no real explanation."[33]

Thus no solution of the problem of suffering is really offered and the author's purpose is, in Fullerton's words:

"to subject the rationalism of the current dogma of retributive suffering and the view of God implied in it, to a thoroughgoing and fearless criticism, but not to set up a rival theory of suffering in its place."[34]

To the orthodox reader, Eliphaz in chapters 4-5 is right to minimize Job's responsibilities for his present plight, to console him and yet to rebuke the tone of Job's speech. But, as Fullerton writes:

---

31  K Fullerton, 1930, shows how the orthodox could have read *Job*.
32  K Fullerton, 1924 (p 130).
33  K Fullerton, 1924 (p 132).
34  K Fullerton, 1924 (p 133).

"The subtlety of [the speech]...lies in its irony and innuendo...not...of Eliphaz at the expense of Job, but...of the author at the expense of Eliphaz and of the orthodox reader whose position he represents."[35]

For example, in 5:2-5 it is suggested that Eliphaz was oblivious to the application to Job of what he was saying. His dogmatism led him to speak in general formulas which Job interpreted from the standpoint of his own suffering, and so misinterpreted. The author deliberately portrays Eliphaz in an ironic light as a type of the orthodox. Job 9:2-4 introduces one of Job's most daring speeches and this introduction helps to anaesthetize the orthodox against what follows but, if taken in their ironical senses, these words provide the real introduction to what follows.[36] The technique of double-entendre is clearly important, although the process for identifying it might be criticized for being too subjective. It is based on an assessment of what the author really meant when he constructed his work, a question that will never be answered by an analysis of objective evidence. However, in my view, the isolation of this technique by Fullerton is not devalued by the subjective nature of the method, since it clearly sheds important light on interpretation of the text.

The use of quotations by the author of *Job* is highlighted by R Gordis.[37] He argues that rather than deleting passages which scholars have found irrelevant or contradictory to the tenor of the book, the use of quotations by the authors of *Job* and Ecclesiastes to expound their own ideas should be posited. These quotations are not obvious in the text as they are not indicated by a system of punctuation (which did not exist in ancient times) and often they lack an introductory verb of speaking or thinking (for example, 'I thought' or 'you said') and so the reader has to recreate these quotations. Different types of

---

[35] K Fullerton, 1930 (p 340). Recently Y Hoffman, 1980, has noted the use of ambiguous, equivocal words in the first speech of Eliphaz which convey the author's opinion about the character of Eliphaz.

[36] K Fullerton, 1938, argues that the word צדק and the preposition עם in 9:2 have double meanings. He argues that the change of מן at 4:17 to עם at 9:2 is not accidental but was utilized by the author deliberately to half conceal and half reveal his meaning. The reverent "no man can be righteous in God's sight" is changed into the sarcastic "no man can be in the right as against God."

[37] R Gordis, 1939-40; R Gordis, 'Quotations as a Literary Usage in Biblical, Oriental and Rabbinic Literature', 1949; R Gordis, 1965, pp 169-189; cf R Gordis 1981.

quotations do not form distinct categories but are closely related developments of the same basic technique. Gordis writes:[38]

> "The term 'quotations' refers to *words which do not reflect the present sentiments of the author of the literary composition in which they are found, but have been introduced by the author to convey the standpoint of another person or situation*. These quotations include, but are not limited to, citations of previously existing literature, whether written or oral. In other words the term...refers to passages that cite the speech or thought of a subject, actual or hypothetical, past or present, which is distinct from the context in which it is embedded."

Gordis cites examples of this use of quotations too numerous to mention here. However, one form of quotation in *Job* isolated by him is of especial interest since it relates to the 'deliberate misuse of forms' technique. This form is described as 'oblique restatement':

> "At times, Job cites the opinion of the Friends, not literally but ironically, in a form bordering on parody. Failure to recognize this fact has vitiated many attempts to interpret chapter 12, one of the most striking utterances of Job..."[39]

Gordis argues that 12:7-8, for example, is *"a restatement by Job of the Friends' admonition to him"*.[40] In 12:5 Job declares "In the thought of one who is at ease there is contempt for misfortune; it is ready for those whose feet slip." Then he recapitulates the friends' position as he sees it - they have to admit that the wicked prosper (v 6) but have tried to turn his attention elsewhere by calling on Job to admire God's perfection as reflected in the natural order (vv 7f; cf 5:9f; 11:7f). Job now meets this attempt to sidetrack the argument by replying that there is nothing new in the idea of the power and greatness of God: "Who among all these does not know that the hand of the Lord has done this?" (v 9). In fact, he is able to portray God's might far more effectively than the friends (vv 13-25). In chapter 13 he reiterates that he knows as much as they do (13:1,2) and yet he still desires to argue with the Almighty (13:3).

---

38 R Gordis, 'Quotations as a Literary Usage in Biblical, Oriental and Rabbinic Literature', 1949 (p 109).

39 R Gordis, 'Quotations as a Literary Usage in Biblical, Oriental and Rabbinic Literature', 1949 (p 142). Other passages containing this oblique restatement include Job 13:14-15 and 19:28-29.

40 R Gordis, 'Quotations as a Literary Usage in Biblical, Oriental and Rabbinic Literature', 1949 (p 143).

ii) Passages in Job showing the deliberate misuse of forms

Examples of the misuse of forms by the author of *Job* can be found throughout the book and a detailed discussion of passages illustrating this is now required. I shall draw on the examples Fohrer gives where applicable throughout this discussion. The possibility of a pattern to be found in the use of this technique by the author of *Job* must also be kept in mind. The misuse can be illustrated by comparison of the form in *Job* with the same form being used in a traditional way in another book of the Old Testament. This will demonstrate that the form did exist and had a 'proper' use opposite to the use the author of *Job* makes of it.

The narrative sections of the book of *Job* do not provide any examples of this misuse of forms; rather, taken together, they resemble traditional kinds of narrative such as those found in the Pentateuch and later 'tales' in the Old Testament and Apocrypha. This observation has led scholars to think that the prologue and epilogue to *Job* originally formed a 'patriarchal' narrative which was well-known in Israel from early times and which was 'spoiled' many centuries later by the author of the dialogue sections of *Job*. The vast majority of examples of the misuse of forms in *Job* come from the dialogue, chapters 3-31, which need to be examined in some detail.

Job 3:11-26 contains the misuse of a lament form. Use of the question 'Why?' and a description of distress are characteristic of a complaint. However laments usually concern distress concerning a particular situation and an attempt to improve it by appeal to God to change it. Death is usually the *un*desirable outcome of being the victim of God's wrath, for example, in Psalm 88:4-5: "I am a man who has no strength, like one forsaken among the dead, like the slain that lie in the grave, like those whom thou dost remember no more for they are cut off from thy hand." In *Job* on the other hand there is a description of death as desirable; for example in 3:11, 3:13 and 3:21, death rather than God's favour is seen as the only release from present misery and is therefore to be longed for. The complaint is that the sufferer is still alive. Fohrer notices this phenomenon and points out furthermore that in 3:20-23, instead of the laments being to God they are *about* God. Further, laments beginning 'Why?' tend to call *God* in question, for example Psalm 74:10-11:

"How long, O God, is the foe to scoff? Is the enemy to revile thy name for ever? Why dost thou hold back thy hand, why dost thou keep thy right hand in thy bosom?" and Psalm 79:5-10, but Job calls his own birth into question. Fohrer notes that in 3:16-19 hymnic sentences are used as laments or reproaches.[41]

Chapter 6:8-10 provides another example. This is an affirmation of loyalty by Job in the form of a death wish and can again be seen as a parody of lament forms - ie passages which long for safety from attack. Psalm 55:6-8, for example - "And I say, 'O that I had wings like a dove! I would fly away and be at rest; yes, I would wander afar, I would lodge in the wilderness, I would haste to find me a shelter from the raging wind and tempest.'" - is a 'straight' longing for a place of safety from attack, whereas for Job, destruction is what he longs for: "O that I might have my request, and that God would grant my desire; that it would please God to crush me, that he would let loose his hand and cut me off! This would be my consolation; I would even exult in pain unsparing; for I have not denied the words of the Holy One." Fohrer notes also that the form of 6:15-21, a curse on Job's friends by Job, would traditionally be used in the Psalms to curse one's enemies.[42]

In 7:7-8 Fohrer points out that 'Remember' is not an appeal to God as in some psalms but is an accusation or reproach.[43] In 7:15 Fohrer notes that a traditional wish for healing becomes a wish for death. In 7:11-21 the intensity of Job's charges against God increases as the parody of hymn forms in Psalm 8 in 7:17-18 shows. In Psalm 8, verse 4 - "what is man that thou art mindful of him, and the son of man that thou dost care for him?" - the Psalmist is expressing awe at the favour God shows to man in his creation and praises his majesty and his name. Job however turns this on its head: "What is man, that thou dost make so much of him, and that thou dost set thy mind upon him,

---

41 Job's opening soliloquy in 3:3-10 is a self-curse. The content is different from a traditional curse. In *Job, man's* actions in bringing him into the world and letting him prosper are called into question rather than God's part in the process. Job's life itself is to be reviled whereas so often the gift of life is praised in the Old Testament, for example in Psalm 100, verse 3a, "Know that the Lord is God! It is he that made us, and we are his". There is a change in the traditional content (resembling a 'reuse' of form) but not a deliberate misuse of the form.
42 See above p 116.
43 See above p 116.

dost visit him every morning, and test him every moment?" Job is remarking on God's constant attention to man, as the Psalmist does, but he sees this as a negative thing - he cannot get away from God and pleads God to "Let me alone" (v 16). Psalm 8 is a thanksgiving for God's concern for man's life whereas Job 7:11-21 accuses God of being a "watcher of man" and longs for release.

Another parody is contained in Job 9:5-10, a hymnic description of God's creative power. These descriptions in *Job* are reproaches against the unassailable God whose actions man cannot predict, for example verse 5, "He who removes mountains and they know it not when he overturns them in his anger". Usually in hymns the unknowability of God and the marvels of his creation are a source of wonder to man and inspire praise, for example, in Psalm 104 and Amos 5:6-9. A parody is contained in Job 9:25-28 where Job complains that he is troubled when he tries to forget his suffering which he regards as an inevitable part of transitory human existence. In Jeremiah 20:7-9 Jeremiah says that trouble comes when he tries to forget God - he admits that God has prevailed and made him a laughingstock: "If I say, 'I will not mention him, or speak any more in his name,' there is in my heart as it were a burning fire shut up in my bones and I am weary with holding it in, and I cannot" (20:9). Job remarks in contrast: "If I say, 'I will forget my complaint, I will put off my sad countenance, and be of good cheer,' I become afraid of all my suffering, for I know thou wilt not hold me innocent." The form of words used in *Job* is very similar to the words used in the Jeremiah passage but the point made is very different by the change of content and context.

Job 10:2-12 contains a misuse of the kind of form found in Psalm 139. Psalm 139 is a prayer for deliverance from enemies, as is made apparent in verses 19-24, and it also praises the fact that God knows a man so thoroughly that he cannot escape - eg verses 7-8: "Whither shall I go from thy Spirit? Or whither shall I flee from thy presence? If I ascend to heaven, thou art there! If I make my bed in Sheol, thou art there!" Thus the all-seeing eye of God is regarded by the Psalmist as something to be praised - he is glad that one cannot escape from God. Job 10:2-12, on the other hand, is a request to be delivered from God. In verses 8-10, praise to God as creator is turned into a reproach against him. Job cannot escape from God's 'care' but this is seen as a bad thing, not something to be praised. Job is trying in this passage to move God against himself, not against his enemies. In the same chapter, verses 13-17 seem also to fit into the category of a misuse of forms. The 'if' motif is used here in the sense 'even if': even if I do what is generally considered to be right you still crush me, as in verse 15: "If I am wicked, woe to me! If I am righteous, I cannot lift up my head, for I am filled with disgrace and look upon my affliction." One might compare this sentiment with Psalm 7 which asks God for punishment if it is deserved, for example verses 3 and 5: "O Lord my God, if I have done this, if there is wrong in my hands,...let the enemy pursue me and overtake me, and let him trample my life to the ground, and lay my soul in the dust." Job on the other hand says that God punishes him even when it is *not* deserved - a lament has become a reproach against God. Fohrer notes that 10:13-17 also contains a parody of a hymn form. He argues that 10:18-19 picks up the lament of chapter 3 and turns it into a 'why' question, a complaint against God. This is an example of deliberate modification of a form. Fohrer argues that 11:7-19 provides another example of the adaptation of hymnic forms from a praise of God's majesty into an interrogation of Job. However this could be seen as a questioning along traditional wisdom lines - evidence of a hymn form is slim here.

Job 12:7-12 is generally seen as a passage supporting Job's claim to wisdom since it contains two wisdom sayings, in verses 11 and 12. But taken out of context verses 7-9 appear to be a misuse of a traditional form of praise to God as creator. Usually nature proclaims God's glory, for example Psalm 98, verses 7-9: "Let the sea roar, and all that fills it; the world and those who dwell in it! Let the floods clap their hands; let the hills sing for joy together before the Lord, for he comes to judge the earth." In *Job* however nature bears witness to the fact that "the hand of the Lord has done this" (v 9). "This" presumably refers to the decline in Job's fortunes - making him a "laughingstock" (v 4). Thus God is here being blamed, not praised, for what has happened to Job - he has inflicted the evil and nature bears witness to his actions. The wisdom sayings that follow in verses 11-12 lose their force in the light of these preceding verses and merely reinforce the idea that God is all-powerful, presumably with the suggestion that God has the power to inflict good or evil.

Job 12:13-25 is a hymnic description of God's wisdom and power, but it is a negative one. R Gordis[44] argues that this passage contains praise to God, couched in negative terms, a parody of descriptions by the friends of God's beneficent power. It can also be seen as a parody of positive praise such as is found in some of the psalms, for example Psalm 107. Psalm 107 describes how God helped the people of Israel in a beneficent way - eg verse 29, "he made the storm be still, and the waves of the sea were hushed" - and then it goes on to praise God's works in a more abstract way, eg verse 33, "He turns rivers into a desert, springs of water into thirsty ground". Job 12:13-25 however sees God's power as destructive - eg verse 20, "He deprives of speech those who are trusted, and takes away the discernment of the elders." - and so it is seen as a danger to mankind, working against their efforts to succeed and to walk in paths of righteousness.

In Job 13:20-22 Job asks God to give him nothing: eg verse 21, "withdraw thy hand far from me, and let not dread of thee terrify me". He wants to be free of God. This contrasts with passages which ask to see the face of God, or accuse God of hiding his face,[45] for Job does not want to see him any more. Psalm 27:4 expresses this desire to see God's face - "One thing have I asked of the Lord all the days of my life, to behold the beauty of the Lord, and to inquire in his temple." (cf also Proverbs 30:7-9). Proverbs 30:7-9 has a very similar form to this passage in *Job* but the writer there conveys a conventional desire for God's blessing in his life - "Remove far from me falsehood and lying; give me neither poverty nor riches; feed me with the food that is needful for me, lest I be full, and deny thee, and say, 'Who is the Lord?' or lest I be poor, and steal, and profane the name of my God."

Job 14:1-12 closely resembles Job 7:11-21 in subject matter and, like 7:11-21, also parodies Psalm 8. This passage in *Job* is a complaint about man's lot. Job describes the human condition (vv 1-3) and then makes a plea for divine

---

44 R Gordis, 1978.
45 See S Balentine, 1984. Balentine gives examples of God hiding his face in the context of lament in the psalms - in psalms of individual lament, eg Pss 10:1; 13:2; 22:25; 27:9; 51:11; 69:18; 88:15; 102:3; 143:7 and in psalms of communal lament, eg Ps 44:25. Either there is a petition to God in question form or there is an imperative. Job, on the other hand, wants to escape from God for a while and then be recognized afresh by him.

clemency (14:4-6). Whilst Psalm 8 praises man as God's highest creation, Job 14:1-12 describes man in human terms as "born of a woman" and instead of seeing man as "little lower than the angels" sees him as "full of trouble". In 14:13 Job pleads with God to recognize him after a sojourn in Sheol - "Oh that thou wouldest hide me in Sheol, that thou wouldest conceal me until thy wrath be past, that thou wouldest appoint me a set time and remember me!" This parodies a similar form in Psalm 55:6-7: "And I say, 'O that I had wings like a dove! I would fly away and be at rest; yea, I would wander afar, I would lodge in the wilderness.'" In Psalm 55, the psalmist wants to escape from his enemies. Job 14:18-22 is another passage about the hopelessness of man's condition and can be compared with 'hopeful' passages in the psalms. In *Job* God is accused directly - "thou destroyest the hope of man" (v19) - whereas throughout the psalms confidence is expressed that God will rescue his people and deliver them from their enemies, eg Psalm 28:6-8: "The Lord is my strength and my shield; in him my heart trusts; so I am helped, and my heart exults, and with my song I give thanks to him."(v 7). Psalm 31 contains complaints closely akin to Job's - "I am the scorn of all my adversaries, a horror to my neighbours, an object of dread to my acquaintances;" (v11) - but in the end the psalmist trusts and hopes in God: "But I trust in thee, O Lord, I say, 'Thou art my God.' My times are in thy hand; deliver me from the hand of my enemies and persecutors!" (vv 14-15). It is this note of trust and hope that Job lacks and which he parodies in his complaints.

Job 16:7-14 is a description of attack from an enemy, not from the enemies of Israel as traditionally but from God himself. This parodies passages where God is seen as giving strength to man, as giving him the will to live, as giving a meaning to his life, for example, Psalm 94:18-19 - "When I thought, 'My foot slips,' thy steadfast love, O Lord, held me up. When the cares of my heart are many, thy consolations cheer my soul." - and verse 22 "But the Lord has become my stronghold, and my God the rock of my refuge." In *Job* however: "God has worn me out" (16:7), "He has torn me in his wrath, and hated me;" (16:9a), "I was at ease, and he broke me asunder" (16:12).

In 19:22 Fohrer notes that a traditional curse on one's enemies becomes a curse on the friends - "Why do you, like God, pursue me? Why are you not satisfied with my flesh?" In Chapter 21:7-13, as noted above when discussing

Fohrer, there is a parody of passages which discuss the prosperity of the righteous, since Job describes the prosperity of the wicked in the same terms. This description can also be compared with passages in which the prosperity of the wicked is described, for example Psalms 10:5-6 and 73:3-9. Fohrer argues that since this kind of parody already existed in the psalms, it is a form simply used in a new context, the content remaining the same. However, in my view, the content is different - the description of the prosperity of the wicked, as in Psalm 73, is critical: "Pride is their necklace; violence covers them as a garment." (73:6) In *Job* however the description of their prosperity is envious: for example verses 9-10: "Their houses are safe from fear and no rod of God is upon them. Their bull breeds without fail, their cow calves, and does not cast her calf." Furthermore in *Job* the message is clearly that the ways of the wicked prosper and they are never apparently brought to judgement. In the psalms however the prosperity of the wicked is only a temporary blessing. Thus the author of Psalm 73 is envious of the prosperity of the wicked, "until I went into the sanctuary of God; then I perceived their end." In 21:17-18 Fohrer points out that commonplaces about the fate of the wicked are made into questions expecting the answer 'no'. In 21:23-26, *Job*, like Ecclesiastes, sets up a contrasting pair between two types of people, one who has prospered in life and the other who has suffered - "never having tasted of good" (v25) - and remarks that the same fate awaits them all: "They lie down alike in the dust and the worms cover them." Ecclesiastes 9:2 recognizes that the wicked and righteous suffer a similar fate - "since one fate comes to all, to the righteous and the wicked, to the good and the evil, to the clean and the unclean..." - and it also sets up contrasting pairs to illustrate this point. Ecclesiastes 8:14 is another example: "There is a vanity which takes place on earth, that there are righteous men to whom it happens according to the deeds of the wicked...I said that this also is vanity." These passages in *Job* and Ecclesiastes contrast with traditional ideas about the reward of the good and the punishment of the wicked, for example Psalm 1, eg verse 6: "for the Lord knows the way of the righteous; but the way of the wicked will perish." Fohrer classifies this example as a 'form transferred to a different area of life' - a wisdom saying about death is being reused to state that the wicked escape punishment. In my view this might better be called a 'misuse' of traditional forms than a reuse. Indeed, Fohrer sees 21:32-33 as 'parodic' noting the happy end of the sinner whilst in its original context such a form referred to the honourable end of the pious man.

Job 23:8-9 is a clear parody of a hymn such as Psalm 23. Here Job complains about God's absence and explores the reason why the desired litigation of verses 3-7 cannot take place: "Behold, I go forward, but he is not there; and backward, but I cannot perceive him; on the left hand I seek him, but I cannot behold him; I turn to the right hand, but I cannot see him." This provides a contrast to passages where Job cannot escape from God's presence. It also parodies psalms, for example where God's presence leads man through life, eg Psalm 23: "He leads me beside still waters; he restores my soul. He leads me in paths of righteousness for his name's sake" (vv 2b-3), or again Psalm 139.

Job 26:5-14 is a hymn in praise of God's power - verses 5-6 tell of God's dominion over the underworld, verses 7-14 of his power reflected in his creative activity. However the unorthodox note here is that God's power in creation is seen as frightening whereas usually in the psalms and in the prophets it is to be praised, eg Isaiah 40:9-11: "Behold, the Lord God comes with might, and his arm rules for him; behold his reward is with him, and his recompense before him. He will feed his flock like a shepherd, he will gather the lambs in his arms..." (vv 10-11a). God's greatness in creation is extolled and is a source of comfort for man. As mentioned above, Fohrer argues that 29:7-17,21-25 belongs to a wisdom context but is deliberately made to refer to the past prosperity of Job rather than to the prosperity of the righteous. Fohrer cites 30:25-26 as an example of a lament used in a new context with an opposite meaning. Here it is not linked with confession of sin but with protestation of innocence.

Finally Job 31, Job's 'negative confession' of integrity which is of the genre 'purificatory oath', is only reused by the author of *Job* since its content is already negative. This passage has judicial elements[46] - Job is the defendant

---

[46] For a discussion of Job 31 as a legal appeal of a defendant for a formal judicial hearing, see M B Dick, 1979. Dick argues that 31:35-37 is an ironic attempt to compel God's presence before a magistrate rather than a traditional plea for God's succour, an incongruity which reduces the legal metaphor to the absurd and makes bankrupt an attempt to see the man/God relationship in legal terms.

against God who is the attacker. In verses 2-4 he asks three questions indicating the punishments to be expected in the light of traditional theology if he had gone wrong; then he makes oaths relative to different things, for example falsehood (vv 5-6), upright conduct (vv 7-8). An extrabiblical parallel to this chapter is the Egyptian 'negative confession' of the dead person before Osiris.[47] This style of confession parodies passages elsewhere where God is the defendant - for example, Micah 6:3-5 in which God wants to know what he has done to his people. He is defending his own actions - "O my people, what have I done to you? In what have I wearied you? Answer me!" (v 3). Job however pleads his own case with a series of sentences beginning, "If I have...then...", implying that he himself does not really believe that he has done these things and therefore that he sees himself as innocent and undeserving of this punishment by God. God will not defend him and so he has to defend himself - God is no longer his "refuge and strength, a very present help in trouble" (Psalm 46:1), he has become Job's enemy against whom Job has to protect himself and argue his own defence. Cox[48] argues for what amounts to a misuse of the traditional ending to a lament in 31:35-37. Here an expected prayer is turned into an accusation by the author of *Job*.

A discussion of the oath in chapter 31 is provided by S H Blank.[49] He points out that chapter 31 is the climax and conclusion of Job's argument with which he rests his case. Thus it contains the strongest declaration of his innocence. This is conveyed by an oath which does not contain any part that is suppressed, unlike the eleven other examples of oaths in the Old Testament that Blank cites,[50] where either the conditional curse is evaded or the part containing the naming of the dire consequences if the oath-taker commits perjury is avoided. (The reason for this is commonly thought to be the fear on

---

47 J B Pritchard, 1950, pp 34-36.
48 D Cox, 1981.
49 S H Blank, 1951.
50 eg II Samuel 3:35, David swears saying, "God do so to me and more also, if I taste bread or anything else till the sun goes down!" (cf I Kings 20) He leaves unspecified the ominous contents of the 'so' and 'more also'. See also Numbers 5:19-27; Exodus 22:9-10.

the part of the biblical authors that once the calamity was named it would possess reality.) Blank writes:[51]

"A complete oath with nothing suppressed occurs in Psalm vii, another in Psalm cxxxvii. The third example is this thirty-first chapter of *Job*. It is the classic Biblical example of an oath in the form of a complete conditional curse upon one's self."

Blank finds four clear instances of the complete oath in this chapter of *Job* - 1) verses 5,7,8; 2) verses 9,10; 3) verses 13,16-17,19-22; 4) verses 38-40. In each oath the final verse contains the apodosis. This is the curse which is to befall Job if he has been guilty of committing any offences or omitting any acts of piety and righteousness listed in the previous conditional clauses. These curses are:- (If I have at all failed in my duty) "then let me sow, and another eat; and let what grows for me be rooted out" (v 8) or "let thorns grow instead of wheat, and foul weeds instead of barley" (v 40); (and if I have been guilty of any offence) "then let my wife grind for another, and let others bow down upon her" (v 10) or "then let my shoulder blade fall from my shoulder and let my arm be broken from its socket." (v 22) In saying things which are customarily left unsaid or at most concealed in the evasive oath-formula, the author of *Job* created a dramatic effect and asserted once and for all Job's innocence and his knowledge of this innocence.

In chapter 38 in the speeches of God there seems to be evidence of the misuse of forms. The genre of the God-speeches is a matter of dispute and an overall genre for them may not exist. Fohrer argues that at least three form-elements (catechetical questions of the wisdom teacher, controversy dialogues of the sages, and judicial examination) have been worked into the overall form of the divine addresses and that when one looks at the smaller genres that make up the speeches they appear to fall into two categories - nature wisdom and legal material. J G Williams[52] makes an interesting suggestion for the form of the God-speeches, proposing that:

"in the God-speeches we are confronted with a *riddle*, a riddle whose theme, in keeping with the dialogue, is irony. This is not only a riddle to us as interpreters but is intended as a

---

51   S H Blank, 1951 (p 107); cf M B Dick, 1983, who also provides a survey of oaths of innocence in the Old Testament and argues that in Job 31 the oath exhibits an affinity to the wisdom tradition.
52   J G Williams, 1971 (p 241).

riddle that Job hears, none of his questions is answered and no demand is placed directly upon him. He hears only a beautiful and glowing recital of the different cosmic forces and wild animals which all have one thing in common: he cannot control them."

This suggestion of a certain irony in these speeches could be developed further. They can perhaps be seen as a parody of set-piece interrogations about the cosmos such as are found in the prophets. For example, Isaiah 40:12-26 contains a series of questions asked by man about God's creative work which are meant to extol him and convey wonder at the greatness of his power and activity. In *Job* the speeches are *by* God and are designed to stop man's questioning by saying that God's ways are too mighty for him to understand. Fohrer argues that God uses legal terms here and in 40:2,8 to show Job the error of his ways and in 40:9-14 a hymn of praise is used as an ironic warning to man to know his proper place. This form is diverted from its proper function into a didactic use. There is an undertone of: who are you to question since you are nothing in the overall scheme of things? - eg 38:4-5: "Where were you when I laid the foundation of the earth? Tell me, if you have understanding. Who determined its measurements, - surely you know! Or who stretched the line upon it?" There is a strong note of sarcasm here. The form of man's praise of God as creator has been misused so that God himself is using it as a weapon to put Job's complaints into perspective. God has become the attacker and Job the defendant. This misuse outside the dialogue sections reinforces the idea that what God is saying is also unorthodox and it adds force to regarding the whole book as a sceptical work.

In conclusion, what was seen in chapter 1 to be true of the book of *Job* on grounds of *content*, is true also on the lower level of individual forms. On a cursory reading of *Job* one instinctively perceives Job as sceptical or unorthodox; maybe part of the reason is that one is unconsciously aware of the misuse of forms technique at work as well as instantly recognizing the forcefulness of Job's complaints against God as untraditional. For, by this technique traditional material is used in a new and radical way to convey a sceptical message. Notably it is what Job himself says that is really unorthodox in content, particularly on issues that are traditionally treated in wisdom and cultic circles, and this is matched by the forms which the author of *Job* uses in order to misuse them. This misuse of forms by the author of

*Job* can be seen as the way to his scepticism since awareness of the importance of the author and his techniques unlocks the door to other aspects of his scepticism as conveyed through the structure of the book (see chapter 4 section c)). It can also be seen as the key to the sceptical nature of *Job*. In the next section I shall look at the possibility of finding a pattern in the use of the technique which might provide a clue as to the extent of the original author's work. Then I shall discuss Ecclesiastes, the wisdom book generally aligned with *Job*, to assess its 'wisdom' element in comparison with *Job*, to see if techniques such as are found in *Job* are common in this other work of 'protest' literature from within the wisdom tradition. This will also help to evaluate whether such activity by authors is common in the Old Testament.

iii) A pattern in the misuse of forms

An interesting pattern can be found in the study of which parts of *Job* contain the misuse of forms. All the examples of misuse of forms in *Job* from within the dialogue section of the book, chapters 3-31, are found to be from the speeches of Job himself rather than from those of the friends, a pattern which may well have been deliberate on the part of the author. It is Job who is saying unorthodox things as regards content: why not also in form? The friends, on the other hand, are maintaining traditional wisdom positions and therefore use traditional forms. The only possible exceptions to this rule are 5:3-7, possibly 4:12-21, 22:15-16 and the occasional parody of what has already been said (eg 9:2-4). Job 5:3, spoken by Eliphaz, contains a typical wisdom form - a first person account as found in Psalm 37:25 - "I have been young, and now am old; yet I have not seen the righteous forsaken or his children begging bread" - or Proverbs 24:30: "I passed by the field of a sluggard, by the vineyard of a man without sense". But in Job 5:6-7 this typical wisdom form is spoilt by a sceptical ending, in a similar vein to Ecclesiastes: "For affliction does not come from the dust, nor does trouble sprout from the ground; but man is born to trouble as the sparks fly upward." Another possible misuse of a form is contained in 4:12-21, for the form here seems to be more like a prophetic or even apocalyptic vision whilst the content is more typical wisdom teaching. Wisdom is being put in an alien context.

This is not an example of a traditional form being used in a sceptical way but does show how this technique of misusing forms can be applied to other material. It does not however affect the argument here, that the misuse of forms in a sceptical way occurs only in Job's speeches themselves in the dialogue sections. A similar example is contained in Job 22:15-16 which is a wisdom saying put into a question form and thus transformed into a warning. The form is again being misused, but not in a sceptical way. Another is 19:23-27 in which the form is legal but the content is a 'confession of confidence' (Westermann[53]) typical of the psalms of lament. More sceptical are the occasional parodies within the book, for example Job 9:2-4 which is a parody of Eliphaz's statement in 4:17-21. This technique serves to highlight the way Job is able to twist what others have said and how the author misuses the forms they use. Eliphaz asks, "Can a mortal man be righteous before God? Can a man be pure before his Maker?" (4:17) and decides that God does not even trust his angels and servants fully; so how can man be free from error? Job parodies this by using the same question - "But how can a man be just before God?" (9:2b) - but twists its meaning to say that a man is not given the opportunity to be just before God because God makes himself inaccessible and is so great and mighty anyway that such an attempt would be futile: "If one wished to contend with him, one could not answer him once in a thousand times" (9:3).

These possible exceptions to the rule are not therefore of great consequence and certainly do not disprove the idea that a deliberate pattern in employing this 'misuse of forms' technique may be attributed to the author of the dialogue of *Job*. But why are only parts of the laments of Job 'misuses' of this sceptical kind? What about the rest of Job's speeches? Can we find any pattern in the type and subject matter of passages misused in this way? A study of such passages that contain misuses in the context of the whole leads to a possible general conclusion that this technique is only used in passages where Job is generalizing about life and man's lot and is not used in passages where he is simply describing his own condition; nor is it used in judicial parts nor in parts addressed to the friends; and finally it is not used in the two traditional

---

53  C Westermann, 1956 (1981).

accounts about the prosperity of the wicked in 21:1-22 and 24:1-17. No misuse of forms can be found in the sections that are generally seen by scholars as inauthentic in the mouth of Job (those which rightly belong in the arguments of the friends in the third round of speeches - eg Job 27:7-23). This might provide support for the idea that they are inauthentic. Whilst I have argued above for a possible misuse of forms in chapter 38, the technique cannot be found in sections which are often seen as later additions - for example the speeches of Elihu and the hymn to wisdom (chapter 28). This factor might provide support for arguments in favour of their being later additions (see discussion in chapter 4, pp 195-198).

iv) The reuse and misuse of forms in Ecclesiastes

In this section I shall discuss Ecclesiastes as a parallel to *Job*. I shall investigate whether similar techniques of form are being used in Ecclesiastes as in *Job* with the intention of conveying a radical message on the level of form as well as content. Ecclesiastes, like *Job*, can be divided up by working with various genre levels. The quest to find an overall genre for the book has been almost as fruitless as the search for an overall genre for *Job*. It has been likened to the Egyptian 'royal testaments' such as the Instruction for Merikare[54] and the Instruction of Amenemophet[55], but similarities in purpose and teaching between these works are not generally considered great enough for a definite genre classification of Ecclesiastes to be made. F Ellermeier[56] argues that Ecclesiastes can be designated a 'māšāl' in terms of genre. Ellermeier in fact deals mainly with 'sayings' and 'reflections' seeing these as the genres that are constitutive of the book, dividing the genre 'reflection' into 'unified' and 'broken'. R Braun[57] moves away from the quest for one overall genre and isolates three basic genres in Ecclesiastes - meditative reflection (betrachtende Reflexion), meditation (Betrachtung) and instruction (Belehrung). He often makes comparisons of Ecclesiastes with Greek diatribe

---

54 J B Pritchard, 1950, pp 414-418.
55 J B Pritchard, 1950, pp 418-419.
56 F Ellermeier, 1967, p 49.
57 R Braun, 1973.

which suggests that he sees this as a possible overall genre for the book. As Murphy[58] writes:

"In conclusion, one may say that no single genre, even diatribe, is adequate as a characterization for *Qoheleth's* book. This seems due to the fact that it is the publication of his teachings, which would have embraced many different genres of writing."

There has been more success in recognizing various subgenres for Ecclesiastes than in recognizing an overall genre. Such subgenres fit my classification 'smaller genres'. Three principal smaller genres emerge from a study of the book. The first is the wisdom saying which abounds, for example, in chapters 7 and 9:17f. Chapter 7 contains a collection of seven wisdom sayings about 'good' (7:1-12). Verses 1-6 follow the pattern of traditional wisdom sayings such as are found in Proverbs (eg Proverbs 12). However the positive nature of the wisdom in these verses is nullified in verse 7 when the author makes the adverse verdict that "this also is vanity". Verses 8-12 however continue in traditional wisdom style, the verses culminating in praise of wisdom (7:11-12). Qoheleth shows by his interpolation in verse 7 that he sees wisdom as a worthless exercise in that man gains no achievement by his effort. In this sentiment in this verse he is showing a scepticism which is at odds with wisdom books such as Proverbs. Here the author uses a traditional wisdom form and then shows its shortcomings by a remark of his own.

The second main smaller genre is the instruction. The rest of chapter 7 (7:13-14) provides a short example of this. Commands and prohibitions are the main components of this genre. Thus in verse 13a there is a command to reflect on the work of God. In verse 13b man's impotence before the work of God is expressed in a rhetorical question and verse 14 contains commands to accept the good and evil day, and make the best of them. These instruction passages tend to follow traditional wisdom forms. They provide a comment upon the various sayings and prohibitions; for example in chapter 7 the 'instruction' found in verses 13-14, in commenting upon verses 1-12, provides the overall genre for the whole chapter.

---

58   R Murphy, 1981 (p 131).

When the author wants to make some comment of his own he uses the third main smaller genre, that of 'reflection'. This genre is a characteristic of Ecclesiastes alone (the other 'smaller genres' above also characterize other wisdom books). The genre 'reflection' refers to texts containing observation and thought, and incorporates within it several subgenres such as sayings or proverbs (eg 2:14; 4:5-6), rhetorical questions (eg 2:2,12,15,19,22,25) and quotations (see below) - all subgenres from the wisdom tradition. This genre 'reflection' both includes traditional wisdom elements and provides room for Qoheleth's own remarks which give the book its distinctiveness. This is Qoheleth's new contribution. He changes the nature of reflection, creating a new style within a traditional one. Qoheleth uses subgenres within the reflection genre, such as the quotation, in order to contradict them in the following line (eg 8:12-13 is negated by the framework in verses 11-14); or else he simply contrasts two proverbs, thus throwing up inconsistencies within the wisdom tradition itself (eg 4:5-6). Alternatively he may quote a proverb to support an argument (5:3) or to provide a text for further commentary (eg 4:9 is commented on in 4:10-12). Elsewhere Qoheleth narrates a tale to make, for instance, an 'example story' in 9:13-16. He uses the traditional form of the example story (see Proverbs 7:6-12; 24:30-34) within his own argument which in content departs from traditional wisdom. He also uses the smaller genres of woe oracle (2:16; 4:10; 10:16) and blessing (10:17) in his passages of reflection.

Much of Qoheleth's protesting nature comes therefore from the unusual features of his own style in which forms are placed in a new context, a technique perhaps best described as a reuse of forms since the content of the forms remains the same (both content and context have to be changed to constitute a *misuse* of forms). Repetition of phrases such as 'pursuit after wind', 'under the sun', and 'eat and drink' and repetition of favourite words such as vanity, do/deed, wise/wisdom, good, time, etc are a main characteristic of this author's style alongside his reflective interpolations, are are the 'yes, but' passages recognized principally by Hertzberg[59]. This is the

---

[59] H Hertzberg, 1963, p 30. cf W Zimmerli, 1962, p 130, and R Kroeber, 1963, p 37. F Ellermeier, 1967, pp 125-238, however denies that this technique exists in Ecclesiastes.

technique by which one statement modifies another without simply contradicting it: for example in 3:17 there is an affirmation of divine justice which follows the statement of the existence of injustice in 3:16. Again in 8:11-12a Qoheleth remarks that the sinner survives but in 8:12b-13 states that it will be well for the God-fearer but otherwise for the wicked.

Other literary techniques in Ecclesiastes include the use of quotations[60] and recognition of polar structures. Gordis finds four methods of the use of quotations in Ecclesiastes. First, there is the straightforward use of proverbial quotations cited to reinforce an argument which is accepted by the writer as true, eg 10:18; 11:1. Secondly, proverbs are also used to reinforce his argument - part of the proverb will be apposite whilst the rest of the saying, though irrelevant, is quoted for the sake of completeness, eg 5:1-2; 11:3-4. Proverbial quotations are used as a text on which the author comments from his own viewpoint, eg 7:1-14; 4:9-12; 5:9-12; 8:2-4 etc. Finally contrasting proverbs are used to contravene accepted doctrines, as in *Job*. Each author uses this device for his own purpose by quoting one proverb and then registering his disagreement by citing another diametrically opposed to it, eg Ecclesiastes 4:5-6; 9:16,18. The proverbs in which the author of Ecclesiastes states his own view are thought to be his own composition whilst the ones apparently quoted may be genuine quotations, or may be original restatements by the author of conventional wisdom doctrines.

The work of J A Loader[61] is devoted to the phenomenon of polarization in Ecclesiastes. Polar structures are "patterns of tension created by the counterposition of two elements to one another"[62] - the term 'polar structure' refers to a 'thought pattern' or 'structure of contents' and is not to be confused

---

60 R Gordis, 'Quotations as a Literary Usage in Biblical, Oriental and Rabbinic Literature', 1949 and R Gordis, 1951, pp 95-101. Gordis proposes that Qoheleth quotes 'old wisdom'. He also finds quotations used in wisdom, in some psalms and in the prophets. R N Whybray, 1981, examines Gordis' hypothesis and isolates eight quotations from earlier wisdom (2:14a; 4:5,6; 7:5,6a; 9:17; 10:2,12) which agree in form and content with proverbs. He argues that these citations were not used to be refuted but to be enlisted as support for Qoheleth's own judgements. Some he quoted because he agreed with their sentiments (7:5-6; 10:2,12) but wished to give them a radically new interpretation. Others he used to confirm the first stage in a two-part argument in which he first posited a truth and then qualified it.

61 J A Loader, 1979. See discussion in J Barton, 1984, pp 130-131.

62 J A Loader, 1979 (p 1).

with the formal structure of the literary units in the book. This technique involves looking at the form of the individual pericopes to find typical forms or structures of individual units. Loader points out that the forms constitute the framework within which the contents or thought-structures function. He sees Ecclesiastes as made of up a number of well-structured pericopes. The author is regarded as constantly counterpoising poles to each other and creating tension by their opposition. Opposing themes such as 'toil and joy' (9:3-7), 'talk and silence' (5:2-7), 'the worth and worthlessness of wisdom' (1:12-2:26) are discussed by the author in passages structured in such a way as to highlight the tension. The figures of style in the book are mainly typical of general wisdom literature although some, Loader argues, have their origin in Hellenistic literature - what is original is the way in which the author "takes over current forms to serve his own purpose."[63]

Many of the typical literary forms to be found in chokmatic literature are used in the book but as part of new structural units, eg 11:1-6. Loader argues that a polar tension may be found in the book between the use of typical forms from wisdom literature (itself a polar relation between the author and wisdom literature) and the use of literary units peculiar to Qoheleth, such as the *Gattung* of the reflection. This exists alongside the polar tension between form and contents. Loader writes:

*"Qoheleth time and time again makes these chokmatic elements function in opposition to general ḥokmā. This is evidence of a formal solidarity with general wisdom - so to speak - and a polemical opposition to general wisdom in the contents."*[64]

Loader then notes that "we often find typical chokmatic proverbs *with chokmatic contents and all.*"[65] He argues that Ecclesiastes' place as wisdom literature is where real wisdom protests against a rigidity foreign to reality:

*"Qoheleth is not merely a hakam with deeper vision than others and he does not practice Lebenskunde as the older wisdom, but he protests."*[66]

Loader argues that polar structures in Qoheleth are fundamental since they occur in almost every passage of the book - polar patterns feature in the form

---

63  J A Loader, 1979 (p 115).
64  J A Loader, 1979 (p 115).
65  J A Loader, 1979 (p 115).
66  J A Loader, 1979 (p 3).

and polar relations exist between form and contents. Qoheleth is not merely a borrower but his borrowing has a specific purpose, viz the polarization of his own view and that of the lending source. Loader concludes:[67]

*"The tension in the contents of the book and between the contents and formal aspects testify to the tension between the views of Qoheleth and those of the general ḥokmā.."*

Thus Qoheleth stands in solidarity with general hokma - he uses its forms and often repeats its types, yet, on the other hand, he is critical of wisdom. Loader writes:[68]

"Reality, as it were, attacks the dogma but does so with the weapons of dogma."

Loader is not the only scholar to have noticed the use of traditional religious vocabulary to express an unconventional world view[69] but he expresses himself more specifically in terms of forms and content and their interrelationship than most other scholars.

This analysis of a specific literary technique by the author of Ecclesiastes demonstrates the importance of techniques concerning form, content and structure and can be seen to be related to my own analysis of *Job* (see chapter 4 section c) on the structure of *Job*). The relationship of Ecclesiastes to wisdom in terms of form and content is also instructive, although in its predominant use of wisdom genres, Ecclesiastes can perhaps be seen to stand closer to the mainline wisdom tradition, despite clearly providing a critique of it. Furthermore Loader's second form/content category resembles in part the 'misuse of forms' technique found in *Job* in that he notes the way that forms can be filled with a surprising content. This also suggests a relationship between types of literary technique used in sceptical literature.

Thus the author of Ecclesiastes is free in using his own stylistic features to convey his own thought concerning traditional wisdom issues. He uses forms predominantly from the wisdom tradition and does not depart from it to the same extent as *Job* does. The form and content are often merely reused in a new context which leads to a change in their meaning. Much of the content of his book is unorthodox and questions accepted values although other parts

---

67  J A Loader, 1979 (p 116).
68  J A Loader, 1979 (p 130).
69  R Gordis, 1951.

remain more traditional - for example 9:13-10:15, which is a collection of wisdom sayings. In 9:13-16 an example story is told which closely resembles example stories in Proverbs (eg 21:22). The moral of the story is given in the quotation of a wisdom saying in verse 16a, but then the author gives his own modification of the saying in the light of the reality exemplified in the story. He 'spoils' the form of example story by adding his own viewpoint to the end of it and shows that he is not altogether following the traditional wisdom line. Again in 9:17-10:1 the author uses traditional sayings about wisdom. In verses 17-18a he is in favour of wisdom; but in 9:18b-10:1 he modifies the advantages of wisdom by using a saying about the sinner, which is in opposition to the saying in verse 18a, and by using a proverb about dead flies and a little wisdom. Here the author is putting different wisdom sayings together to highlight the contradiction between them.

Later in chapter 10 other traditional wisdom themes are used, though usually they are used by the author as part of a wider context, given to them by his comments and stylistic devices. Thus 10:2-3 contains sayings about the wise use of one's ability. Verses 12-15 on the other hand contain sayings about the fool, and in verse 15 the author adds his own comment on the futility of the fool's toil, thus underlining the uncertainty of life. In 9:13-10:15, therefore, the wisdom sayings in both form and content are put in a wider context which says that there is no profit for man in his achievements in this life, for all is vanity. R E Murphy[70] recognizes the mixture of traditional and untraditional in Qoheleth when he writes:

"This work is clearly at odds with the views of traditional wisdom teaching, especially the doctrine of retribution... This negative stance should not be allowed to conceal certain important emphases: the insistence upon God's transcendence and sovereignty, and upon the task of man to meet the present as it is, as it comes from the hand of God, with joy."

A closer look at a few chapters will illustrate the way Qoheleth deals with wisdom material and will show where his technique parallels and yet differs from that found in *Job*. Chapter 1 begins with a superscription. The title, "words of..." is paralleled in other wisdom books, for example in Proverbs 22:17; 30:1 and 31:1, and it is comparable to introductions in Egyptian

---

70 R E Murphy, 1981 (p 131).

instructions, for example, the Instruction of Ptahhotep.[71] The identification of Qoheleth as "son of David, king in Jerusalem" (1:1) is in accordance with the tradition of ascribing wisdom books to Solomon as in Proverbs and the Wisdom of Solomon. Ecclesiastes 1:2 contains a saying emphasizing the motto "vanity of vanities" which recurs throughout the book. The author here sets the tone of the book in a stylistic feature of his own. This is followed by a reflection about human toil in 1:3-11 which is clearly the author's own work - a thesis is stated (that there is no profit in man's toil) which is then illustrated in verses about the absence of any progress in natural phenomena. The author uses the form of a poem here and then justifies it by a prose comment in verses 9-11 which states that nothing is new, and there is simply no remembrance of what has been. The poem and commentary contain an analysis of life that is characteristic of a wisdom teacher (eg in the examples drawn from the world of nature). Ecclesiastes 1:12-18 contains another reflection characteristic of the style of the author. The author makes statements here and then quotes traditional proverbs in support of his statement. He uses proverbs in a new context in order to criticize wisdom and introduce the theme of the bankruptcy of wisdom: "For in much wisdom is much vexation, and he who increases knowledge increases sorrow." (1:18)

Another chapter containing many examples of the author's original treatment of his material is Ecclesiastes 5:1-20 (Hebrew 4:17-5:19). In this chapter the author uses two instruction genres and follows them by a reflection. In the two instructions many traditional wisdom genres are used, such as the command, the comparative saying, the prohibition, the quotation of a proverb, a 'better' saying and a rhetorical question. In the reflection three wisdom sayings are cited but with a "this is vanity" addition in verse 10b. These are followed by an example story about the uncertainty of riches for all one's toil which leads Qoheleth to his own conclusion about enjoying toil and life as a gift of God. Then there is a second example story about the uncertainty of possessions followed again by a conclusion about toil and desire in which a wisdom saying about human appetite and two rhetorical questions relative to the wise and the poor are apparent. There is a 'better' saying about desire

---

71   J B Pritchard, 1950, pp 412-414.

(a favourite stylistic device of this author) and a reiteration of the phrase, "vanity and a striving after wind." Wisdom forms are used throughout the chapter and are left in their traditional form, though the context in which the author puts them presents them in an untraditional light and, accompanied by Qoheleth's clever stylistic techniques, provides a sceptical strain. Qoheleth thus uncovers the weaknesses and inconsistencies of the wisdom tradition by the 'reuse' and 'misuse' of its own forms.

A final example is chapter 8 which uses much traditional wisdom, showing clearly Qoheleth's own reflection on wisdom and the methods he adopts. The chapter opens with an instruction concerning the relationship between man and the king, a common theme in wisdom (cf Ecclesiastes 10:4; Proverbs 14:35; 20:2). This is followed by three reflections. The first is a reflection upon time and judgement. In verses 5-6a there is a quotation of wisdom sayings and in 6b-8 a counterstatement to these sayings by the author. This is followed by a reflection on injustice in verses 9-15 which is evidence of Qoheleth's own views on the issue. This is a genre which allows room for both the citation of traditional sayings and comment upon them. In verses 12b-13 traditional wisdom about God's judgement upon the God-fearer and the evil man is to be found. This is however closely followed by a 'yes, but' statement modifying verses 12b-13 by giving two examples of vanity. Finally in verses 16-17 Qoheleth reflects on man's inability to know the 'doing' of God. These reflections provide examples of the 'new' scepticism found in Qoheleth's thought, but it is the content that is new, not the form. Where traditional forms are used they are put into a context of reflective thinking which changes their nature. The three reflections in this chapter are at one in agreeing about the absence of justice and (divine) judgement in the affairs of the world and man's impotence in dealing with these things.

This survey of Ecclesiastes makes it clear that there is a use of forms similar to that found in *Job*, often merely a 'reuse' but at times a 'misuse' of forms. It shows that there are significant similarities in the literary techniques used by authors who wish to question tradition - that is, the use of an existing tradition to criticize it in a radical way. It also confirms that it is legitimate to posit the use of such literary techniques by biblical authors. In using almost exclusively wisdom forms, the author of Ecclesiastes remains much closer to mainline wisdom than the author of *Job* does. Ecclesiastes stands at the end of the biblical wisdom tradition and the author uses the characteristic forms and genres of that tradition in order to criticize it. *Job* does this too but its author does not only employ wisdom forms. The scepticism of the author of Ecclesiastes is often expressed in reflective passages which show up the weaknesses of wisdom by providing traditional material with a new context. This study supports the conclusion already reached by the traditional route of historical study of the wisdom literature that Ecclesiastes represents a protesting or sceptical strain which arises closely out of the wisdom exercise whereas *Job* is on the sidelines of that tradition. The protesting elements of *Job* have been seen to be characterized by the misuse of forms technique. In a similar way the author of Ecclesiastes conveys his protest by his use of form. Thus, as well as providing an interesting parallel to *Job*, the argument for the classification of Ecclesiastes as protest literature of a profound kind is strengthened. The alignment of the two books as protest literature of a radical nature is more informative than their traditional alignment as 'wisdom literature'.

### b) A NEW OVERALL GENRE FOR JOB, THE PARODY

It was decided at the end of chapter 2 that *Job* is either a disparate collection of various genres or it is *'sui generis'* and cannot be categorized in terms of genre. The change in opinion about the genre of *Job* between C Westermann[72] and N C Habel[73] noted in that chapter was the result of a corresponding change in method - from searching for a single genre to classify the book to a realization that more than one genre is to be found in *Job* and that a single genre fails to do justice to the whole. However to posit an amalgamation of genres is really leading back in a full circle to older scholars who saw no possibility of classifying *Job* within the confines of a narrow literary term. This suggested that the quest for a genre in terms of literary

---

72 C Westermann, 1956 (1981).
73 N C Habel, 1985.

classification has failed to find the key to the overall interpretation of *Job* on the level of form. A new way of looking at the problem is required.

All that has been said by scholars so far on the question of overall genre should not in any way be seen as invalid but a new dimension can perhaps be found in the suggestion that *Job* indeed does not belong to a genre EXCEPT IMPROPERLY. In other words, in *Job* we are seeing by the author a deliberate IMPROPER USE OF GENRE to convey on the level of form what is already conveyed in the content, namely the radical scepticism of the book. The author is here deliberately stepping outside literary conventions to make a protest. My suggestion is that the whole book is characterized by a deliberate *misuse*, or improper use, of genre. In the same way that the *misuse* of smaller genres conveys a sceptical message on a more detailed level, the overall genre of the book is one which misuses various genres in order to enhance this impression. When discussing smaller genres in *Job* above we often used the word 'parody' to describe the misuse of forms technique. An example of this is the parody of Psalm 8 in Job 7:11-21 and the parodies in 9:5-10; 9:25-28 and 10:8-12 (a parody of Psalm 139). Job 14:1-12, like 7:11-21, also parodies Psalm 8; and 21:7-13 parodies a wisdom poem which would originally and properly have described the punishment of the wicked but here presents the prosperity of the wicked. Job 23:8-9 is a clear parody of a hymn such as Psalm 23.

Of modern literary genres, the parody is the one which is parasitic on other genres and uses any genre for its own purposes. It is not a normal genre because its very existence depends on the presence of other 'proper' genres which it can use, or more precisely *misuse*; for another characteristic of parody is that it uses other genres in such a way that it mocks the original genre. Parody is 'improper' in that it is not the name of a genre in the generally accepted sense but is the name of a parasitic element that can use any genre.

i) Definitions of parody

Modern literary definitions of parody vary in some degree from the way I wish to use it in relation to *Job*, in that there is a comic element which has existed in parody from early times. However it will be seen below that it is not at the heart of the meaning of the word. In recent centuries the parody as a tool of comedy has become dominant to such an extent that many modern literary definitions see this as fundamental to the definition of the genre. For example T R Frosch[74] sees the comic element as parody's major characteristic:

> "Parody as we ordinarily understand it, is an imitation of a writer's manner done so as to extract humour from the original."

He acknowledges however that parody can operate as "a tool of serious criticism, exposure, correction"[75] (for example in *The Pooh Perplex* by F Crews[76]) but sees the "impulse to parody" as a "comic tendency"[77] This definition of parody is clearly not applicable to *Job* which, whilst sceptical and ironic, is not 'comic' in the humorous sense - not even J W Whedbee[78], who argues that *Job* is a comedy would argue that it was a comedy in this sense. An examination of the meaning of 'parody' shows that this comic element does not fully describe its true nature. The *Oxford English Dictionary*[79] defines parody as:

> "A composition in prose or verse in which the characteristic turns of thought and phrase in an author or class of authors are imitated in such a way as to make them appear ridiculous, especially by applying them to ludicrously inappropriate subjects, an imitation of a work more or less closely modelled on the original, but so turned as to produce a ridiculous effect."

A *Dictionary of literary terms*[80] says:

> "A parody (from the Greek 'counter-song') is a literary composition that imitates the style of another work. Although it amuses us it need not make us devalue the original."

Dr Johnson[81] perhaps comes closest to a purer definition of parody when he defines it as:

> "a kind of writing in which the words of an author or his thoughts are taken and by a slight change adapted to some new purpose."

---

74 T R Frosch, 1973 (p 372).
75 T R Frosch, 1973 (p 373).
76 F Crews, 1963.
77 T R Frosch, 1973 (p 371).
78 J W Whedbee, 1977.
79 *OED*, s.v. 'parody'.
80 S Barnet, M Berman, W Burbo, 1964.
81 S Johnson, 1755, s.v. 'parody'. D MacDonald, 1960, calls Johnson's definition "imprecise and incomplete" (p 557).

Finally, D MacDonald[82] makes some useful points about parody, for example, "that it concentrates on the style and thought of the original" and that "at its best, it is a form of literary criticism."[83] He contrasts parody with "its poor relations" travesty and burlesque and comments:

"If burlesque is pouring new wine into old bottles, parody is making a new wine that tastes like the old but has a slightly lethal effect."[84]

I will look briefly here at a few early examples of parodies, to show that comedy is not the key characteristic of this genre and that a basic definition of parody needs to be more general, as Dr Johnson's is. Then I will judge whether the category of 'parody' is useful in application to *Job*. D MacDonald writes of parody that it:

"seems not to have appealed to the ancient Hebrews or the early Christians; at least there is no trace of it in either the Old or New Testament."[85]

I wish to show that this is not the case.

Information on early parodies is sparse. The literary form which gave us the word was the *parodia* of Athenian drama. This was contained in a satyr play which took place after a tragedy and was performed by the same actors wearing grotesque costumes. The only surviving examples are the *Cyclops* of Euripides[86] and *Ichneutai* attributed to Sophocles[87]. The most celebrated was the *Gigantomachia*.[88] The first 'true' parodist is generally seen as Aristophanes[89] who imitates Aeschylus, Euripides and Socrates in a satirical way in such comedies as *The Frogs, The Birds, The Acharnians* and *The Clouds*.[90] In *The Clouds* Socrates is presented as saying and doing many laughable things. In *The Frogs* Euripides is discomfited by Dionysus' use of

---

82  D MacDonald (ed.), 1960.
83  D MacDonald (ed.), 1960 (p 559).
84  D MacDonald (ed.), 1960 (p 559).
85  D MacDonald (ed.), 1960 (p 562).
86  Euripides, *Cyclops*, ed W Buhl, 1983; R Seaford, 1984.
87  Sophocles, *Ichneutai* - Only fragments of this play still exist. First published by Hunt and Wilanowitz, *Oxyrhynchus Papyri*, volume 9, 1912. See R J Carden, 1974.
88  No longer extant.
89  F H Sandbach, 1977, argues that Aristophanes' parodying of contemporary tragedy is largely guesswork since the original has not been preserved.
90  Aristophanes' works in B B Rogers, 1902.

lines which he had himself written. For example lines 1471 and 1475 distort verses from Euripides' plays:

Dionysus: 1471: "My tongue is sworn - but I'll choose Aeschylus."
["My tongue is sworn - my mind did never swear." Euripides]
1475: "What's shameful, if the audience think not so?"
["What's shameful, if the doers think not so." Euripides][91]

Aristophanes criticizes the philosophy of the characters he parodies as well as their manner whereas earlier burlesques only satirized the manner of certain writers, for example in the *Batrachomyomachia*[92] he treats frogs and mice as if they were Homeric heroes and describes them in an elevated style imitating Homer. Aristophanes is probably the first parodist where the comic element begins to predominate and at this early stage there is little distinction in this area between the parody and the burlesque. Parody, unlike burlesque, is necessarily a late form in that it needs something existing to work on - this is inherent in its parasitic nature. K J Dover[93] discusses the parodies of Aristophanes and finds two purposes contained within parody, a distinction which assists the attempt to assign a serious work such as *Job* to such a genre since it separates the humorous element from the primary element of parody. He writes:

"Parody has two quite distinct purposes, which may be realized simultaneously but can also be realized in isolation from each other. One purpose is to hold up the serious poetry itself to criticism and ridicule; parody suggests, by selection and exaggeration... The second, and commoner purpose of parody is to exploit the humorous potentialities of incongruity by combining high-flown tragic diction and allusions to well-known tragic situations with vulgarity or trivial domestic predicaments."[94]

Chaucer can be accredited with a mediaeval parody which was written at the end, rather than at the beginning of a culture - *The Tale of Sir Thopas*.[95] His

---

91 Aristophanes, *Frogs* (405 BC) in W B Stanford, 1903.
92 For a recent edition of the *Batrachomyomachia*, see R Glei, 1984.
93 K J Dover, 1972.
94 K J Dover, 1972 (p 73).
95 F N Robinson, 1974, pp 164-167. An example of the parody at work is provided in lines 712-717:
"Listeth, lordes in good entent,
And I wol telle verrayment
Of myrthe and of solas,
Al of a knyght was fair and gent

mastery of form in this mock romance is shown in his use of the tail-rhyme stanza (which he uses nowhere else), the favourite form of the popular poets at the time. He parodies both the form and the content of the English romances of his day, for example, the romances of Bevis of Hampton and Guy of Warwick (whom he even mentions in the tale itself). Sir Thopas can be appreciated fully only by a reader thoroughly familiar with the clichés of popular romance. Even the Host who interrupts the story in the Tales fails to see the point of this brilliant parody. It is "a parody of the romances which gains its effect by exaggerating their already incredible events and descriptions."[96]

The distinction between serious and comic parody is perhaps not to be taken too far, for parody is often very much a product of its time and can only be appreciated fully by those who realize what is being parodied. Thus the distinction between what is serious and what is funny becomes very subjective - what to eighteenth century listeners might have been comic may not seem to us to have much satirical value, for example the parodies of H Fielding.[97] The point is that the definition of parody should not necessarily have to contain comedy - a mild 'irony' or 'scepticism' is all that is required. Its keynote is the way in which it uses existing material in order to show up the weaknesses of that material, on the level of form as well as content.

Could parody, as an already existing classification, be used to explain what is happening in *Job* in relation to known literary techniques? The basic meaning of parody applies to *Job* in that the well-known forms of a number of traditions are being 'parodied' by the author by giving them a new content and context. The author is using parody as a technique to create a certain 'ironic' or 'sceptical' effect (see argument in chapter 4). 'Parody' can perhaps therefore be used as a useful overall classification for *Job* in terms of genre.

---

       In bataille and in tourneyment,
       His name was sire Thopas."
Certain features highlight the parody: eg, the appeal to 'lordes' would probably have been seen as a vulgar address amongst Chaucer's contemporaries. 'Thopas' is itself a fanciful name and the prefacing of a knight's name with the title 'Sir' is regarded by Chaucer and his French contemporaries as a vulgarism. He overuses the term in this tale, extending its use even to the enemy giant 'Sir Olifaunt'.

96  M W Bloomfield, 1986 (p 187).
97  eg Henry Fielding, *The Tragedy of Tragedies or The Life and Death of Tom Thumb the Great*, 1931. This parody depends on incongruities for its effect.

Furthermore I shall argue that it is possible to regard the entire book of *Job* as a parody of the folk tale since a new content is given to a traditional tale thereby spoiling the original and 'parodying' the original form (see chapter 4).

Finally I wish to focus on the use of parody by the author of *Job*, which is distinctive because it evolved within Hebrew culture. This kind of parody is a literary technique which developed outside 'wisdom' and outside the influence of Egyptian literature (in which parody is not found). It is not dependent on parodies from other cultures nor are they dependent on it. Elements of parody with which to compare this technique in *Job* can be found in another protesting work - the book of *Jonah*, which I shall discuss in the next section.

Thus parody as a description of what is happening in *Job* on the level of form is a valid and useful classification to use, even though *Job* does not fit all the modern requirements of a definition of parody. A definite procedure can be seen to have been at work on the level of form with implications for the content and context of the book. Therefore in the improper genre called 'parody' we have the key to the improper use of forms by the author of *Job*. It is also a suitable genre classification to provide a solution to the issue of overall genre, if indeed parody is considered to be a genre at all. Parody is an improper genre but it provides the clue to an 'overall genre' in a new sense with attention being paid to the possibility of *use* by an author, rather than just *classification* when making genre judgements.

ii) Parody in *Jonah*[98]

"Biblical scholars have had as much difficulty digesting Jonah's song as the great fish had with Jonah."[99]

The book of *Jonah* can be classified as a 'parody' in terms of genre since it satirizes and parodies the prophetic tradition with much use of irony and innuendo. It was produced at a time when prophecy was on the wane. Prophecy is often seen to have failed and B Vawter[100] argues that Jonah is not only a failed prophet but has become for the author of the book "almost a

---

98  As with Job/*Job*, Jonah refers to the character, *Jonah* to the book.
99  J S Ackerman, 1981 (p 213).
100 B Vawter, 1983 (p 98).

buffoon of prophecy." The author's intention is important in *Jonah* and Vawter lays an emphasis on this. The song of Jonah in 2:3-10 is often thought to be an existing psalm appropriated by the author,[101] but Vawter argues for its originality to the author. Vawter argues that the author appropriated for his own purpose this pastiche of psalmic verses which is unrelated to the historical character of the prophet Jonah. These verses are important for discerning what this author thought were valuable spiritual insights. Vawter argues that whilst Jonah's lament has no real point (and this is not the Jonah of the rest of the book), chapter 2 is "an integral part of the author's sardonic reflection on a still venerated institution of the irrecoverable past which had sadly failed its mission."[102] Vawter sees the author of *Jonah* deliberately setting forth the incongruity of a dutiful prophet, ordained by destiny to do what he is inspired to do, but refusing the mission - an action totally out of character for the prophets (compare the anguish to Jeremiah caused by God's call to him).[103]

J S Ackerman[104] sees the song of Jonah as providing the key to the genre of the book. He argues that it plays an important part in the story as a whole:

"it establishes major dissonances between the prophet's perception of reality and that of his narrative world. These dissonances...are set in the context of the bizarre and unexpected. Thus, they move the entire work in the direction of satire and compel an ironic reading throughout."[105]

The song performs two functions. It helps to establish a genre, that of satire, through which to understand the story. It is also "the crucial vortex into and out of which all of the story's main images move, helping us to integrate and properly interpret the symbolism with which the work abounds."[106] The prose narrative provides unexpected amusement by showing us a protagonist who is consistently out of step with his surroundings. Jonah's actions and speeches are caricatures of the prophetic tradition and, Ackerman argues, the result is a farce.

---

101 eg E M Good, 1965, who argues that it is an interpolated psalm which produces an ironic effect, but not intentionally on the part of the author or glossator who inserted it.
102 B Vawter, 1983 (p 101).
103 E M Good, 1965, also points out that in 1:2 there is incongruity in "a prophet's unhesitating and total abandonment of his prophetic task" (p 42).
104 J S Ackerman, 1981.
105 J S Ackerman, 1981 (p 216).
106 J S Ackerman, 1981 (p 217).

Ackerman makes some general comments about the importance of context in determining meaning which relate to my findings in this monograph. He argues that the location in which a song is sung is important:

"Context helps us evaluate analyses which conclude that a song is not an original part of the setting because its language is more archaic or because it represents a later corruption of a particular genre."[107]

Stylized, archaic language may well occur in Jonah's song. Ackerman writes:

"May we not also assume that the broken genre, jolting us with its unexpected pattern and unusual setting, reflects conscious literary artistry?"[108]

Furthermore "context helps us determine the sometimes obscure line between genuine religious devotion and its parody."[109] He quotes G Highet who points out that:

"some of the best material parodies are those which might, by the unwary, be accepted as the genuine work of the...style parodied."[110]

He cites as a biblical example of parody, an example only discernible by its context, Hosea 6:1-3, and writes of this passage:

"How are we to interpret it? Is the prophet urging Israel to return to YHWH? Is it a repentance liturgy of the people, expressing faith in God's healing power and willingness to restore the relationship once they return? The context gives us the interpretation. The prayer is hypothetical, placed by YHWH in the people's mouths (5:15); and in 6:4-6 we see YHWH's response to it: 'What shall I do with you, O Ephraim...your love is like a morning cloud, like the dew that goes early away...' The repentance liturgy of the people, we see, is heavily ironic. YHWH is exasperated by it because Israel perceives her god as a vegetation deity whose return is as sure as the spring rains - not dependent on Israel's return to and respect for covenant law. Biblical literature is also capable of highly sophisticated irony which, taken out of context, can be missed entirely."[111]

Ackerman lists verbal and dramatic ironies and decides that the song of Jonah is a satire. He writes:

"The song develops the story's satiric elements forcing us to judge the prophet's perception of reality as illusory...The ironic mode in which the satire is presented invites us to laugh at

---

107 J S Ackerman, 1981 (p 218).
108 J S Ackerman, 1981 (p 218).
109 J S Ackerman, 1981 (p 218).
110 G Highet, 1962 (p 72).
111 J S Ackerman, 1981 (p 220).

the prophet's erratic behavior while acknowledging in ourselves the impulses that motivate such behavior."[112]

Therefore it can be seen that the song of Jonah provides a starting point for regarding the whole book as imbued with irony. E M Good[113] argues that the entire book of *Jonah* is a satire which is ironic through and through since it portrays the prophet and highlights his attitude in relation to God's in order to ridicule him. He notes that even the phrase 'son of Amittai' is ironic, translating it 'son of faithfulness or truth' and pointing out that Jonah "abandons his faithfulness at the first opportunity and speaks truth only under duress, even then not understanding it."[114] It is clear that a knowledge of what usually happens to prophets in the Old Testament highlights the incongruities in the book. The author of *Jonah*, standing at the end of prophecy, is able to use this technique of irony to great effect. Jonah's effort to escape God's presence on the sea contrasts with passages where a storm on the sea is a sign of divine presence rather than absence (eg Psalm 29; 77:16f; 97:2-5; 107:23f; 148:7-8); there is incongruity between Jonah's confession of Yahweh as creator of the sea and his attempt to escape; Jonah's offering of himself as a sacrifice contrasts with his unwillingness to proclaim the word to Nineveh; the repentance of the people of Nineveh is exaggerated by the author so as to contrast with the reluctance of Jonah - his success and his unexpected reaction are ironic; finally, the Ninevites are presented as appearing to understand more about the divine grace than Jonah does. The irony comes to a climax when God repents and Jonah is vexed with God. Good argues that Jonah mouths a liturgical cliché - "He speaks the pious and well-worn words but he thoroughly disapproves of their being true."[115] The wish for death is phrased in words similar to Elijah in I Kings 19:4 but whilst Elijah is in despair over his failure to turn the hearts of idolatrous Israel, Jonah's despair is caused by vexation at God's forgiveness of pagan Nineveh. Good writes, "his sullen death wish is surely a parody of Elijah's profound

---

112 J S Ackerman, 1981 (p 244).
113 E M Good, 1965.
114 E M Good, 1965 (p 42).
115 E M Good, 1965 (p 50).

discouragement."[116] God makes Jonah look absurd in the incident of the castor oil plant. Jonah, in his desperation, wishes for death and Yahweh corners him. Good concludes that the author's purpose was "to expose absurdity by the irony of satire. Like all ironists, he took his stand upon an ultimately serious truth."[117] Good's interpretation clearly rests largely on his own interpretation of the message of the book of *Jonah* and the juxtaposition of its various parts. However the work of the scholars discussed in this section is of value in showing how an author can be seen using the techniques of irony and parody to convey his message (These techniques are closely interrelated in *Job* ).

In conclusion, *Jonah* appears to mock the forms of the prophetic tradition in a similar way to *Job*'s misuse of the forms of the wisdom, legal and psalmic traditions. *Jonah* stands at the end of prophecy and so parodies its traditional forms and content by using them in a new context. Parody can thus be seen as a valid classification for the literary techniques employed by biblical authors who are trying to make a protest on the level of form as well as content by using genre in a new way. Irony, an important tool for conveying 'scepticism', is also fundamental to an understanding of *Jonah* and indeed of *Job*, as I shall argue in chapter 4. It is asserted by S R Hopper[118] that irony directed at one's own culture is a late development. At first the archetypes of a culture are full of power and give form to the world of a particular society. But these archetypes become hardened into a canon and eventually lose their 'depth dimension'. When this happens irony develops and the creative author has to step outside the culture to use the old forms in new ways. For the authors of both *Job* and *Jonah*, who both stood at the end of their own traditions, the time was ripe for such techniques.

---

116 E M Good, 1965 (p 51). B Vawter, 1983, also notes that Jonah appears as a reflection of Elijah in a prophetic parody, cf I Kings 19:4-12.
117 E M Good, 1965 (pp 54-55).
118 S R Hopper, 1962.

## Chapter 4

## THE 'SCEPTICAL' SETTING, CONTENT AND STRUCTURE OF *JOB*

## The scepticism of Job and of the author of the book

### a) THE QUEST FOR A CONTEXT FOR *JOB*

"What is surprising about the book of Job is not that its author was familiar with these various forms, which would be part of Israel's literary and cultural heritage, but that he felt free to use them as he chose. This certainly does not suggest that he was trammeled by the conventions of a narrow group."[1]

In the first part of this chapter I shall discuss the purpose of the author of *Job* in using parody as a literary tool and the kind of setting he might have come from. This will involve questions both of dating and of social setting. The intention of the author is a crucial issue - he could not accidentally have employed the technique of misuse of forms or parodied forms from many other traditions. He deliberately used such a method both to disguise and to convey his very radical message. The forms appear to be traditional, thus appeasing traditionalists and leading to the book's acceptance by orthodox readers from the earliest period (see chapter 1 section a)) but in fact they convey a very unconventional message. The very form of a folk tale disguised the true nature of the work and led interpreters to focus on the themes aired in the parts of the book of that genre (see chapter 1 section b)). Thus the use of this technique of parodying material has considerable implications for the content of *Job*; for here the author of *Job* is parodying a facile tale with a more

---

[1] R N Whybray, 1974 (p 63).

profound content in the dialogue section. The radical message of the book will be considered in section ii) below, first, however, I shall consider the author and his milieu.

It has been argued in chapter 3 that many of the books that use parody as a technique stand at the end of a tradition, notably *Jonah* which stands at the end of 'prophecy' and provides a satirical critique of it. It is the same with *Job*. Parody itself is a late kind of genre in that it feeds on other genres. This observation would support a late date for the book, possibly the late fourth century at the beginning of the period of a widening of intellectual interests which came to fruition in the Hellenistic era.

i) A wider intellectual setting for *Job*?

In chapter 2 the idea was raised that a wider intellectual milieu outside the wisdom context might provide a setting for the authorship of *Job*. There might even be a possibility of finding a different 'group' representing another mainline tradition alongside wisdom (or developing out of wisdom as a refinement of it) to which *Job* belongs.

Attempts to find an author, a date and a setting for *Job* are generally inconclusive and usually subjective. The quest for an author for *Job* started by trying to find one named author for the book[2] but this was soon abandoned in favour of a general search for an unnamed author.[3] Literary-critical analysis of *Job* developed an awareness of different levels of authorship so that it was questioned whether a single author with skills of varied style in his adaptation of material to the structure of the book could really be posited. The only section which could be ascribed to a single author was perhaps the dialogue. The final form could be merely an accidental compilation of various pieces or

---

[2] Mosaic authorship is still maintained by some conservative scholars who point to the reference in Baba Bathra, 14b, 15a - "Moses wrote his own book, and the passages about Balaam and Job" - eg G W Hazelton, 1914. The rabbis dated the lifetime of Job or of the author at various periods extending from the time of Isaac and Joseph to that of Cyrus and Ahasuerus. The apocryphal addition to *Job* in the LXX identifies the hero with Jobab King of Edom (Gen. 36:33), a grandson of Esau, who thus predates Moses.

[3] eg A B Davidson and C H Toy, 1911, to avoid the issue of a named author, argued that the spiritual energy of the nation expressed itself impersonally in the period when *Job* was written. J P Naish, 1925, saw the author as an unnamed Babylonian exile who eventually returned to Judah and wrote his own story down in *Job*.

the product of a later editor. Alternatively there could be a purpose behind the ordering of the material and *Job* could be the composition of a creative and original author.[4] There is a clear circularity in these arguments.

The attempt to assign a date to *Job* has been equally unfruitful. Pre-critical scholars argued that *Job* belongs in patriarchal times since the book is set in this age.[5] More recent scholars have argued for the monarchic period, notably the time of Solomon (following Gregory Nazianzen (died ca 390)) on the grounds that it was during his reign that Hebrew literature received its greatest development and the wisdom literature was produced.[6] Many scholars have assigned *Job* to the Exilic age either on the basis of the message of *Job* or as a result of comparisons with other biblical texts in an attempt to work out where the ideas in *Job* fit into the historical development of Hebrew thought[7] - as in arguments which urge that, for example, the same kind of questions are discussed in Psalms 49 and 73 which are also to be assigned to the Exilic age.[8] Others prefer a post-exilic date sometimes on the grounds that *Job* is a type

---

4   eg K Budde, 1876 and 1896 and, more recently, J F A Sawyer, 1978, who suggests that a redefinition of the term 'author' is needed in the light of literary-critical analysis. He argues in favour of an overall author with his own creative design who deliberately inserted some older material such as the Elihu speeches and incorporated some original compositions of his own to give the book structure and symmetry.
5   Other reasons include the fact that there is no reference to the Mosaic law, to the later history of Israel or to pre-patriarchal times and that older names of God (Shaddai, El and Eloah) are used in *Job*. These arguments often referred only to the prose parts of the book (the rest was seen as a later product) and they ignored later indications in the book that the author had knowledge of a later age, for example small details such as habitual use of the name Yahweh in the prose narrative, and more general factors such as the nature of the language and the type of issues discussed (see E C S Gibson, 1919, who argued on such grounds against the production of *Job* in the patriarchal period, preferring the Exile.)
6   eg E J Young, 1949 and F I Andersen, 1976, cf an earlier scholar F Delitzsch, 1866.
7   eg H Creelman, 1917, argues in favour of an exilic origin for *Job* because of the advanced state of society, the condition of disorder and distress at the time and the reflective nature of the problem in the book. He argues that the Exile furnished a fitting occasion for discussion of a great moral problem. He also asserts that parallels of language and thought between *Job* and Isaiah 40-55 favour the same period for both. However he prefers a post-exilic date for the book. The problem with dating *Job* is that the text offers no explicit historical allusion to suggest a particular period. See recent discussion by J J M Roberts, 1977. Coincidence of language with other books is often considered close enough to point to indebtedness on one side or the other. However the direction in which such interdependence occurs is often indeterminable, eg Job 3 could be imitating Jeremiah 20:14-18, but the dependence could work the other way.
8   The dating of Psalms 49 and 73 to the Exile is by no means conclusive, in fact dating the psalms is in general a tenuous operation. They should not be used as fixed points by which to date other material.

representing Israel and at other times on the grounds that the Satan is a character named only in post-exilic literature and that the angelology of the book finds its closest parallel in the late book of Daniel, 167-165 BC.[9] It can be seen that the criteria for establishing the date of *Job* are inconclusive - one can either see the question of dating as unimportant as N C Habel does,[10] or one can attempt an absolute date beginning from other conclusions. I shall suggest that an approach which begins from questions of context or social setting might be of value in elucidating *Job*. Starting from such considerations, I shall posit the idea that *Job* should be given a late date and be assigned either to the Hellenistic period or to the years immediately preceding it - late 4th or early 3rd century BC.

As for place of writing, Uz is questioned as a real location but it is often thought to refer to a district near Edom.[11] Edom is preferred by scholars[12], Babylon has also been suggested[13] but these arguments are thwarted by the fact that the book clearly has an Israelite flavour.[14] The best approach is to relate place of writing to the issue of the author's milieu or situation in Israelite

---

9   eg T K Cheyne, 1887, pp 79-82; K Budde, 1896 (1913, pp 44f); A S Peake, *Job*, 1904. See discussion of the Satan passages, pp 200-203.

10  N C Habel, 1984, stresses that the universality of the work is more important than an assessment of its date. He writes (p 42), "Consistent with the orientation of traditional wisdom thinking, the author of *Job* has created an artistic work with universal dimensions rather than a text directed at a particular historical situation or theological issue alive in Israel at a specific time...Thus, while the cumulative evidence may tend to suggest a postexilic era, the book's literary integrity, paradoxical themes, heroic setting, and uncomfortable challenge are pertinent for students of wisdom and life in any era and far more important than the precise date of this ancient literary work."

11  P Dhorme, 1911, examined archaeological evidence to situate Uz. There are two traditions concerning the location of Uz in the Old Testament. There are references to Uz in Genesis 10:23; 22:21; 36:28. In Genesis 10 Uz is the son of Aram, son of Shem. Aram gave his name to the Mesopotamian district called in Genesis, Aram-Naharaim and Padan Aram; and Uz, migrating further southward, gave his name to a district near Edom. There was another Uz 400 years later, a descendant of Esau. J Lindblom, 1945, argues for an Edomite setting from details in Job, eg Eliphaz is an Edomite name, Teiman is in Edomite land.

12  R H Pfeiffer, 1926 and 1948, refutes the arguments of Dhorme that the author is a Jew and argues that his thought and language are Edomite. This is questioned by H H Rowley, 1970 and R Gordis, 1965, who argues that the book was written by a "highly intellectual Hebrew" (p 212).

13  This is argued with extra-biblical parallels in mind. eg M Jastrow, 1906, argues for a conscious borrowing by the author of *Job* from a Babylonian poem from the library of Assurbanipal concerning a high official or king of Nippur called Tabi-utul Bel.

14  eg J Lindblom, 1945, writes, "The foreign piece received an Israelite imprint. The Edomite sheik became a biblical patriarch."

society, as reconstructed from the concerns of his book. This brings us back to our consideration of the author as part of the wisdom tradition and the questioning of this assumption and hence to the suggestion that a Greek setting might be appropriate for the production of *Job*. This is not a new idea. G H Box[15], for example, provides a historical argument for *Job* in its final form as the product of the Hellenistic period and argues that the wisdom school became particularly prominent in this period. He suggests that the wise tended towards secularism in their outlook in the pre-exilic period but that after the destruction of Jerusalem they became religious teachers as well. He writes:

"The fundamental change in the conditions of Jewish life after the Exile profoundly affected Judaism generally. With the destruction of the old-fashioned life and institutions there came into existence a new balance of forces...With the advent of Greek culture and civilization the disintegration of the old order was completed. One striking result of the new conditions was the rise of the individual into prominence."[16]

A study of Hellenistic influences on the literature of the Israelites is undertaken by M Hengel[17] who admits that it is hard to prove direct Hellenistic influence in the literature, let alone dependence on Hellenistic works, but who points to a few areas of possible contact between the two cultures. He discusses briefly the book of *Job*. He notes that Theodore of Mopsuestia saw *Job* as an imitation of a Greek tragedy[18] and in recent times the suggestion has also been put forward that *Job* is dependent on Aeschylus' *Prometheus Bound*.[19] Comparison of *Job* with Greek tragedy has featured in discussions of the literary genre of *Job*, but hypotheses of literary dependence have been widely rejected.[20] The comparison between *Job* and Greek tragedy should clearly not be taken too far. Its main value is to underline how different *Job* is from other books in the Bible.[21] Hengel writes:

---

15  G H Box, 1932.
16  G H Box, 1932 (p 118).
17  M Hengel, 1974.
18  L Pirot, 1913, pp 131-4. cf J M Vost, 1929. C Kuhl, 1953, pp 204-306, surveys recent attempts to connect *Job* with the Greek tradition.
19  See discussion in chapter 2, pp 98-100.
20  J Barr, 1971-2, argues that there is no literary dependance between the two.
21  For example, on the basis of affinities between *Job* and Greek tragedy, R B Sewall, 1959, identifies a literature of dissent in Israel and a movement within Judaism which he calls the 'Hebraic tragic vision' (p 22). He refers to this literature as "protest literature" (p 23) and reconstructs a picture of the unknown poet of *Job*, seeing in the folktale the possibility for a tragic drama. The poet saw *Job* not as illustrating the

"In form and theme the book of *Job* is completely dependent on the ancient East; despite some analogies with themes from Greek tragedy, the contrasts are 'in part of a fundamental nature'. On the other hand, the book of *Job* shows how, in the thought of the period of the Achaemenides, determined by 'wisdom', intellectual development was preparing to move in the direction of the Hellenistic epoch even without demonstrable Greek influence."[22]

Hengel sees as signs of Greek influence the tendency in *Job* towards the propagation of encyclopaedic knowledge, a completely universalist view of God[23] and an individual critical attitude towards the doctrine of retribution as represented in the school tradition. Hengel writes of *Job*:

"Its conclusion is neither resignation nor Promethean defiance, nor even a change in God from arbitrariness to righteousness - the speech of God shows God's sovereign right - but the humble submission of Job to God's superior power."[24]

He dates *Job* to the fifth or fourth century BC.

Hengel cites the view of M Friedländer[25] who has found traces of Greek philosophy in the Hebrew wisdom literature - in *Job*, Proverbs 1-9, Ecclesiastes and some psalms - but this 'Panhellenism' has not met with much support from scholars. Hengel writes:

---

ancient piety - that is, a good man blessing the Lord even in his afflictions and being rewarded for his constancy - but as throwing it into grievous question. Job was a righteous man to whom suddenly and unaccountably suffering came. The tragic element was not that he suffered misfortune but that there was no human cause or explanation for his sufferings, nothing in his past to account for these repeated blows. Job knew nothing of the wager suffered at the hands of a God whom to worship and to love had been his daily blessing; he only saw God turning suddenly hateful and malign. This questioned all his beliefs about God and justice. Job was thus caught in a dilemma, and it was this dilemma of which the poet was aware. Sewall writes, "From the depths of an ancient scepticism and a sense of justice which dared to hold Deity itself to account, the Poet saw the story in the light of the tragic vision. The resolution of the folk story by which Job, for all his piety and suffering, was rewarded by twice his former possessions and a new family, was unacceptable." (p 22)

22  M Hengel, 1974 (p 109) (Quotation from G Fohrer, 1963, p 47).
23  R H Pfeiffer, 1948 (p 679) terms the author 'the most learned man up to his time known to us', cf H Richter, 1958, pp 1-20. Even R H Pfeiffer, pp 678-683, who rejects any dependence of *Job* on Greek models and believes it was composed about 600 BC by an Edomite, stresses the peculiarity of Job's conception of God: "*Job*'s theology is more akin to the Greek than to the Israelite notion...the function and attributes of the Deity in *Job* indicate that the author conceived his God primarily as a cosmic force, not as the patron God of a nation." (p 703)
24  M Hengel, 1974 (p 109) and G Fohrer, 1963, pp 552-557.
25  M Friedländer, 1904; objections are however raised by W Swart, 1908, and E F Sellin, 1905, p 17f. Sellin does however allow some traces of the influence of Greek culture and lifestyle in Proverbs 1-9 and Job 28; 29:18 (Phoenix saga); cf a critical survey in P Heinisch, 1913, p 15f.

"At best we may say that the Jewish wisdom schools of the pre-Hellenistic period prepared the ground for the penetration and rejection of Hellenistic civilization after the rule of the Ptolemies by the 'international' and practical-rational character of their teaching."[26]

R Kittel[27] also expressed the situation in these terms:

"If one draws this conclusion, even before the real onslaught of Hellenism on Judaism, the latter had produced in its wisdom teaching an intellectual trend which was related to Greek popular philosophy and at the same time was destined to work against it."

Hengel finds the main Hellenistic influences in the book of Ecclesiastes and then, to a lesser extent, in Sirach and the Wisdom of Solomon.

Hengel then goes on to discuss the tendency of Jewish literature in the Persian and early-Hellenistic period towards development. He notes the *"astonishing richness and pluriformity"*[28] of the literature, for example, in works like *Job* and Ecclesiastes "a critical reflection could break through the traditional religious view".[29] Hengel remarks that it is astonishing that such a small Jewish state could develop such creative forces. M Smith[30] sees there "indications of an educated laity which was in contact with the culture of its environment" and changed its "literary production with international fashion." Hengel writes:

"Whether individual works were written before or after Alexander's expeditions is also of secondary importance, as obviously 'Greek' influences are hardly directly demonstrable before Koheleth; rather we find rational, critical, speculative and universalist tendencies which prepared the ground for the encounter with Hellenistic civilization. In all probability, groups of the priesthood, the Levitical writing schools and the lay nobility shared in producing this rich writing."[31]

Hengel notes the appearance of a division in the middle of the third century BC first hinted at in Ecclesiastes. He argues that in Palestine:

"an active, aristocratic minority became open to the critical and universalist spirit of early Hellenism, whereas conservative circles, in deliberate antithesis, opposed it by referring to

---

26  M Hengel, 1974 (pp 109-110).
27  R Kittel, 1929, III, 2 (p 733); W Bousset and H Gressmann, 1926 (1966, p 497, note 2).
28  M Hengel, 1974 (p 112).
29  M Hengel, 1974 (p 113).
30  M Smith, 1965 (p 365); cf R H Pfeiffer, 1948, p 655 and M Hadas, 1959, who writes of the Hellenistic era under Alexander the Great, "a new literature arose to answer the needs of ordinary people." (p 23).

the national tradition, with the help of certain arguments taken from the thought of the new period."[32]

Thus Hengel opens up a few new lines of thought regarding Hellenistic influence on biblical books. With regard to *Job*, Hellenistic influence cannot be proved. Yet *Job* seems to be the product of the period leading up to the infiltration of Greek ideas into Israelite literature and represents part of a general development or widening of the concerns of the Hebrews. This is probably as far as Hengel's conclusions can take us. They open up the possibility of a wider intellectual context at the time, a wider context which includes a tendency towards producing critical literature.

The idea of a broader intellectual milieu for *Job* is also supported by the findings of scholars such as J J M Roberts[33] who argues, largely after undertaking a study of *Job* in relation to other ancient Near Eastern parallels, for a wider sphere of traditions from which the author of *Job* has taken material and by which he has been influenced. This is supported by the variety of small genres found in *Job*. This might suggest a greater interchange between groups in Israel and a broad intellectual environment from which an author could draw. Can we only talk in such general terms or can we define the context of *Job* more closely and find a part of the general intellectual milieu in which *Job* might belong?

ii) Job - the product of a philosophical group?

Many 'philosophical' ideas are raised in the dialogues of *Job*. Musing on the mysteries of life and human existence may in itself be called a philosophical tendency. Rather than seeing this as the way in which unconventional wise men developed their ideas[34], perhaps we should see it as a separate tendency from wisdom. It may have arisen out of wisdom but should be distinguished from it. *Job* is regarded by Finkelstein as a 'Plebeian Paradox'.[35] He argues

---

31   M Hengel, 1974 (p 113).
32   M Hengel, 1974 (pp 113-114).
33   J J M Roberts, 1977, pp 107-114.
34   R Gordis, 1971.
35   L Finkelstein, 1938.

for the existence of a separate philosophical group among the Plebeians producing protest literature. He writes:

"The continued and iterated protest against injustice, which becomes one of the main motifs of the book, marks it as a product of the plebeian mind. Neither Job nor his opponents in the debate have anything in common with the Wisdom teachers and their ideal of prudence and success, or Ben Sira and his insistence on human freedom of choice."[36]

He sees Job as deeply influenced by his Persian environment and its theology. His view is a very imaginative reconstruction of the setting in which *Job* was produced. For example he writes:

"Projected into the land of Uz, among the patriarchal nomad chieftains of the desert, the work yet bears the ineradicable marks of its origin in Jerusalem of the fourth century B.C.E. Behind the shifting curtains of Arab sheiks, we can discern the cunning faces and expressive gestures of Jerusalem traders, arguing in tones and cadences far more suitable to metropolitan sophistication than to pastoral simplicity."[37]

Such optimism for reconstructing a precise milieu for *Job* is unfounded. However Finkelstein's imaginative reconstruction has some possible value in that it stresses how unlike normal wisdom the debates in *Job* are, and it raises the possibility of a more philosophical group or tradition as a background for *Job*. Rather than talking in terms of a Plebeian group, the posited existence of which rests on tenuous foundations, we might be better to take a different starting-point - the forms and message of *Job* - and discuss possibilities arising out of these results.

The kind of questions asked by *Job* and the techniques by which its radicalism is conveyed suggest to me that a more philosophical group might be envisaged as the background to the production of the book. A certain affinity of spirit might be found between *Job* and the Greek sceptics (in the same way that an affinity was found between *Job* and Greek tragedy) and an interesting parallel might be drawn, without involving any suggestion of dependence of one group on another.[38] This will be worked out fully below. The parallel might be useful in reconstructing a philosophizing, intellectual tradition or

---

36 L Finkelstein, 1938 (pp 232-233).
37 L Finkelstein, 1938 (p 231).
38 Although M Hengel, 1974, argues for the possibility of minor influence from Hellenism on *Job* and it is true that the existence of such groups may have occurred in the same period.

'school'[39] that existed in Palestine and produced literature of a sceptical kind (which might include other works which display a sceptical approach on the levels of form and content, such as Ecclesiastes and Jonah). Such a group would have had its beginnings in wisdom circles but would have broken away from them by stepping outside the bounds of the wisdom tradition. It may have arisen out of a crisis in wisdom, which had failed to provide the answers from experience that men desired, and formed a separate tradition in Israel and the ancient Near East (as evidenced by ancient Near Eastern parallels). Such a group may also have had knowledge of the cult and legal traditions having arisen out of the widening intellectual milieu in the period before the Greek era. This suggestion may have a far-reaching effect on traditional ideas of the social structure of Israel.

## b) THE SCEPTICISM OF *JOB* AS SHOWN IN THE CONTENT OF THE BOOK

### i) Scepticism and the Greek sceptics

At the core of the various meanings of the word 'sceptic' and its derivatives is the action of questioning or doubting. The Oxford English Dictionary sums it up well in its simple definition:[40]

"The word 'sceptical'...is used to describe anything that questions the truth of a particular fact or theory or takes a cynical viewpoint."

'Sceptical' has the general meaning 'inclined to or imbued with scepticism' and can be used in reference to people or doctrines. 'Scepticism' refers to 'a sceptical attitude in relation to a particular branch of science or to doubt or unbelief with regard to the Christian religion' or to 'doubt or incredulity in general; mistrustfulness or a sceptical temper.' However it has a more specialized, original meaning in relation to the Greek Sceptics. It refers to the doctrine of the Sceptics - "the opinion that real knowledge of any kind is

---

39 The 'sceptics' themselves did not form a distinct 'school' of philosophical thought so the word 'tradition' is perhaps preferable.
40 OED s.v. 'sceptical'.

unattainable." The word 'sceptic' originally refers to a group in Greek antiquity (4th century BC)[41] which, like Pyrrho and his followers, "doubts the possibility of real knowledge of any kind; one who holds that there are no adequate grounds for certainty as to the truth of any proposition whatever."[42] As J Annas and J Barnes write:[43]

> "Sceptics are doubters: they neither believe nor disbelieve, neither affirm nor deny. To be sceptical on any given matter is to suspend judgement on it, to subscribe to no positive opinion either way. A sceptical philosophy recommends doubt and suspension of judgement over a substantial range - perhaps even over the whole range - of human investigations."

The ancient sceptics did not attack knowledge (although they denied certainty in knowledge), but belief:

> "They argued that, under sceptical pressure, our beliefs turn out to be groundless and that we have no more reason to believe than to disbelieve. As a result, they supposed, our beliefs would vanish. We should, of course, lose all knowledge; but that would be merely a trivial consequence of our general loss of belief."[44]

The ancient sceptics expected to induce ordinary, non-philosophical doubt which excluded beliefs and was therefore a practical doubt:

> "Indeed, it was precisely by reference to the practical corollaries of their doubt that they used to recommend their philosophy: scepticism, they claimed, by relieving us of our ordinary beliefs, would remove the worry from our lives and ensure our happiness."[45]

The cynical element that crept into later meanings of the word 'sceptical' was not present in the earliest definition. Rather the 'sceptic' maintained a neutral

---

[41] The sceptical movement lasted over a period of six centuries but was not a continuous line. Mainline scepticism is attributed to Pyrrho. A second version then grew up in the New Academy who considered themselves followers of Plato rather than Pyrrho. For a history of the movement see C L Stough, 1969. See also A A Long, 1974 and M F Burnyeat, 1983.
[42] OED s.v. 'sceptic'.
[43] J Annas and J Barnes, 1985 (p 1).
[44] J Annas and J Barnes, 1985 (p 8).
[45] J Annas and J Barnes, 1985 (p 9); cf C L Stough, 1969 who writes, "The practical orientation of Skepticism never disappeared completely...The concern of all skeptics with the relation of philosophy to ordinary life led them to look for workable solutions to problems unearthed by their own epistemological criticism." (p 4) The earliest sceptic Pyrrho was chiefly "a moralist whose teachings embodied a way of life rather than a systematic philosophy." (p 6) This information is known from Timon of Phlius, his pupil, whose views survive only as quotations in other writers.

stance refusing to come down in definite criticism of the opponent. Sextus Empiricus in *Outlines of Pyrrhonism* gives this definition of 'scepticism':

"Scepticism is an ability which sets up antitheses among appearances and judgements in any way whatever: by scepticism, on account of the 'equal weight' which characterizes opposing states of affairs and arguments, we arrive first at suspension of judgement and second at 'freedom from disturbance'."[46]

The ancient sceptics labelled their opponents 'dogmatists', an appelation which in modern English hints at an irrational rigidity of opinion and a refusal to look impartially at the evidence. In its ancient sense the word lacked that tone: a dogmatist was simply one who subscribed to dogmas or doctrines. The meaning is closer to our modern term 'orthodox' which means holding correct or the currently accepted opinions especially on religious doctrine, the stance of Job's three comforters.

The author of *Job* 'suspends belief' in a similar way to the Greek sceptics when he does not provide a resolution in the God speeches to the arguments raised in the dialogue and when he retains the epilogue as the traditional happy ending to *Job*. Job, the character, starts with a framework of belief of some kind but becomes less and less sure what precisely his beliefs are in the light of the experiences he has so that he comes close to denying the possibility of belief of any kind, in the manner of the Greek sceptics - compare Ecclesiastes, which similarly can be seen to be 'sceptical' of the possibility of any certain beliefs. The author of *Job* also attacks 'dogmatists', ie those who adhere to certain traditional dogmas. He portrays Job as wanting to subscribe to such dogmas in that they make life much more straightforward and he is in fact terrified by the insights he gains when that framework is taken away. However his experience dictates otherwise. It drives him to question and to doubt in a profound and radical way what traditional religious belief teaches about God and about retribution. Thus Job questions that the righteous and wicked get their just deserts and he begins to realize that there is another side to God - an arbitrariness combined with a power that is frightening. The sentiments of Job in the dialogue are 'sceptical' in that they doubt and question

---

46 Sextus Empiricus, *Pyrrhoneioi hypotyposeis*, (Outlines of Pyrrhonism), Loeb Classical Library.

tradition. He attacks the reasoning of the traditionalists who hold certain dogmas about God and his action in the world and puts experience before beliefs which do not begin to answer his questions. Job does not leave any stone unturned in his inclination to doubt. He also questions the possibility of belief in a God that can behave in this way and he is doubtful of the possibility of reasoning with him.

The scepticism in *Job* works on two levels: Job himself says sceptical things, and the author displays his own scepticism by the use that he makes of individual forms (see chapter 3, pp 125-136) and by his design for the structure of the book (see below, section c)). In a sense the two levels are scarcely distinguishable in that the character of Job is clearly born of the author's own experience. But the distinction needs to be made in order to understand the nature of the scepticism in *Job*. In Job's radical reversals of the friends' arguments not only the scepticism of Job but the orthodoxy of the friends is highlighted. Admittedly, the speeches of the friends and those of Job do not correspond - questions raised by the one are not directly answered or refuted by the other; but, out of sequence, Job does answer and refute the friends' arguments, or at least indirectly attack their presuppositions. The friends' arguments are based on the wisdom teaching of just deserts, Job's are based on the conflict of personal experience with such teaching. The friends make a few generalizations about man's lot whilst *Job* provides a much more fundamental questioning. The main thrust of the arguments of the friends is to accuse Job of having sinned - he is to blame and God is in the right. Job on the other hand sees God as being the one at fault. Whilst the friends' arguments are generally directed at Job, Job's arguments are predominantly directed at God. Thus a study of the dialogue section will also uncover what it is that Job says that is sceptical about God. In the next sections therefore I shall examine the exact nature of the 'sceptical' content of Job's speeches. Then in the final part of this chapter I shall discuss the overall structure of the book in which the scepticism of the author of *Job* is revealed.

ii) The Dialogue section of *Job*

(1) The first cycle of speeches

The message of the friends is that Job must have sinned and that he only has to repent to be restored. All three friends are in agreement on this point. Job's sin is the reason for his punishment. Bildad adds that Job's children must have sinned since they were killed (8:4) and Zophar rejects Job's claims to innocence - "Know then that God exacts of you less than your guilt deserves." (11:6b) God knows Job's sins even if Job seems to be unaware of them. Furthermore, God does not pervert justice. Bildad argues that God does not reject a blameless man but he does punish the godless (8:20-22). Zophar claims that man cannot understand God and his ways (11:7-12) and asserts that Job must seek God and make supplication to him, repent and be restored (11:13-20). Eliphaz asserts furthermore that Job has instructed many yet now has lost confidence in God as the one who rewards the innocent and punishes the guilty. In 4:12-5:7 he describes a vision he experienced which teaches that only God is righteous and holy - even angels fall short of God's standards - so men can only expect to perish for they are born to trouble. Eliphaz tells Job what he would do if he were in Job's position: he would seek God and commit his cause to him because God is known to bind up and heal those who accept God's reproof and chastening. Crafty and wily people are destroyed by God (5:8-27).

Job in his opening reply in chapter 6 appears not to have heard Eliphaz, possibly a deliberate technique by the author to demonstrate the incompatibility of the two approaches represented here. Job addresses God rather than the friends. Rather than regarding himself as the one who has sinned, Job argues that either God has turned against him or he is arbitrary in his treatment of man. Job regards God as against him - his arrows have been fired[47] and his terrors are apparent to him (6:4). Like the friends, Job believes that his affliction is from God (in fact he finds his pains the harder to bear because he believes they are from God). However the God he now experiences seems

---

[47] The figure of God as an archer is frequent in the Old Testament, eg Psalms 7:12-13; 21:12 and 45:5, but nowhere else does God fire poisoned arrows. Here we may have a deliberate reversal of the traditional image.

irreconcilable with the God he knew before and this is seen as a justification for his complaints (6:2-13). In chapter 7 Job openly charges God with being his tormentor, coming perilously near to fulfilling Satan's prediction in the prologue that he would curse God to his face. God's constant attention is seen as oppressive and Job calls him a 'watcher of men'.[48] God guards him like the sea monster (7:12) and scares him with terrifying visions (7:13-14). He wishes to be left alone and asks, "What is man, that thou dost make so much of him, and that thou dost set thy mind upon him?" (7:17)[49] He asks why God should mind if he sins, questioning the traditional teaching that sin offends God because he is concerned for man. In these chapters Job has raised two fundamental issues that are never approached by the friends. The first is the question why man is important to God and why his sins and weaknesses are the subject of divine concern. The second is why a man, even a sinner, should be made to suffer, seeing that he is not master of his destiny.

In his second speech in chapters 9 and 10 Job addresses the doctrine of retribution. Eliphaz had stated that Job had lost confidence in God as the one who metes out retribution. This is seen to be true. But Job takes this further by talking in terms of contending with God. If one wished to do so one could not answer him - God would overwhelm man by posing unanswerable questions (this is in fact just what God does later in the book). Like the friends he upholds the wisdom and might of God but he gives it a negative application - God always comes off best. Man has no power to appeal against God who is both enemy and judge. Eliphaz had asked in 4:17 how a man could be righteous before God and Bildad had argued in 8:3 that God is invariably just. Job argues that God sets the standard of justice but there is no higher court to which appeal can be made against his decisions.[50] Therefore Job launches a vigorous attack upon God's moral government of the world. He recognizes that God is mighty and man too feeble to argue with him.

---

48 God is often spoken of in the Old Testament as watching over men to guard them from danger but here his watch is depicted as hostile.
49 This contrasts vividly with Psalm 8:4 where God's constant attention is seen as a thing to be praised and with Psalm 33:18 where the sense of God's gracious eye brings comfort.
50 A S Peake, 1905, writes, "Job here touches on the problem whether a thing is right because God declares it to be so, or whether He declares it right because it is so." (p 111).

Eliphaz expressed God's power in his first speech and Job demonstrates that he can do so too but he stresses the negative and destructive aspects of God's might and thus produces a searing attack upon God's irresponsible and unjust power.

In chapter 9 Job asserts that God's anger is unshakeable and arbitrary in that he vents his wrath on anyone he pleases. This is a contradiction of Bildad in 8:20. He returns to the impossibility of facing God by referring to God's power. The friends see God's power as positive but Job finds a negative aspect (eg 9:12). God is mighty in overcoming the monsters of chaos (9:9,13). How then can Job expect to face him or find words to answer him? Job asserts, "Though I am innocent, my own mouth would condemn me; though I am blameless, he would prove me perverse" (9:20). The idea that God causes all things is used by Job to blame God for everything, for example, for causing Job to speak these bitter words (9:18) and for the wickedness of the earth (9:24). In verse 22 Job returns to the problem of retribution. God is arbitrary - he destroys the blameless and the wicked (here Job contradicts Bildad in 8:20 and Eliphaz in 4:7). In verse 23 there is a further contradiction of the words of Eliphaz. Eliphaz had said (5:22) that if Job patiently bore the discipline of God, he would laugh at destruction and famine. Job retorts that it is God who mocks when disasters come. Job returns to the thought of the impossibility of meeting God on equal terms before a fair court. There is no equality and no umpire who is able to take both parties under his authority and protection (9:32-33).

Another of Job's arguments against the doctrine of retribution occurs in 10:4 when he asks God if he sees things the way man does - for example is his conception of right and wrong the same?[51] He is so convinced that he has not sinned that there must be another reason for his punishment: perhaps this is it. However, he then contradicts himself by asserting that God knows that he is not guilty (10:7). This implies that God does have the same standards. The problem to which Job again and again returns is that there is no one to justify Job against God as God himself is the only judge who has control of him.

---

51 C J Ball, 1922, and H H Rowley, 1970, interpret this verse as meaning "Art Thou liable to errors of judgement? Hast Thou no more insight than my friends?" (Ball).

God has created him and then destroyed him (10:8). In verse 14, God his protector has become his warder. There is deliberate irony in the choice of the words 'work wonders' in verse 16 - God's wonderful works in the creation of Job are now matched by his wonders in tormenting him.

Job often appears to agree with the friends but then reveals a profound disagreement. So in chapter 12 Job states in the manner of positive praise to God that God's created things bear witness that God's hand is always at work. Life and death are in God's hands (12:10). Yet later he says that God is to blame for misfortune and for the evil happenings of nature since he is the all-powerful God. Job maintains his right to question wisdom maxims by asserting that wisdom is not with the aged; it is with God alone and is therefore a redundant exercise for man. God knows how to cope with every situation and there is no opposition to his will. The problem is that God often acts capriciously and arbitrarily in nature (12:13-25). He reverses human fortunes, mocking the good in man and making fun of man's attempt to serve him. In 12:23 the rise and fall of nations does not appear to be governed by any moral principle and provides another example of God's arbitrary use of his power. Thus, against the friends' assertion of God's wisdom which can be understood according to certain rules, Job's stresses God's arbitrariness. In chapter 13 Job pleads with God for an opportunity to state his case, a matter which does not concern the friends. He expresses confidence that God will not dispute his case. He wants to know why God has turned against him and his only satisfaction will come from a personal answer from God. This contrasts with the friends' call to Job to repent. He will not repent when he has not sinned - God must explain himself for his apparently arbitrary action. In chapter 14 Job returns to God's oppressive watch over man. God has already determined the length of man's life, a boundary which man cannot pass. Two views of God struggle for predominance in Job's thoughts. He longs for the old fellowship with God from which he feels cut off, since his sufferings are to him as to his friends the evidence that he is abandoned by God. He believes that God will one day long for his fellowship. If God loved him he would number his steps, not keep watch over his sin. However man cannot escape destruction. God has the power to destroy the greatest mountain. In the same way he destroys man's hope.[52]

A recurring feature of these speeches is Job's criticisms of the friends. In 6:6-7 Job alludes to Eliphaz's empty consolations which lack human sympathy. He reveals that he has heard Eliphaz but found his words tasteless, meaningless and nauseating. In 6:14 Job clearly thinks that the friends should remain loyal, even if he, as Eliphaz has already begun to insinuate, has turned from God.[53] In 6:24-27 Job rebukes them for reproving him and accuses them of exploiting situations to their own advantage rather than wanting to help others. However he pleads with them to change their minds. In chapter 12 Job charges the friends with trying to curry favour with God. He asserts that he recognizes God's wisdom and might, as they do, but believes that no moral purpose governs God's exercise of his power and wisdom so that it is often destructive. In 12:1-2 Job allows the friends' claim to a monopoly of wisdom but goes on to deny it later when he asserts that so far from the friends having wisdom, the beasts could teach them. He asserts that his own position is not inferior to theirs and bewails the fact that he has become a laughing-stock and asserts his blamelessness. He aligns the friends with the prosperous who look down on the unfortunate and excuse themselves from giving sympathy by the assumption that they have brought it upon themselves. In chapter 13 Job claims to have as much wisdom as the friends and desires to argue his case with God (13:3). He attacks the friends as worthless - he does not even try to reason with them.[54] However, he wants them to listen to him. In verses 7-12 he tries to frighten the friends - what will happen to them if they try to deceive

---

[52] In 14:19 תקוה 'hope' is thought to refer to hope of a return to life. However, H H Rowley, 1970, argues that it refers to man's hope of a continuance of life - death shatters man's hopes. It could just refer to God's constant opposition to man, making his life difficult which makes man lose heart. God prevails against him (possibly referring to the struggle for life). He changes man's countenance (a description of death) and man is sent away. N C Habel, 1985, argues that here 'hope' means "that deep confidence and capacity to survive the worst disasters, even death", a hope which is crushed by God.

[53] This verse could have a general application - ie he who is not kind to a friend will not know the fear of God. Job might see this as a benefit for the unkind person who would not suffer his torment of knowing God and living under his constant supervision.

[54] The friends tell lies and are 'worthless physicians'. This could mean 'healers of worthlessness' who try to cover up the holes in their arguments uncovered by Job. Alternatively it could mean that friends who came to minister comfort and healing are unable to do so.

God? Job is full of scorn for the friends' servility towards God which leads them to patronize him. God is too great to be deceived by this - he will penetrate their shallow souls and see through this insincerity. Job scorns the maxims of the friends: "Your maxims are proverbs of ashes, your defences are defences of clay" (13:12).

In conclusion, Job is largely preoccupied in the first round of speeches in assessing God's character in the light of his bitter new experience of his Maker. He is sceptical of his former beliefs, notably of his conception of God. The friends, on the other hand, point their fingers at Job himself - in their view God cannot be at fault. Thus the two sides talk past each other - the orthodox line represented by the friends offers Job no comfort. Job believed these doctrines once, but his suffering has made him sceptical of the possibility of holding such orthodox beliefs.

(2) The second cycle of speeches

In the second cycle the friends' criticisms become more personal. Eliphaz asserts that Job's words condemn him (15:3-6) and show that he has rightly been punished - Job shows a lack of humility. He knows no more than any other man (verse 8, "Have you listened in the council of God? And do you limit wisdom to yourself?"). He describes the punishment of the wicked in 15:17-35. Bildad also describes what wicked men will suffer. He remarks on Job's lack of respect for the friends - "Why are we counted as cattle? Why are we stupid in your sight?" (18:3). He points out that Job must not expect to be treated differently from other men (18:4) (with the implication that other wicked men is meant here). Zophar asserts that the triumph of the wicked is short and sin brings its own punishment. God is quick to punish the wicked - it is part of God's decree (Job 20). In this round there are few arguments for Job to refute and he levels criticisms at the friends in chapters 16 and 17. He calls them 'miserable comforters' (16:2)[55] and uses their own words (in 8:2

---

55 H H Rowley, 1970, argues that מנחמי עמל means literally 'comforters of trouble', ie comforters who increase trouble instead of giving comfort (Job picks up the word Eliphaz has just used in 15:35). R Gordis, 1978, argues similarly that the Hebrew denotes 'worthless comforters' rather than 'comforters causing anguish' because of the parallelism with 15:35, ie עמל with און.

and 15:2) against them. However this attack really disguises his true complaint which is against God. God has abandoned him and it is God's attack that has made men turn against him. God is compared to a wild beast: "He has torn me in his wrath, and hated me; he has gnashed his teeth at me; my adversary sharpens his eyes against me" (16:9). In verse 10 men are massed against him, gape at him and abuse him. God has cast him into the hands of the wicked and broken him. In verse 12 Job emphasizes the unexpectedness of God's onslaught and its violence: "I was at ease, and he broke me asunder; he seized me by the neck and dashed me to pieces." However, despite God's treatment of him, he is his only witness and to him Job must appeal (16:18-17:9). He is determined to maintain his rights before God and begs that these be maintained. In 9:33 he had lamented that there was none to whom he might appeal to stand between him and God, but he now longs that God would himself take up his case. He is sure that death is imminent and is worried that if he dies he will not be vindicated. This theme reappears in 17:13 where Job longs for death but then asks ther question - if he seeks Sheol and gives in to darkness and its creatures where then is his hope of vindication?[56] In 16:20 he again reiterates that his friends scorn him and have become his accusers, but he later accuses God of making the friends not understand (in 17:4). In chapter 17 the lines become shorter, perhaps to convey the idea that Job is speaking under great emotional strain. He criticizes the friends, asserting that one day their children will suffer for their heartlessness. (17:5) In verses 8-10 he asserts that upright men are appalled at this treatment of a righteous man. He is here appealing to the doctrine of just retribution and at the same time trying to frighten the friends. Job bewails the fact that he has become as one to whom no respect is given and he again blames God. Chapter 19 repeats these sentiments. Job rebukes his friends for their cruel words which torment and wrong him, and he reiterates his assurance that God has unjustly persecuted him. His opening words - 'How long' - mock Bildad's opening words in two of his speeches. In verse 6 Job's thought turns to God: "know then that God has put me in the wrong and

---

[56] Alternatively these verses assert that Sheol is the best that Job can hope for and that he will carry any hope with him to the grave.

closed his net about me" (verse 6), as a hunter deals with animals. God has stripped Job of the honourable reputation he once enjoyed.

In 19:23-29 Job wishes his avowal of innocence were inscribed in a book or in rock forever so that they are not forgotten. He is sure that one day God will vindicate him. One day he will see God on his side, even if it is after his death (or anyway after his skin has been destroyed which presumably means that he would then be dead). "From my flesh I shall see God" (19:26)[57] suggests that Job will be aware of his own vindication. At this thought Job's heart faints within him - he is overcome by the thought which seems too wonderful to be possible. This section (vv 25-7) has been seen as evidence of a belief in an Afterlife.[58]

However it can be seen as Job's striving towards a solution. In 14:21f Job had spoken of the ignorance of the dead of all that transpires on earth. Here he is borne by the inner logic of his faith in God, despite his suffering which he believes to come from the hand of God, to look for a break in that ignorance and the immense relief of knowing that his innocence has been vindicated. His conflicting opinion of God - between the God who now torments him and the God he has always loved and served - is clearly shown in this chapter which moves from despair to a ray of hope. In 19:28-29 Job warns the friends against persecuting him under the mistaken idea that the origin of his

---

57 ואחר עורי literally, 'from behind my skin' is usually translated 'without my flesh' (RSV), or 'in my flesh' (AV). Rowley asserts that either interpretation is possible. It is usually argued that this verse cannot refer to Job seeing God after his body decays (S R Driver and G B Gray, 1921). R Gordis, 1978, argues that "it is best interpreted as meaning that he sees the vision of God vividly in his own person unmediated by any other being or tradition" (p 206). N C Habel, 1985, also favours 'within my flesh'. He writes, "It is clear from Job's desire to come face to face with God (13:15,20,24) that he wants to see God as Job the human being, not as an ethereal spirit" (pp 293-294). The reference to seeing with his own 'eyes' also suggests a physical seeing.

58 Many translations of these verses are offered - see the surveys in H H Rowley, 1963. The discussion centres upon whom Job is referring to as his 'redeemer' - the majority see it as 'God' but sometimes it is seen as a separate vindicator (eg S Mowinckel, 1925, pp 207-212; W A Irwin, 1962; S Terrien, 1962; M H Pope, 1965). Is this a vision of future resurrection in which Job will be in a disembodied form, or 'in his flesh' in which case does it refer to a present vision? The crescendo of faith is the 'I know' - a vision of God seen in his own person. This is generally thought not to refer to resurrection after death in view of Job's rejection of the doctrine in Job 14:7-23. אחזה אלוה is thought to be only a momentary vision (eg by A S Peake, 1905). Rowley writes, "Though there is no full grasping of a belief in a worthwhile Afterlife with God, this passage is a notable landmark in the progress toward such a belief" (p 174).

sufferings is in himself. He reminds them that they are as much under God's judgement as he is and will be judged for their false accusation of him.

Chapter 21 begins with an appeal for a hearing. Verse 5a - "Look at me, and be appalled" could refer either to Job's physical condition at which the friends are appalled, or to the words he is about to say. "Lay your hand upon your mouth" is a gesture of awed silence. Then Job refutes the friends' arguments about the certain punishment and short triumph of the wicked. In 21:7-16 he asks why they prosper and live long, grow mighty and happy and have a peaceful end. In contrast to Zophar, who said in 20:11 that the wicked die prematurely, Job declares that they live to old age. Their prosperity continues unbroken and is not fleeting as the friends had said in 15:20; 18:5 and 20:5. They see their children settled in prosperity (21:8) (compare the friends' statements in 15:33f; 18:19 and 20:21). In 21:17-22 Job asks how often the godless suffer - "How often is it that the lamp of the wicked is put out?" Bildad in 18:5 had said that the light of the wicked *is* put out - Job questions this. Verse 19 is thought to be a reply to an objection which Job supposes the friends might offer, namely, that even if the wicked man should escape punishment himself, his children will have to suffer it. In 20:10 the friends had spoken of the inheritance of suffering that the wicked man leaves to his children, as well as heaping disaster on himself. Job here protests that it would be no justice for a man to sin and his children to suffer. The sinner himself should be corrected and disciplined. Job questions whether a man takes interest in the affairs of his family once he is dead. Verse 22 could be a reproach to the friends for imposing their own rigid doctrine on God himself. It could however refer to God who, since he is judge, needs to realize that the wicked do not care for what comes after. This could imply a limitation on God's knowledge of man and his ways and would be a much more radical statement. In 21:23-26, death levels all - the wicked man dies at ease and in prosperity and the good man dies in bitterness but the same fate is meted out to both - and in the grave the bodies of both rot away. In verse 27 Job accuses the friends of schemes to wrong him, possibly referring to Job's realization that when his friends talked of the fate of the wicked they really meant himself. Job anticipates that they will declare that the wicked leave no memory among men (cf 8:14-19; 15:34; 18:15-19; 20:26-29). However in fact the wicked man is spared and no one requites him: "When he is borne to the grave, watch is kept over his tomb. The clods of the valley are sweet to him" (21:32, 33a).

Job's scepticism revealed in this cycle is clearly not a detached theorizing about the possibility of knowledge about God. It is the result of an anguished personal experience which conflicts with the need to make demands on God in the old manner. The more personal attacks of the friends of Job serve to heighten his bitter criticism. Whilst being sceptical of God's ways and the possibility of a relationship with him, Job clings to the hope that, after all, God is just and listens to man. Occasionally his hope resurfaces and his scepticism disappears - but these sentiments are only momentary. His desire to find God becomes for Job the only way out of his predicament.

(3) The third cycle of speeches

In the third cycle Eliphaz asserts that Job's suffering is proof of his sins because God is impartial (a just judge). Some suitable sins are then outlined of the kind Job might have committed. Job may think God is indifferent but righteous people are glad he is not. If only Job would "agree with God and be at peace" (22:21a), humble himself, remove unrighteousness, pray and renew his vows, God would deliver him. Bildad asserts that God is greater than his creation - his power is not limited - so how can man be righteous before God? (25:1-6). Zophar does not have a third speech although many reconstructions of it have been suggested.[59] The friends are here moving onto Job's ground in talking about God rather than simply providing a critique of Job as in the last round. They claim to know God's ways.

In chapter 23 Job expresses the desire to find God and come to his dwelling, then, "I would lay my case before him and fill my mouth with arguments." (23:4) He appears to talk in the categories of the friends in that he wants to understand his suffering (which he can only do if God answers him and lays his counterchanges against him) and he is confident that God will give him a fair hearing and will not simply overwhelm him by his power.[60] God will allow an upright man to reason with him and he will be forever acquitted

---

[59] See discussion in chapter 1, pp 52-53.
[60] Earlier he had feared that God would do just that (9:34-35; 13:21) and in fact God does overwhelm him in this way in the Yahweh speeches.

(verse 7). In 23:8-17 Job contradicts the certainty of the friends that they know God's ways and that God is just when he talks of the inaccessibility and power of God - he cannot find God and yet God knows his ways. This contrasts with the Psalmist who can conceive of no place where he may escape God (Psalm 139:7-12); it also contrasts with earlier sentiments of feeling closed in by God. Once tried, Job is sure that he will be vindicated for he has done nothing wrong, but God does what he likes and he treats Job in this way for his own reasons. When Job thinks of God's inscrutability, he is frightened and God has made him so: "for I am hemmed in by darkness and thick darkness covers my face." (23:17)

In chapter 24[61] Job argues that God is inactive in the face of human oppression and injustice - he takes no notice of the poor, the suffering, the godly, nor even of the wicked. Furthermore, why does he not let those who follow him see that he brings such wickedness to judgement? The evil deeds of men are then enumerated. In chapter 26 Job becomes once more critical of the friends and sarcastically refers to their sound knowledge and its origin, suggesting that false wisdom is plentiful.[62] In chapter 27 Job repeats that God has taken away his right and made his soul bitter. God has wronged him and yet he swears an oath by this God - this outlines how the two conceptions of God, against whom and to whom he appeals, lie side by side in Job's thought. He affirms that as long as he is alive he will speak the truth and will hold onto his integrity and to righteousness in the face of the friends' opposition. Here he does not regret his life at all - his conscience does not reproach him.[63]

In conclusion, Job displays scepticism in the way he suspends belief in traditional categories, as demonstrated by the fluctuation in his thought. Neither side is convinced by the other and the dialogue ends in a stalemate. The speeches of the friends lack the depth contained in Job's speeches and no

---

61   Verses 18-24 are generally regarded as being the words of another speaker since the sentiments flatly contradict what Job has been saying. They fit better into the mouth of one of the three friends and are often regarded as part of the misplaced third speech of Zophar. Verses 18-21 counter Job's charge that the wicked prosper. Verses 22-24 try to resolve the contradiction between the presence of the wicked and the tradition that they are destined to be forgotten after a brief accursed life.

62   The rest of the chapter is regarded as part of Bildad's speech. In fact some scholars (eg J Strahan, 1913; B Duhm, 1897; S R Driver and G B Gray, 1921 and G Hölscher, 1937) regard verses 2-4 also as part of Bildad's speech, representing sarcasm directed at Job.

63   The rest of 27 (and 24:18-24) is regarded as the third speech of Zophar.

satisfactory answers are provided to his questions. The message seems to be that there are no answers to the questions posed. The progressively shorter speeches of the friends suggest that their arguments are becoming less effective. Reiteration of the orthodox position becomes weak and they resort to outspoken criticism of Job, particularly in the second cycle. Job's speeches on the other hand get longer and grow in strength and determination. The irony contained in them is marked, and his criticisms of the friends and of the orthodox position concerning God and his dealings with man become more sceptical as his fervour increases.

However there is much contradiction contained in Job's words and at times he shows that many of the same presuppositions as held by the friends are ingrained in his thought. He is sceptical of the possibility of holding such beliefs and the contradictions may demonstrate that he is suspending judgement rather than coming down fully against the orthodox position. Most of all, Job is sceptical of the understanding of God he previously had. Throughout the speeches it is God on whom Job rests his complaint and his most unorthodox sentiments come from his criticisms of God which contrast markedly with the assertions about God by the friends. Job's new experience of God makes him sceptical of all traditional answers to his suffering.

So much for the scepticism of Job, the character. As to the author of *Job*, he displays his scepticism in his ordering of the structure of the whole book, for example in the raising of issues to which he deliberately does not supply an answer and by his juxtaposition of different sections of the book and themes. This will be illustrated in the next section.

## c) THE SCEPTICISM OF THE AUTHOR OF *JOB* AS SHOWN IN THE OVERALL STRUCTURE OF THE BOOK

"Form and content interrelate and interact - the character and organizing principle of the story derive from its form and form determines the arrangement of the basic elements within the whole and their relationship to the whole and moulds whatever is expressed therein."[64]

### i) The interrelationship of structure and content

In this section I shall discuss the views of scholars who have come closest to a recognition of the influence of the author's intention on the overall structure of the book. M Weiss makes the statement above when discussing the structure of the prologue of *Job*, but I should want to suggest that it is equally applicable to the whole book - or rather the book as the original author intended it. The meaning of each part becomes apparent only when seen in relation to the whole and the meaning of the whole can be known only by looking at how the different sections interrelate. Literary-critical conclusions take us part of the way in deciding which sections of the book should be regarded as the author's own work. But more decisive is the structure of the book - the relation of overall form to content. The intention of the author is important in this matter. By the use of the prose parts (whether they already existed as a story in some form or not - see below), the author was able to set up the framework within which the dialogue was to be read - as an ironic comment upon the saintly man of the prologue and as a parody of traditional folk tale genres. Clear structural pointers in the text show that it was not meant to be read as an orthodox wisdom work. It was meant to provide a sceptical critique of such orthodoxy, by making the reader suspend belief in the possibility of holding such views.

The scepticism of the author of *Job* is revealed in the most profound way in the overall structure of the book. The different parts are juxtaposed in such a way as to convey its sceptical message. This idea, in relation to smaller parts

---

64 M Weiss, 1983 (p 13).

of the book, is not altogether new - compare G Fohrer[65], on sections deliberately placed next to each other in order to create a certain effect - but scholars have not argued that the entire work is subject to this process and that the author arranged his material *with sceptical intent* . But there is much to be said for reading the book in this way. Thus the traditional folk tale genre is spoiled by the dialogue - the lament in chapter 3 breaks into the narrative and contradicts the words of the patient Job in the prologue. The speeches of Yahweh deliberately spoil the genre of a wisdom-type discussion which has preceded it in the dialogue.

It is useful to describe the tension between different sections in *Job* as deliberate irony on the part of the author.[66] An extremely helpful study is undertaken by Y Hoffman[67] who highlights ironies in the text and argues that a single author composed both the prose parts and the poetic dialogues, each of which cannot be understood without the other. He also argues that the prologue did not exist independently so that all seeming discrepancies are the deliberate work of the author.[68] The tension between the two parts of *Job* - prologue/epilogue and dialogue - suggests deliberate irony by the author of *Job* with different audiences in mind. Hoffman writes,

"This irony, the author's wink from between the lines, which breaks the literary illusion, is a clearly alien element."[69]

He suggests that the ambivalence found between prologue and dialogue is premeditated and that it represents the author's dialectic approach to the problems he raised. The author intended to present a naive tale in which the heavenly judgement was decisive, and a happy ending was expected, in order

---

65 G Fohrer, 1959 - relevant here is the fourth category of the way old forms are used in a new way, see pp 117-118.
66 W C Booth, 1971, argues that whether a work is ironic depends on two factors:
   i) the intentions of the author
   ii) the reader's catching the proper clues to those intentions.
   In *Job*, E M Good, 1965, finds irony working on different levels, in the speeches of the friends and Elihu, as exemplars of a certain irony regarding Job; in Job's speeches and in the portrayal of God (as in the interchange between God and Job in 38:1-42:6). On another level there is the irony of the poet as artificer of the whole.
67 Y Hoffman, 1981.
68 The issue of whether the author composed the prose tale or not is not fundamental to this view since, even if it existed in some form beforehand, the crucial thing is that the author *used* it (or misused it) for his own purposes.
69 Y Hoffman, 1981 (p 169).

to satisfy his more orthodox readers. However his conjunction of prologue and dialogue has other readers, 'the sceptics', in mind. They were to realize the irony which masks the hidden truth that man's problems cannot be solved in such clear cut terms as the orthodox believe.

An example of Hoffman's approach is that he sees the Job of the prologue (1:8 where he is described as a perfect saint) as a deliberately idealized figure in order to meet the demands of the dialogue. He writes,

"The abstract and theoretical problem in the dialogues, whether or not the Lord judges people according to criteria of justice intelligible to a human mind, necessitates an axiomatic (hence a theoretical) presupposition about Job's absolute righteousness. Thus the author emphasized this in the Prologue."[70]

A second example used by Hoffman is 1:11, Satan's declaration that Job "will curse thee to thy face", which he regards as intelligible only against the background of the dialogue. He argues that this declaration does not fit the prologue - it does not make sense that Job should be allowed to behave wickedly but with the proviso that he does not curse God to his face so that he can still be regarded as righteous. The author added this in order to shift the centre of gravity from deeds to words which become the sole criterion for Job's personality, thus linking prologue and dialogue and giving room for manoeuvre in the words of Job who does not actually curse God. Hoffman's final example is 1:5 which, he argues, adds nothing to the prologue - it suggests that Job's righteousness might be impaired by his sons' lack of righteousness and it spoils a basic assumption of the prologue that all the calamities were not a punishment but a necessary consequence of the wager between Satan and God. Three speeches of the dialogue clarify this issue since in 5:4; 8:4 and 20:10 Job's friends allude to the possibility that the sons' death was a consequence of their own wickedness, and Job has no reason to complain. The author of *Job* rejects this solution, but, Hoffman argues, in order for "this possibility to be considered seriously by the readers...he must not introduce it *a priori* as an absurdity. Such a chance is indeed given by expressing Job's apprehension about the uprightness of his sons."[71] Hoffman

---

70  Y Hoffman, 1981 (p 166).
71  Y Hoffman, 1981 (p 167).

tries to evaluate the author's ironic attitude. He regards it as the irony of "the hesitating sceptic, who makes irony a device for discovering the truth, which is not always unequivocal," as Socrates did. He quotes M Swabey who writes:

"With irony the contradiction between the hidden reality and outward show, between the temporal and eternal, between the relative and the absolute, appears."[72]

Hoffman concludes:

"Thus the dialectic relations between the prologue and the speeches are by no means merely an external literary device, but an honest reflection of the author's ambivalence towards his subject...This standpoint was already chosen by the author when he opted to make the popular tale a basis for his work. Thus, by referring to the popular myth about Job the righteous, not only does the writer find a common denominator for most of his audiences, but also hides himself dialectically behind a legend that provides him with an ambivalent overview of presuppositions which he himself set down, but to which he is nevertheless not fully committed."[73]

The intention of the author is therefore decisive for an interpretation of *Job*. This intention can be characterized as 'sceptical' in the manner in which ironies are contained within the text and within the tensions between different parts. Hoffmann's idea of a tension between the prologue/epilogue and dialogue can be taken further to include the tension between the dialogue and Yahweh-speeches and the tension between those and Job's reply (see discussion below, pp 205-208). J G Williams,[74] for example, discusses the irony of the God-speeches and of Job's reply. The greatest paradox is that, after Job has been overwhelmed and humbled, God, who has not answered any of Job's questions and seems to substantiate what the friends have said, justifies Job by saying that he has spoken truth (נכונה) and the friends have not, when in fact Job has accused God of injustice (eg Job 9). G Fohrer[75] argues that it is Job's reply that is the truth about God which God praises. However in the replies, 40:4-5 confirms what he has already said in the dialogue and 42:2-6 says

---

72  M Swabey, 1961 (p 53).
73  Y Hoffman, 1981 (p 169).
74  J G Williams, 1971; cf J G Williams, 1978, where he argues that "what is *said* but unspoken is what constitutes the meaning of the speeches of God" (p 64).
75  G Fohrer, 1963.

nothing about God directly.⁷⁶ Williams argues that Job's 'nekona' must therefore relate to Job's attitude to God rather than his words. Williams argues furthermore that in 42:7 God is not merely condemning the naive orthodoxy of the friends, he is presenting a condemnation of himself.⁷⁷

Williams follows a similar approach to Hoffmann in isolating contradictions and tensions attributable to the author. He sees the transition from 38:1-42:6 to 42:7f as constituting a break since the reader is not prepared after God's display of power for the divine approval of Job. A break is also found in chapter 3 in the transition from the prose prologue with its folk-tale atmosphere to the poetic dialogue in which we encounter real characters. The poet modifies the folk tale to suit his purpose, the modification being seen most clearly in 2:11-13 and 42:7-9 where the three friends appear.⁷⁸ Williams writes:

"It seems clear that the poet does not take the theological solution of the folk tale seriously, if it is considered by itself. The significance of the framing story must be seen in its juxtaposition against the dialogue and God-speeches and calls completely into question the world of retributive justice that is presupposed in the folk tale and the dialogue."⁷⁹

He interprets this juxtaposition as irony which, he argues, always arises out of a two-fold experience of the present state of things and a reality over against it. In the light of this reality, which in Job is still a mystery, the status quo is felt to be radically wrong. So Williams argues that ironic speech is the only way the author can find to express his disillusion at the disintegration of his world. He then goes on to give examples of this irony which correspond quite closely to the examples I gave under the title 'misuse of forms'. He groups examples from the dialogue together as Job's ironic speech - in 6:15-21, Job's

---

76   Job 42:2 has already been said by Job in the dialogue; 42:3a is a quotation of God (38:2). 42:3b could be construed as irony; 42:4 is a partial quotation of God's words in 38:3 and 40:7, and 42:5-6 says nothing *about* God.
77   D Cox, 1978, on the other hand, suggests that in his striving after truth and knowledge, as opposed to the complacent attitude of the friends, Job was in the right (42:7) but, in his expectation of being able to understand the human situation and find a pattern that would give meaning to existence, Job darkened counsel (38:2) and frustrated the justice of God (40:8).
78   J G Williams, 1971, sees these verses as the author's later addition to the original prose tale and cites the work of Fohrer on the issue of different stages of the development of the prose sections.
79   J G Williams, 1971 (pp 236-237).

friends have now become to Job as the Satan to God - the use of the lament over one's enemies indicates the change of the friends to enemies. In 7:17-18 he accuses God and the irony is apparent in the way he employs hymnic motifs to express Job's lament and implied accusation.[80] In 7:21 Job reverses the Jewish scheme of values as expressed by Eliphaz (in chapter 5) by crying out for death; in 16:18-22 Job cries out in a lament of the innocent dead before he is dead. He hopes for a witness against God but this could be none other than God - an impossible hope both because of its paradoxical nature and because of what Job has already said about and to God. In 9:2 Job parodies Eliphaz's statement in 4:17-21 - the accepted truth is reversed in ironic fashion. For Eliphaz it means that man is inferior to God in every way. For Job it means that man is *juridically inferior*, that is unable to get a fair hearing with God (he also anticipates what actually happens when God appears and does not respond to his questions). In 12:12-25 Job agrees with some of the friends' words about God's wisdom, for example in 12:12, Job agrees with Bildad who says that wisdom is with the aged (8:8-10). Zophar, likewise, has said that true wisdom is with God (11:7-8) and Job agrees (12:13) but Job then turns their words against them and describes God's wisdom for himself - if that is God's wisdom it is capricious and chaotic.

Williams' approach does not emphasize enough the juxtaposition of larger sections nor does he explain satisfactorily the way irony is apparent in the tension between God's words and Job's reply. He argues that God realizes that Job is speaking ironically and "rushes on with his *coup de grace*."[81] He quotes Jung[82] who suggests that God reacts as though he does not see Job and so taunts him by never really answering the questions and by parading his cosmic power, as Job predicted. Williams argues that the Behemoth and Leviathan speeches are depicted as true representations of God, Behemoth is described as the first of all God's works (40:19a), usually the description of wisdom in its ordering and creating role (Proverbs 8:22). Behemoth is a symbol of chaos and destruction and this description therefore plays into Job's hands since he depicted God's relation to man as chaotic. God is also

---

80   G Fohrer, 1963 (p 166).
81   J G Williams, 1971 (p 246).
82   C Jung, 1954.

presented as a divine version of the friends. In the light of all this the restoration of Job is ironic - God is shown up and reacts as Job predicted in 9:16-17 and God does not realize that he has been exposed. Job repents, tongue in cheek, realizing that it is the only way to deal with a deity who is easily threatened and does not observe covenants.[83] When we re-enter the folk-tale world in 42:7, God pronounces Job as in the right and the friends as wrong and Job is proved morally superior to God.

Williams suggests alternatively that Job is overwhelmed by God's speeches and is exposed as "one (man) who cannot endure the quest for justice, for vindication, for an answer to or resolution of the suffering that he and other men experience."[84] The speeches of God are the expression of dissolution of faith in creation - faith that the world is God's creation for man for him to enjoy and dominate - since man's place in the cosmos is not even mentioned; they shatter the Israelite affirmation of God's relation to the world. Williams regards *Job* as forging a new understanding of the God-man relationship which sees God as neither just nor unjust and which may reflect "a dishabilitation of a covenant-oriented mythos."[85] Job is not valued in the book except when we see his restoration in the epilogue, and, according to the friends, man needs to know that he is valued in order to live; yet when we return to the folk tale Job is valued and God, in effect, condemns himself. The supreme irony of the book is that in the folk tale Job becomes intercessor for the friends who have defended God. Thus Williams concludes that "the poet does not take the epilogue seriously, except insofar as it enhances the irony of the dialogue and theophany."[86]

Williams' conclusions concerning which sections display irony rest heavily on his own particular interpretation of the message. His study is however important in highlighting a number of ironies which are clearly present in the text, for example the final irony of Job as intercessor for the friends. In fact, it is the way of reading the book which usually determines the extent of the irony detected. If the whole book is read in the pious way described in chapter 1

---

[83] C Jung, 1954 (p 50).
[84] J G Williams, 1971 (p 249).
[85] J G Williams, 1971 (p 252).
[86] J G Williams, 1971 (p 250).

then none of it would be seen to express irony, but if the prologue and epilogue are read in the light of the sentiments expressed in the dialogue section, the tensions that expose the sceptical nature of *Job* can be seen as highly ironic. The author's use of irony is a clear indication of his scepticism.

A method employed by D A Robertson[87] is to ask continually - 'What does this part of the text mean when it is read in the light of all the other parts?'[88] Robertson's answer in almost every case is that it has an ironic rather than a straightforward meaning. His conclusion is that "irony pervades the entire book and provides the decisive key to understanding its complicated theme."[89] Once again the terminology of irony is used of a particular interpretation of the message of the book. The structural relationship of one part to another on a literary-critical level is however neglected. Robertson argues that the prose sections have the genre of a didactic folk tale and that the plot is reversed in chapter 3 when Job does just what Satan says he will and curses God:

"What began as a test of Job's loyalty to God has turned into a test of God's loyalty to Job."[90]

Robertson's ideas about the relation of the Yahweh speeches to the dialogue and to Job's replies follow similar lines to Jung's: Job is the wise one by the end of the book. These ideas about irony relate closely to my investigations in this chapter as they presuppose the essential unity of the book and see the inconsistencies as deliberate and therefore ironic.

Inconsistencies should therefore be recognized in the book and their significance emphasized - traditional literary-criticism has all too often avoided inconsistencies by the removal of verses.[91] (On the other hand, one should not try to integrate all inconsistencies so that they cease to be inconsistencies). As R M Polzin[92] writes:

"Literary-historical inconsistencies are as much a feature of the book's structure as its content. It is wrong to peel much of the book away."

---

87 D A Robertson, *The Old Testament and the Literary Critic*, 1977.
88 D A Robertson, *The Old Testament and the Literary Critic*, 1977 (p 34).
89 D A Robertson, *The Old Testament and the Literary Critic*, 1977 (p 34).
90 D A Robertson, *The Old Testament and the Literary Critic*, 1977 (p 37).
91 R M Polzin, 1974; cf R D Moore, 1983.
92 eg K Budde, 1896.

He characterizes the attempt to remove these inconsistencies as academic 'failure of nerve'. He describes how they are essential to the message of *Job*. He writes:

"Insight is conferred not by the avoidance of contradiction and inconsistency but precisely by the courageous integration of contradiction and resolution."

Likewise, R D Moore,[93] in discussing the relation of chapter 3 to the prologue writes:

"the poet, in presenting Job, has not sought thematic continuity with the narrative but rather thematic disjunction. Job 3 is a negative commentary upon Job 1:21."

He sees a tension here between the real and the ideal - the author has affirmed his own integrity here by presenting Job as a real person.

The whole book is seen by N C Habel[94] as having a "forceful underlying plot". He argues that inconsistencies are worked into the overall plan of the author and describes the book as a 'rich paradoxical totality.' He writes:

"Subtle ironies, blatant sarcasm, ambiguities of language and complexities of plot all unite to portend a theology of paradox."[95]

He acknowledges the interweaving of ambiguous images of the world with conflicting perspectives about the world and finds the meaning of *Job* in the interplay of literary design and theological idea. In an article on various polarities and contradictions in *Job*, Habel argues that:

"none of these oppositions are neatly juxtaposed. Job and his friends seem to talk past each other in their disputations. Responses to their respective speeches are deferred and tangential. The grand retort of God from his whirlwind seems to bypass the crux of Job's complaint. The happy ending...appears such a ludicrous non-sequitur that recent scholars have dubbed the literary genre of Job a classical comedy."[96]

He looks for a progression of argument in the book but finds it lacking. He discusses structuralist studies of *Job* but criticizes them for not attempting to explore the way themes interact within the book - they concentrate rather on the superstructure of the book. He writes:

---

93 R D Moore, 1983.
94 N C Habel, 1985. See N C Habel, 1984.
95 N C Habel, 1985 (p 60).
96 N C Habel, 1981 (p 373).

"It is the contention of this paper that a study of the mythic themes and ancient traditions about humanness in *Job* reveals another primary set of oppositions which highlight a major message of the book. The fundamental polarity lies with destiny and inheritance, ie between a divinely appointed destiny for humans and their inherited human condition."[97]

This is clearly an attempt to find an overall message for *Job* and yet it is not of the same kind as attempts to stress one theme in the book over all the others. It is an attempt to integrate the contradictions of structure into a thematic unity. Job the tragic hero in the dialogue is juxtaposed with the suffering saint of the prose narrative to bring out this polarity which is evident in the movement from the prologue to the opening monologue of Job. There is a similar tension between the closing speech of Job and the pious portrait of Job the intercessor found in the epilogue. There is thus a continuity of theme into which contradictions are built and which gives the book a unity.

This points the way to the kind of method required when attempting to show how scepticism and irony are built into the structure and themes of *Job*. An example of such a polarity might be the lack of characterization in the prologue/epilogue as compared with characterization at a high level in the dialogue. The orthodox Jewish view only works in stories that are not highly characterized. The prose tale, taken on its own, works because Job has no individuality apart from being an obedient servant of God. In such tales the just and wicked get the right rewards for their actions. Usually in the Old Testament it is assumed that there is some reward, some possibility of fathoming God's ways, some way for man to understand God. But in the dialogue of *Job* there are no rewards, there is only the agonized questioning of one who dares to stand up for his rights before God. Job is well-characterized and it is in his characterization that the interest of the book lies. He is a morally ambiguous character and his statements are difficult to fit into the traditional mould. For example, in 27:2 he directly blames God for acting unjustly, "As God lives, who has taken away my right, and the Almighty, who has made my soul bitter..."

Thus the author of the dialogue section of *Job* juxtaposed the traditional folk story about Job which was known in the early days of Israel with the speeches

---

97  N C Habel, 1981 (p 373).

of Job and the friends (and of God), to transform a trite story about a patient man bearing the suffering sent from God into a work with profound meaning. This deliberate juxtaposition of various parts into a new structure was done with sceptical intent in order to heighten the contradictions inherent in the situation and provides the clue to the overall design of the author and to the message of the book.[98] The speeches of Yahweh contain ironies which are the work of the same author who juxtaposed both sections with an original form of the folk tale in order to heighten the contradiction between the questions of Job and the answers given both by God and by the traditional prose tale.

Literary-critical questions need to be discussed in relation to these juxtapositions since the full extent of the work of the original author needs to be defined. In the light of the recent positing of the unity of the book the question of primary and secondary material in *Job* is often regarded as dated. The bid for unity has the advantage of taking the text as it stands which is preferable to carving it up into small pieces, a criticism that may be reasonably levelled at older scholars such as K Budde.[99] On the other hand there is no merit in enforcing a unity on disparate material and a criticism of modern interpretations, for example, R Gordis[100], is that interpretations of individual passages and sections are often forced to fit in with a very subjective view of the unity of the whole book. The question of which parts of the book are original to the author is clearly important but it is perhaps less decisive than scholars have argued in the past. The very lack of conclusions on the issue means that any attempt to make absolute judgements is futile. In the next two sections I present my own views on this issue, using my own conception of the book's message and author's technique to reach such conclusions. I shall first consider secondary additions, and then show how the rest of the book can be seen as the work of the original author and how he juxtaposed different sections.

---

98 As J G Williams, 1971 and Y Hoffman, 1981, argue, the author took over a stereotyped, formulaic prose tale and spoiled it with an ironic intent and, as R D Moore, 1983, argues, there is deliberate thematic disjunction in *Job*.
99 K Budde, 1896.
100 R Gordis, 'Quotations as a Literary usage in Biblical, Oriental and Rabbinic Literature', 1949.

ii) Secondary material

The speeches of Elihu and Chapter 28, the hymn to wisdom, are the focus of discussion in this section.[101] Most arguments for and against the authenticity to the author of these sections rest on a subjective assessment of the importance of the message of each section to the rest of the book. It is important to ask if a section adds anything in terms of ideas or themes to the book. The speeches of Elihu have been seen both as the central message of the book and as entirely subsidiary to the main theme.[102] They do not however add much to the main themes of the book in the way that they repeat ideas from the other sections, both dialogue and God speeches.[103] They spoil the climax to come by anticipating the God speeches and slow down the main movement of the plot.[104] The hymn to wisdom has been highlighted by those wishing to

---

[101] I shall consider arguments for the second speech of Yahweh as a secondary addition in section iv), footnote 128.

[102] J T Marshall, 1905 and L Dennefield, 1939 highlighted the Elihu speeches as essential to the message of *Job*, whilst S R Driver and G B Gray, 1921 and W A Irwin, 1937, saw them as of subsidiary importance. J T Marshall considered the speeches superior to other parts of the book, particularly in their conception of a more anthropocentric God than the remote, majestic God of the rest of the book.

[103] The Elihu speeches were often assessed by early scholars in terms of what they added to the problem of suffering. The repetition of material means that Elihu adds little that is new with the exception of the idea that suffering acts as a discipline, ie God sends suffering as a warning in order to safeguard man against sin (eg 33:19-25, cf Eliphaz in 5:17). K Budde, 1876 and 1896, and J T Marshall, 1905, saw this as the author's main answer to suffering but are generally considered to have overstated their case.

[104] The majority of scholars have seen the Elihu speeches as secondary for the following reasons. There is no mention of Elihu in the prologue and epilogue but rather a long justification of his appearance in 32:6-22 which differs greatly from the single epithet that introduces each of the three friends of Job. He ends his speech abruptly at the end of chapter 37 and then in 38:1 Yahweh disregards Elihu's intervention to address Job. Neither the Yahweh speeches nor the epilogue refer to Elihu's solution. Furthermore, in the dialogue each speaker expounds his views rarely confuting previous arguments, certainly not immediately after they have been stated. Elihu, on the other hand, attacks Job directly and criticizes each side in the debate. For example, in 32:2-3 he is shown to be angry at both Job (cf 34:35) and the friends (cf 32:12). He also addresses Job by name (33:1) which is not done by the friends. He gives the impression of being familiar with the whole conflict (eg in 32:1-12 he describes his attention to the discussion before speaking) which might suggest that *Job* in an original form was already in existence, enabling a later writer or editor to single out from the dialogue assertions to which he considered the friends had given no adequate reply. Recent scholarship stresses unity of authorship and purpose in the book and the authenticity of these speeches becomes a secondary issue, eg N C Habel, 1984, finds a role for Elihu in the design of the book rather than focusing on the contribution to the whole of the content of the speeches.

affirm the importance of the 'wisdom' tradition to the author of Job.[105] Other grounds for assessing authenticity are literary-critical concerns and those of style and language which can be seen as inconclusive in both cases.[106] A suggestion was raised in chapter 3 that those parts of Job which do not show evidence of the deliberate misuse of forms (or parodying of traditions) might be seen as unoriginal to the author since this technique is clearly a characteristic feature of his work. This might provide a more objective criterion to add to the weight of evidence from other approaches. Neither the speeches of Elihu nor the hymn to wisdom display this technique. In fact it is only used in Job's speeches in the main dialogue and in the first Yahweh speech.

---

[105] The hymn to wisdom provides a summary of the familiar wisdom doctrine which Job and the friends held and which becomes the cause of Job's despair when he finds that it does not work in practice. Its poetic form has been seen as an expansion on a short proverb which consists of a question (28:12-20) and an answer (v 23) (see C Westermann, 1956 (1981)). Its inclusion in *Job* generally enhances the impression that the book is wisdom literature, whilst its exclusion is more commonly on literary-critical grounds rather than on those of unity of the message. The hymn forms an independent literary unit with its own refrain (28:12 and 28:20); it is very different from the preceding dialogue in both style and content; it does not answer the arguments of the previous speaker - but then nor does 27:11-23 which immediately precedes it; it is inappropriate in Job's mouth (it could be the lost third speech of Zophar, a suggestion which would restore the pattern of rounds of speeches found earlier in the dialogue); it does not add any major new ideas to the book and it is lyrical rather than polemic as the dialogue is, providing no indication of listeners or of antagonists in the debate. The message of chapter 28 is that "in humble reverence towards God and obedience to His will man's truest wisdom is to be found." (H H Rowley, 1958, p 192). As Rowley points out this is in fact the position that Job reaches *after* the divine speech - in anticipating the Yahweh speeches the hymn makes the rest of the book an anticlimax. Furthermore the message of the main part of the hymn is that wisdom and the secrets of the universe and of divine providence are inaccessible to man - a sentiment which does not agree with Job's desire to bring God into court and question him, and which would belong better with the theophany (M H Pope, 1965). Some scholars argue that the speeches do not fit at this juncture in the book and attempts have been made to move it (eg P Szczygiel, 1931, moves it to follow 42:6). Others regard the insertion of the hymn at the present juncture as a deliberate technique by the author to provide a pause, indicating that the dialogue is at an end, eg C Westermann, 1956 (1981). E A Dhorme 1926 (1967) regards it as a general judgement on the previous discussion. Other issues of concern to scholars are the authenticity of verse 28 of Chapter 28 (see discussion in C Westermann, 1956 (1981)) and the hymn's similarities with other hymns to wisdom elsewhere in the Old Testament.

[106] On style, use of divine names and vocabulary used in the Elihu speeches, see discussions in E A Dhorme, 1926 (1967). Dhorme concludes that the speeches of Elihu are a new stage in the composition of the book, the work of an author using an already completed book and adding to it. On linguistic evidence for and against the secondary nature of the hymn to wisdom and a discussion of the characteristic stylistic traits of the author of the dialogue and Yahweh speeches, which are also to be found in Job 28, see E A Dhorme, 1926 (1967).

After weighing the arguments discussed and applying this more objective criterion, I am of the opinion that neither section can be assigned to the main author of *Job*. In regard to the Elihu speeches, even scholars who advocate unity of the book, such as N C Habel,[107] have problems with this section and recent arguments that one author wrote the main dialogue and the Elihu speeches but at different periods in his life[108] are clearly unsatisfactory because of the fictitious nature of these reconstructions. The hymn to wisdom is often regarded as an independent hymn but added by the main author.[109] This is, of course, plausible if the author wished to stress his affinity to the wisdom tradition but, unless its addition is ironic, it does not concur with the radical critique of the wisdom tradition that he offers in the mouth of Job in the dialogue.

The case for seeing some parts of the books as later additions is strengthened if there can be found some purpose by an author or editor for adding them at a later date. The purpose of the addition of the Elihu speeches must therefore be assessed. R N Cartensen[110] argues that the speeches of Elihu represent the views of a community of faith, the 'Elihu' school, which had a distinctive outlook, also found in the Wisdom of Solomon and Psalms 49, 73 and 139. He argues that this group which grew up within later wisdom corrected and supplemented the book of *Job* as it existed without them. He sees this approach as of value in ascertaining earlier strands in *Job* but does not pursue this line. He sees Elihu as adding a distinctive idea regarding the saving power of knowledge and the importance of immortality and argues that these ideas are at the beginning of later apocalyptic and gnostic systems which represented an impulse away from the traditional approach to God in history

---

107 N C Habel, 1985.
108 For example, R Gordis, 'Quotations as a Literary Usage in Biblical, Oriental and Rabbinic Literature', 1949, 1965, and 1978, argues that the use of quotations, a basic characteristic throughout the dialogue, is intensified in the Elihu speeches and provides evidence in favour of unity of authorship. In this section the author cites the words of Job either directly (33:11 from 13:27) or obliquely, in irony (33:7 from 9:34) or in restructured form (33:20 from 6:7) (see discussion of the use of quotations in chapter 3, pp 123-124).
109 eg R Gordis, 1965, argues that it is a preliminary effort by the same author as the rest of the book, when he was young, to express his basic ideas in a lyrical form. It was integrated by a later editor when parts of the dialogue were lost, cf N Snaith, 1968.
110 R N Cartensen, 1967.

and national election, in law and temple, which, he asserts, the rest of *Job* illustrates. This view may be thought over-imaginative but it illustrates the point that if a context or purpose for the addition of the speeches can be found, this is a valid approach to the question of relative dating.

In my opinion the addition of the Elihu speeches was an attempt to strengthen orthodox views already to be found in the speeches of the comforters concerning the problem of suffering. Such views included the idea that God only punishes wicked people and does not punish righteous people; therefore anyone suffering affliction must be wicked. Calamity does not fall on good and bad alike, so virtue is not useless, nor do the wicked enjoy an uninterrupted prosperity. Exact justice is meted out by God and no wickedness escapes his notice or action. God sends pain as a warning to wicked people to turn them from evildoing and to the righteous so that they may be cleansed of sin and pride, making pain a discipline to refine the righteous. Finally, God is not affected by men's virtue or their sin. Men who cry to God in vain for help do not cry aright or have not learned their lesson. Why was this kind of orthodox addition thought to be necessary and what kind of orthodox writer added it? In my view, it was added because the author of it thought that the answers of the friends failed in some way, and he could express his own solution to the problem of suffering more clearly. However his mind was not as original as that of the author of the dialogue and his attempts to sharpen the argument merely result in repetition of arguments employed by the friends and by God. As said above, the presence of the speeches at this juncture spoils the climax of God's appearance to Job; they have been added in rather an unskilful manner. The hymn to wisdom is plausibly added by an orthodox wise man, anxious to affirm the orthodox nature of *Job* as a characteristic product of wisdom circles. Alternatively the main author added the wisdom poem with a view to disguising his intentions and making it palatable to the orthodox. But if this was the case, it makes little sense that he should place the words in the mouth of Job.

iii) The prologue, epilogue and dialogue

(1) The prologue and epilogue - Literary-critical questions

The relationship of the prologue and epilogue, and of both to the dialogue, is crucial for an understanding of the technique of the author of *Job*. It is important to assess what is precisely attributable to him and what may have existed beforehand.[111] The prologue/epilogue and dialogue sections should be considered separately in order to avoid the pitfall of reading one in the light of the other (usually the latter in the light of the former).[112] It is only then that the truly questioning nature of the dialogue and the very different Job that it portrays comes to the fore. It is necessary to separate the prologue and epilogue from the dialogue and see if they make a consistent whole before discussing the relationship of the two sections with the dialogue. Did the author take over an existing story? If so, is that what we now have as the prologue/epilogue? Was this an an original prose story that circulated independently in early Israelite circles or was only part of it in existence? Because of the awkward transition from the prologue to the dialogue and the very different style, language and portrayal of Job of the two sections, it is hard to imagine that the author did not use something existing and see the potential for expressing his message through the simple tale. Most scholars therefore regard the prologue and epilogue as early and the dialogue as added

---

111 The traditional nature of the prose tale has been questioned because of its artificial character and 'stereotyped formulae' (E J Kissane, 1939). Kissane considered it impossible to say how much of the story is derived from tradition and how much is due to the author's artistry. T K Cheyne, 1899-1903, argued that the book "has no literary purpose. It has grown; it has not been made. The different parts of the book, however, had their purpose which must be sought for by an exegesis unfettered by a priori theories." (c 2489) Cheyne posited the original existence of different speeches in the prose tale in order to avoid the contradictions seen to exist between the submissive Job of the prologue and the questioning Job of the dialogue. See also discussion of K Budde in chapter 1, pp 33-34.
112 eg K Fullerton, 1924 argued that the dialogue was deliberately surrounded by a framework of the prologue, Yahweh speeches and confession of Job by the author in order to weave a veil around the real purpose of the book, as expressed in the dialogue where the author outpours his heart. He also argued that the book ends at Job's submission, a conclusion based on the fact that the epilogue does not refer to the wager in heaven in the prologue.

to an already existing framework. But some scholars regard the prologue/epilogue as late.[113]

The motif of the divine assembly, often cited as a reason for a late date, is a feature of early Near Eastern theology encountered in Mesopotamian literature and in the Ugaritic mythological texts and is echoed in some psalms and in Second Isaiah. An older scholar, T K Cheyne[114], argued that the prominence of the figure of 'the Satan' in the prologue shows that it is late, for the only parallel text in which 'the Satan' appears in the same sense as 'the accuser' is in Zechariah 3 (dated c 519 BC) where the conception of the Satan is actually less developed than in Job 1 and 2.[115] However it will be seen below that these arguments for the lateness of the entire prologue are not conclusive.

A fresh approach to the question of the prologue and epilogue and their relation to the dialogue was pursued by L W Batten[116] to whom the epilogue was of prime concern. He regards it as a witness to an original folk tale. His ideas raise a few interesting questions. By focusing on just the epilogue, instead of using the prologue as his starting point, as most scholars do, he brings to light some features that are often glossed over. He divides the epilogue into three parts. Verses 7-9 form the first part in which the striking feature is the commendation of Job not for his endurance of misery as in 2:3 but for what he has said - usually taken to mean what has been said in the dialogue with the friends. His friends are then condemned because they had not spoken right of Yahweh as Job had - they can be forgiven only if Job intercedes for them. Job is condemned by Elihu and God in the speeches, so that this reproof, read in the context of the whole book, comes as a surprise. It is also surprising that the friends are condemned since at every point they

---

113 For example, M H Pope, 1973, argues that the presence of the Satan in the prologue is evidence that the prologue and epilogue can be dated to the Persian period, the rest of the book having been written earlier and later grafted on to this tale. G Hölscher, 1937, and E A Dhorme, 1926, suggested that the author of the dialogues himself wrote the prose parts since he could not have simply begun in chapter 3 without a prose framework. For a discussion of the role of the Satan figure in *Job*, see R S Kluger, 1967.
114 T K Cheyne, 1899-1903.
115 A Dillmann, 1891, wrote, "In Zechariah (1:10f; 3:1f; 6:5) the Prologue of *Job* is *already used* and imitated" implying that *Job* is earlier; cf O Baab, 1951, who also sees the references to angels as late.
116 L W Batten, 1933.

maintained an orthodox position. And it is even more surprising that Job's radical position is justified since he openly accuses God of being unjust. Batten argues that originally this part of the epilogue was in a different place, possibly after chapter 31. He argues that since the epilogue ignores the material in chapters 32:1-42:6 it could not have been written by one familiar with those chapters. It also ignores the prologue and, Batten asserts, "may have been composed before that part was prefixed to the poem."[117] He argues that this piece is quite unconcerned with Job's fortunes and relates only to the dialogue section. He writes:[118]

"The author stands as a referee in the debate and awards the laurels to Job. In this judgement he goes further than the great poet who wrote the debate, for that author apparently intends to do no more than show that the orthodox position is not always consistent with the facts."

Batten's discussion of the second section of the epilogue is of interest. He points out that verses 10-11 ignore the Satan sections of the prologue. He writes:

"Here the statement is specific that the evil that Job suffered was inflicted by Yahweh himself. This confirms the inference that the Satan stories are the latest addition to the book, for they are inconsistent with every other part. In the long discussion between Job and the opponents there is no hint from either party that Job's woes sprang from any source other than God himself."[119]

Here is a fact that is often overlooked: that Satan appears merely in the prologue and not in the epilogue. If we pursue the idea that the Satan passages are later than the rest and omit them from the original form of the story, does that story make sense? I believe that it does.[120]

According to this suggestion, the prologue then starts with the folk-tale introduction to Job and his possessions and stresses the piety of Job. Then 1:6-12 are omitted and the story continues with an account of the afflictions that are sent upon Job which are in fact said to come from God. Job then

---

117 L W Batten, 1933 (p 127).
118 L W Batten, 1933 (p 127).
119 L W Batten, 1933 (p 127).
120 This view is supported by E König, 1893, p 415; L Finkelstein, 1938, p 235; and R H Pfeiffer, 1948, who sees the later addition of the Satan passages as part of his argument for an original Edomite folk tale, to which elements such as these were added by a Jewish redactor.

speaks, "Naked I came from my mother's womb, and naked shall I return; the Lord gave, and the Lord has taken away; blessed be the name of the Lord." He is thus responding as a patient man would respond to suffering - he is a model believer. Then 2:1-8 are removed and the plot continues with the words of Job's wife and Job's reply. Then the three friends appear and cannot speak to him - they are shocked by his condition and they see that no words will appease his suffering. Turning to the epilogue (42:7f), it is possible that God condemns the friends for not having spoken words of comfort to Job and tells them to make a sacrifice, Job acting as intercessor on their behalf. Then the fortunes of Job are doubled and a happy ending closes the book.

Batten's third section consists of verses 12-17 where the wealth Yahweh bestows is doubled - except for the number of children which is left the same. He writes:

"It is clear therefore that this section is closely related to a part of the prologue, but not to all, for in Job's restoration there is ample concern with his property, but not a word about the healing of his disease."[121]

In the prologue the infliction of the disease is attributed to Satan but not the destruction of Job's property. In the prologue, raids and storms are agencies controlled by God himself, for example in 1:16 where the fire of God is described as having fallen from heaven, something Satan could not have controlled. Another feature of this section is the pre-eminence of the daughters - they alone are named and their beauty and wealth stressed. Batten suggests that the reference to sons could be a later interpolation by an editor who thought it would not do to give Job daughters only. In the prologue however the sons are the central figures.

It seems therefore that an argument can be constructed which asserts that the author of the dialogue section of *Job* used an original folk story which did not contain the God/Satan controversy as the framework for his plot. These additions were then made by one concerned to make his own contribution to the problem of God's infliction of suffering on Job for it was unthinkable to the orthodox (probably orthodox wise men) that God should be seen as inflicting men with this kind of misery - it must be the work of Satan. This

---

121 L W Batten, 1933 (p 127).

suggestion that the prologue/epilogue as we now have it contains both an original early prose tale and the orthodox sentiments of later editors, removes the tension between scholars who assert that the section is early and those who assert that it is late - it is both!

(2) The interplay of structure and themes between the prose tale and poetic dialogue

N C Habel[122] talks of themes anticipated in the prose story which are taken up in the dialogue. Major issues are introduced in the prologue, such as the doctrine of reward and retribution, God's arbitrariness and innocent suffering. This argument is used to demonstrate unity of plot and theme. But in my view these themes are introduced in the prologue in order to be deliberately reversed in the dialogue. What is evidenced here is ironic discontinuity. In the prose tale the conventions of the folk-tale genre are apparent. It is a 'once upon a time' tale. Even the location could be imaginary, and certainly would not be well known to an Israelite audience; the patriarchal setting may also be imposed; the characters are not realistically drawn but are defined by stereotyped formulae; the plot is conventional, and there is a repetition of set formulae and economy of language. The switching of scenes from earth to heaven gives it an unreal quality. The reader of course realizes that man cannot have knowledge of a debate that took place in heaven. The hero is presented as the paragon of humanity and the idea of perfection is further emphasized by the arithmetic of his possessions. There is a stress on Job's blamelessness and integrity, demonstrated by his ritual purification of his sons by sacrifice in case they had sinned when celebrating feast days. Although Satan reduces Job's possessions and his family to nothing, Job blesses God and when stricken with disease he also blesses God. His words in 1:21 and 2:10 are key verses in demonstrating his patience. God also vouches for Job's integrity and his innocence. Then the close construction of the plot is broken by the arrival of the friends just as we are expecting to return to heaven and hear God claim his victory. They are portrayed in a favourable light at first since they are respectful to Job and speak no word because his suffering is great.

---

122   N C Habel, 1985.

In the dialogue many aspects of the plot set up in the prose story are deliberately reversed to make a sceptical point. The doctrine of retribution does not work; there is innocent suffering that is totally unjustified; and God is a cruel and arbitrary tyrant with whom reasoned argument is impossible. Job ceases to be patient; he becomes impatient, even blasphemous. He almost does as his wife advises - 'Curse God and die'. He falls short of doing it directly but certainly utters curses, for example against the day of his birth. Job becomes a real character with real feelings and the friends, although they do not come to life in the same way, become argumentative and more and more disrespectful of Job as the dispute develops. There is an ironic refutation of the original words of Job in the prologue. Thus when one compares 1:21 with chapter 3 one can find directly opposite assertions. For example in 1:21 Job reverently accepts the womb but in 3:11 he regrets his emergence from it. Further in 1:21 Job accepts the fact that he will return to the womb but in 3:17 he regrets that he is not in the tomb since he would find rest there. In 1:21 Job accepts God's ways and blesses him. Finally, in 3:20 he questions God's ways and in 3:1 invokes curses.[123] These reversals are surely deliberate on the part of the author, designed to shock the reader and provoke debate. The curious thing is that instead of losing sympathy with this character who suddenly utters blasphemies, one sympathizes with him because his reaction is real and comprehensible - the reader is able to identify with it.

In the dialogue section Job's blamelessness and integrity are really put to the test. Curiously the speeches do not logically follow on one from another and in this way even the dialogue form itself is mocked. There is no real dialogue between Job and the friends - ie between personal experience and the arguments of the orthodox - because they are talking past each other; they do not understand each others' needs. The author is mocking the friends who miss the point just as God later on misses the point. Job also puts God on trial in the dialogue, whereas in the prologue he was prepared to accept good and evil from God. Now he longs for justice and realizes that the only judge is God who has turned against him. He is thus on the verge of despair. His

---

[123] R D Moore, 1983.

only hope is that God will answer him. When he does so, it looks as though Job is vindicated. But the reader is not prepared for what God is about to say.

iv) The speeches of Yahweh and Job's replies

(1) Literary-critical concerns

By its position, length and literary power, the reply of Yahweh stands as the climax of the book and if it is genuine it must be central in the poet's plan.[124] The major objection to the Yahweh speeches is that they do not answer the questions raised with vehemence by Job in the dialogue. God merely silences Job with ironic questions and provides no explanation of his sufferings. However, this viewpoint presupposes that a positive solution should have been provided. Is it not possible that one author deliberately left his questions unanswered knowing from experience that such questions are not answered? A number of scholars regard the speeches as deliberate irony[125] and so the issue of the author's intention comes once again to the forefront of the discussion. *Some* intervention by God in response to Job's plea is generally considered a structural necessity to the plot and to the symmetry of the book.[126] However the problem is that what Yahweh says to Job is anticipated in the earlier speeches of each of the three friends, of Elihu and of Job himself. This has led some scholars to argue that the present Yahweh speeches are not the original form the solution took. A further complication is that in 42:7 Job is described by God as having spoken what is "right", an odd assertion for the author to make if the aim of his inclusion of the Yahweh speeches was to prove just the opposite.[127]

---

124 There is considerable debate about the authenticity and contribution of each speech - both have been either evaluated highly or dismissed as repetitive, inferior or unnecessary - eg compare the views of S R Driver, 1906, with C Cornhill, 1907, on the first speech and those of R Gordis, 1964, and C Kuhl, 1953, on the second. A recent monograph on the unity and relationship of the Yahweh speeches is that of J van Oorschot, 1987.
125 eg R A F MacKenzie, 1959, sees the Yahweh speeches as ironic in the way they ignore questions of justice and retribution and instead stress the divine mystery.
126 H H Rowley, 1970, holds that "it is hard to suppose that the book ever existed without any speech of Yahweh, for without some speech from him the structure of the book collapses." (p 14).
127 If one accepts the placing of 42:7 here - cf L W Batten, 1933 above.

The main purpose of the dialogue section and of the sceptical utterances of Job, highlighted by the technique of the deliberate misuse of forms, is to launch an attack upon God. It is clear from this that the author of *Job* intended the Yahweh speeches to form the climax to the original book as a response to Job. He deliberately made them ironic in tone and largely irrelevant to Job's questions in order to show that Job's presupposition that God would answer his questions is all wrong. The question of whether both speeches or only one is original to the author remains.[128] If one denies an ironic tone to these speeches, one has more ground for arguing that they are secondary. However they do add a new dimension to the book and to the argument and in that sense contribute to the overall themes of the book. The first speech implies that the suffering of the just, like all phenomena of nature, enters into the scheme of divine providence and that man has to accept that God's motives regarding individuals are his own affair. The second speech maintains that if God spares the wicked it is not because he lacks the power to overthrow them.

The main point of dispute is not whether there are any God speeches in the design of the main author but whether both speeches are original to him. My own criterion of the use of the 'misuse of forms' technique and its appearance

---

[128] The authenticity of Yahweh's second speech is most frequently questioned. It is widely regarded as "uncalled for, since it adds nothing essentially new, but merely continues in an inferior way what the first speech had said." (H H Rowley, 1958, p 90). The style is long and heavy and is often attributed to a different author. Scholars reject varying amounts of the speech as secondary or suggest different rearrangements to cope with inconsistencies in both structure and message eg S R Driver and G B Gray, 1921, argue that 40:6-42:1 is secondary because in 40:4b Job has already thrown up his case so there is no further need for Yahweh to speak. They also argue that whilst there is a new subject in the second speech there is not sufficient distinctness of purpose, nor does it draw from Job a really distinct confession for he does not withdraw his impugnment of God's righteousness. However R Gordis, 1978, draws a clear distinction between the first and second speeches and between Job's two confessions. S R Driver and G B Gray, 1921, set out the standard arguments for regarding the Behemoth-Leviathan section as secondary - there are linguistic and stylistic differences between this section and the rest of the book; there is an incongruity between the length of the descriptions of the beasts in the first speech and in this section (and the physical aspect rather than the temperament or habits of the animals is described); the question form which is frequent in the first speech is much less common here and results in a lack of vividness in this speech; and Behemoth and Leviathan, if they are respectively the hippopotamus and the crocodile, are predominantly Egyptian animals as opposed to the Palestinian animals described in the first speech; whilst if they are mythical monsters they also differ from the actual animals of Palestine described in the first speech. The loss of the Behemoth-Leviathan section does not radically affect the overall theme of the speeches so that the question of their authenticity can be regarded as of secondary importance.

in different sections reveals that it is used only in the first speech of God. However if the two speeches form a unit, this is not a strong argument. In the way that they both basically emphasize the same point about God's power and might over creation, they can be seen as a single unit. My inclination is to incorporate both speeches as part of the original author's intention since they do not contradict or anticipate his thought in the way that the Elihu speeches do. However Schmid[129] accommodates only the first Yahweh speech by arguing that it is a response to the problem of the innocent sufferer which belongs to genuine wisdom (the second speech he sees as secondary since it reasserts dogmatic wisdom and regards it as added by the proponents of later orthodoxy). He writes of the first Yahweh speech:[130]

"Sein Leiden wird nicht rational erklärt, wie es von den drei Freunden und Elihu versucht wird, sondern Hiob wird angehalten, sein Geschick im Horizont der kosmischen Ordnung zu sehen und anzunehmen."

A reasonable conclusion might be that the original author of the dialogue wrote the first Yahweh speech and the first few verses of the second which together formed a whole. Then came Job's reply which we have after the second speech. The animal passages, notably the Behemoth and Leviathan passage, were possibly added by an orthodox editor who wished to reinforce the point about God being all-powerful to counteract the limitations on God imposed by Job in the dialogue.

(2) The juxtaposition of the dialogue, speeches of Yahweh and Job's reply

Basically God does not answer the questions posed by Job and apparently has no intention of doing so. He merely stresses his power - as Job anticipated he would do in chapter 9. His reply is deliberately disappointing and an anticlimax. It also presents a picture of God which is in contradiction to the rest of the Old Testament and which confirms Job's worst fears about the impossibility of communion with him. And yet Job repents. He admits his fault. This, again, seems incongruous. The reader has been in agreement

---

129 H H Schmid, 1966.
130 H H Schmid, 1966 (p 180-181), "His [Job's] suffering is not explained rationally, as the three friends and Elihu have tried to explain it; instead Job is instructed to see his own fate within the horizons of cosmic order and to accept it in that context."

with Job all along - he too wants to be assured of a just God - and yet here Job loses all his grandeur and repents in dust and ashes. He does not however answer God's questions directly - once again characters are talking past each other. It is ironic that he lays his hand on his mouth despite not having been given an answer (see discussion of J G Williams'[131] idea of Job's 'tongue in cheek' repentance, pp 187-190). It suggests to me that this is the author's experience - that often one does not receive a satisfactory answer but all one can do before such a God is to bow down and repent.

(3) The Epilogue

With the epilogue the irony reaches its peak. Job is said by God to be in the right after he has just repented of his wrongdoing and despised himself still further than in the dialogue. In the context of the prose tale alone God could have been praising Job for the words uttered by the patient character of the prologue - and this is probably how the pious read the book. However in its present position it is ironically made to refer to his words in the dialogue, with all their curses and blasphemies. It is generally regarded as a justification of Job against the orthodoxy of the friends by demonstrating that it is better to question than to accept rigid orthodoxy which falsifies things just as much. Job is presumably also right in his questioning of the God-man relationship - perhaps it was his curses and blasphemies that he was repenting of in his reply, although this is not explicitly said. This statement of God's is in fact the most helpful thing that God says in the whole debate - he at last shows Job some recognition and support, but only after Job has repented. But this again presents a strange view of God, and seems out of character with what we have already seen of God. Perhaps the author's intention was to emphasize further God's arbitrariness.

A further irony of the epilogue is that Job has to intercede for the friends who all along have been defending traditional concepts about God and suffering and who, until 42:7, seem to be supported by God. N C Habel[132], in an article on the friendship motif in *Job*, remarks that it is given an ironical

---

131 J G Williams, 1971.
132 N C Habel, 1977.

twist both in 42:7 and in Job's intercession for the friends. The Lord then accepts Job's prayers for the first time since all his other petitions have apparently fallen on deaf ears. The final irony is, of course, that the theme of the dialogue is reversed - there is an unsatisfactory rewarding of Job with material possessions which appears to justify the friends' position, supports the doctrine of retribution overturned by Job in the dialogue, and contradicts God's vindication of Job in 42:7. This puts Job back into the same position as he was at the start, even more baffled and yet assured of a real relationship with God.

It is clear therefore that the way the book is now arranged by an author is critical for an interpretation of it. Irony is the key to its complicated contradictions and opposing themes. The arrangement was made with sceptical intent and the content is moulded into this structure by polarities of theme and contradictory answers. Thus the main concern of the author was not to give a solution to the problem of innocent suffering, the doctrine of retribution or to the nature of the relationship between God and man. Rather he purposefully shows that there are no solutions. The problem of why the innocent suffer is not answered, rather innocent suffering is seen to be simply a fact of life. The doctrine of retribution is shown to contradict the findings of personal experience, and yet at the end it seems to be the only answer. In terms of the God-man relationship, one is no nearer a solution. God is not portrayed as a God who cares for man's plight, and the only justification Job receives is in 42:7. There is no straightforward meaning to the book. Rather, simple solutions to the problems raised are shown, by the irony used and the inconsistencies highlighted by the author, to be non-existent. In this way the author conveys his profound scepticism.

Thus the final form of the book as the author intended it is deliberately contradictory. However some editorial redaction occurred which accounts for the Elihu speeches, for the hymn to wisdom, for the addition of the Satan passages and possibly for the animal passages in the second speech of Yahweh and dislocation of the third cycle of speeches (although I prefer to regard the latter as an accident of transmission). Why then did not a final editor remove the contradictions and make the book more palatable to the orthodox reader? The answer must surely be either that these contradictions could not be removed because they formed an intrinsic part of the story or that the editor did not recognize them as contradictions, wishing to read the book in an orthodox manner and misled by the pious prologue.

The author had taken the traditional tale of Job and made the central character say unorthodox things within the confines of traditional discussion of the doctrine of retribution. These contradictions were not recognized to a sufficient extent to lead later editors to remove them. However the additions were attempts to enhance the orthodox flavour of the book, which was seen to be lacking in the dialogue. The portrayal of the character of Job and the techniques of the author provides us with a clue that there was a stage in Hebrew thought where moral ambiguities were present and where sceptical questioning endangered traditionally-held beliefs. This stage however was not allowed to develop further due to a widespread reserve towards the criticism of traditional values, for many were of the opinion that such a hardening of an individual in radical positions was destructive.

It has been argued above that the keynote of *Job* is its scepticism, working on the dual levels of sceptical questioning by the *character* Job and a sceptical juxtaposition of the various incongruous parts of the book by the *author*. This can be related to the context of a group, similar in kind to the Greek sceptics, or to a wider sceptical tradition which existed at a certain time in the development of Israelite religion. A stage of 'scepticism' in Israel has been recognized by some scholars. J F Priest[133], for example, refers to a useful suggestion made to him by P Berger in a private letter:

"that skepticism may best be understood as 'an intellectually articulated challenge to the ultimate legitimations of society; that is, a radical questioning of the religious, philosophical or ethical presuppositions upon which society rests.'"

This can be seen to relate closely to what is going on in *Job* - it provides a challenge to the traditional beliefs of a society which has become hardened into a certain pattern of thinking. It stands on the edge of a tradition which the believer has in a sense grown out of, in the same way that *Jonah* stands at the close of prophecy and points to its shortcomings. However it does not decide

---

133 J F Priest, 1968 (p 319).

in favour of one side or another - it merely throws up the inconsistencies. However Priest then asserts that:

"one seldom raises the question of skepticism in ancient Israel, for almost all that we know of ancient Israelite thought comes to us through the medium of the books of the Hebrew Bible which are themselves "official" statements legitimating that society."[134]

This suggests that none of the books can have a sceptical intent, but maybe this statement merely reflects the pious way in which they were read. This, we have seen, led to the inclusion of *Job* in the canon without any question being raised. Priest then goes on to talk of "an informal kind of skepticism operative at all stages of Israel's history...the formal, intellectual articulation does indeed come after the Exile."[135] This statement suggests that scepticism formed an undercurrent in Israelite life before it became explicit in *Job* which provides support for the quest for 'protest literature' in the Bible.

The precise nature of this scepticism is examined by Crenshaw.[136] His method is to define scepticism in the context of a study of the difference between scepticism, pessimism and cynicism. Crenshaw writes:

"In my view, skepticism includes both a denial and an affirmation. The negative side of a skeptic's mental outlook consists of the doubting thought, whereas the positive affirmation of a hidden reality indicates that it is altogether inappropriate to accuse skeptics of unbelief. This vision of a better world is inherent in skepticism."[137]

This pinpoints the tension that is to be found in *Job* between Job's desire to affirm and to deny God. Perhaps this tension can also be found both in the author's negative criticism of the tradition and in his extension of the boundaries of that tradition through his questioning. There is a further tension between the author's mocking of the tradition, and yet using the forms of that tradition. Crenshaw writes of Israel:

"The matrix formed by the disparity between the actual state of affairs and a vision of what should be both sharpened critical powers and heightened religious fervor. Doubt, it follows, is grounded in profound faith. Once skeptics lose all hope of achieving the desired transformation, pessimism sets in, spawning sheer indifference to cherished convictions."[138]

---

134 J F Priest, 1968 (p 319).
135 J L Crenshaw, 'The Birth of Skepticism in Ancient Israel', 1980 (p 1).
136 J L Crenshaw, 'The Birth of Skepticism in Ancient Israel', 1980 (p 1).
137 J L Crenshaw, 'The Birth of Skepticism in Ancient Israel', 1980 (p 1).
138 J L Crenshaw, 'The Birth of Skepticism in Ancient Israel', 1980 (p 1).

It is certainly true that Job and the author of *Job* have a profound faith which comes through in various passages in the book and yet the realization that traditional answers are shallow and unsatisfying and inimical to personal experience inspires the scepticism and doubting which is embedded deep in the book. The positive value of such questioning should however be stressed. Scepticism forges a new and difficult path and involves much painful questioning of traditional beliefs but in the end Job was 'in the right' to question - not to do so falsifies life even more.

In conclusion, the book of *Job* can be regarded as 'sceptical' literature on two levels. The first is in terms of the content of Job's speeches. Job dares to challenge God and protest vehemently against his apparent arbitrariness. His words contrast with the dogmatism of the friends. His sentiments are 'sceptical' because they suspend belief in a God that can be known and comprehended. The second level is in terms of the arrangement of the book - its form and structure and the intention of its author whose techniques and milieu are revealed by a form-critical approach to the book. This study has revealed that the scepticism of the author is shown by his use of the 'misuse of forms', a technique akin to 'parody' as a literary use, rather than a classification. It is also revealed by his juxtaposition of different sections of the book which appear to be inconsistent but in fact display irony and sceptical intent. The work of the author is made comprehensible against the background of a context outside the mainline wisdom tradition which bears more resemblances to the Greek 'sceptics' than to traditional wisdom circles.

The author of *Job* is presenting a new and revolutionary outlook on the status of the individual before God and in the face of suffering. He breaks the bounds of convention in the way in which he portrays the character of Job challenging God with 'sceptical' questions. He displays his 'scepticism' however on a more profound level in his parodying of the established tradition on the level of form and in his juxtaposition of parts of the book so that, for example, Job is not only asking awkward questions but is being praised for doing so. This scepticism is positive and daring, but it was not a genre that was taken up by subsequent biblical authors or fully understood by interpreters from early times. The book's very originality and unorthodoxy led to its omission from the mainstream of Hebrew literature.

# Conclusion

This monograph has presented arguments which lead to the conclusion that the book of *Job* is best described and understood as 'sceptical' literature. In the introduction it was noted that this description is rarely used by scholars and rarely satisfactorily defined. Furthermore, whilst the content of Job's utterances in the dialogue has at times been described as 'sceptical', literary aspects concerning the form, genre and overall structure of the book which reveal the 'scepticism' of the author have been neglected, as have considerations regarding the role of the author and the circles or tradition responsible for its production. I have attempted to rectify this imbalance in this monograph.

I took traditional and critical approaches to the message of *Job* as my starting point to demonstrate the range of differing interpretations of Job that are possible and to show the one-sidedness of many attempts to find an overall message for *Job*. I then assessed the assignation of *Job* to 'wisdom' or 'wisdom literature' which has also suffered from imprecision of terminology and definition because it has been part of an attempt to find an overall classification for the book. I concluded that, on a narrow definition of 'wisdom', *Job* fails as a wisdom text, although in broad terms it can be seen to have sprung from the same intellectual and spiritual quest as other wisdom books. I suggested that it may represent part of a more general intellectual exercise with its context outside wisdom circles, or may be the product of a different mainline group distinct from wisdom circles. Finally I assessed attempts by scholars to find an overall classification for *Job* in terms of 'genre' which was also found to be unsatisfactory. It was seen that the presence of small genres in the text is not sufficient to classify the whole in terms of that genre, nor is it satisfactory to decide the overall genre of a work and then try to fit all smaller genres into this picture. The validity of the quest for an overall genre was thus questioned and a new methodology suggested which breaks the whole book down into smaller genres and gradually builds up a complete picture at various genre levels.

Deliberate concentration on small passages in *Job* revealed a striking variety of different genres not only from 'wisdom', but from 'legal' and 'psalmic' or 'hymnic' origins too. A good mix of these genres was found in each chapter of the book (excepting the 'narrative' genre of the prologue/epilogue), none of which were found to predominate to any significant extent. It was clear that this diversity of small genres was significant and it led to a new form-critical approach to *Job* being undertaken. This led to the discovery that a characteristic feature of *Job* is that it constantly 'misuses' the forms it contains. Diverse forms from many areas of Israelite life are deliberately misused by the author of *Job* to convey his sceptical message - a traditional form is used with a different content and context and thus has a different function. A detailed discussion of passages showing the deliberate misuse of forms reveals the main examples of this technique in Job 3:11-26; 6:8-10; 7:1-21; 9:5-10,25-28; 10:2-12,13-17; 12:7-12,13-25; 13:20-22; 14:1-12,13; 16:7-14; 19:22; 21:7-13,23-26; 23:8-9; 26:5-14; 31 and in chapter 38 which parodies set-piece interrogations about the cosmos such as are found in the prophets. The occurrence of the 'misuse of forms' technique only in Job's speeches in the dialogue section and in the first speech of Yahweh raises the possibility that parts of the book in which such techniques are not found may not be original to this author. These parts were found to correspond to sections generally regarded by scholars as secondary - for example the speeches in the third cycle, commonly seen as inauthentic in the mouth of *Job*, the speeches of Elihu, and the hymn to wisdom. It was seen that this misuse is best illustrated by comparison of the form in *Job* with the same form being used in a *traditional* way in another book in the Old Testament. Furthermore the distinctiveness of *Job* was highlighted by a comparison with Ecclesiastes. In Ecclesiastes the author uses similar techniques of forms on the smallest genre levels to a similar unorthodox end, but his use is almost exclusively of wisdom forms. In this he stands closer to mainline wisdom, despite clearly providing a critique of it.

A more suitable genre for *Job* than traditional classifications, one which characterizes this misuse of forms technique in order to convey a radical message, is 'parody', a genre which is by its nature parasitic and makes a deliberate improper use of other genres. By his use of parody the author deliberately stepped outside literary conventions to make a protest. 'Parody' does not necessarily contain a comic element, as in modern definitions, and a brief study of early parodies confirms that a basic definition of parody needs to be more general. Its keynote is the way in which it uses existing material to show up the weaknesses of that material on the level of form as well as content. Parody as a literary technique by a biblical author was also found in the book of *Jonah* in which the author's intention is to satirize and parody the prophetic tradition with much use of irony and innuendo.

Finally an attempt was made to characterize *Job* as 'sceptical' in terms of its setting, content and structure. This was discussed on two levels - that of the scepticism of Job the character and that of the author of *Job*. It was concluded that a 'sceptical' tradition as a context for this author's activity may be sought both in a broader intellectual milieu which lies outside the main wisdom tradition (to be dated to the 4th century BC in the period immediately preceding the Hellenistic era) and in a narrower philosophical group which can be likened to the milieu of the Greek sceptics. The scepticism conveyed by the author of *Job* resembles the 'suspending of belief' practised by the early Greek sceptics, this definition being at the core of the meaning of the word, and whilst no interdependence of cultures can be found, the parallel is instructive. The scepticism in *Job* is working on two levels. Firstly, Job the character in his doubting comes close to denying the possibility of belief in a God who behaves as Yahweh has to him, and he attacks 'dogmatists', in the form of the friends, and the tradition they represent in the manner of the Greek sceptics. Secondly, the author of *Job* suspends belief when he does not provide a resolution to the arguments raised in the dialogue in the God speeches. The sceptical content of Job's speeches is revealed in his radical reversals of the friends' arguments (which also demonstrates their orthodoxy) and by his attitude in the dialogue towards God. He suspends belief in the orthodox position of the friends regarding retribution and in his previous understanding of God. However the contradictions in his thought suggest that he is suspending judgement rather than coming down fully against the orthodox position.

## Conclusion

The juxtaposition of different sections and themes in *Job* (the prologue/epilogue with the dialogue, and God's speeches with Job's reply) is not in my view evidence of inconsistency by the author, or of secondary addition, but is fundamental to his sceptical intention. The tensions between different sections reveal deliberate irony on the part of the author. Inconsistencies are significant, scepticism and irony being built into the polarities and contradictions contained in the book's structure and themes. The author of the dialogue juxtaposed a traditional folk story about Job (which did not contain the Satan passages) with the speeches of Job, the friends and God to transform a trite story about Job into a work with profound meaning. This deliberate juxtaposition of various parts into a new structure was done with sceptical intent in order to heighten the contradictions inherent in Job's situation. This provides the clue to the overall design of the author and to the message of the book.

The author does not provide solutions to the questions he raises, rather he shows by his use of irony that issues such as innocent suffering do not have a simple answer. The final form of the book as the author intended it is deliberately contradictory. These contradictions were reduced in their effect by the additions of later editors. There was a short stage in Hebrew thought, which was not allowed to develop, where moral ambiguities were present and where sceptical questioning endangered traditionally held beliefs. This stage is reflected in the sceptical approach of the author of *Job* which, however, is positive and daring since it highlights the inadequacy of traditional answers, throws up the tensions in the thought of a culture and exposes false doctrines and inadequate beliefs.

In conclusion, this monograph has highlighted the importance of studying techniques of form when seeking to understand the 'scepticism' of *Job*. It highlights particularly the deliberate misuse of form to make a sceptical point in the manner of 'parody'. This fresh, form-critical approach to *Job*, which takes into account questions of genre, overall structure and the interrelationship between form, content and context, is a crucial key for unlocking the meaning of the book and may well provide a starting-point for the analysis of other books and passages in the Old Testament. This thesis has highlighted the 'sceptical' content of *Job* in terms of Job's own radical 'suspending of belief' in traditional wisdom categories. It has also placed a new emphasis on the scepticism and irony employed by the author of the book and has suggested that a 'wisdom' context may not be the most appropriate for the production of *Job* - rather an intellectual tradition or more philosophical group outside wisdom circles with close similarities to the Greek 'sceptics' may be posited. This suggestion throws into question traditional groupings of biblical literature and holds that new alignments of material may be more instructive for an understanding of the development of Israelite religion. *Job* is witness to a profoundly sceptical stage of thought in Israel which questioned traditionally-held beliefs.

# Abbreviations

| | |
|---|---|
| AJSL | American Journal of Semitic Languages |
| AJSLL | American Journal of Semitic Languages and Literatures |
| ALUOS | Annual of Leeds University Oriental Society |
| ANCL | The Anti-Nicene Christian Library, eds A Roberts & J Donaldson, Edinburgh, 1867-97. |
| AO | Archiv für Orientforchung |
| ASTI | Annual of the Swedish Theological Institute |
| AThR | Anglican Theological Review |
| AV | Authorized Version |
| BJRL | Bulletin of the John Rylands Library |
| BK | Biblischer Kommentar |
| BS | Bibliotheca Sacra |
| BTB | Biblical Theology Bulletin |
| BWANT | Beiträge zur Wissenschaft vom Alten und Neuen Testament |
| BZAW | Beihefte zur Zeitschrift für die alttestamentlich Wissenschaft |
| CBQ | Catholic Biblical Quarterly |
| CJT | Canadian Journal of Theology |
| EB | Encyclopaedia Biblica |
| EJ | Encyclopaedia Judaica |
| ET | Expository Times |
| EvTh | Evangelische Theologie |
| HTR | Harvard Theological Review |
| HUCA | Hebrew Union College Annual |
| IB | The Interpreter's Bible |
| IDB | Interpreter's Dictionary of the Bible |
| JAAR | Journal of the American Academy of Religion |
| JBL | Journal of Biblical Literature |
| JBR | Journal of the Bible and Religion |
| JDTh | Jahrbücher für deutsche Theologie |
| JJS | Journal of Jewish Studies |
| JQR | Jewish Quarterly Review |
| JR | Journal of Religion |
| JRAS | Journal of the Royal Asiatic Society |
| JSOT | Journal for the Study of the Old Testament |

| | |
|---|---|
| JSOTS | Journal for the Study of the Old Testament Supplement Series |
| JSS | Journal of Semitic Studies |
| JTS | Journal of Theological Studies |
| OTS | Oudtestamentische Studien |
| PIBA | Proceedings of the Irish Biblical Association |
| PL | Patrologiae [Latinae], Cursus Completus, 221 volumes, Paris 1844-65. |
| RB | Revue Biblique |
| RevExp | Review and Expositor |
| RHPhR | Revue d'Histoire et de Philosophie Religieuses |
| RHR | Revue de l'Histoire des Religions |
| RR | Review of Religion |
| RSV | Revised Standard Version |
| RThPh | Revue de Theologie et de Philosophie |
| SAIW | Studies in Ancient Israelite Wisdom, ed J L Crenshaw, New York, 1976. |
| SBL | Society of Biblical Literature |
| SJT | Scottish Journal of Theology |
| StUNT | Studien zur Umwelt des Neuen Testaments |
| TGOS | Transactions of the Glasgow Oriental Society |
| ThR | Theologische Rundschau |
| VT | Vetus Testamentum |
| VTS | Vetus Testamentum Supplement Series |
| ZAW | Zeitschrift für die alttestamentliche Wissenschaft |
| ZTK | Zeitschrift für Theologie und Kirche |
| | |
| (NF | Neue Folge) |
| (NS | New Series) |

# Bibliography

Ackerman, J.S., 'Satire and Symbolism in the Song of Jonah', *Traditions in transformation, turning points in Biblical Faith*, eds. B. Halpern and J.D. Levenson, Winona Lake, 1981, pp 213-46.

Aharoni, R., 'An Examination of the Literary Genre of the Book of Job', *Tarbiz* 49 (1979), pp 1-13.

Aked, C.F., *The Divine Drama of Job*, Edinburgh, 1913.

Alonso-Schökel, L.A., 'Toward a Dramatic Reading of the Book of Job', *Semeia* 7 (1977), pp 45-61.

Alt, A., 'Zur Vorgeschichte des Buches Hiob', ZAW 55 (1937), pp 265-8.

Ambrose, *De interpellatione Job et Daniel* (PL 14), cc 797-871.

Anderson, F.I., 'Another perspective on the book of Job', *TGOS* 18 (1959/60), pp 53-6.

—, *Job*, (Tyndale Old Testament Commentaries), Leicester, 1976.

Annas, J. and Barnes, J., *The Modes of Scepticism*, (Ancient Texts and Modern Interpretations), Cambridge, 1985.

Anthes, R., 'Lebensregeln und Lebensweisheit der alten Ägypter', AO 32(2) (1933).

Apocrypha, The, *The Oxford Annotated Apocrypha* (RSV), Expanded edition, ed. B.M. Metzger, New York, 1965.

Augustine, *De patientia* (PL 40), cc 611-626.

Baab, O.J., 'The Book of Job', *Interpretation* 5 (1951), pp 329-343.

Bacher, I.W., 'Das Targum zu Hiob', *Monatschrift für die Geschichte und Wissenschaft des Judentums* 20 (1871), pp 208-23, 283-4.

Baker, J.A., 'The Book of Job: Unity and Meaning', JSOTS 2 (Studia Biblica) (1978), pp 17-26.

Balentine, S., *The Hidden God: the hiding of the face of God in the Old Testament*, Oxford, 1984.

Ball, C.J., *The Book of Job*, Oxford, 1922.

Bardtke, H., 'Prophetische Züge im Buche Hiob', *Das Ferne und Nahe Wort* (L. Rost Festschrift), 1967, pp 1-10.

Barnet, S., Berman, M. and Burbo, W. (eds), *A Dictionary of Literary Terms*, London, 1964.

Barr, J., 'Review of Rowley's New Century Bible Commentary on Job', *JSS* 16 (1971), p 103.

—, 'Hebrew Orthography and the Book of Job', JSS 30/1 (Spring 1985), pp 1-33.

—, 'The Book of Job and Its Modern Interpreters', BJRL 54 (1971-2), pp 28-46.

—, 'Why? in Biblical Hebrew', JTS (1985), pp 1-33.

Barth, K., *Church Dogmatics* 4/3 (First Half), translated by G.T. Thompson, Edinburgh, 1936-81, pp 384-9; 398-409; 420-434; 452-461.

Barton, G.A., 'The Composition of Job 24-30', *JBL* 30 (1911), pp 66-77.

—, 'The original home of the Story of Job', *JBL* 31 (1912), pp 63-71.

Barton, J., 'Gerhard von Rad on the world-view of early Israel', JTS N.S. 35/2 (1984), pp 301-323.

—, *Reading the Old Testament*, London, 1984.

Batley, J.Y., *The Problem of Suffering in the Old Testament*, Cambridge, 1916.

Batten, L.W., 'The Epilogue to the Book of Job', AThR 15 (1933), pp 125-8.

Baumer, F.L., *Religion and the Rise of Scepticism*, New York, 1960.

Baumgartel, F., *Der Hiobdialog: Aufriss und Deutung*, BWANT 61 (1933).

Baumgartner, W., 'Die literarischen Gattungen in der Weisheit des Jesus Sirach', ZAW 34 (1914), pp 161-198.

—, *Die Klagegedichte des Jeremia*, BZAW 32 (1917).

—, *Israelitische und Altorientalische Weisheit*, Tübingen, 1933.

—, 'The Wisdom Literature', *The Old Testament and Modern Study*, ed. H.H. Rowley, Oxford, 1951, pp 210-237.

Bentzen, A., *Introduction to the Old Testament* Vol 2, Copenhagen, 1948 (2nd edn. 1952).

Bergant, D., *Job, Ecclesiastes*, (Old Testament Message 18), eds. C. Stuhlmueller and M. McNamara, Delaware, 1982.

Bertie, P., *Le Poeme de Job*, Paris, 1929.

Besserman, L.L., *The Legend of Job in the Middle Ages*, Cambridge Mass., 1979.

Beveridge, H., 'The Date of the Book of Job', JRAS, 1919, p 234.

Beyerlin, W. (ed.), *Near Eastern Religous Texts relating to the Old Testament*, London, 1978.

Bickell, G., *Das Buch Hiob*, Vienna, 1894.

Bishop, E.F.F., *Job, the Patriarch of East Palestine*, Cambridge, 1973.

Blank, S.H., 'The Confessions of Jeremiah and the meaning of prayer', *HUCA* 21 (1949), pp 331-354.

—, 'An effective literary device in Job 31', *JJS* 2/2 (1951), pp 105-7.

—, 'Men against God: The Promethean Element in Biblical Prayer', *JBL* 72 (1953), pp 1-13.

—, 'Wisdom' *IDB* 4, Abingdon, 1962, pp 852-861.

—, 'The Prophet as paradigm', *Essays in Old Testament Ethics*, eds. J.L. Crenshaw and J.T. Willis, New York, 1974, pp 111-130.

Bleek, F., *Introduction to the Old Testament* 2, English translation by G.H. Venables, 1894.

Bleeker, L.H.K., *Job*, 1926.

Blenkinsopp, J., *Wisdom and Law in the Old Testament*, London, 1983.

Blommerde, A., *Northwest Semitic Grammar and Job*, Rome, 1969.

Bloomfield, M.W., 'Chaucerian realism' in *The Cambridge Chaucer Companion*, eds. P. Boitani, and J. Mann, Cambridge, 1986, pp 179-193.

Booth, W.C., *A Rhetoric of Irony*, Chicago, 1971.

Bottéro, J., 'Le "Dialogue pessimiste" et la transcendance', *RThPh* 16 (1966), pp 7-24.

Bousset, W. and Gressman, H., *Die Religion des Judentums im späthellenistichen Zeitälter*, Tübingen, 1926. (reprinted 1966).

Box, G.H., *Judaism in the Greek Period*, Oxford, 1932, pp 119-132.

Bradley, A.C., *Shakespearian Tragedy*, London, 1904.

Bradley, G.G., *Lectures on the Book of Job*, Oxford, 1888.

Braun, R., 'Kohelet und die frühhellenistische Popularphilosophie', BZAW 130 (1973).

Brennecke, E., 'Job' in H.C. Alleman and E.E. Flack, *Old Testament Commentary*, Philadelphia, 1948.

Brenner, A., 'God's Answer to Job', VT 31 (1981), pp 129-137.

Bright, J., 'A prophet's lament and its answer: Jeremiah 15:10-21', *Interpretation* 28 (1974), pp 59-74.

Brock, S.P. (ed.), *Testamentum Iobi*, Pseudepigrapha Veteris Testamenti Graece, Leiden, 1967.

Brook, P.M., *Job, an interpretation*, London, 1967.

Bruce, W.S., *The Wisdom Literature of the Old Testament*, London, 1928, pp 13-30.

Buber, M., 'The Heart Determines (Psalm 73)', *Biblical Humanism*, New York, 1968, pp 199-210.

Budde, K., *Beiträge zur Kritik des Buches Hiob*, Bonn, 1876.

Budde, K., *Das Buch Hiob*, Handkommentar zum AT, 1st edn. Göttenburg, 1896; 2nd edn. Göttingen, 1913.

Buhl, F., *Kanon und Text des Alten Testaments*, Leipzig, 1891; English translation, 1892.

—, 'Zur Vorgeschichte des Buches Hiob', *BZAW* 41 (1925), pp 52-61.

Buhl, W., Euripides: *Cyclops*, Leipzig, 1983.

Burnyeat, M.F., *The Skeptical Tradition*, Berkeley Los Angeles, London, 1983.

Burrows, M., 'The Voice from the Whirlwind', JBL 47 (1928), pp 117-132.

Bussler, E., 'Hiob und Prometheus, zwei Vörkampfer der göttlichen Gerechtigkeit', Hamburg, 1897.

Buttenweiser, M., *The Book of Job*, London, 1922.


Calvin, J., *Sermons...sur le livre de Job*, 1569 (English translation: A. Golding, London, 1574).

Caquot, A., 'On the Meaning and Study of Israelite Wisdom, Israelite perceptions of wisdom and strength in the light of the Ras Shamra Texts', in J. Gammie et al. (eds) *Israelite Wisdom: Theological and Literary Essays in Honour of Samuel Terrien*, Missoula, 1978.

Carden, R.J., *The Papyrus Fragments of Sophocles*, Berlin, 1974.

Carroll, R.P., 'Postscript to Job', *The Modern Churchman* N.S. 19 (1975-6), p 166.

—, *From chaos to covenant: Prophecy in the book of Jeremiah* , New York, 1981.

Cartensen, R.N., 'The Persistence of the "Elihu" Tradition in Later Jewish writings', *Lexington Theological Quarterly* 2 (1967), pp 37-46.

Causse, A., 'Sagesse égyptienne et sagesse juive', *RHPhR* (1929/2), pp 149-169.

Ceresko, A.R., *Job 29-31 in the Light of Northwest Semitic*, Rome, 1980.

Chaine, J. and Robert, A., in Robert Tricot, *Initiation Biblique*, 3rd edn. 1954.

Charles, R.H., *Apocrypha and Pseudepigrapha of the Old Testament*, Volume 2, Oxford, 1913.

Charlesworth, J.H., *The Old Testament Pseudepigrapha*, Vol. 1, London, 1983.

Cheyne, T.K., *Job and Solomon*, London, 1887, pp 11-115.

—, *Jewish Religious Life after the Exile*, New York, 1898.

—, 'Job', EB, eds. T.K. Cheyne and J.S. Black, (4 vols), 1899-1903, cc. 2464-2491.

Childs, B.S., *Isaiah and the Assyrian Crisis*, Studies in Biblical Theology Second Series 3, London, 1967.

—, *Introduction to the Old Testament as Scripture*, Philadelphia, 1979.

Churgin, P., *Targum Kethubim*, New York, 5705=1945.

Clements, R.E., *Prophecy and Tradition*, Oxford, 1975.

Clines, D.J.A., 'Job', *A Bible Commentary for today*, ed. G.C.D. Howley, London and Glasgow, 1979, pp 559-592.

—, 'The Arguments of Job's three friends', *Art and Meaning: Rhetoric in Biblical Literature*, (JSOTS 19), eds, D.J.A. Clines, D.M. Gunn and A.J. Hauser, Sheffield, 1982, pp 99-214.

—, 'In search of the Indian Job', VT 33 (1983), pp 398-418.

—, Job 1-20 (Word Biblical Commentary), Dallas, Texas, 1989.

Coats, G.W., *Rebellion in the Wilderness*, Nashville, 1968.

—, *Saga, Legend, Tale, Novella, Fable: Narrative forms in Old Testament literature*, JSOTS 35, Sheffield, 1985.

Cornill, C., *Introduction to the Canonical Books of the Old Testament*, translated by G.H. Box, New York, 1907.

Couroyer, B., "Qui est Behemoth?', *RB* 82 (1975), pp 418-443.

Cox, D., *The Triumph of Impotence: Job and the Tradition of the Absurd*, Analecta Gregoriana 212, Rome, 1978.

—, 'The Structure and Function of the Final Challenge: Job 29-31', *PIBA* 5 (1981), pp 55-71.

—, *Proverbs* (Old Testament Message volume 17), Delaware, 1982.

Cranfield, C.E.B., 'An interpretation of the book of Job', *ET* 54-5 (1942/3), pp 295-298.

Creelman, H., *Introduction to the Old Testament*, New York, 1917, p 239.

Crenshaw, J.L., 'Method in determining wisdom influence upon "historical" literature', *JBL* 88 (1969), pp 129-142.

—, 'Popular Questioning of the Justice of God in Ancient Israel', *ZAW* 82 (1970), pp 380-395.

—, *Prophetic Conflict*, BZAW 124 (1971).

—, 'The Eternal Gospel (Ecclesiastes 3:11)', *Essays in Old Testament Ethics*, eds. J.L. Crenshaw and J.T. Willis, New York 1974, pp 23-55.

—, 'Wisdom', *Old Testament Form Criticism*, ed. J.H. Hayes, San Antonio, 1974, pp 225-264.

—, *Hymnic Affirmation of Divine Justice*, SBL Dissertation Series 24, Missoula, 1975.

—, *Studies in Ancient Israelite Wisdom*, New York, 1975.

Crenshaw, J.L., 'The Human Dilemma and Literature of Dissent', *Tradition and Theology in the Old Testament*, ed. D. Knight, Philadelphia, 1976, pp 235-258.

—, 'Theodicy', *IDBSupp*, Nashville, 1976.

—, 'Wisdom in Israel by Gerhard von Rad', *Religious Studies Review* 2/2 (1976), pp 6-12.

—, 'Wisdom in the Old Testament', *IDBSupp* (1976), pp 952-956.

—, 'The Twofold Search: A Response to Luis Alonso Schökel', *Semeia* 7 (1977), pp 63-69.

—, 'The Birth of Skepticism in Ancient Israel', *The Divine Helmsman: Studies in God's control of human events* (presented to Lou H. Silberman), eds. J.L. Crenshaw and S. Sandmel, New York, 1980, pp 1-9.

—, *Old Testament Wisdom: An Introduction*, Atlanta, 1981; London, 1982.

—, (ed.) *Theodicy in the Old Testament*, (Issues in Religion and Theology 4), London and Philadelphia, 1983.

—, *A Whirlpool of Torment*, (Overtures to Biblical Theology 12), Philadelphia, 1984.

—, *Ecclesiastes*, London, 1988.

Crews, F., *The Pooh Perplex*, London, 1963.

Crook, M.B., *The Cruel God, Job's Search for the Meaning of Suffering*, Boston, 1959.

Curtis, J.B., 'On Job's Witness in Heaven', *JBL* 102 (1983), pp 549-562.

Cyprian, *Liber de bono patientia* (PL 4), cc. 645-662.


Dahood, M.J., 'Some Northwest-Semitic Words in Job', *Biblica* 38 (1957), pp 306-320.

Dancy, J.C., *The Shorter Books of the Apocrypha*, (Cambridge Bible), Cambridge, 1972.

Davidson, A., *The Book of Job*, (Cambridge Bible for Schools and Colleges), Cambridge, 1884; revised by H.C.O. Lanchester, 1918.

Davidson, A.B. and Toy, C.H., 'Job', *Encyclopaedia Britannica*, 1911, pp 422-427.

Davidson, R., 'Some Aspects of the Theological Significance of Doubt in the Old Testament', *ASTI* 7 (1968-9), pp 41-52.

—, *The Courage to Doubt*, London, 1983.

Davidson, S., *Introduction to the Old Testament* 2, 1862, pp 174-233.

Davies, G.I., 'Review of H.P. Müller - Das Hiobproblem. Seine Stellung und Entstehung im alten Orient und im Alten Testament', *VT* 33 (1983), pp 366-8.

Delitzsch, F., *Biblical Commentary on the Book of Job*, 2 volumes, translated by F. Bolton, Edinburgh, 1866 (original edn. 1864).

Dennefield, L., 'Les discours d' Élihou', *RB* 48 (1939), pp 163-180.

Dhorme, E.A., 'Les chapitres 25-28 du livre de Job', *RB* 33 (1924), pp 343-358.

Dhorme, E.A., *A Commentary on the Book of Job*, Paris, 1926 (English translation, 1967).

—, *Le Livre de Job*, (Biblioteque de la Pleiade 2), Reprinted Paris, 1972, pp 1221-1348.

Dhorme, P., 'Le Pays de Job', *RB* N.S. 8 (1911), pp 102-7.

Dibelius, M., *James*, (Hermeneia), Philadelphia, 1976 (revised edition in original translation by H. Greeven).

Dick, M.B., 'The legal metaphor in Job 31', *CBQ* 41 (1979), pp 37-50.

—, 'Job 31 The oath of innocence and the sage', *ZAW* 95 (1983), pp 31-53.

Dillmann, A., *Das Buch Hiob*, Kurzgefasstes exegetisches Handbuch zum Alten Testament, Leipzig, 1891.

Dillon, E.J., *The Sceptics of the Old Testament*, London, 1895.

Dover, K.J., *Aristophanic Comedy*, London, Berkeley and New York, 1972.

Driver, S.R., *The Book of Job in the Revised Version*, Oxford, 1906.

—, *Introduction to the literature of the Old Testament*, Edinburgh, 1909 (8th edn), pp 408-435.

—, 'Problems in Job', *AJSLL* 52 (1935-6), pp 160-170.

—, and Gray, G.B., *The Book of Job*, (International Critical Commentary), Edinburgh, 1921.

—, Dubarle, A-M, *Les Sages d'Israel*, Lectio Divina, Paris, 1946.

Duesberg, H. and Fransen, I., *Les Scribes Inspirés*, Belgium, 1966.

Duhm, B., *Das Buch Hiob*, (Kurzer Handkommentar zum Alten Testament), Freiburg, 1897.

Eaton, J.H., *Job*, (Old Testament Guides 1), Sheffield, 1985.

Eerdmans, B.D., *Studies in Job*, Leiden, 1939.

Eichhorn, J.G., *Einleitung in das Alte Testament*, Leipzig, 1823-4. (originally published 1787).

Eissfeldt, O., *Einleitung in das Alte Testament*, Tübingen, 1934. (English translation P.R. Ackroyd, Oxford, 1965, pp 454-490, 764-5.)

Ellermeier, F., 'Randbemerkung zur Kunst des Zitierens: Welches Buch nannte Heinrich Heine "das Hoheleid der Skepsis"?', *ZAW* 77, N.F. 36, 1965, pp 93-4.

—, *Qohelet* 1/1, Herzberg, 1967.

Ellison, H.L., *From Tragedy to Triumph, the message of the book of Job*, London, 1958.

Emerton, J.A., 'Wisdom', *Tradition and Interpretation*, ed. G.W. Anderson, Oxford, 1979, pp 214-237.

Ewald, G.H.A. von, *Commentary on the Book of Job*, translated by J.F. Smith, London and Edinburgh, 1882.

Feinberg, C.L., 'The Book of Job', *BS* 91 (1934), pp 78-86.

—, 'Job and the Nation Israel', *BS* 96 (1939) pp 405-511; *BS* 97 (1940) pp 27-33, 211-216.

Fichtner, J., *Die altorientalische Weisheit in ihrer israelitisch-jüdischen Ausprägung*, BZAW 62 (1933).

—, 'Jesaja unter den Weisen', *Theologische Literaturzeitung* 74 (1949), pp 75-80. (reprinted in *Gottes Weisheit*, Stuttgart,1965, pp 18-26).

—, 'Hiob in der Verkündigung unserer Zeit', *Wort und Dienst* 2 (1950), pp 71-89.

Fielding, H., *The Tragedy of Tragedies or The Life and Death of Tom Thumb the Great*, London, 1731.

Fine, H.A., 'The Tradition of a Patient Job', *JBL* 74 (1955), pp 28-32.

Finkelstein, L., *The Pharisees* 1, Philadelphia, 1938.

Fisch, H., *Poetry with a purpose*, Bloomington and Indianapolis, 1988.

Fishbane, M., 'Jeremiah 4 and Job 3: A Recovered Use of the Creation Pattern', *VT* 21 (1971), pp 151-167.

Fohrer, G., 'Zur Vorgeschichte und Komposition des Buches Hiob', *VT* 6 (1956), pp 249-267; reprinted in *Studien zum Buche Hiob*, 1983.

—, 'Review of Westermann, *Der Aufbau des Buches Hiob*', *VT* 7 (1957), pp 107-111.

—, 'Form und Funktion in der Hiobdichtung', *Studien zum Buche Hiob*, 1963, pp 60-77. Originally published in *Zeitschrift der Deutschen Morgenländischen Gesellschaft* 109 (1959), pp 31-49.

—, 'Remarks on modern interpretations of the prophets', *JBL* 80 (1961), pp 309-319.

—, 'Gottes Antwort aus dem Sturmwind, Hiob 38-41' *Theologische Zeitschrift* 18 (1962), pp 1-24.

—, *Das Buch Hiob*, (Kommentar zum Alten Testament), Gütersloh, 1963.

—, *Introduction to the Old Testament*, London, 1970, pp 323-334 (originally published 1968).

—, 'The righteous man in Job 31', *Essays in Old Testament Ethics*, eds. J.L. Crenshaw and J.T. Willis, New York, 1974, pp 3-22.

—, 'Sophia', *SAIW*, 1976, pp 63-83.

—, *Studien zum Buche Hiob* (1956-1979), (2nd Auflage), BZAW 159 (1983).

Fortes, M., *Oedipus and Job in West African Religion*, Cambridge, 1983.

Foster, H., 'Is the Book of Job a Translation from an Arabic Original?', *AJSL* 49 (1982-3), pp 21-45.

Fowler, H.W. and Fowler, F.G (eds.), *Concise Oxford Dictionary*, Oxford, 5th edn. 1964.

Franklyn, P., 'The Sayings of Agur in Proverbs 30: Piety or Scepticism?' *ZAW* 95 (1983), pp 238-252.

Freedman, D.N., 'The Elihu Speeches in the book of Job', *HTR* 61 (1968), pp 51-9.

Friedländer, M., *Griechische Philosophie im Alten Testament: eine Einleitung in die Psalmen und Weisliteratur*, Berlin, 1904.

Fries, K., *Das philosophische Gespräch von Hiob bis Plato*, Tübingen, 1904.

Frosch, T.R., 'Parody and the Contemporary Imagination', *Soundings* 56/3 (1973), pp 371-393.

Fullerton, K., 'The Original Conclusion to the Book of Job', *ZAW* 42 (1924), pp 116-135.

—, 'Double Entendre in the First Speech of Eliphaz', *JBL* 49 (1930), pp 320-341.

—, 'Job: Chapters 9 and 10', *AJSL* 55 (1938), pp 225-269.

Gammie, J.G., 'Behemoth and Leviathan: On the didactic and theological significance of Job 40:15-41:26', *Israelite Wisdom*, 1978, pp 217-231.

—, et al. (eds.), *Israelite Wisdom: Theological and Literary Essays in honour of Samuel Terrien*, Missoula, 1978.

Gard, D.H., *The Exegetical Method of the Greek Translator of the Book of Job*, (SBL Monograph Series 8), Princeton, 1952.

Gardiner, A.H., *Ancient Egyptian Onomastica*, Oxford, 1947.

Gautier, L., *Introduction à l'Ancien Testament*, (2nd ed.), Paris, 1914, II, pp 98-99.

Gehman, H.S., 'The Theological Approach of the Greek Translator of Job 1-15', *JBL* 68 (1949), pp 231-240.

Gemser, B., *Sprüche Salomos*, Handbuch zum Alten Testament 6 (1937).

—, 'The Instructions of Onchsheshonqy and Biblical Wisdom Literature', *SAIW*, 1976, pp 134-160. Originally published in VTS 7 (1960), pp 102-28.

Genung, J.F., 'The Book of Job as literature', *The Bible as Literature*, eds. R.G. Moulton and A.B. Bruce, London, 1899, pp 77-121.

Gerleman, G., *The Book of Job*, (Studies in the Septuagint 1), Lund, 1946.

—, 'נסה (piel) versuchen' in E. Jenni and C. Westermann (eds), *Theologisches Handwörterbuch zum Alten Testament* 2, Munich, 1976, cc 69-71.

Gerstenberger, E., 'The Woe Oracles of the Prophets', *JBL* 81 (1962), pp 249-263.

Gerstenberger, E., 'Covenant and Commandment', *JBL* 84 (1965), pp 38-51.

—, 'Zur alttestamentlichen Weisheit', *Verkundigung und Forschung* 14 (1969), pp 218-221.

—, 'Psalms' in *Old Testament Form Criticism*, ed. J.H. Hayes, San Antonio, 1974, pp 218-221.

Gese, H., *Lehre und Wirklichkeit in der alten Weisheit*, Tübingen, 1958.

—, 'Die Frage nach dem Lebenssinn: Hiob und die Folgen', *ZTK* 79 (1982), pp 161-9.

Gibson, E.C.S., *The Book of Job*, Westminster Commentaries, 3rd edn., London, 1919.

Gibson, J.C.L., *Job* (The Daily Study Bible), Edinburgh, 1973.

Gilbert, M. (ed.), *La Sagesse de l'Ancien Testament*, Gembloux, 1979.

Ginsberg, H.L., 'Job the patient and Job the impatient', *VTS* 17 (1969), pp 88-111.

—, 'Job', *Encyclopaedia Judaica*, 10 Jes-Lei, Jerusalem, 1972, cc 111-128.

Ginzberg, L., *Legends of the Jews* Vols II, IV and V, Philadelphia, 1913-38.

Glatzer, N.N., 'The Book of Job and its interpreters', *Biblical Motifs*, ed A. Altmann, Philip W. Lain Institute of Advanced Judaic Studies, Brandeis University, 1966, pp 197-220.

—, (ed.), *The Dimensions of Job: A Study and Selected readings*, New York, 1969.

Glei, R., *Die Batrachomyomachie*, (Studien zur klassischen Philologie 12), Frankfurt am Main, 1984.

Glenville, S.R.K., 'The Instructions of Onchsheshonqy', *Catalogue of Demotic Papyri*, Volume 2, British Museum, 1955.

Godbey, A.H., 'The Hebrew Māšāl', *AJSLL* 39 (1922-3), pp 89-108.

Goldsmith, R.H., 'The Healing Scourge', *Interpretation* 17 (1963), pp 271-9.

Good, E.M., *Irony in the Old Testament*, London, 1965.

Gordis, R., 'Job and the Literary Task: A response (to David Robertson)', *Soundings* 56 (1973), pp 470-484.

—, *The Biblical Text in the Making*, Philadelphia, 1937, pp 50ff.

—, 'Quotations in Wisdom Literature', *JQR* 30 (1939-40), pp 123-147. Reprinted in *SAIW*, 1976, pp 220-244.

—, 'The Social Background of Wisdom Literature', *HUCA* 18 (1944), pp 77-118. Reprinted in *Poets, Prophets and Sages*, pp 160-197.

—, *The Wisdom of Ecclesiastes*, New York, 1945.

—, 'All Men's Book - A New Introduction to Job', *Menorah Journal* 37 (1949). Reprinted in *Poets, Prophets and Sages*, 1971.

Gordis, R., 'Quotations as a Literary Usage in Biblical, Oriental and Rabbinic Literature', *HUCA* 22 (1949). *Reprinted in Poets, Prophets and Sages*, 1971.

—, *Koheleth, The Man and His World*, (Texts and Studies of the Jewish Theological Seminary of America 19), New York, 1951.

—, 'The Temptation of Job,, *Judaism* 4 (1955), pp 195-208.

—, 'The Conflict of Tradition and Experience', *Great Moral Dilemmas in Literature*, ed. R.M. McIver, New York, 1956, pp 155-178.

—, 'Elihu the Intruder: A study of the Authenticity of Job (chapters 32-33)', *Biblical and Other Studies*, ed. A. Altmann, 1963, pp 60-78.

—, 'The Lord out of the whirlwind. The climax and meaning of Job', *Judaism* 13 (1964) pp 48-63.

—, *The Book of God and Man*, Chicago, 1965.

—, *Poets, Prophets and Sages*, Bloomington, 1971, pp 280-324.

—, *The Book of Job: Commentary*, New York: Jewish Theological Seminary of America, 1978.

Gray, G.B., 'Job, Ecclesiastes, and a New Babylonian Literary Fragment', *ET* 31 (1919-20), pp 440-3.

Gray, J., 'The Book of Job in the Context of Near Eastern Literature', *ZAW* 82 (1970), pp 251-269.

Green, W.H., 'The Dramatic Character and Integrity of the Book of Job', *Presbyterian and Reformed Review* 8, (1897), pp 683-701.

Gregory the Great, *Morales sur Job*, (Sources Chrétiennes), Paris, 1950. English translation ed G. Marriot, 4 parts in 3 volumes, Oxford, 1848-1850.

Gressmann, H., *Altorientalische Texte zum Alten Testament*, Berlin, 1926.

Griffith, M., *The authenticity of Prometheus Bound*, Cambridge, 1977.

—, *Aeschylus: Prometheus Bound*, Cambridge, 1983.

Grill, J., *Zur Kritik der Komposition des Buches Hiob*, Tübingen, 1890.

Gros Louis, K.R.R., 'Abraham II', *Literary Interpretations of Biblical Narratives*, II, Nashville, 1982.

Grossouw, W. and Epping, C., in A van den Born et al., *Bijbels Woordenboek*, 2nd edn, Roermond, Netherlands, 1954-57, col. 847.

Guillaume, A., 'Job', *A New Commentary on Holy Scripture*, eds. C. Gore, H.L. Goudge and A. Guillaume, London, 1951, pp 311-340.

Guillaume, A., 'The Unity of the Book of Job', *Annual of Leeds University Oriental Society*, volume 4 (1962-3), pp 26-46.

—, 'The Arabic Background of the book of Job', *Promise and Fulfilment*, (Festschrift S.H. Hooke), Edinburgh, 1963, pp 106-127.

—, *Studies in the book of Job*, (ALUOS Supplement 2), Leiden, 1968.

Gunkel, H., *Hiobbuch*, (Die Religion in Geschichte und Gegenwart 3), Tübingen, 1928.

—, *Einleitung in die Psalmen: Die Gattungen der religiösen Lyrik Israels*, Göttingen, 1933.

Habel, N.C., *Job*, (Cambridge Bible Commentary}, London, 1953.

—, 'He who stretches out the heavens', *CBQ* 34 (1972), pp 417-430.

—, 'Appeal to ancient tradition as a literary form', *ZAW* 88 (1976), pp 253-271.

—, 'Only the Jackal is My Friend: On Friends and Redeemers in Job', *Interpretation* 31 (1977), pp 227-236.

—, '"Naked I came..."': Humanness in the Book of Job', *Die Botschaft und die Boten*, (Festschrift für H.W. Wolff zum 70. Geburtstag), eds. J. Jeremias and L. Perlitt, Neukirchen-Vluyn, 1981, pp 373-392.

—, 'Of things beyond me: Wisdom in the Book of Job', *Currents in Theology and Mission* 10 (1983), pp 142-154.

—, 'The Narrative Art of Job: Applying the Principles of Robert Alter', *JSOT* 27 (1983), pp 101-111.

—, 'The role of Elihu in the Design of the Book of Job', *In the shelter of Elyon: Essays on Ancient Palestinian Life and Literature in Honour of G.W. Ahlström*, (Journal for the Study of the Old Testament Supplement 31), eds. W.B. Barrick and J.R. Spencer, Sheffield, 1984.

—, *The Book of Job*, (Old Testament Library), London, 1985.

Hadas, M., *Hellenistic Culture: Fusion and Diffusion*, New York, 1959.

Hamblen, E.S., *The Book of Job Interpreted*, New York, 1949.

Hanson, A. and M., *Job*, (Torch Bible Commentaries), London, 1953.

Hastoupis, A.P., 'The Problem of Theodicy in the book of Job', *Theologia* (1951), pp 657-668.

Hatch, E., *Essays in Biblical Greek*, Oxford, 1889.

Hazelton, G.W., 'The Book of Job - Who wrote it?', *Bibliotheca Sacra* 71 (1914), pp 573-581.

Heater, H., *A Septuagint translation technique in the Book of Job*, (CBQ Monograph Series 1), Washington, 1982.

Heaton, E.W., *Solomon's New Men*, New York, 1974.

Heinisch, P., 'Griechische Philosophie und Altes Testament', Biblische Zeitpagen 6/7, 1913, p 15ff.

Hempel, J., 'Das theologische Problem des Hiob', ZST 7/4 (1929-30), pp 114-173. Reprinted *BZAW* 81 (1961).

Hempel, J., 'The Contents of the Literature', *Record and Revelation*, ed. H.W. Robinson, Oxford, 1938.

Hengel, M., *Judaism and Hellenism*, Volumes 1 and 2, Tübingen, 1973; London, 1974.

Hennecke, E. and Schneemelcher, W. (eds), *New Testament Apocrypha*, Vol II 1963, pp 533-6.

Hermisson, W-J., 'Notizen zu Hiob', ZTK 86 (1989), pp 125ff.

Hertzberg, H.W., 'Der Aufbau des Buches Hiob', *Festschrift A. Bertholet zum 80. Geburtstag*, ed. W. Baumgartner et al., Tübingen, 1950, pp 233-258.

—, *Der Prediger*, (Kommentar zum Alten Testament XV 11/4), Gütersloh, 1963, p 30.

Highet, G., *The Anatomy of Satire*, Princeton, New Jersey, 1962.

Hirzel, L., *Hiob*, Kurzgefasstes exegetisches Handbuch zum Alten Testament 2, Leipzig, 1839.

Hitzig, F., *Geschichte des Volkes Israel*, Leipzig, 1869.

Hoffman, G., *Hiob*, Kiel, 1891

Hoffman, Y., 'The Use of Equivocal Words in the First Speech of Eliphaz (Job 4-5)', *VT* 30 (1980), pp 114-118.

—, 'The Relation between the Prologue and the Speech Cycles in Job: A Reconsideration', *VT* 31 (1981), pp 160-170.

Holbert, J.C., '"The Skies will uncover his iniquity": Satire in the Second Speech of Zophar (Job 20)', *VT* 31 (1981), pp 171-9.

—, '"Deliverance Belongs to Yahweh!" Satire in the Book of Jonah', *JSOT* 21 (1981), pp 59-81.

—, 'The Rehabilitation of the Sinner: The Function of Job 29-31', *ZAW* 95 (1983), pp 229-237.

Hölscher, G., *Das Buch Hiob*, (Handbuch zum Alten Testament), Tübingen, 1937.

Holzmann, O., 'Das Buch Hiob', in B. Stade, *Geschichte des Volkes Israel* II, 1888, pp 348-352.

Hoonacker, A. van, 'Une question touchant la composition du livre de Job', *RB* 12 (1903), pp 161-189.

Hopper, S.R., 'Irony and Pathos of the Middle', *Cross Currents* 12, (1962), pp 31-40.

Horst, F., *Hiob*, (Biblischer Kommentar Altes Testament 16), Neurkirchen, 1960-2; 3rd edn. 1974.

Horst, P.W. van der, 'The Role of Women in the Testament of Job', *Nederlands Theologisch Tijdschrift* 40 (1986), pp 273-289.

Hulsbosch, A., 'Sagesse créatrice et éducatrice. 1. Job 28', *Augustinianisme* 1 (1961), pp 217-235.

Humbert, P., *Recherches sur les sources égyptiennes de la littérature sapientiale d'Israël*, Neuchâtel, 1929.

—, 'Le modernisme de Job', *VTS* 3 (1960), pp 150-161.

Hurvitz, A., 'The Date of the Prose Tale of Job Linguistically Reconsidered', *HTR* 67 (1974), pp 17-34.

Irwin, W.A., 'An Examination of the Progress of Thought in the dialogue of Job', *JR* 13 (1933), pp 150-164.

—, 'The First Speech of Bildad', *ZAW* 51 (1933), pp 205-216.

—, 'The Elihu Speeches in the Criticism of the Book of Job', *JR* 17 (1937), pp 37-47.

—, 'Job and Prometheus', *JR* 30 (1950), pp 90-108.

—, 'The Wisdom Literature', *IB* 1, Nashville, 1952, pp 212-219.

—, 'Job', *Peake's Commentary on the Bible*, eds. M. Black and H.H. Rowley, London, 1962, pp 391-408.

—, 'Job's Redeemer', *JBL* 81 (1962), pp 217-229.

James, M.R., *Apocrypha Anecdota* (ii), Cambridge, 1877.

—, The Apocryphal New Testament, Oxford, 1924.

Jastrow, M., 'A Babylonian Parallel to the Story of Job', *JBL* 25 (190), pp 135-191.

—, *The Gentle Cynic*, Philadelphia, 1919.

—, *The Book of Job, its origin, growth and interpretation*, Philadelphia and London, 1920.

Jepsen, A., *Das Buch Hiob und seine Deutung*, (Arbeiten zur Theologie 1/14), Stuttgart, 1963.

Job, J.B., *Where is my father? Studies in the book of Job*, London, 1977.

Johnson, S., *Dictionary of the English Language*, London, 1755.

Jones, E., *The Triumph of Job*, London, 1966.

Jowett, B. (tr.), *The Dialogues of Plato*, (4th edn.), Oxford, 1964

Jung, C., *Answer to Job*, London, 1954 (originally published, 1952).

Kaiser, O., *Introduction to the Old Testament*, Gütersloh,1969, Bristol, 1975

Kallen, H.M., *The Book of Job as a Greek Tragedy Restored*, New York, 1918.

Kautzsch, K., *Das sogenannte Volksbuch von Hiob und der Ursprung von Hiob*, Leipzig, 1900.

Kellett, E., '"Job": an Allegory?', *ET* 51 (1939-40), pp 250-1.

Kelly, B.H., 'Truth in Contradiction. A study of Job 20 and 21', *Interpretation* 15 (1961), pp 147-156.

Kissane, E.J., *The Book of Job*, Dublin, 1939.

Kittel, R., *Geschichte des Volkes Israels* III 2, (1929), p 733.

Kluger, R.S., *Satan in the Old Testament*, Evanstone, Illinois, 1967.

Knibb, M.A. and van der Horst, P.W., *Studies on the Testament of Job*, Society for New Testament Studies Monograph Series 66, Cambridge, 1989.

Knight, H., 'Job (considered as a contribution to Hebrew Theology)', *SJT* 9 (1956), pp 63-76.

Koch, K., 'Is there a Theme of Retribution in the Old Testament?', *ZTK* 52 (1955), pp 1-42. Reprinted in J.L. Crenshaw ed. *Theodicy in the Old Testament*, Philadelphia and London, 1983, pp 57-87.

Koehler, L., *Die Hebräische Rechtsgemeinde*, Zürich, 1931 (translated by P.R. Ackroyd, London, 1956). (Originally published Tübingen, 1953.)

Kohler, K., 'The Testament of Job', *Semitic Studies in Memory of Dr Alexander Kohut*, ed. G.A. Kohut, Berlin, 1897, pp 264-338.

König, E., *Einleitung in das Alte Testament*, Bonn, 1893, p 415.

—, *Das Buch Hiob*, Gütersloh, 1929.

Kraeling, E.G., *The Book of the Ways of God*, London, 1938.

—, 'Review of J. Lindblom, *La Composition du livre de Job*', *RR* 10 (1946), pp 425-9.

Kramer, S.N., 'Man and His God: A Sumerian Variation on the "Job" motif', *VTS* 3 (1960), pp 170-182.

Kraus, H.J., *Theologie der Psalmen*, (Biblischer Kommentar Zum Alten Testament 15), Neukirchen, 1979.

Kroeber, R., *Der Prediger*, (Schriften und Quellen der alten Welt 13), Berlin, 1963.

Kroeze, J.H., 'Die Elihu-reden im Buche Hiob', *OTS* 2 (1943), pp 156-170.

Kubina, V., *Die Gottesreden im Buche Hiob*, Herder, 1979.

Kuhl, C., 'Neuere Literarkritik des Buches Hiob', *ThR* N.F. 21 (1953), pp 163-205, 257-317.

—, 'Vom Hiobbuche und seinen Problemen', *ThR* 22 (1954), pp 261-316.

Kuntz, J.K., 'The Canonical Wisdom Psalms of Ancient Israel - their rhetorical, thematic, and formal dimensions', *Rhetorical Criticism*, eds. J.J. Jackson and M. Kessler, Pennsylvania, 1974, pp 186-222.

—, 'The Retribution Motif in Psalmic Wisdom', *ZAW* 89 (1977), pp 223-233.

Lake, K. (translator), *I Clement* XVII (The Apostolic Fathers), (Loeb Classical Library), London and New York, 1930.

Lambdin, T.O., 'Egypt: Its Language and Literature' in G.E.Wright (ed.), *The Bible and the Ancient Near East* (Essays in honour of W.F. Albright), London, 1961, p 292.

Lambert, W.G., *Babylonian Wisdom Literature*, Oxford, 1960.

Lamparter, H., *Das Buch der Anfechtung*, (Botschaft des Alten Testaments 13), Stuttgart, 1955.

Landsberger, B., 'Die babylonische Theodizee: akrostichisches Zwiegespräch sog. "Kohelet", *Zeitschrift für Assyriologie* XL III (1936), pp 32-76.

Langdon, S., *Babylonian Wisdom*, 1923, pp 67ff.

Larcher, C., *Le livre de Job* (La Sainte Bible), 2nd edn. Paris, 1957.

Laue, L., *Die Composition des Buches Hiob*, Halle, 1896, pp 1-7, 118-43.

Laurin, R., 'The Theological Structure of Job', *ZAW* 84 (1972), pp 86-89.

Lefevre, A., 'Le Livre de Job', in L. Pirot's *Supplément au Dictionnaire de la Bible* 14 (1949), col. 1079.

Lévêque, J., *Job et son dieu*, Paris, 1970.

—, 'Anamnese et disculpation: la conscience du juste en Job 29-31', *La Sagesse de l'Ancien Testament*, ed. M. Gilbert, Louvain, 1980, pp 231-248.

Lewalski, B.K., *Milton's Brief Epic: The Genre, Meaning and Art of Paradise Regained*, Providence and London, 1966.

Lewin, M., *Targum und Midrasch zum Buche Hiob*, Mainz, 1895.

Licht, J., *Testing in the Hebrew Scriptures and in Post-biblical Judaism*, Jerusalem, 1973.

Lindblom, J., 'Job and Prometheus', *Acta Instituti Romani Regni Sueciae* 2/1 (1939), pp 280-7.

Lindblom, J., *Boken om Job och hans lidande*, Lund, 1940.

—, *La Composition du livre de Job*, Lund, 1945.

—, 'Wisdom in the Old Testament Prophets', *VT* Supplement 3 (1955), pp 192-204.

Littlehales, H. (ed.), *The Prymer*, 2 vols, London, 1891.

Loader, J.A., *Polar Structures in the book of Qoheleth*, BZAW 152 (1979).

Lods, A., "Recherches récentes sur le livre Job", *RHPhR* XIV (1934), pp 501-19.

—, *Historie de la littérature hébraïque et juive*, Paris, 1950.

Lohr, M., 'Die drei Bildad-Reden im Buche Hiob', *BZAW* 34 (1920), pp 107-112.

Long, A.A., *Hellenistic Philosophy*, London, 1974.

Luther, M., *Preface to the book of Job*, in Works of Martin Luther, (The Philadelphia edition), Philadelphia, 1932 VI, pp 383f.

Luyten, J., 'Psalm 73 and Wisdom', *La Sagesse de l'Ancien Testament*, ed. M. Gilbert, Leuven, 1979, pp 59-81.

Maag, V., Hiob: *Wandlung und Verarbeitung des Problems in Novelle, Dialogdichtung und Spätfassungen*, Göttingen, 1982.

Mack, B.L. *Logos und Sophia: Untersuchungen zur Weisheitstheologie im hellenistichen Judentum*, StUNT 10, Göttingen, 1973, pp 21-33.

MacDonald, D. (ed.), *Parodies: An Anthology from Chaucer to Beerbohm - and after*, London, 1960.

MacDonald, D.B., 'The original form of the legend of Job', *JBL* 14 (1895), pp 63-71.

—, 'Some External Evidence on the Original Form of the Legend of Job', *AJSLL* 14/3 (1898), pp 137-164.

—, *The Hebrew Literary Genius*, Princetown, 1933, pp 23-32, 192-5.

McFadyen, J.E., *Introduction to the Old Testament*, (2nd edn.) New York, 1906, pp 274-77.

Luyten, J., 'Psalm 73 and Wisdom', *La Sagesse de l'Ancien Testament*, ed. M. Gilbert, Leuven, 1979, pp 59-81.

—, *The Problem of Pain, A study in the book of Job*, London, 1917.

McKane, W., *Proverbs*, Philadelphia, London, 1970.

McKenzie, J.L., 'Reflections on Wisdom', *JBL* 86 (1967), pp 1-9.

MacKenzie, R.A.F., 'The purpose of the Yahweh speeches in the book of Job', *Biblica* 40 (1959), pp 435-445.

—, *Job* (Jerome Bible Commentary 1), London, 1968, pp 511-533.

—, 'The Transformation of Job', *BTB* 9 (1979), pp 51-57.

MacLeish, A., *J.B. A Play in Verse*, London, 1959.

Magonet, J., *Form and Meaning - Studies in Literary Techniques in the book of Jonah*, Berne and Frankfurt, 1976.

Mai, A. (Cardinal), *Scriptorium Veterum Nova Collectio*, Vol VII, Rome, 1825-38.

Mansi, J.D. (ed.), *Sacrorum conciliarum nova et amplissima collectio*, IX, Venice, 1759-98, cc. 223m-225.

Marcus, R., 'Job and God', *RR* 14 (1949-50), pp 5-29.

Marshall, J.T., *Job and his Comforters*, London, 1905.

Massebieau, L., 'L'Epitre de Jacques est-elle l'oeuvre d'un Chrétien?', *RHR* 32 (1895), pp 249-283.

Matthews, I.G., *The Religious Pilgrimage of Israel*, New York and London, 1947, pp 168-181.

May, H.G., 'Prometheus and Job', *AThR* 34 (1952), pp 240-246.

Meinhold, J., *Einführung in das Alte Testament*, Leipzig, 1919.

Merx, E.O., *Das Gedicht von Hiob*, Jena, 1871.

Mettinger, T.N.D., *Solomonic State Officials*, (Coniectanea Biblica: Old Testament Series 5), Lund, 1971.

Michel, D., *Untersuchungen zur Eigenart des Buches Qohelet*, BZAW 183, 1989.

Miles, J.A. Jr., 'Gagging of Job or The Comedy of Religious Exhaustion', *Semeia* 7 (1977), pp 71-126.

Miskotte, K.H., *When the Gods are Silent*, New York, 1967.

Mohr, J.C.B., *Kurzer Hand-Commentar zum Alten Testament*, 1897.

Möller, H., *Sinn und Aufbau des Buches Hiob*, Bonn, 1955.

Montet, E., *Le Livre de Job*, Geneva, 1926.

—, 'Job', *La Bible du Centenaire* 3, 1947.

Moore, G.F., *Judaism* (Volumes 1-3), Cambridge, 1927.

Moore, R.D., 'The Integrity of Job', *CBQ* 45 (1983), pp 17-31.

Mowinckel, S., 'Hiobs go'el und Zeuge im Himmel', *BZAW* 41 (1925), pp 207-212.

—, *The Psalms in Israel's Worship*, Volume 2, translated by D R Ap-Thomas, Oxford, 1962.

Muller, H-P., 'Wie sprach Qohalat von Gott?', *VT* 18 (1968), pp 507-21.

—, 'Altes und Neues zum Buch Hiob', *EvTh* 37 (1977), pp 284-304.

Müller, H-P., *Das Hiobproblem und seine Stellung und Entstehung im alten Orient und im alten Testament*, Darmstadt, 1978.

Murphy, R.E., 'A Consideration of the Classification "Wisdom Psalms"', *VTS* 9 (1962), pp 160-1.

—, 'Assumptions and Problems in Old Testament Wisdom Research', *CBQ* 29 (1967), pp 101-112.

—, 'Form Criticism and Wisdom Literature', *CBQ* 31 (1969), pp 475-483.

—, *Wisdom Literature*, (The Forms of the Old Testament Literature 13), eds. R. Knierim and G.M. Tucker, Michegan, 1981.

Murray, G., 'Promctheus and Job', *Twentieth Century Interpretations of the book of Job*, ed. P.S. Sanders, 1968. (originally 'Aeschylus as a Poet of Ideas' from chapter 3 of Aeschylus, *The Creator of Tragedy*, Oxford, 1940.)

Murray, J.A.H., *A New English Dictionary*, Volume 8, Oxford, 1914.

Naish, J.P., 'The Book of Job and the Early Persian Period', *Expositor* 9th Series/3 (1925), pp 34-49, 94-104.

Neher, A., 'Job: the Biblical Man', *Judaism* 13 (1964), pp 37-47.

Nichols, H.H., 'The Composition of the Elihu Speeches', *AJSL* 27 (1910-11), pp 97-128.

Noth, M., 'Noah, Daniel und Hiob in Ezekiel 14', *VT* 1 (1951), pp 251-260.

—, and Thomas D.W. (eds), *Wisdom in Israel and in the Ancient Near East*, Leiden, 1960.

Oesterley, W.O.E. and Robinson, T.H., *An Introduction to the Books of the Old Testament*, New York, 1934, London, 1941 (4th edn.), pp 166-178.

—, *Hebrew Religion*, London, 1937, pp 310-316.

Olivier, J.P.J., 'Schools and Wisdom Literature', *Journal of Northwest Semitic Literature* 4 (1975), pp 49-60.

Oorschot, J. van, *Gott als Grenze*, BZAW 170, 1987.

Origen, 'Letter to Africanus', *ANCL* 10 (1869), p 373.

Orlinsky, H.M., 'Some Corruptions in the Greek Text of Job', *JQR* 26 (1935-6), pp 133-145.

—, 'Studies in the Septuagint of the Book of Job', *HUCA* 28 (1957), pp 53ff; 29 (1958), pp 229f; 30 (1959), pp 153f; 32 (1961), pp 239f; 33 (1962), pp 119f; 35 (1964), pp 57f; 36 (1965), pp 37f.

Paterson, J., *The Wisdom of Israel: Job and Proverbs*, London and Nashville, 1961.

Patrick, D., 'Job's Address of God', *ZAW* 91 (1979-80), pp 268-282.

Paulus, J., 'Le thème du Juste Souffrant dans la pensée grecque et hebraique', *RHR* 121 (1940), pp 18-66.

Peake, A.S., *The Problem of Suffering in the Old Testament*, London, 1904, pp 83-103.

—, *Job*, (The Century Bible), Edinburgh, 1905.

Peake, A.S., 'The art of the book', in P.S. Sanders (ed.), *Twentieth Century Interpretations of the Book of Job*, New Jersey, 1968, pp 109-113. Originally published in *Job*, (The Century Bible), Edinburgh, 1905.

Pedersen, J., 'Scepticisme Israelite', *RHPhR* 10 (1930), pp 317-370.

Perdue, L.G., *Wisdom and Cult*, (SBL Dissertation Series 30), Missoula, Montana, 1977, pp 286-291.

Pfeiffer, R.H., *Le problem du livre de Job*, Geneva, 1915.

—, 'Edomitic Wisdom', *ZAW* 44 (1926), pp 13-25.

—, 'The Priority of Job over Isaiah 40-55', *JBL* 46 (1927), pp 202-206.

—, *Introduction to the Old Testament*, London, 1948, pp 660-707.

—, *History of New Testament Times*, New York, 1949.

—, 'Wisdom and Vision in the Old Testament', *SAIW*, 1976, pp 305-313.

Philonenko, M., *Le Testament de Job*, (Semitica 18), 1968.

Picard, J-C. (ed), *Apocalypsis Baruchi graece*, (Pseudepigrapha Veteris Testamenti Graeci, Volume 2), Leiden, 1967.

Pirot, L., *L'oeuvre exégétique de Théodore de Mopsueste*, Rome, 1913.

Plöger, O., *Sprüche Salomos*, BK XVII, Neukirchen-Vluyn, 1984.

Pohlman, K.-F., *Die Ferne Gottes: Studien zum Jeremiabuch*, BZAW 179, 1989, pp 63-111.

Polzin, R.M., 'The Framework of the Book of Job', *Interpretation* 28 (1974), pp 182-200.

—, 'John A. Miles on the Book of Job: A Response', *Semeia* 7 (1977), pp 127-133.

—, 'An attempt at structural analysis: The Book of Job', *Biblical Structuralism*, Missoula and Philadelphia, 1977, pp 54-125.

Pope, M.H., *Job*, (The Anchor Bible), New York, 1965; 3rd edn. 1973.

Potter, R., 'Job', *A new Catholic Commentary on Holy Scripture*, 2nd edn., London, 1969, pp 417-438.

Priest, J.F., 'Where is wisdom to be placed?', *JBR* 31 (1963), pp 275-82.

—, 'Humanism, Skepticism and Pessimism in Israel', *JAAR* 36 (1968), pp 311-326

Pritchard, J.B. (ed), *Ancient Near Eastern Texts*, Princeton, 1950; 3rd edn. 1969.

Procksch, O., *Theologie des Alten Testaments*, Gütersloh, 1949.

Proctor, F. and Wordsworth, C. (eds), *Breviarium ad usum insignis ecclesiae Sarum*, Volume 2, Cambridge 1879-1886, cc. 271-282.

Rad, G. von, 'The Confessions of Jeremiah', *EvTh* 3 (1936), pp 265-76, reprinted in J.L. Crenshaw (ed), *Theodicy in the Old Testament*, Philadelphia and London, 1983, pp 88-99.

—, 'Job 38 and Ancient Egyptian Wisdom', in *The Problem of the Hexateuch*, Munich, 1958; London, 1966, pp 281-291.

—, *Old Testament Theology*, Volumes 1 and 2, Edinburgh and London, 1965.

—, *Wisdom in Israel*, London, 1972.

Rahlffs, A., *Septuaginta* (2 vols.), Stuttgart, 1935.

Rahner, K., *Encounters with Silence*, New York, 1960.

Rankin, O.S., *Israel's Wisdom Literature: Its Bearing on Theology and the History of Religion*, Edinburgh, 1936.

Raphael, D.D., 'Tragedy and Religion', *The Paradox of Tragedy*, Bloomington and London, 1960, pp 37-51. Reprinted in *Twentieth Century Interpretations of the book of Job: A Collection of critical essays*, (ed. P.S. Sanders), Englewood Cliffs, New Jersey, 1968, pp 46-55.

Reddy, M.P., 'The Book of Job - A Reconstruction', *ZAW* 90 (1978), pp 59-94.

Reese, J.M., *Hellenistic Influence on the Book of Wisdom and Its Consequences*, Analecta Biblica 41, 1970.

Regnier, A., 'La distribution des chapitres 25-28 du livre de Job', *RB* 33 (1924), pp 186-200.

Renan, J.E., *Le Livre de Job*, Paris, 1859.

Reventlow, H.G., 'Tradition und Redaktion in Hiob 27 im Rahmen der Hiobreden des Abschnittes Hi, 24-27, A.H.J. Gunneweg zum 60 Geburtstag am 17.5.82.', *ZAW* 94 (1982), pp 279-293.

Richter, G., *Studien zum Buche Hiob*, (BWANT 3/7), Stuttgart, 1927.

Richter, H., 'Die Naturweisheit das Alten Testaments im Buche Hiob', *ZAW* 70 (1958), pp 1-20.

—, *Studien zu Hiob*, Theologische Arbeiten 11, Berlin, 1959.

Richter, W., *Recht und Ethos*, (Versuch einer Ortung des Weisheitlichen Mahnspruches), München, 1966.

Ringgren, H., *Word and Wisdom*, (Studies in the 'hypostatization' of divine qualities and functions in the ancient Near East), Lund, 1947.

Roberts, A and Donaldson, J., *The Anti-Nicene Christian Library*, VII, New York, 1913, p 482.

Roberts, J.J.M., 'Job and the Israelite Religious Tradition', *ZAW* 89 (1977), pp 107-114.

Roberts, J.J.M., 'Job's summons to Yahweh: the Exploitation of a legal metaphor', *Restoration Quarterly* 16 (1973), pp 159-165.

Robertson, D.A., 'The book of Job, a literary study', *Soundings* 56 (1973), pp 446-69; reprinted in slightly different form in *The Old Testament and the Literary Critic*, Philadelphia, 1977, pp 33-54.

—, 'The Comedy of Job: A Response', *Semeia* 7 (1977), pp 41-44.

Robin, E., *Job* (La Sainte Bible 4), eds. L. Pirot and A. Clamer, Paris, 1949, pp 699-868.

Robinson, F.N. (ed), 'The General Prologue' in *The Works of Geoffrey Chaucer*, 2nd edn., Oxford, 1974, lines 477-528.

Robinson, H.W., *The Old Testament: its making and meaning*, London, 1937, pp 152-157.

Robinson, T.H. *Job and his Friends*, London, 1954.

Rogers, B.B., *The Comedies of Aristophanes*, London, 1902.

Römheld, D., *Wege der Weisheit: Die Lehre des Amenemope und Prov. 22:17-24:22*, Diss Marburg 1988, BZAW 184, 1989.

Ross, J.F., 'Psalm 73', *Israelite Wisdom*, ed. J.G. Gammie et al., Missoula, Montana, 1978, pp 161-175.

Roth, W.M.W., *Numerical Sayings in the Old Testament*, VTS 13, 1965.

Rowland, C., *The Open Heaven: a study of apocalyptic in Judaism and early Christianity*, London, 1982.

Rowley, H.H., 'The Book of Job and its meaning', *BJRL* 41 (1958), pp 167-207.

—, *From Moses to Qumran*, London, 1963, pp 141-83, (first published in Bulletin 41 (1958-9), pp 167-207).

—, (ed.), *Job*, (The New Century Bible), London, 1970.

Ruprecht, E., 'Das Nilpferd im Hiobbuch', *VT* 21 (1971), pp 209-231.


Sandbach, F.H., *The Comic Theatre of Greece and Rome*, London, 1977.

Sanders, J.A., *Suffering as Divine Discipline in the Old Testament and Post-Biblical Judaism*, Rochester, New York, 1955.

Sanders, P.S., *Twentieth Century Interpretations of the Book of Job. A collection of critical essays*, Englewood Cliffs, New Jersey, 1968.

Sarna, N.M., 'Epic Substratum in the prose of Job', *JBL* 76 (1957), pp 13-25.

Sawyer, J.F.A., 'The authorship and structure of the Book of Job', JSOTS 2 (Studia Biblica) (1978), pp 253-7.

Schmid, H.H., *Wesen und Geschichte der Weisheit: Eine Untersuchung zur altorientalischen und israelitischen Weisheitsliteratur*, BZAW 101, 1966.

Schmidt, J., 'Studien zur Stilistik der alttestamentlichen Spruchliteratur', *Alttestamentliche Abhandlungen* 13/1 (1936).

Schmidt, J.M., *Die Jüdische Apokalyptik*, Neukirchen, 1969.

Schmidt, L., *'De Deo': Studien zur Literarkritik und Theologie des Buches Jona, des Gesprächs zwischen Abraham und Jahwe in Genesis 18:22f und von Hiob 1*, BZAW 143, 1976.

Schofield, J.N., 'Job in the Framework of his time', *Modern Churchman* (1958), pp 238-244.

Scott, R.B.Y., *Proverbs, Ecclesiastes*, New York, 1965.

—, 'The Study of Wisdom Literature', *Interpretation* 24 (1970), pp 20-45.

—, 'Wisdom; Wisdom Literature', *EJ* 16 (1971), cc. 557-563.

—, *The Way of Wisdom*, New York, 1972.

—, 'Wise and Fookish, Righteous and Wicked', *VTS* 23 (1972), pp 146-165.

Seaford, R., *Euripides: Cyclops*, Oxford, 1984.

Sellin, E.F., *Die Spuren griechischer Philosophie im Alten Testament*, Leipzig, 1905.

—, *Introduction to the Old Testament*, English translation by Montgomery, London, 1923, pp 212-223.

—, *Das Hiobproblem*, Berlin, 1931.

Sewall, R.B., 'The Book of Job', *The Vision of Tragedy*, New Haven, 1959, pp 9-24.

Sextus Empiricus, *Outlines of Pyrrhonism* (Loeb Classical Library), London, pp 1933-49.

Shapiro, D.S., 'The Problem of Evil and the book of Job', *Judaism* 5 (1956), pp 46-52.

Siegfried, C., 'The Book of Job', *The Sacred Books of the Old Testament* 17 (ed. P. Haupt), Leipzig, 1893.

Skehan, P.W., 'Strophic Patterns in the Book of Job', *CBQ* 23 (1961), pp 125-42.

—, 'Job's final plea (Job 29-31) and the Lord's reply (Job 38-41)', *Biblica* 45 (1964), pp 51-62.

Slotki, J.J., 'The origin of the book of Job', *ET* 39 (1927-8), pp 131-5.

Smith, M., *Fischer Weltgeschichte*, Vol 5, 1965.

Snaith, N., *The Book of Job: its origin and purpose*, London, 1968.

Spitta, F., 'Der Brief des Jakobus', *Zur Geschichte und Literatur des Urchristentums*, Volume 2, Göttingen, 1896, pp 1-239.

Stanford, W.B., *Aristophanes' Frogs*, London, 1903.

Staples, W.E., *The Speeches of Elihu*, University of Toronto Studies, Philological Series 8, 1925.

Steiner, G., 'Tragedy; Remorse and Justice', *The Listener* 102 (1979), pp 508-11.

Steinmueller, J.E., *A Companion to Scripture Studies* 2, 2nd edn. London, 1944; 7th edn. 1951, pp 160-170.

Steuernagel, C., 'Das Buch Hiob', *Die Heilige Schrift des Alten Testaments*, ed. E.F. Kautzsch, Tübingen, 1922, pp 323-7 (originally published 1892).

Stevenson, W.B., *The Poem of Job*, Oxford, 1947.

Stockhammer, M., 'The righteousness of Job', *Judaism* 7 (1958), pp 64-71.

Stough, C.L., *Greek Skepticism*, Berkeley and Los Angeles, 1969.

Strahan, J., *The Book of Job interpreted*, Edinburgh, 1913.

Studer, G., *Hiob*, Bremen, 1881.

Stuhlmann, M.H., *Hiob*, Hamburg, 1804.

Styan, J.L., *The Dark Comedy: The Development of Modern Comic Tragedy*, Cambridge, 1968.

Sutcliffe, E.F., *A Catholic Commentary on Holy Scripture*, London, 1953, p 418.

—, *Providence and Suffering in the Old and New Testaments*, London, 1953, pp 110-119.

Swabey, M., *Comic Laughter*, New Haven, Connecticut, 1961.

Swart, W., *De invloed van der Griekschen geest op de boeken Spreuken, Prediker, Job*, Groningen, 1908, pp 23-106.

Szczygiel, P., *Das Buch Hiob*, (Die Heilige Schrift des Alten Testaments), Bonn, 1931.

Talmon, S., 'Wisdom in the book of Esther', *VT* 13 (1963), pp 419-455.

Terrien, S., *Job: Poet of Existence*, Indianapolis and New York, 1957.

—, 'Quelques remarques sur les affinités de Job avec Deutero-Esaïe', *VTS* 15 (1960), pp 295-310.

—, 'Amos and Wisdom', in B.W. Anderson and W Harrelson (eds.), *Israel's Prophetic Heritage*, London, 1962, pp 108-15.

—, 'Job', *IB*, Volume 3, New York and Nashville, 1962, pp 877-1197.

—, *Job*, (Commentaire de l'Ancien Testament 13), Paris, 1963.

—, 'Le Poéme de Job: drame para-rituel du nouvel-an?', *VTS* 17 (1968), pp 220-235.

Terrien, S., *The Elusive Presence: Toward a New Biblical Theology*, (Religious Perspectives 26), New York, 1978, pp 350-389.

—, *Israelite Wisdom*, New York, 1978.

Tertullian, *De patientia*, (PL I), cc. 1223-1274.

Thelen, M.F., J.B., Job and the Biblical Doctrine of Man', *JBR* 27 (1959), pp 201-5.

Thilo, N., *Das Buch Hiob*, Bonn, 1925.

Thompson, K., 'Out of the Whirlwind: The Sense of Alienation in the Book of Job', *Interpretation* 14 (1960), pp 51-63.

Tischendorf, C. (ed), *Apocalypses Apocryphae Mosis, Esdrae, Pauli, Johannis*, (translated by J. Perkins), Leipzig (Lipsiae), 1866, pp 34-69.

Torrance, J.B., 'Why does God let Man suffer?', *Interpretation* 15 (1961), pp 157-163.

Torrey, C.C., *The Apocryphal Literature*, New Haven, 1945, pp 140-145.

Tournay, R., 'Le proces de Job ou l'innocent devant Dieu', *La vie spirituelle* 95/2 (1956), pp 339-54.

Tsevat, M., 'The Meaning of the Book of Job', *SAIW*, 1976, pp 341-374, (originally *HUCA* 37 (1966), pp 73-106).

—, *The Meaning of the Book of Job and other Biblical Studies*, New York, 1980, pp 1-37.

Tur-Sinai, N.H., *The Book of Job*, Jerusalem, 1957.

Urbrock, W.J., 'Reconciliation of opposites in the dramatic ordeal of Job', *Semeia* 7 (1977), pp 147-153.

—, 'Job as Drama: Tragedy or Comedy?' *Currents in Theology and Mission* 8 (1981), pp 35-40.

Van der Ploeg, J. and Van der Woude, A.S., *Le Targum de Job de la Grotte 11 de Qumran*, Leiden, 1971.

Vawter, B., *Job and Jonah; Questioning the Hidden God*, New Jersey, 1983.

Vellacott, P. (trans.), *Aeschylus, The Oresteian Trilogy*, London, 1956.

— (trans.), *Aeschylus, Prometheus Bound*, London, 1961, pp 20-52.

Vermeylen, J., 'Dieu et ses representations antagonistes dans le livre de Job', *Qu'est-ce que c'est Dieu?* Hommage a L'abbe Daniel Coppicters de Gibson (1929-1983), Brussels, 1985, pp 591-611.

Vernes, M., 'Bulletin critique de la religion juive', *RHR* I (1880), 232-33.

Vischer, W., *Hiob. Ein Zeuge Jesu Christi*, Zurich, 1947.

Vischer, W., 'God's Truth and Man's Lie, A Study of the Message of the book of Job', *Interpretation* 15 (1961), pp 131-46.

Volz, P., *Das Buch Hiob*, Schriften des Alten Testament 3/2, Göttingen, 1911 (2nd edn. 1921).

—, *Hiob und Weisheit*, Göttingen, 1921, (2nd edn), pp 8-9.

Vosté, J.M., 'L'oeuvre exégétique de Théodore de Mopsueste au 110 Concile de Constantinople', *RB*, 38 (1929), pp 382-95 (esp. pp 390-3).

Weber, J.J., *Le livre de Job, L'Ecclésiaste*, Paris, 1947.

Webster, E.C., 'Strophic patterns in Job 3-28', *JSOT* 26 (1983), pp 33-60.

Weill, R., 'Le Livre du Desespere. Le sens, L'intention et la composition de l'ouvrage', *Bulletin de l'Institut Francais d'Archeologie Orientale du Caire* 45 (1947), pp 89-154.

Weinfeld, M., 'The Origin of the Humanism in Deuteronomy', *JBL* 80 (1961), pp 241-7.

Weiser, A., *Das Buch Hiob*, (Das Alte Testament Deutsch 13), Göttingen, 1951.

Weiss, M., *The story of Job's Beginning*, Jerusalem, 1983.

Wellhausen, J., 'Review of Dillmann's Hiob', *JDTh* 16 (1871), pp 552-7.

Wertheimer, S., *Leket Midrashim*, Jerusalem, 1904.

West, M.S., 'The Book of Job and the Problem of Suffering', *ET* (1928-9), pp 358-364.

Westermann, C., *The Structure of the book of Job*, Philadelphia, 1981; translated by C.A. Muenchow from German (1st edn. 1956).

—, *Isaiah 40-66* (Old Testament Library Series), London, 1969.

—, 'The role of the lament in the Theology of the Old Testament', *Interpretation* 28 (1974), p 30.

—, *Genesis*, (Biblischer Kommentar: Altes Testament 1/16), Neukirchen-Vluyn, 1979.

Wette, W.M.L. de, *Introduction to the Old Testament*, Volume 2, 1817 (English translation by T. Parker, 1843, pp 554-570).

Whedbee, J.W., *Isaiah and Wisdom*, Nashville, 1971.

—, 'The Comedy of Job', *Semeia* 7 (Studies in the Book of Job, eds. R. Polzin and D. Robertson), Missoula, 1977, pp 1-39.

Whybray, R.N., *Wisdom in Proverbs*, London, 1965.

—, *The Succession Narrative*, London, 1968.

—, *The Intellectual Tradition in the Old Testament*, BZAW 135, 1974.

—, *Isaiah 40-66* (New Century Bible), London, 1975.

—, *Two Jewish Theologies: Job and Ecclesiastes*, Hull, 1980.

Whybray, R.N., 'The Identification and Use of Quotations in Ecclesiastes', *Congress Volume*, ed. J.A. Emerton (Vienna, 1980), *VTS* 32, Leiden, 1981, pp 435-451.

—, 'Prophecy and Wisdom' in R. Coggins, A. Phillips and M. Knibb (eds), *Israel's Prophetic Tradition*, 1982, pp 187-9.

—, 'Qoheleth, Preacher of Joy', *JSOT* 23 (1982), pp 87-98.

Wiernikowski, I., *Das Buch Hiob nach der Auffasung der Rabbinischen Literatur*, Breslau, 1902.

Wildeboer, G., *Die Literatur des Alten Testaments*, Göttingen, 1895.

Williams, J.G., '"You have not spoken truth of me", Mystery and Irony in Job', *ZAW* 83 (1971), pp 231-254.

—, 'Deciphering the Unspoken: The Theophany of Job', *HUCA* 49 (1978), pp 59-72.

Williams, P.J., 'Theodicy in the Ancient Near East', *CJT* (1956), pp 14-26.

Williams, R.J., 'Wisdom in the Ancient Near East', *IDBSupp*, Nashville and New York, 1976, pp 949-52.

Wilson, J.V.K., 'A Return to the Problem of Behemoth and Leviathan', *VT* 25 (1975), pp 1-14.

Wolff, H.W., 'Amos' geistige Heimat', *Wissenschaftliche Monographien zum Alten und Neuen Testament*, 18 (1964).

Wood, J.D., 'The Idea of Life in the Book of Job', *TGOS* 18 (1959-60), pp 29-37.

Young, E.J., *Introduction to the Old Testament*, London, 1949, pp 319-331.

Zerafa, P.P., *The Wisdom of God in the Book of Job*, Rome, 1978.

Zimmerli, W., *Sprüch/Prediger*, (Das Alte Testament Deutsch 16/1), Göttingen, 1962, pp 123-253.

—, 'The Place and Limit of the Wisdom in the Framework of the Old Testament Theology', *SJT* 28 (1964), pp 146-158.

—, *I am Yahweh*, Atlanta, 1978, pp 11-40 (originally published Munich, 1969).

—, 'Concerning the Structure of Old Testament Wisdom', *SAIW*, 1976, pp 175-207.

Zimmern, H., 'Babylonische Hymnen und Gebete', *Der Alte Orient* VII, Leipzig, 1905.

Zink, J.K., 'Impatient Job: An Interpretation of Job 19:25-27', *JBL* 84 (1965), pp 147-152.

# Indices

## A. Subject Index

Apocalypse of Paul 23, 24
Author
  suffering of 32, 86
  named author 160-1
  sceptical questioning of 210
Author's intention 4, 33, 45, 107, 111-13, 122-3, 134-5, 159, 184, 200, 202, 209-12
  deliberate irony 45-6, 96-7, 184-5
  importance of inconsistencies 45, 191-3, 207-9
  imposed unity to book 45, 193-4, 203
  unorthodoxy 136, 204-5
Author's techniques 33-4, 45, 66, 121-2, 136, 143, 146-7, 153, 159, 172, 188
  double-entendre 121-3
  form/function 112, 114, 118-20
  - forms modified for use in a new context 113
  - discourse given fresh function 117
  - forms used in a different context 114-15
  - reapplication of forms 116
  misuse of forms 110-12, 115, 121, 124-5, 127-8, 131-7, 136-8, 143, 148, 188-9, 206-7, 212
  mixture of genres 112
  oblique restatement 124
  reuse of forms 110, 113, 116-17
  suspending belief 170
  use of forms 69, 109, 110, 112, 114-15
  use of imagery 112
  use of quotations 84, 123-4

Canon, Job's inclusion in 44, 45
Comedy 96-7, 149
Context
  author 160-1
  date 160-4
  place 162-3
  philosophical tendency 166-7
  wider intellectual tradition 86-8, 160-8
  wisdom setting 3, 61, 83, 162

Daniel 6, 12, 51, 60, 162
Death
  afterlife 79, 81, 179
  desirability of 125-6
  Sheol 178
Deutero-Isaiah 92, 93
Deuteronomy, Deuteronomistic
  Deuteronomy as wisdom 60
  Deuteronomistic theology of history 36
Dialogue
  arguments of Job and friends 36, 94, 111
  character of dialogue 94
  particular emphasis on 35, 38
  tension with prologue/epilogue 36-7, 39
  third cycle of speeches 52-3, 181-3
Disinterested righteousness 6, 29
Doctrine of retribution 35-6, 39, 177-8, 180
  as a wisdom issue 35, 38, 73-4, 79
  historical context 36
  Job's view of 52-4, 79, 174
  parody of 31

Ecclesiastes
  ancient Near Eastern parallels 138
  as a protest 44, 50, 147
  as sceptical literature 1, 36
  as wisdom 2, 63-88, 142-7
  author's unorthodoxy in use of forms 144-7
  autobiographical stylization in 66
  comparison with Job 51
  critique of doctrine of retribution 131
  genre levels 138
  instruction 139
  overall genre 138-9
  polar structures in 141-3
  reflection 140
  repetition of phrases 140
  reuse of forms 140
  techniques of form 138-147
  use of quotations 141
  use of subgenres 140
  wisdom saying in 139
  yes/but technique 141

## Indices

Elect 81-2
Elihu speeches
  author's purpose 197-8
  question of secondary addition 12, 33, 85, 195-8
Elijah 23
Elisha 23
Epistle of James 6, 12-13, 19, 23
Esther 60
Ezekiel 6, 12, 19, 23, 33, 51, 118

Folk Story 19, 22, 33, 202-3
  Moslem knowledge of 22
  spoiled 184-5, 193, 199, 203
Form   - see similar categories under Genre
  forms used in Job 3, 71-2
  hymnic forms 71-2, 116, 119
  legal forms 72, 114-15, 118
  misuse of forms   -see under author's technique
  oath of innocence 117, 133-4
  psalmic forms 116, 118
  prophetic forms 116
  reuse of forms   -see under author's technique
  wisdom forms 3, 59, 64-72, 116, 118, 128
    - autobiographical narrative 65-6
    - citation of proverbs 64
    - debate 70
    - didactic elements in Job 67-9
    - didactic poetry 66-7
    - hymn to wisdom 68
    - interpretation accompanying proverb 64
    - lament 70, 111, 115-17, 125
    - numerical proverbs 64-5
    - onomastica 64, 118
    - prayers 67
    - proverbs 64-5
Form/function
  in Job   -see under author's intention
  in the prophets 118-20
    - borrowing 119
    - imitation 119
    - opposite meanings 119
Friends of Job
  arguments in the dialogue 36, 52-4, 111, 124, 172-83
  ironic portrayal of 122-3
  portrayal in Hebrew text and LXX 14
  reason for Job's sin 172
  relation to dogmatists 170
  relationship with Job 10, 47-8, 52-4, 171-83
  view of God 172, 181

Genesis 1-11 60
Genre 3, 57, 88, 101-2, 106-7, 110-11, 118, 147-8, 185
  -see similar categories under Form
  comedy   -see separate entry
  criteria for identifying genre 89
  curse 116, 118, 130
  disputation 111
  drama 97
  dramatization of a lament 89-95, 100, 111-2
  lament genres 88, 90, 94, 111, 115-17, 119
  legal genres 91, 104-5, 114-15, 119, 132-3
  misuse of genre   -see under misuse of forms
  mixture of 101, 104-5, 107, 112
  overall 88, 92, 95, 100-3, 111-12, 121, 147-8, 153
  paradigm of answered lament 95, 112
  parody   -see under separate entry
  psalmic/hymnic genres 92, 104-5, 113-14, 116, 119
  Streitgespräch 92-4
  tragedy   -see under Greek tragedy
  wisdom genres 89, 102, 104-5, 113-14, 116
Genre levels 102-4, 147-8
God
  appearance of 48
  as an oppressive presence 46-7, 126-9, 173, 175
  character of 41, 43, 47-8, 130
  God/man relationship 39-43, 173, 182, 208
    - in Sirach 78
    - in Wisdom of Solomon 76
  justice of 35-6, 137, 173, 181
  nature of 40, 79, 175-6, 180, 182
  perceived as an enemy 130
  power to inflict good or evil 128, 132, 174, 176
Greek tragedy 3, 51, 98-100, 162-3

Haggadic legend 8
Hellenistic influence 163-7
  universalist tendency 165
Hypostatization of wisdom 59, 82-3

Innocent suffering 29-32
  Job as model or type 32
  understanding of God 31-2, 34
Irony 96-7, 122-3, 208-9
  of author   -see under author's intention
  in Yahweh speeches 135

## Indices

Jeremiah, confessions of 32, 50-1
   Form/function in 119
   Jeremiah 15 51
Job
   arguments in the dialogue 36, 52-4
   as a Promethean figure 51
   challenge to traditional doctrines 49, 52-4, 78-9, 83, 111, 211
   comparison with patriarchs 7
   critique of wisdom 83-4, 172-183
   emphasis on character 11, 12
   Job's conflict 77, 81, 175, 179-82
   just sufferer 22
   need for justification 174, 178-9
   patient 4, 6, 12-13, 17, 22-3, 25, 28-9, 31
   patron saint 28
   pious 6, 8-9, 11-12, 22, 29
   rebelliousness 9-10, 44, 52-5
   relationship with friends 10, 47-8, 52-4, 94, 124, 130, 171, 172-83
   relationship with God 41, 42, 48, 52-4, 77, 94
   response to God 41, 43, 47-8, 52-4, 187-8
   scepticism in dialogue 172-183
   suffering 8, 175, 178, 182
   two different Jobs 37, 204
   type of Christ 23-5, 28
   view of God 40, 52-4, 77, 130, 171, 183, 189, 211
   vindication in 42:7 36, 49, 208-9
Job tradition 12-13, 17-20, 28
Jonah 44
   author's intention 154-7
   context 155
   genre 154-7
   irony 156-7
   parody in 153-7
   song (chapter 2) 154
Joseph narrative 60, 85
Judges 36

Linguistic concerns 83
Literary-critical issues 194
   dislocation in third cycle of speeches 52-3
   effect on interpretation of book 32
   history of scholarly discussion 5
   hymn to wisdom 95-8
   prologue/epilogue 12, 200-3
   reconstructions of growth of book 42-3
   unity of authorship 33-4, 45
   unity of message 33-4
Liturgy
   Commendatio Animae 26
   Little Job 26-8
   Office of the Dead 26-8

Moses 10, 23, 51

Parody 109, 114, 116, 124, 132, 137, 159, 160, 184, 212
   as a genre 148-53, 212
   of doctrine of retribution 131
   of hymn forms 126-9, 132
   of lament forms 126, 128
   of Psalm 8 46, 126, 129, 130
   parody in Yahweh's speech 135
Patriarchs
   comparison with Job 7
   Aaron 10
   Abraham 7, 9-10, 23, 50
   Adam 10
   Dinah 7
   Enoch 9
   Esau 7
   Jacob 7, 50
   Melchizedek 9
   Noah 6, 12, 51
Patristic writings
   Ambrose 25
   Augustine 26
   Cyprian 26
   Gregory the Great 24, 25
   Tertullian 25
Prologue/Epilogue (Prose tale)
   framework for book 38
   irony in 122, 190-1, 208-9
   literary-critical issue 12, 200-3
   overemphasis on 6, 12, 31, 33-4
   story of 29-30
   tension with dialogue 36-7, 39, 125, 199-200
   unsatisfactory nature 37
Protest
   criteria for texts as 49-51
   Job as protest literature 3, 46, 49
   nature of Job's protest 2, 44, 47, 52-4
   protest literature in the Old Testament 46, 49-51, 147
Proverbs 58-9, 63-88
Psalms
   classification of Job as dramatization of psalms of lament 111-2
   of lament 50, 94, 113-14, 118
   proverbial sayings in 65
   wisdom 50, 61, 63-88

Rabbinic interpretation and elaboration 7-11
Reformers
   Calvin 29
   Luther 29

Samuel 51
Satan 8, 12, 19, 29-31, 162, 200-2
Sceptical
  as a description of *Job* 1-6, 168, 212
  as intention of author 45, 135, 137, 152-3
  meaning of 168-71
Scepticism
  as a description of *Job* 1-3, 171, 210
  in context of doctrine of retribution 36
  in structure of book 4, 136
  meaning of 168, 170
  of author 3, 110, 171, 184, 209-12
  of Job -see under Job
  on level of genre 148
Sceptics, Greek 3, 167-70, 185, 212
  against dogmatists 170
Septuagint 12-20
  additions 16-18
  deliberate theological changes 14-16, 19
  method of translator 14-16
  motives of translator 13-14
  portrayal of friends 14
Sirach 58, 63-88
  prophecy in 66
  refrains 66
Solomon 70
  attribution of authorship of wisdom
    books 86-7
Structure
  juxtaposition of parts 4, 184-7, 193-4, 203, 207-9, 212
Succession Narrative 60, 85

Testament of Job 20-2
  attitude to women 21
  elaborations 21
  influence of 22
  negative attitude towards Elihu 21
Theodore of Mopsuestia 19
Tobit 17-18
Torah 10
  wisdom link 76, 80-1

Wisdom
  content
    - ambiguity of events and the
      meaning of life 77-8
    - confidence in wisdom 81-2
    - life as the supreme good 80-1
    - order in the world 75-6
    - predestination 79
    - punishment and reward 78-9
  crisis in wisdom 3, 168
  criteria for wisdom influence 62-3
  definition of 58-63, 65
  development of 59, 74-5, 83
  doctrine of retribution as a wisdom issue
    -see separate entry
  elements of wisdom lacking in Job 71, 87-8
  wisdom forms -see separate entry
  wisdom genres -see separate entry
  Job as wisdom 3, 39, 57-8, 72-4, 83, 87-8, 103, 175
  limits of 61, 82
  personification of 82-3
  theological wisdom 59, 74-6, 80, 82
Wisdom literature 39, 72
  ancient Near Eastern wisdom 38, 58, 64, 69-70, 85, 93, 95
  characteristic themes 74-83
  classification of Job by scholars as 23, 55, 57, 63, 73-4, 87-8, 103
  didactic elements 84-5
  impetus for study of 38
  Job as wisdom in revolt 73, 83
  other wisdom literature 58, 63-4
  tradition of authorship 86-7
Wisdom of Solomon 58, 63-88
Wise the, wisdom movement, wisdom
  setting 23, 38-9, 57, 61
  criteria for including Job 85-8, 160
  orthodox additions 202-3, 209-10
  schools 70, 83-5
  widening interests of wise 66, 84, 86, 163, 166, 168
  wise man's task 79

Yahwistic history 85
Yahweh speeches 37, 40, 117, 181-91, 193
  genre 106, 121-2, 134
  irony 135
  literary-critical issue 40, 43, 205-6, 207
  overemphasis on 42-3
  parody 135
  picture of God 207

## B. Index of Authors

Ackerman, J.S. 153, 154, 155, 156
Aharoni, R. 102
Aked, C.F. 93
Alonso-Schökel, L.A. 97
Alt, A. 31
Ambrose 25

| | |
|---|---|
| Andersen, F.I. | 161 |
| Annas, J. | 169 |
| Augustine | 26 |
| | |
| Baab, O.J., | 38, 200 |
| Baker, J.A. | 57 |
| Balentine, S. | 129 |
| Ball, C.J. | 174 |
| Barnes, J. | 169 |
| Barnet, S. | 149 |
| Barr, J. | 83, 84, 98 |
| Barth, K. | 41, 97 |
| Barton, G.A. | 53 |
| Barton, J., | 141 |
| Batten, L.W. | 36, 200, 201, 202, 205 |
| Baumgartel, F. | 100 |
| Baumgartner, W. | 38, 58, 62, 68 |
| Bentzen, A. | 69, 70, 92, 100, 111 |
| Bergant, D. | 73 |
| Berman, M. | 149 |
| Besserman, L.L. | 6, 17, 18, 19, 25, 26, 27, 28 |
| Bickell, G. | 33 |
| Bishop, E.F.F. | 83 |
| Blank, S.H. | 35, 51, 74, 133, 134 |
| Bloomfield, M.W. | 152 |
| Booth, W.C. | 185 |
| Bousset, W. | 165 |
| Box, G.H. | 42, 163 |
| Bradley, A.C. | 99 |
| Braun, R. | 138 |
| Budde, K. | 32, 33, 34, 43, 53, 161, 162, 191, 194, 195, 199 |
| Buhl, W. | 150 |
| Burbo, W. | 149 |
| Burnyeat, M.F. | 169 |
| Buttenweiser, M. | 31, 100 |
| | |
| Calvin, J. | 29 |
| Caquot, A. | 75 |
| Carden, R.J. | 150 |
| Carroll, R.P. | 48 |
| Cartensen, R.N. | 197 |
| Ceresko, A.R. | 83 |
| Charles, R.H. | 17 |
| Charlesworth, J.H. | 20 |
| Cheyne, T.K. | 33, 162, 199, 200 |
| Childs, B.S. | 37, 102 |
| Clements, R.E. | 65 |
| Clines, D.J.A. | 21, 22, 30 |
| Coats, G.W. | 50, 89, 110 |
| Cornill, C. | 43, 205 |
| Cox, D. | 84, 112, 133, 188 |
| Creelman, H. | 161 |
| Crenshaw, J.L. | 31, 38, 46, 47, 49, 50, 59, 60, 61, 62, 66, 78, 92, 93, 94, 95, 211 |

| | |
|---|---|
| Crews, F. | 149 |
| Curtis, J.B. | 42 |
| Cyprian | 26 |
| | |
| Dancy, J.C. | 17 |
| Davidson, A. | 32, 34 |
| Davidson, A.B. | 160 |
| Davidson, R. | 46, 47, 48, 49, 50, 51 |
| Davidson, S. | 34 |
| Davies, G.I. | 92 |
| Delitzsch, F. | 35, 161 |
| Dennefield, L. | 195 |
| Dhorme, E.A. | 196, 200 |
| Dhorme, P. | 162 |
| Dibelius, M. | 13 |
| Dick, M.B. | 132, 134 |
| Dillmann, A. | 200 |
| Dover, K.J. | 151 |
| Driver, S.R. | 31, 32, 35, 43, 53, 98, 179, 182, 195, 205, 206 |
| Duesberg, H. | 38 |
| Duhm, B. | 33, 73, 182 |
| | |
| Eerdmans, B.D. | 12 |
| Eissfeldt, O. | 38, 70 |
| Ellermeier, F. | 1, 44, 138, 140 |
| Emerton, J.A. | 65 |
| | |
| Fichtner, J. | 35, 65, 100 |
| Fielding, H. | 152 |
| Fine, H.A. | 38 |
| Finkelstein, L. | 31, 166, 167, 201 |
| Fisch, H. | 3 |
| Fohrer, G. | 30, 31, 32, 42, 70, 72, 85, 103, 105, 106, 107, 109, 112, 113, 114, 115, 116, 117, 118, 119, 120, 121, 124, 125, 126, 128, 131, 132, 135, 164, 185, 187, 189 |
| Fortes, M. | 98 |
| Foster, H. | 83 |
| Fransen, I. | 38 |
| Friedländer, M. | 164 |
| Fries, K. | 98 |
| Frosch, T.R. | 149 |
| Fullerton, K. | 31, 32, 53, 121, 122, 123, 199 |
| | |
| Gard, D.H. | 14, 15 |
| Gardiner, A.H. | 64 |
| Gautier, L. | 33 |
| Gemser, B., | 35, 64, 78 |
| Genung, J.F. | 93 |
| Gerleman, G. | 13, 14 |
| Gerstenberger, E. | 61, 65 |
| Gese, H. | 35, 39, 62, 95, 112 |
| Gibson, E.C.S. | 161 |

| | | | |
|---|---|---|---|
| Ginsberg, H.L. | 37 | Kittel, R. | 165 |
| Ginzberg, L. | 8, 9 | Kluger, R.S. | 200 |
| Glatzer, N.N. | 22, 23, 24, 29 | Knibb, M.A. | 22 |
| Glei, R. | 151 | Koch, K. | 35, 36, 78 |
| Good, E.M. | 154, 156, 157, 185 | Kohler, K. | 21 |
| Gordis, R. | 12, 13, 16, 21, 35, 40, 52, 53, 64, 84, 123, 124, 129, 141, 143, 162, 166, 177, 179, 194, 197, 205, 206 | König, E. | 31, 201 |
| | | Kraeling, E.G. | 42 |
| | | Kroeber, R., | 140 |
| Gray, G.B. | 32, 35, 43, 53, 69, 98, 179, 182, 195, 206 | Kuhl, C. | 32, 163, 205 |
| | | Kuntz, J.K. | 35, 59, 60, 61, 82 |
| Gray, J. | 38 | | |
| Green, W.H. | 34, 93 | Lake, K. | 23 |
| Gregory the Great | 24, 25 | Lambdin, T.O., | 74 |
| Gressmann, H. | 70, 165 | Lambert, W.G. | 69, 95 |
| Griffith, M. | 98 | Landsberger, B. | 69 |
| Gros Louis, K.R.R. | 50 | Laue, L. | 33 |
| Guillaume, A. | 83 | Laurin, R. | 42 |
| Gunkel, H., | 58, 59, 70 | Licht, J. | 50 |
| | | Lindblom, J. | 31, 33, 98, 119, 162 |
| Habel, N.C. | 45, 100, 101, 102, 107, 147, 162, 176, 179, 192, 193, 195, 197, 203, 208 | Littlehales, H. | 26, 27 |
| | | Loader, J.A., | 141, 142, 143 |
| | | Lods, A. | 33 |
| Hadas, M. | 165 | Long, A.A. | 169 |
| Hastoupis, A.P. | 40 | Luther, M. | 29 |
| Hazelton, G.W. | 160 | | |
| Heaton, E.W. | 61, 62, 85 | Maag, V. | 43 |
| Heine, H. | 1, 44 | Mack, B.L. | 83 |
| Heinische, P. | 164 | MacDonald, D. | 149, 150 |
| Hengel, M. | 69, 163, 164, 165, 166, 167 | MacDonald, D.B. | 33, 40, 97 |
| Hennecke, E. | 23 | McKane, W. | 59, 68 |
| Hermisson, W-J. | 53 | McKenzie, J.L. | 60 |
| Hertzberg, H.W. | 140 | MacKenzie, R.A.F. | 42, 43, 205 |
| Highet, G. | 155 | Mai, A. (Cardinal) | 20 |
| Hoffman, Y. | 123, 185, 186, 187, 188, 194 | Mansi, J.D. | 19 |
| Hölscher, G. | 182, 200 | Marcus, R. | 38 |
| Holzmann, O. | 98 | Marshall, J.T. | 195 |
| Hopper, S.R. | 157 | Massebieau, L. | 13 |
| Horst, P.W. van der | 21, 22 | Matthews, I.G. | 36, 84 |
| Humbert, P. | 38 | May, H.G. | 98 |
| | | Meinhold, J. | 36 |
| Irwin, W.A. | 42, 74, 98, 179, 195 | Mettinger, T.N.D. | 84 |
| | | Michel, D. | 51 |
| | | Miskotte, K.H. | 40 |
| James, M.R. | 20, 23 | Mohr, J.C.B. | 33 |
| Jastrow, M. | 1, 31, 40, 53, 162 | Möller, H. | 53 |
| Johnson, S. | 149, 150 | Montet, E. | 32 |
| Jones, E. | 35, 38, 102 | Moore, G.F. | 35, 74 |
| Jowett, B. | 98 | Moore, R.D. | 45, 191, 192, 194, 204 |
| Jung, C. | 39, 189, 190 | Mowinckel, S. | 42, 67, 179 |
| | | Müller, H-P. | 64, 92 |
| Kaiser, O. | 100 | Murphy, R.E. | 102, 103, 110, 139, 144 |
| Kallen, H.M. | 98 | Murray, G. | 98 |
| Kautzsch, K. | 12, 31 | | |
| Kellett, E. | 32, 92 | Naish, J.P. | 160 |
| Kissane, E.J. | 35, 36, 43, 199 | Noth, M. | 38 |

| | | | |
|---|---|---|---|
| Oesterley, W.O.E. | 31, 32, 33 | Simon, R. | 12, 31 |
| Olivier, J.P.J. | 84 | Skehan, P.W. | 12 |
| Oorschot, J. van | 205 | Slotki, J.J. | 98 |
| | | Smith, M. | 165 |
| Peake, A.S., | 31, 102, 162, 173, 179 | Snaith, N. | 42, 53 |
| Pfeiffer, R.H. | 12, 22, 31, 40, 41, 53, 102, 162, 164, 165, 201 | Spitta, F. | 13 |
| | | Stanford, W.B. | 151 |
| Pirot, L. | 163 | Staples, W.E. | 43 |
| Plöger, O. | 39 | Steiner, G. | 98, 99 |
| Pohlman, K.-F. | 51 | Stevenson, W.B. | 12, 36 |
| Polzin, R.M. | 45, 191 | Stough, C.L. | 169 |
| Pope, M.H. | 42, 46, 48, 101, 107, 179, 196, 200 | Strahan, J. | 182 |
| | | Studer, G. | 34 |
| Potter, R. | 66 | Swabey, M. | 187 |
| Priest, J.F. | 3, 74, 210, 211 | Swart, W. | 164 |
| Pritchard, J.B. | 3, 38, 69, 77, 85, 133, 138, 145 | Szczygiel, P. | 196 |
| Procksch, O. | 32 | Talmon, S. | 60 |
| | | Terrien, S. | 30, 42, 48, 53, 65, 101, 179 |
| | | Tertullian | 25 |
| Rad, G. von | 2, 3, 30, 39, 60, 61, 65, 66, 67, 68, 69, 70, 76, 77, 78, 79, 80, 94, 97 | Thomas, D.W. | 38 |
| | | Tischendorf, C. | 23 |
| | | Torrey, C.C. | 20, 22 |
| Rankin, O.S. | 35, 43, 73 | Toy, C.H. | 160 |
| Raphael, D.D. | 99, 100 | Tsevat, M. | 29, 30, 32, 47, 48 |
| Reddy, M.P. | 53 | Tur-Sinai, N.H. | 32 |
| Reese, J.M. | 69 | | |
| Regnier, A. | 53 | Urbrock, W.J. | 97 |
| Richter, H. | 91, 92, 102, 119, 164 | | |
| Richter, W. | 61 | | |
| Roberts, J.J.M. | 84, 161, 166 | Vawter, B. | 153, 154 |
| Robertson, D.A. | 191 | Vernes, M. | 33 |
| Robinson, F.N. | 151, 152 | Volz, P. | 33, 35, 37, 78, 100 |
| Robinson, H.W. | 34, 35 | Vost, J.M. | 163 |
| Robinson, T.H. | 31, 32, 33 | | |
| Rogers, B.B. | 150 | Weinfeld, M. | 60 |
| Römheld, D. | 64 | Weiser, A. | 85, 100 |
| Roth, W.M.W. | 64, 65 | Weiss, M. | 184 |
| Rowland, C. | 60 | Wellhausen, J. | 33 |
| Rowley, H.H. | 32, 41, 43, 48, 162, 174, 176, 177, 179, 196, 205, 206 | Wertheimer, S. | 8 |
| | | Westermann, C. | 70, 89, 90, 92, 100, 101, 102, 111, 119, 137, 147, 196 |
| | | Whedbee, J.W. | 65, 96, 101, 149 |
| Sandbach, F.H. | 150 | Whybray, R.N. | 3, 59, 60, 61, 62, 64, 65, 85, 86, 120, 159 |
| Sawyer, J.F.A. | 161 | | |
| Schmid, H.H. | 3, 38, 62, 72, 73, 74, 75, 87, 207 | Wiernikowski, I. | 8 |
| | | Wildeboer, G. | 43 |
| Schmidt, J. | 59 | Williams, J.G. | 134, 187, 188, 189, 190, 194, 208 |
| Schmidt, J.M. | 60 | | |
| Schneemelcher, W. | 23 | Wolff, H.W. | 65 |
| Scott, R.B.Y. | 32, 35, 39, 60, 73, 74 | | |
| Seaford, R. | 150 | Young, E.J. | 161 |
| Sellin, E.F. | 33, 164 | | |
| Sewall, R.B. | 44, 46, 98, 163 | | |
| Sextus Empiricus | 170 | Zimmerli, W. | 140 |

## C. Index of Biblical References

| Genesis | | | | | | | |
|---|---|---|---|---|---|---|---|
| 10:23 | 162 | 2:2 | 140 | 5:1-2 | 141 | | |
| 22 | 50 | 2:3 | 96, 200 | 5:1-11 | 113 | | |
| 22:1,12 | 50 | 2:7-9,11 (Sept additions) | 16 | 5:1-27 | 111 | | |
| 22:21 | 162 | 2:9 | 30 | 5:2-5 | 123 | | |
| 36:28 | 162 | 2:10 | 10, 30, 203 | 5:2-7 | 113 | | |
| 36:33 | 162 | 2:10b | 66 | 5:3 | 136, 140 | | |
| | | 2:11a | 65 | 5:3-5 | 71 | | |
| | | 2:11-13 | 188 | 5:3-7 | 136 | | |
| Exodus | | 2:12 | 140 | 5:4 | 14, 186 | | |
| 20:18-20 | 49 | 2:13 | 96 | 5:6-7 | 71, 136 | | |
| 22:7 | 117 | 2:14 | 140 | 5:8f | 113 | | |
| 22:9f | 117 | 2:15 | 140 | 5:8-13 | 71 | | |
| 22:9-10 | 133 | 2:16 | 140 | 5:8-27 | 172 | | |
| | | 2:19 | 140 | 5:9 | 116 | | |
| Numbers | | 2:22 | 140 | 5:9f | 124 | | |
| 5:19-27 | 133 | 2:25 | 140 | 5:9-12 | 141 | | |
| | | 3 | 37, 45, 81, 96, | 5:11 | 116 | | |
| Deuteronomy | | | 111, 128, 161, 188, | 5:12-16 | 116 | | |
| 8:2-16 | 49 | | 191, 192, 204 | 5:17-18 | 54 | | |
| | | 3:1 | 204 | 5:17-21 | 71 | | |
| Judges | | 3:3-10 | 104, 116, 126 | 5:19-21 | 65 | | |
| 2:2-3 | 36 | 3:11 | 125, 204 | 5:22 | 174 | | |
| 2:11-15 | 36 | 3:11-13 | 115 | 5:26 | 96 | | |
| 2:20-23 | 36, 49 | 3:11-16 | 90 | 5:27 | 104 | | |
| 3:1-4 | 49 | 3:11-26 | 125 | 6 | 172 | | |
| | | 3:13 | 125 | 6:2-13 | 172 | | |
| II Samuel | | 3:16 | 141 | 6:2-27 | 90 | | |
| 3:35 | 133 | 3:16-19 | 126 | 6:4 | 47, 172 | | |
| | | 3:17 | 141, 204 | 6:5-6 | 65 | | |
| I Kings | | 3:17-19 | 116 | 6:6-7 | 176 | | |
| 4:32-34 | 86 | 3:17-26 | 90 | 6:7 | 197 | | |
| 19:4 | 156 | 3:20 | 204 | 6:8-10 | 115, 126 | | |
| 19:4-12 | 157 | 3:20-23 | 116, 125 | 6:9 | 54 | | |
| 20 | 133 | 3:21 | 125 | 6:10 | 52 | | |
| | | 3:21f | 115 | 6:11-13 | 116 | | |
| II Chronicles | | 4 | 121, 122 | 6:14 | 176 | | |
| 32:31 | 49 | 4:2-19 | 111 | 6:15-21 | 116, 126, 188 | | |
| | | 4:3-4 | 116 | 6:21-30 | 72 | | |
| Job | | 4:5-6 | 140 | 6:22-23 | 77, 114 | | |
| 1 | 24, 200 | 4:7 | 54, 113, 174 | 6:24 | 114 | | |
| 1:1 | 9 | 4:7-11 | 113 | 6:24-27 | 176 | | |
| 1:1-2:12 | 104 | 4:8-11 | 113 | 6:26-29 | 114 | | |
| 1:5 | 186 | 4:9 | 140 | 6:30 | 52 | | |
| 1:6 (Sept) | 15 | 4:9-12 | 141 | 7 | 46, 96, 139, 173 | | |
| 1:8 | 30, 186 | 4:10 | 140 | 7:1-12 | 139 | | |
| 1:9 | 30 | 4:10-11 | 113 | 7:1-14 | 141 | | |
| 1:10 | 9 | 4:10-12 | 140 | 7:3 | 116 | | |
| 1:11 | 186 | 4:12-16 | 116 | 7:5-8 | 116 | | |
| 1:14 | 9 | 4:12-21 | 104, 136 | 7:7-8 | 116, 126 | | |
| 1:16 | 202 | 4:12-5:7 | 172 | 7:9-10 | 117 | | |
| 1:21 | 192, 203 | 4:17 | 123, 137, 173 | 7:11 | 117 | | |
| 1:22 | 30, 66 | 4:17-21 | 116, 137, 189 | 7:11-12 | 139 | | |
| 2 | 200 | 5 | 71, 121, 122, 189 | 7:11-21 | 126, 127, 129, 148 | | |

| | | | | | | | |
|---|---|---|---|---|---|---|---|
| 7:12 | 113, 114, 173 | 9:15 | 54 | 11:2-6 | 104 |
| 7:12-14 | 47 | 9:16-17 | 190 | 11:2-20 | 111 |
| 7:13-14 | 139, 173 | 9:17 | 10 | 11:3-4 | 141 |
| 7:15 | 18, 116, 126 | 9:17f | 139 | 11:6 | 54 |
| 7:16 | 127 | 9:17-24 | 47 | 11:6b | 172 |
| 7:16-21 (Vulg) | 27 | 9:17-10:1 | 144 | 11:7f | 124 |
| 7:17 | 173 | 9:18 | 174 | 11:7-8 | 189 |
| 7:17-18 | 96, 116, 126, 189 | 9:18b-10:1 | 144 | 11:7-9 | 113 |
| 7:17-21 | 47 | 9:19-21 | 115 | 11:7-12 | 172 |
| 7:21 | 54, 188 | 9:20 | 174 | 11:7-19 | 114, 128 |
| 8:2 | 177 | 9:21 | 52 | 11:10 | 113 |
| 8:2-3 | 54 | 9:22 | 36, 174 | 11:13-16 | 113 |
| 8:2-4 | 72, 104, 115, 141 | 9:23 | 174 | 11:13-20 | 172 |
| 8:2-22 | 111 | 9:24 | 115, 174 | 11:17-19 | 113 |
| 8:3 | 173 | 9:25-26 | 116 | 11:20 | 113 |
| 8:4 | 172, 186 | 9:25-28 | 127, 148 | 12 | 96, 175, 176 |
| 8:5-7 | 113 | 9:25-35 | 90 | 12:1-2 | 176 |
| 8:7-12 | 104 | 9:28b | 115 | 12:2-3 | 96 |
| 8:8f | 113 | 9:32-33 | 174 | 12:2-6 | 104 |
| 8:8-10 | 189 | 9:33 | 178 | 12:4 | 128 |
| 8:8-13 | 102, 104 | 9:34 | 197 | 12:4 (Sept) | 14 |
| 8:11 | 67 | 9:34-35 | 181 | 12:5 | 124 |
| 8:11-12 | 65 | 10 | 121, 144, 173 | 12:6 | 124 |
| 8:11-12a | 141 | 10:1 (Vulg) | 27 | 12:7f | 124 |
| 8:11-13 | 65 | 10:1-7 (Vulg) | 27 | 12:7-8 | 124 |
| 8:11-14 | 140 | 10:1-22 | 90 | 12:7-12 | 102, 128 |
| 8:11-22 | 113 | 10:2 | 14 | 12:9 | 124 |
| 8:12-13 | 140 | 10:2-3 | 144 | 12:10 | 175 |
| 8:12b-13 | 141 | 10:2-12 | 127 | 12:11-13 | 104 |
| 8:13 | 102 | 10:2-17 | 78 | 12:12 | 189 |
| 8:13-20 | 104 | 10:4 | 174 | 12:12-13 | 65 |
| 8:14-19 | 180 | 10:4-7 | 115 | 12:12-25 | 189 |
| 8:20 | 174 | 10:6-7 | 52 | 12:13 | 189 |
| 8:20-22 | 172 | 10:7 | 10, 174 | 12:13-25 | 79, 104, 124, 129, 175 |
| 9 | 96, 121, 173, 174, 187, 207 | 10:8 | 175 | | |
| | | 10:8,16-17 | 47 | 12:23 | 175 |
| 9:2 | 123, 189 | 10:8-12 | 116, 148 | 13 | 175, 176 |
| 9:2b | 137 | 10:8-12 (Vulg) | 27 | 13:1-3 | 124 |
| 9:2f | 115 | 10:12-15 | 144 | 13:1-5 | 104 |
| 9:2-4 | 123, 136, 137 | 10:13-17 | 116, 128 | 13:3 | 115, 176 |
| 9:2-10 | 96 | 10:14 | 175 | 13:4-12 | 114 |
| 9:3 | 137 | 10:14-15 | 115 | 13:4-13 | 111 |
| 9:3-4 | 97 | 10:15 | 52 | 13:5 | 96 |
| 9:4 | 117 | 10:16 | 140, 175 | 13:6-16 | 105 |
| 9:5-10 | 127, 148 | 10:17 | 115, 140 | 13:7-12 | 176 |
| 9:9 | 174 | 10:17 (Sept) | 15 | 13:12 | 96, 177 |
| 9:11-12 | 77, 97 | 10:18 | 141 | 13:13-28 | 115 |
| 9:12 | 174 | 10:18f | 113 | 13:14-15 | 124 |
| 9:12-13 | 116 | 10:18-19 | 114, 128 | 13:16 | 94 |
| 9:13 | 174 | 10:18-22 (Vulg) | 26 | 13:17-27 | 90, 105 |
| 9:13-16 | 140, 144 | 10:20 | 46 | 13:20-22 | 65, 129 |
| 9:13-20 | 77 | 11 | 104 | 13:21 | 181 |
| 9:13-24 | 91 | 11:1 | 141 | 13:23 | 54 |
| 9:13-10:15 | 144, 144 | 11:2 | 103 | 13:24-28 | 47 |
| 9:14-16 | 115 | 11:2-3 | 115 | 13:27 | 197 |

| | | | | | |
|---|---|---|---|---|---|
| 14 | 175 | 18:5-21 | 113, 114, 117 | 22:21a | 181 |
| 14:1-12 | 129, 130, 148 | 18:12 | 113 | 22:23 | 104 |
| 14:1-22 | 90, 117 | 18:15-19 | 180 | 22:26-27 | 104 |
| 14:4-6 | 130 | 18:19 | 180 | 22:27 | 116 |
| 14:13 | 130 | 18:21 | 102 | 22:28-30 | 104 |
| 14:18-22 | 130 | 19 | 32, 178 | 23 | 181 |
| 14:19 | 176 | 19:1-12 | 91 | 23:2-12 | 117 |
| 14:21f | 179 | 19:2-4 | 114 | 23:2-24:25 | 90 |
| 15:2 | 178 | 19:5-12 | 47 | 23:3 | 46 |
| 15:2-35 | 111 | 19:6 | 54, 178, 179 | 23:3-7 | 132 |
| 15:3-6 | 177 | 19:6-7 | 37 | 23:4 | 181 |
| 15:7-8 | 117 | 19:13-22 | 90 | 23:7 | 182 |
| 15:8 | 177 | 19:20-27 (Vulg) | 26 | 23:8-9 | 46, 131, 148 |
| 15:9-10 | 117 | 19:22 | 47, 116, 130 | 23:8-17 | 182 |
| 15:14 | 10 | 19:23-27 | 90, 137 | 23:13 | 116 |
| 15:17-35 | 102, 113, 116, 117, 177 | 19:23-29 | 179 | 23:16-17 | 47 |
| | | 19:25 | 115 | 23:17 | 182 |
| 15:20 | 180 | 19:25-26 | 48 | 24 | 182 |
| 15:33f | 180 | 19:25-27 | 179 | 24:1-17 | 138 |
| 15:34 | 180 | 19:26 | 179 | 24:18-24 | 182 |
| 16 | 177 | 19:28-29 | 114, 124, 179 | 24:23 (Sept) | 15 |
| 16:2 | 89, 177 | 20 | 177 | 25:1-6 | 181 |
| 16:2-5 | 96 | 20:2-29 | 111 | 25:4 | 55 |
| 16:7-14 | 130 | 20:4-29 | 102, 113, 114, 117 | 26 | 182 |
| 16:7-17:16 | 90 | 20:5 | 180 | 26:2-4 | 96 |
| 16:8 | 115 | 20:10 | 180, 186 | 26:5-14 | 132 |
| 16:9 | 178 | 20:11 | 180 | 27 | 38, 182 |
| 16:9a | 116 | 20:19 | 180 | 27:1 | 104 |
| 16:9-14 | 47 | 20:21 | 180 | 27:2 | 47, 193 |
| 16:10 | 178 | 20:22 | 180 | 27:2-6 | 48, 117 |
| 16:12 | 178 | 20:26-29 | 180 | 27:3-4 | 115 |
| 16:12-14 | 116 | 20:29 | 102 | 27:7-23 | 138 |
| 16:13-14 | 15 | 21 | 111, 180 | 27:11-23 | 196 |
| 16:17 | 54 | 21:1-22 | 138 | 27:13-23 | 52 |
| 16:18 | 115 | 21:5a | 180 | 28 | 22, 32, 38, 59, 68, 83, 90, 138, 196 |
| 16:18-22 | 189 | 21:6-34 | 117 | | |
| 16:18-17:9 | 178 | 21:7-9 | 52 | 28 (Sept) | 14 |
| 16:19-22 | 115 | 21:7-13 | 113, 114, 130, 148 | 28:12-20 | 196 |
| 16:20 | 178 | 21:7-16 | 180 | 28:28 | 196 |
| 16:21a | 14 | 21:8 | 180 | 29 | 106, 117 |
| 17 | 177, 178 | 21:13-15 | 52 | 29-31 | 111, 112 |
| 17:2 (Vulg) | 28 | 21:17 | 52 | 29:2 | 114, 117 |
| 17:3 | 115 | 21:17-18 | 113, 131 | 29:7f | 113 |
| 17:4 | 178 | 21:17-22 | 180 | 29:7-17 | 113, 114, 132 |
| 17:5 | 65, 178 | 21:23-26 | 114, 131, 180 | 29:15-16 | 54 |
| 17:8-10 | 178 | 21:27 | 180 | 29:21-25 | 113, 114, 132 |
| 17:11-16 | 116 | 21:32-33 | 115, 132, 181 | 30:1-31 | 90 |
| 17:13 | 178 | 21:34 | 90 | 30:12-14 | 116 |
| 17:15 (Vulg) | 28 | 22:2-30 | 111 | 30:19 | 54 |
| 18:2-4 | 115 | 22:3 | 54 | 30:19-23 | 47 |
| 18:2-21 | 111 | 22:6-9 | 116 | 30:25-26 | 116, 132 |
| 18:3 | 177 | 22:6-14 | 104 | 30:26 | 54 |
| 18:4 | 177 | 22:13-14 | 117 | 31 | 91, 132, 133 |
| 18:5 | 180 | 22:15-16 | 113, 136, 137 | 31:1-34 | 117 |
| 18:5-6 | 113 | 22:19-20 | 116 | 31:1-40 | 104 |

| | | | | | |
|---|---|---|---|---|---|
| 31:2-4 | 133 | 42:1-2,6 | 7 | 51:11 | 129 |
| 31:5-6 | 133 | 42:1-6 | 97, 104, 118, 122 | 52:8-9 | 116 |
| 31:5-8 | 134 | 42:2-6 | 187 | 55:6-7 | 130 |
| 31:7-8 | 133 | 42:7 | 36, 49, 188, 190, | 55:6-8 | 126 |
| 31:9-10 | 134 | | 205, 208, 209 | 55:13-15 | 116 |
| 31:13 | 134 | 42:7f | 202 | 58:11 | 116 |
| 31:16-17 | 134 | 42:7-9 | 21, 188, 200 | 62:11 | 64 |
| 31:19-22 | 134 | 42:7-16 | 104 | 69:8-12 | 116 |
| 31:35-37 | 90, 111, 112, | 42:10 | 6 | 69:18 | 129 |
| | 117, 132, 133 | 42:10-11 | 201 | 69:33 | 116 |
| 31:38-40 | 117, 134 | 42:10-17 | 37 | 73 | 59, 79, 131, 161, 197 |
| 32:1-12 | 195 | 42:12-17 | 202 | 73:3-9 | 114, 131 |
| 32:2-3 | 195 | | | 73:6 | 131 |
| 32:6-22 | 195 | Psalms | | 73:9-10 | 131 |
| 32:8-9 | 85 | 1 | 113, 131 | 73:23-26 | 81 |
| 33:1 | 195 | 1:6 | 131 | 74:2 | 116 |
| 33:7 | 197 | 6 (Vulg) | 27 | 74:10-11 | 125 |
| 33:9-11 | 85 | 7 | 128 | 77:16f | 156 |
| 33:11 | 197 | 7:3 | 128 | 78:2 | 114 |
| 33:14-18 | 85 | 7:5 | 128 | 79:5-10 | 126 |
| 33:14-30 | 65 | 7:12-13 | 172 | 88:4-5 | 125 |
| 33:19-25 | 195 | 8 | 46, 96, 126, 127, | 88:8 | 116 |
| 33:20 | 197 | | 129, 148 | 88:15 | 129 |
| 34:2-9 | 105 | 8:4 | 126, 173 | 88:18 | 116 |
| 34:5 | 85 | 8:5 | 116 | 89:50-51 | 116 |
| 34:5-6 | 52 | 10:1 | 129 | 91 | 113 |
| 34:9 | 52, 85 | 10:5-6 | 114, 131 | 94:18-19 | 130 |
| 34:10-15 | 105 | 13:2 | 129 | 94:22 | 130 |
| 34:16-20 | 105 | 21:12 | 172 | 97:2-5 | 156 |
| 34:21-23 | 105 | 22:25 | 129 | 98:7-9 | 128 |
| 34:23-27 | 105 | 23 | 132, 148 | 100:3a | 126 |
| 34:31-37 | 105 | 23:2b-3 | 132 | 102:3 | 129 |
| 34:35 | 195 | 26:2 | 49 | 103:14 | 116 |
| 35:2f | 85 | 27:4 | 129 | 104 | 127 |
| 37 | 195 | 27:9 | 129 | 104:12-21 | 64 |
| 38 | 134, 138 | 28:6-8 | 130 | 107 | 129 |
| 38:1 | 195 | 29 | 156 | 107:23f | 156 |
| 38:1-8 | 21 | 31 | 130 | 107:29 | 129 |
| 38:1-42: 6 | 32 | 31:11 | 130 | 107:33 | 129 |
| 38:2 | 188 | 31:11-12 | 116 | 107:42 | 116 |
| 38:2-3 | 115, 118 | 31:14-15 | 130 | 111 | 82 |
| 38:2-5 | 96 | 33:18 | 173 | 111:10 | 82 |
| 38:3 | 188 | 37 | 59, 76, 79 | 119 | 82 |
| 38:4-5 | 135 | 37:16 | 65 | 128 | 113 |
| 38:4-39:30 | 104 | 37:25 | 136 | 139 | 127, 132, 148, 197 |
| 40:1-2 | 96 | 37:37 | 81 | 139:7-8 | 127 |
| 40:2 | 115, 117, 135 | 38:11 | 116 | 139:7-12 | 182 |
| 40:3-5 | 97, 118, 121, 122 | 41:9 | 116 | 139:19-24 | 127 |
| 40:4-5 | 187 | 44:25 | 129 | 143:7 | 129 |
| 40:6-14 | 96, 117 | 45:1 | 69 | 144:3 | 116 |
| 40:7 | 188 | 45:5 | 172 | 148:7-8 | 156 |
| 40:8 | 115, 135, 188 | 46:1 | 133 | Proverbs | |
| 40:9-14 | 116, 135 | 49 | 59, 69, 79, 161, 197 | 1:10-19 | 67 |
| 40:15-41:26 | 104 | 49:5 | 114 | 1:19 | 66 |
| 40:19a | 189 | 49:16-17 | 79 | 1:20-33 | 68 |

| | | | | | | | |
|---|---|---|---|---|---|---|---|
| 1:22-23 | 66 | 1:17,18 | 81 | 12:1 | | | 32 |
| 2:1-5 | 77 | 2:1-11 | 70 | 14:7-9 | | | 119 |
| 2:1-22 | 67 | 2:11 | 75 | 14:19-22 | | | 119 |
| 3:9-18 | 80 | 2:14 | 76 | 15 | | | 51 |
| 5:15-23 | 68 | 2:18-19 | 64 | 18:18 | | | 86 |
| 7:6f | 68 | 2:18-21 | 76 | 20:7-9 | | | 127 |
| 7:6-27 | 65 | 2:24 | 64, 76 | 20:14-18 | | | 161 |
| 8 | 59, 68 | 2:26 | 76 | | | | |
| 8:4-36 | 59 | 3:1-9 | 59 | | Ezekiel | | |
| 8:22 | 189 | 3:2 | 64 | 14:12-14 | | | 6, 12 |
| 8:22-23 | 82 | 3:2-8 | 67 | 14:14,20 | | | 51 |
| 11:15-20 | 79 | 3:10-15 | 66 | 14:14-20 | | | 33 |
| 11:21 | 78 | 3:11 | 76, 81 | 14:19-20 | | | 6, 12 |
| 12 | 139 | 3:17 | 79 | 16:23f | | | 118 |
| 14:13 | 75 | 4:5-6 | 141 | | | | |
| 14:20 | 75 | 5:1-6 | 79 | | Hosea | | |
| 14:35 | 146 | 5:1-20 | 145 | 6:1-3 | | | 119, 155 |
| 15:16 | 65 | 5:2-7 | 142 | 14:2b-3 | | | 119 |
| 16:18 | 75 | 7:1 | 80 | | | | |
| 17:6f | 79 | 7:12 | 81 | | Amos | | |
| 20:1-2 | 59 | 7:14 | 80 | 3:3-6 | | | 119 |
| 20:2 | 146 | 7:15 | 79 | 3:3-8 | | | 67 |
| 21:22 | 144 | 7:19 | 81 | 5:1-3 | | | 119 |
| 22:17 | 145 | 7:23-39 | 75 | 5:6-9 | | | 127 |
| 22:17-19 | 77 | 8 | 146 | | | | |
| 22:17-22 | 77 | 8:5-6a | 146 | | Jonah | | |
| 22:17-23:14 | 85 | 8:6b-8 | 146 | 2 | | | 154 |
| 22:17-24:20 | 77 | 8:6b-17 | 146 | 2:3-10 | | | 154 |
| 22:17-24:22 | 81 | 8:9-15 | 146 | | | | |
| 23:29-35 | 59 | 8:12b-13 | 146 | | Micah | | |
| 23:32 | 21 | 8:13 | 79 | 6:3-5 | | | 133 |
| 24:16 | 78 | 8:14 | 79, 131 | | | | |
| 24:30 | 136 | 9:2 | 131 | | Zechariah | | |
| 24:30-34 | 65 | 9:3-7 | 142 | 1:10f | | | 200 |
| 25:11 | 75 | 9:7 | 79 | 3 | | | 200 |
| 25:23 | 75 | 9:14-15 | 70 | 3:1f | | | 200 |
| 30:1 | 145 | 9:16 | 70, 141 | 6:5 | | | 200 |
| 30:1-4 | 39, 70 | 9:18 | 141 | | | | |
| 30:7-9 | 67, 129 | 10:4 | 146 | Wisdom of Solomon | | | |
| 30:18 | 64 | 11:1-6 | 142 | 1:2-5 | | | 79 |
| 30:29-31 | 68 | 11:5 | 75, 77 | 2:1-20 | | | 66 |
| 31:1 | 145 | 12:1-8 | 68 | 3:1 | | | 82 |
| 33:14-15 | 64 | 12:9-11 | 71 | 3:9 | | | 76, 81 |
| 39:33-34 | 64 | | | 3:13 | | | 79 |
| | | | Isaiah | 3:14 | | | 79 |
| Ecclesiastes | | 11:8 | 21 | 4:1 | | | 79 |
| 1 | 144 | 28:23-29 | 119 | 5:3-13 | | | 66 |
| 1:1 | 145 | 40:9-11 | 132 | 5:15-23 | | | 79 |
| 1:2 | 145 | 40:12-26 | 133 | 6:12-22 | | | 68 |
| 1:3 | 81 | 47 | 119 | 7:7-8 | | | 76 |
| 1:3-11 | 145 | 59:5 | 21 | 7:22 | | | 83 |
| 1:4-9 | 67 | | | 7:22-8:21 | | | 68 |
| 1:12-18 | 145 | | Jeremiah | 7:17-20 | | | 64 |
| 1:12-2:26 | 142 | 3:21-25 | 119 | 7:17-22 | | | 82 |
| 1:14 | 71 | 8:17 | 21 | 8:1 | | | 83 |

| | | | | | | | |
|---|---|---|---|---|---|---|---|
| 8:6 | 83 | 2:7-18 | 66 | 32:14-24 | 79 |
| 8:7 | 83 | 4:11-19 | 67 | 33:7-15 | 78 |
| 10-19 | 82 | 6:18-31 | 78 | 33:13-15 | 76, 80 |
| 12:12-18 | 82 | 6:37 | 76, 81 | 37:12-16 | 77 |
| 13:1-15:19 | 76 | 15:11 | 66 | 39:16-35 | 78 |
| 15:1-2 | 81 | 15:16 | 79 | 41:1-2 | 78 |
| 16:17 | 79 | 16:24-30 | 67 | 42:15-43:33 | 68 |
| 16:24 | 79 | 17:1-12 | 67 | 43 | 64 |
| 17:16 | 80 | 19:20 | 76, 78, 81 | 44:1-50:21 | 80 |
| 17:17-21 | 80 | 21:6 | 76 | 50:27 | 68 |
| | | 21:11 | 76, 81 | 51:23 | 85 |
| **Sirach** | | 23:1-6 | 67 | | |
| 1:1-20 | 67 | 23:27 | 76, 81 | **Epistle of James** | |
| 1:16 | 76 | 24 | 76, 83 | 1:1 | 13 |
| 1:26 | 76, 81 | 24:1-22 | 68 | 2:1 | 13 |
| 1:27 | 76 | 24:30-34 | 68 | 5:7,8 | 13 |
| 2:5-6 | 66 | 28:1-7 | 80 | 5:11 | 6, 12, 13, 23 |

# ZEITSCHRIFT FÜR DIE ALTTESTAMENTLICHE WISSENSCHAFT

In Connection with *Hans Christoph Schmitt, Gunther Wanke*
edited by *Otto Kaiser*
1991. Volume 103 (3 issues) ISSN 0044-2526
Complete DM 174,–; Single issue DM 61,–
Student price DM 68,–
Sample copies available upon request

The **Zeitschrift für die Alttestamentliche Wissenschaft,** which is published in three issues of 160 pages each **plus supplements,** has been the leading international and interconfessional periodical in the field of research in the Old Testament and Early Judaism for over one hundred years. Open to various ways of posing the questions of scholarship, the journal features high quality contributions in English, German, and French. Through its review of periodicals and books, it provides fast and reliable information concerning new publications in the field.

Prices are subject to change

Walter de Gruyter    Berlin · New York

# BEIHEFTE ZUR ZEITSCHRIFT FÜR DIE ALTTESTAMENTLICHE WISSENSCHAFT

### SA-MOON KANG
## Divine War in the Old Testament and the Ancient Near East
1989. Large-octavo. XV, 251 pages. Cloth DM 118,–
ISBN 3 11 011156 X (Volume 177)

### JOHN HA
## Genesis 15
**A Theological Compendium of Pentateuchal History**
1989. Large-octavo. XII, 244 pages. Cloth DM 82,–
ISBN 3 11 011206 X (Volume 181)

### BARUCH MARGALIT
## The Ugaritic Poem of AQHT
**Text – Translation – Commentary**
1989. Large-octavo. XVIII, 534 pages. Cloth DM 198,–
ISBN 3 11 011632 4 (Volume 182)

### DWIGHT R. DANIELS
## Hosea and Salvation History
**The Early Traditions of Israel in the Prophecy of Hosea**
1990. Large-octavo. IX, 148 pages. Cloth DM 78,–
ISBN 3 11 012143 3 (Volume 191)

### MARTIN L. BRENNER
## The Song of the Sea; Ex 15: 1–21
1991. Large-octavo. VIII, 193 pages. Cloth DM 88,–
ISBN 3 11 012340 1 (Volume 195)

*Prices are subject to change*

**Walter de Gruyter**  **Berlin · New York**

GTU Library
2400 Ridge Road
Berkeley, CA 94709
For renewals call (510) 649-2500
All items are subject to recall.